Strange, Surprising, Sure

Strange, Surprising, Sure

Essays in Uncommon Philosophy

ROBERT CUMMINGS NEVILLE

Cover painting by Beth Neville. "Great Wall Crisis" (detail). Tempera paint on paper, cut and pasted in a collage.

Published by State University of New York Press, Albany

© 2024 State University of New York

All rights reserved

Printed in the United States of America

No part of this book may be used or reproduced in any manner whatsoever without written permission. No part of this book may be stored in a retrieval system or transmitted in any form or by any means including electronic, electrostatic, magnetic tape, mechanical, photocopying, recording, or otherwise without the prior permission in writing of the publisher.

Links to third-party websites are provided as a convenience and for informational purposes only. They do not constitute an endorsement or an approval of any of the products, services, or opinions of the organization, companies, or individuals. SUNY Press bears no responsibility for the accuracy, legality, or content of a URL, the external website, or for that of subsequent websites.

For information, contact State University of New York Press, Albany, NY
www.sunypress.edu

Library of Congress Cataloging-in-Publication Data

Name: Neville, Robert Cummings, author.
Title: Strange, surprising, sure : essays in uncommon philosophy / Robert Cummings Neville.
Description: Albany : State University of New York Press, [2024] | Includes bibliographical references and index.
Identifiers: ISBN 9781438499611 (hardcover : alk. paper) | ISBN 9781438499635 (ebook) | ISBN 9781438499628 (pbk. : alk. paper)
Further information is available at the Library of Congress.

For
Gwendolyn
Anselm
Evangeline
Mary

Contents

The Painter's Contribution ... ix

Preface ... xi

Prologue ... xvii

Part One: Philosophy

Chapter 1   Being-Itself ... 3

Chapter 2   Eternity ... 17

Chapter 3   Aesthetics ... 31

Chapter 4   Experience ... 53

Chapter 5   Emergence ... 69

Chapter 6   Indeterminacy ... 83

Chapter 7   Wisdom ... 99

Chapter 8   Shallow Roots ... 115

Chapter 9   Pragmatism and Confucianism ... 125

Chapter 10 Philosophy ... 145

Part Two: Philosophers

Chapter 11	On Josiah Royce	177
Chapter 12	On Alfred North Whitehead	195
Chapter 13	On Robert Corrington	213
Chapter 14	On Stefan Alkier	227
Chapter 15	On Nancy Frankenberry	241
Chapter 16	On Charles Taylor	251
Chapter 17	On Ray L. Hart	279
Chapter 18	On Wesley Wildman	297
Notes		323
Index		333

The Painter's Contribution

For several years, this volume's title was *Weird, Surprising, and Sure*. All this time Beth Neville, my wife, opposed that name because "weird" for her meant something very wrong. Mistaken. Illogical. She argued that I had not kept up with the changes in its meaning. I knew my philosophy was probably mistaken and that I was brazen for promoting it. All philosophers share that failing. But not illogical: my philosophy is eminently logical, even beautiful in its logic. So weird had to go. The world is strange, not weird. "Surprising" characterizes our own subjectivity, not the world's characters. And "sure" characterizes my confidence that in the future people would agree with me. But I fear that she is right about weirdness, and so I have changed the title to *Strange, Surprising, Sure*.

Her artwork for my cover here is tempera paint on paper, cut and pasted in a collage. It is part of her larger painting, *The Great Wall Crisis*, which is on YouTube. I thank her for her artwork here and for her dogged insistence on her reading of my title.

Preface

My friend Wesley Wildman once suggested that my philosophy would become popular in fifty years. That was about twenty years ago. Still waiting for applause, I'm tempted to start his count from today, saying its time will arrive fifty years from now. But much has happened in the last twenty years. Strangely, many philosophers now say that we need to start from comparative viewpoints and that all the world's philosophies need to be taken seriously, not just our own. Surprisingly, many philosophers are less fixed in their religions now and are willing to entertain the paradoxical position that ontology is utterly contingent and that true piety is gratitude that it has just happened. Surely, this vast shift in perspectives is coming and our discussions will be contextualized as I predict in fifty more years. So there is the future: strange, surprising, and sure.

When he was rather young, thirty-eight, Ralph Waldo Emerson published a book he called *Essays: First Series*. Three years later, in 1844, he brought out *Essays: Second Series*. Each of the essays was preceded by a poem of moderate distinction, very moderate. His essay "The Poet," was better than his own practice in poetry. But he wrote genuine essays, formed from his lectures given to public audiences, not to an academy. This is not to say he lacked a system: he was a singularly important transcendentalist. But each essay was a view of the whole from its own perspective.

Now that I am old, eighty-five, I dare follow Emerson. Like Emerson, I preface each chapter in this volume with a poem of moderate distinction. His poems err on the side of taking themselves too seriously. My poems are an indirect commentary on his, being more light-hearted. My essays, however, are exactly as serious as his. Although they began with an academic audience in mind, often it was a slightly tipsy audience, for which I gave an after-dinner speech. I have rewritten all of them here, each chapter a view of the whole of my philosophy from its own perspective.

Wildman was the friend who persuaded me to rewrite these chapters as essays rather than as parts of an interconnected system. He would want me to write in an even more freewheeling way than I have here, say, for a church audience rather than for an academic one. He himself can do that, and he has. But our situation has changed a great deal from Emerson's. In his time, undergraduates were fourteen to eighteen years old, Emerson's own age at Harvard. In our time, I write for adults. In Emerson's Boston, the truly intellectual people met in various venues for lectures. In our time, only a few old clubs still have lectures of my (or any) sort and most people go out for entertainment of a nonintellectual sort. In Emerson's time, there were no graduate schools, only undergraduate ones, until late in his career. In our time, there are powerful graduate schools at many levels and they are in chaotic patterns of definition and redefinition; these are the people in diverse departments and faculties for whom I write these chapters. True, I am a philosopher and in some chapters write what only serious philosophical types will follow. But generally I write for people in literature and physics, history and chemistry, critical studies of culture and cognitive science, and the professions of law, medicine, the arts, dentistry, and education. I hope before too long that all these labels change.

All of these chapters are invitations to engage what I presume are fairly unfamiliar topics and methods to the readers. So they all include a kind of introduction as well as commentary and special pleading to take up my own engagement. Like any essays, these stand on their own. Because they are independent, they cumulatively involve some repetition. Repetition means that the first time they are read, they are strange; the second time, surprising that others do not know of them; and the third time, surely true, or false. They also stand together and therefore reinforce one another, as in a system, though with loose joints. This "loosely jointed" system is true for all the chapters here.

The prologue presents the main surprise with three sermons. This is *strange* because I am a global philosopher and the sermons are all Christian and were preached at the same church, the University Church where I was pastor. The *surprise* is that the world is utterly contingent on being created by an ontological creative act which in turn is utterly contingent on the determinations created. In human terms, this means that the world *surely* is filled with ambiguities, especially suffering and death, and that "religious truth" is on a higher level. The rest of the writings in this volume explain all this.

There are two parts here, "Philosophy" and "Philosophers." I thank all those from whom permission is required and for cheers from many editors.

Part one, "Philosophy," has ten chapters.

Chapter one, "Being-Itself," is the most strange, surprising, and sure of the chapters. It attempts to give an ontological approach to my system at its most general. As a purely metaphysical essay, it stands in rhetorical contrast to the sermons in the prologue. But it says much of the same thing. "Being-Itself" borrows from and vastly reworks many of my previous writings as well as introduces much new material. I can hardly cite any given previous work, although a lot of it comes from presentations made to meetings of Jerry L. Martin's group Theology without Walls, including "Tale of a Theology without Walls," published in the *Journal of Ecumenical Studies* 51, no. 4 (Fall 2016): 464–78. Another source is a talk I gave called "An Ontology of Otherness: A Hermeneutic of Compassion."

Chapter two, "Eternity," is an academic essay about eternity as the source of all change. Although many of the chapters in this book brush with eternity, this one is a direct and fulsome approach. The original for this chapter was published in *Time, Space, and Mind: Roots of Humanity*, edited by Linyu Gu, Chung-ying Cheng, and Gary R. Mar, a thematic series to vol. 42 (2015) of the *Journal of Chinese Philosophy*. The version here is quite different from its original, which was called "Space, Time, and Eternity."

Chapter three, "Aesthetics," completes the three main theses in this book, namely that everything with form is good, in addition to the claim that being-itself is an act, not a thing, and that this has important bearing on the claim that everything determinate is a change, or at least almost everything. "Aesthetics" comes from an earlier essay entitled "Harmony, Existence, and the Aesthetic," in *American Aesthetics: Theory and Practice*, edited by Walter B. Gulick and Gary Slater (Albany: State University of New York Press, 2020). It presents my system as giving rise to the experience of harmony in art. The crucial component here is the explication of form as having value.

Chapter four, "Experience," studies five senses of religious transcendence, each a kind of religious experience. "Experience" distinguishes how we relate to the ontological ultimate from how we relate to the four cosmological ones. It came from a talk I gave at a meeting of the Institute for American Religious and Philosophical Thought.

Chapter five, "Emergence," details how change gives rise to emergence of novel forms. It began as a paper at a conference on the cognitive science of the emergence of mind from matter at Arizona State University, focusing on the work of Terrence Deacon. The chapter here keeps that form, but it provides a strange account of creative process within time. No part of this chapter has been previously published.

Chapter six, "Indeterminacy," restates my central surprise: the contingency of both creation and of the origin of creation. It promotes both Western and Chinese versions of this notion. It was originally commissioned in an altered version as "Indeterminacy in Chinese Thought: Spontaneity and the Dao" in *The Significance of Indeterminacy: Perspectives from Asian and Continental Philosophy*, edited by Robert H. Scott and Gregory Moss.

Chapter seven, "Wisdom," had its first appearance as "Wisdom in Chinese Confucian Philosophy" in *Wijsbegeerte*, vol. 112, no. 3, edited by Natascha Kienstra. Its emphasis on Chinese philosophy put it in contrast with most of the other articles in that journal, although it is perfectly complementary here. It is rewritten for this volume.

Chapter eight, "Shallow Roots," was written at the invitation of Cheng Chung-ying and originally published by Springer Nature as "On the Confucian Virtue of Shallow Roots" in *International Communication of Chinese Culture* 4, no. 2 (2017): 139–46. This paper is rewritten. Of course, it stands in ironic contrast to the usual Confucian emphasis on deep roots, which is also true. But here it addresses the question of what Confucianism consists in when made global.

Chapter nine, "Pragmatism and Confucianism," turns explicitly to pragmatism as one of my main heritages and compares that with phenomenology and, to a lesser extent, with analytic philosophy. It develops the Confucian/pragmatic theme of culture and begins the creation of a theory of selfhood. Its main themes are creation, continuity, self-cultivation, and scholar-official, only the last two not being surprises regarding Confucianism. Part of this chapter was originally prepared for an Eastern Division American Philosophical Association panel with Cheng Chung-ying and Edward Casey, chaired by Linyu Gu. An early version of this portion of the chapter appeared under the title "Value and Selfhood: Pragmatism, Confucianism, and Phenomenology," *Journal of Chinese*

Philosophy 42, no. 1–2 (March–June 2015): 197–212. This chapter also draws material from "Confucianism beyond Asia," written as a lecture.

Chapter ten, explicitly called "Philosophy," casts a retrospective glance at the philosophy in the first nine chapters of this volume. It interprets the impoverished state of the discipline and urges that we learn to work equally from the resources of East Asian and South Asian philosophies. Taking these to be paradigmatic of all philosophical traditions, it argues that they have trajectories of reflection that lead to their versions of the Ultimate. I can hardly cite any previous work as a source for this chapter, although a lot of it comes from presentations made to meetings of Jerry L. Martin's group Theology without Walls. Another source is a talk I gave called "An Ontology of Otherness: A Hermeneutic of Compassion."

Part two has eight chapters.

Chapter eleven, "On Josiah Royce," works within the American tradition—Royce claimed to be an "absolute pragmatist"—to distinguish his overweening unity from my wholly contingent unity. It began as a paper in a conference in 2015 in Hamburg, Germany, on Josiah Royce and a version of it was published in *Josiah Royce*, edited by Christoph Seibert and Christian Polke (Tubingen, GR: Mohr Siebeck, 2021), 164–79, under the title "Royce's Philosophy of Religion: A Critical Appraisal."

Chapter twelve, "On Alfred North Whitehead," is gathered from many sources. The one that's derived in its second half is from Demian Wheeler and David E. Conner's edited book *Conceiving an Alternative: Philosophical Resources for an Ecological Civilization*, published under the title "Balancing What Is Useful in Western Philosophy for Present Philosophy" (2019). The first half of the chapter is gathered from various unpublished sources.

Chapter thirteen, "On Robert S. Corrington," is appearing in another version called "Robert S. Corrington and Psychoanalysis," in *The Mind in Nature: Extensions of Ecstatic Naturalism*, edited by Leon Niemoczynski and Iljoon Park, yet to appear.

Chapter fourteen, "On Stefan Alkier," gives my theory of interpreting scripture. It began as a symposium presentation on the contemporary use of scripture and focused especially on Alkier's book *The Reality of the Resurrection: The New Testament Witness*, trans. Leroy Huizenga, foreword by Richard B. Hayes (Waco, TX: Baylor University Press, 2013). The chapter has been rewritten.

Chapter fifteen, "On Nancy Frankenberry," continues my long correspondence with her on the issues of contingency and necessity. In it I argue that, for all her lauding of contingency, she still does not get the full contingency of creation ex nihilo. I take her to be excellent on cosmological contingency but lacking regarding ontological contingency. The first version of my paper was given at a Metaphysical Society of America meeting and was published in *American Journal of Theology and Philosophy* 40, no. 1 (January 2019): 54–61. Its original title was "Cosmological and Ontological Contingency."

Chapter sixteen, "On Charles Taylor," is a criticism of his theory of modernity for being too narrow. This allows me to join with him in many ways, especially his theory of religion. It was written for the volume *Modernity and Transcendence: A Dialogue with Charles Taylor*, edited by Anthony J. Carroll and Staf Hellemans. It was published first as a journal article in the *Journal for Theology and the Study of Religions* 75 ¾ (2021): 397–428, and then as a book with that title (Amsterdam: Amsterdam University Press, 2021), 95–126. My original essay was entitled "Confucian Modernity, Ultimacies, and Transcendence." It was rewritten for the present volume.

Chapter seventeen, "On Ray L. Hart," is about my close friendship with Ray and our ongoing disputes about God. Specifically, it addresses four major questions: Is all thought temporal? Can God be perceived? What about eternity and temporality? And is *Creatio ex nihilo* a surprise? This chapter was commissioned as a contribution to a volume on Hart's work edited by Alina Feld, which has yet to appear.

Chapter eighteen, "On Wesley Wildman," is about my best and closest friendship. In fact, we are so close in theories that I work hard to make out some very significant differences. The chapter was published in its original form in *Religion in Multidisciplinary Perspective: Philosophical, Theological, and Scientific Approaches to Wesley J. Wildman*, eds. F. LeRon Shults and Robert Cummings Neville (Albany: State University of New York Press, 2022).

Prologue

Religions look for ultimacy
Through leaking tunnels.
The West pursues the tunnel of agency, intentions, and desires.
South Asia tracks consciousness toward purity.
The East passes over persons and looks toward natural nothingness.
Each leaks on the others, however, with time and space traversed,
And churches have yoga on Tuesdays, taiji on Wednesdays, and Humanists on Thursday.
Religions' tunnels run from rental space to deepest thought.
Most people enjoy offering fruit to the statue.
A few become doctors of teachings.
Very few see teachings as penultimate
To love only the Ultimate beyond ultimacies.
Religions agree that ultimately we all are fine
And that we should ultimately laugh.
Is this not what Jesus taught?
Of course he whipped the dealers from the Temple.
To be sure, he demanded obedience.
His ethic sacrifices self even as it
Calls selves to stand in for each other.
Yet the train for Heaven stops for all
And we should ultimately laugh.

"It Is Finished"

Jesus was right after all! According to the Gospel of John, Jesus said he had already overcome the world. This was in the large middle portion of the Gospel before he went out to be arrested, tried, and crucified. In the final chapter of the Gospel, probably by a different author, Jesus hailed his disciples who were fishing without luck, told them where to cast their nets, fixed them breakfast on the shore, and then walked off with Peter. He described the death that will come to Peter and asked him three times whether he loves him, to which Peter always answered yes. Jesus commissioned Peter to carry on Jesus's earthly ministry. Peter turned and saw the Beloved Disciple following behind at a distance. He asked what will happen to him, meaning whether the Beloved Disciple too would die. Jesus said quite plainly that was none of Peter's business, and the writer repeated Jesus's phrase to indicate that it does not mean the Beloved Disciple will not die, only that it was not Peter's business. The first chapter of the Gospel of John, perhaps by yet another author, said that God's creative Word became incarnate in Jesus. The world, with its darkness, had not overcome it. Jesus was the light of the world, and the darkness of the world had not overcome it. But Jesus did not say that the light overcame the darkness. The world remained the same no matter what, only that it now contained the light of the world. Jesus said of his life, his last words during the crucifixion, "It is finished" (John 19:30).

I take all of this to mean that Jesus had already overcome the world in his life, the world had not changed, people still will all suffer and die, and that religious truth consists in a higher kind of happiness that absorbs suffering and death. Surprise!

The Synoptic gospels, though less metaphysical than John, continue this theme. All three are structured on the scheme of a single trip from Galilee to Jerusalem where Jesus is arrested, tried, and executed. The Synoptics all, as well as the Gospel of John, begin Jesus's ministry with some version, though different, of the Prophesy of the Baptist and Jesus's baptism. The Synoptics all, though not John, account the crucifixion as a failure of Jesus; John marks it a success. Matthew and Luke, though not Mark, begin with infancy narratives of Jesus, telling different stories. Matthew and Luke both give genealogies of Jesus, Matthew beginning with Abraham and Luke going back to "Son of Adam, Son of God." Matthew and Luke, though not the earliest version of Mark, have post-crucifixion resurrection appearances of Jesus, albeit in different places, Matthew in

Galilee and Luke in Jerusalem. In all the Synoptic accounts, the world is depicted as full of suffering and death, which are not promised to end despite the triumphs of Jesus variously depicted.

All this, of course, we can take as metaphorical, mythological, or legendary speech. In this vein, when we look at the metaphors of other religious traditions, despite the ills of the world, there is transcendent creation and goodness that we can celebrate. In Judaism, it is possible to see the ending of the creation not as stopping the world, though it may stop, but as subsumed in the Creator with the peace that passes understanding. In Islam, despite the heavy focus on the end of the world, its mystical traditions depict our true residence *now* in the glorious Creator. In Buddhism, the ills and joys of the world are but passing dharmas and the existence of something transcendent is denied, though there is a mystery to the creation of the dharmas. In some forms of Hinduism, the ills of the world are sharply separated from our true reality, which is atman, which is Brahman with qualities, which is Brahman without qualities, that we mightily seek and already are. In Daoism, we find our way in the Dao that is the mother of our circumstances while resting serene in the Dao that underlies temporal process. In Confucianism, things begin in absolutely nothing, which is revealed with the move to potentiality for something, the yang, the yin, and finally temporal oscillation. Confucianism, and perhaps Daoism, is very clear that persons among whom we live are pretty far down the evolutionary line. Whatever the metaphors, however they differ regarding the world and anything transcendent, they all allow of the world being interpreted as filled with suffering and death, while religious truth finds a happiness that is compatible with this.

What I have said here is very surprising, although it is not particularly new. All the religions, even Confucianism, have highly metaphorical means of expressing victory in the world, or in a hereafter. The worse things get in this life, the more attractive are these this-worldly victories. Except when they fail. We all suffer and die. "Next lives" gets boring. When this-worldly things get bad enough, we are sorely tempted by the image of Jesus and the Archangel Michael leading an army of angels to our rescue. Or Guan Yin at least getting our children married to doctors. So it becomes surprisingly important to remember the special transcendent, whatever it is called, that is compatible with all our suffering and death. Most of us, of course, will stick with the this-worldly hope. If things go too bad, we might reject the entire religion business. Or we might deny the legitimacy of the failure. Or we might postpone our expectation of succor to some life hereafter. Only a few of us will rest easy, however, in the disastrous failures of a life of suffering and death, because we find our way to a transcendent Creation whose creation is still all right.

To make the point that this is a religious as well as philosophical surprise, what follows in this chapter are three Christian sermons. I am indeed a Christian pastor and was dean of Marsh Chapel at Boston University before the current incumbent, Robert Allen Hill, who invited me to deliver these messages. Although thoroughly Christian, I do not hold to all kinds of Christianity, only those kinds compatible with certain kinds of Confucianism in which I also have held offices. Slightly less, I also practice Buddhism and Hinduism of various sorts, and even less wholeheartedly I practice Judaism and Islam, in all of which I have directed dissertations, beginning with my own. In this book, however, I want to emphasize the significance of religion, and hence in this chapter I begin with sermons.

The first sermon, "Everything Saved Together, or, The High Point of Suburban Life," was for the Easter Vigil, March 31, 2018, in Robinson Chapel beneath Marsh Chapel. The second, "Changes," was preached in Marsh Chapel the Seventh Sunday after Epiphany, February 24, 2019. The third was preached in Marsh Chapel on the First Sunday in Advent, November 29, 2020.

Everything Saved Together, or, The High Point of Suburban Life: Mark 16:1–8; Romans 6:3–11

The Easter Vigil is central to the liturgical story of Jesus's last days, which begins in the wilderness; goes to a suburb, Bethany; then to the city of Jerusalem with nightly returns to Bethany; then to the cross at the hand of Rome; away to Heaven; and finally back home where God fulfills us. I stress this arc because at this season we are tempted to focus on resurrection and getting away from this life. The point of Christianity, nevertheless, and contrary to what many might believe, is not to get away to heaven but to embrace God with us as our creator. The incarnation is fundamental, God with us and in us, that by which we are made and fulfilled. Resurrection is an intensification of incarnation for the human point of view. The Easter Vigil is at once the end of Holy Saturday and the beginning of Easter day (remember that the Jewish day begins with sunset). According to our text in Mark, the women went out to buy spices on Saturday evening after the Sabbath was officially over and then waited until morning to go to the tomb. We can imagine this vigil as a pivot of reflections for tying together a much larger story.

Last weekend I went to a conference where one speaker argued that "the city" is the central locale of Christianity, indeed any, religion. Cities grew up around central worship places, such as temples. The density of urban population fostered farming in the countryside and the need for government, especially a king with a protective army. The speaker claimed that the New Testament notion of "the Kingdom of God" really meant the City of God where the city with its king controlled the surrounding countryside. His commentator lamented the fact that she herself lived and worked in Alexandria, Virginia, a suburb of Washington, DC, and bemoaned the sterile homogeneity of suburbs, agreeing that cities instead are the center of things. I believe that this search for the "center" of things missed the continuity of creation, hence of incarnation, and the bite of resurrection. Here is the arc of the Jesus story: from wilderness to suburb to city to empire to Heaven to back home.

Let's begin with the wilderness. According to John's gospel, Jesus had gone to Judea, near Bethany, to raise his friend Lazarus, which caused such furor and plots on his life that Jesus fled to the wilderness near the little town of Ephraim to hide out with his disciples. I gather that "wilderness" in those days meant nature little modified by human habitation, settlements, farms, and domestic animals. Jesus frequently escaped to the wilderness to pray. Matthew, Mark, and Luke recount that after his baptism in the wilderness near Bethany by John the Baptist, Jesus stayed in the wilderness for forty days and nights to come to terms with temptation. John's gospel, by contrast, says Jesus skipped the temptation in the wilderness and took his new disciples straight back to Galilee, although, as I say, John does refer to the wilderness later in the gospel.

Because wilderness means nature unmodified by human beings, we today understand it to have a much greater extent than was assumed in biblical times. We know the universe goes back at least to the big bang over thirteen billion years ago and has many more galaxies than could be imagined until recently, and there might be many big bangs. The main action of the universe is expanding gasses, wildly clumping for brief durations of astronomical time into solar systems and planets where life can evolve such as on the human habitat of Earth. The end of the universe might be a final dissipation where anything identifiable becomes so distant from anything else than nothing identifiable is left. Or it might be a big crunch where everything flies back together into a super black hole with nothing left outside. Both of these outcomes and their variants are so far in the future that our minds are stretched almost beyond imagination to feel its connection with us. Nevertheless, the whole of nature constitutes the creation shaped by the logos or Word of God in which all things have their being, the Word that was with God from the beginning and that shall be the Omega also. Whereas biblical people could imagine the wilderness as portions of Earth, its mountains and seas not yet humanized, for us the wilderness is wild, distant, intergalactic, and connected beyond imagination. Or rather, to be religious and worship the Creator of all creation, we need poets of a new imagination broad enough for contemporary piety. The image of the *Kingdom* of God is so small as to be mainly harmful now, exaggerating the importance of the human sphere within cosmic creation and imposing anthropomorphic metaphors on God appropriate for super-kings that make divine nonsense. When Jesus went to the edge of the wilderness to hide out, we have to think of him as the incarnation of the Alpha and Omega of all creation. Jesus in the wilderness must be understood as the Pantokrator, Creator of All.

When the festival of Passover was nearing, Jesus and his disciples went back into Bethany, the suburb of Jerusalem, to plot with Mary, Martha, and Lazarus his entry into the Royal City. He was to establish himself as teacher and king, the messiah, the true kind of "king of the Jews." Mary and Martha gave a party at which they anointed Jesus with oil as a king or messiah would be anointed. On what we call Palm Sunday Jesus rode into Jerusalem on a young donkey, which was the way kings rode, and was hailed by many as king. He returned to Bethany that night, and then for the next several days traveled into Jerusalem to teach at the temple, going back to Bethany each evening. Most of our famous teachings of Jesus come from those several days of going to teach in the city by day and returning home at night. For our holy geographic arc, the suburb of Bethany was the pivotal home base for Jesus and his intended establishment of the kingdom of God. The city of Jerusalem was significant for Jesus at that time because he could enter and leave it from the safety of those who loved him in Bethany, where his friends had their home. In the city was controversy with Pharisees,

Sadducees, temple authorities, scribes, and others. Those of us who live in the suburbs and work in the city should take comfort from Jesus's suburban home model.

If Jesus's aim was to restore the kingdom of God in the City of David, he was rudely awakened to discover that the real power in Jerusalem was Rome in the person of Pontius Pilate. The kingdom of the Jews was not really there for Jesus to take, and he was captured, tried, and executed by the Romans for the sake of keeping the peace. Rome's motives had little or nothing to do with Jesus's own teachings or ambitions, which were quite happy to render to Caesar the things that are Caesar's. Pilate seemed quite happy, for his part, to call Jesus "king of the Jews" on the cross. One message to take away from this locus on the holy arc is that religious plans for worldly success are vain and misplaced, whether they be establishment plans that wanted a Jewish state-organized temple or Jesus's own plans for a purification of Judaism. Success in managing a kingdom, however religious and centered in a place of worship, is not what religion is about. Jesus was executed and his disciples went into hiding, although no evidence exists that the Roman authorities tried to arrest them. Pilate was not concerned about the Jesus movement except as a source of political unrest and conflict with the Jewish leaders.

The next step in the arc of Jesus's movement through the creation is the disappearance of his dead body from the tomb. All the gospels agree upon this. Mark has nothing more to say about post-resurrection appearances of Jesus and ends with the women running from the empty tomb in shock and awe. Matthew has the resurrected Jesus meet the disciples in Galilee and ends the gospel with him commissioning them to baptize in his name; Matthew has no account of Jesus's departure, and indeed Jesus's last word in Matthew is that he will be with the disciples until the end of the age. Luke has the resurrected Jesus meet with some disciples on the road to Emmaus and then with the original disciples in Bethany where he blesses them and ascends into heaven. Note again the importance of suburban Bethany as the place of glorious ascension into heaven in contrast to Jerusalem, the failed City of David and the place of execution. John has the post-resurrection Jesus cook breakfast for the disciples in Galilee, commission Peter to lead the church, and then tell Peter that Jesus's personal relationship with the Beloved Disciple is none of Peter's business. For John, there was no ascension into heaven, although Jesus had already begun to morph into a heavenly body when he encountered Mary Magdalen in the garden outside the empty tomb. The gospels have no unanimity about what happened to the resurrected Jesus except to say that after a while he was gone and that his life had been victorious. We can rest with the image that this victory means Heaven for Jesus.

The end of the arc of salvation in Jesus is not his resurrection, however. It is rather what Luke/Acts calls Pentecost when the Holy Spirit comes to direct the life of living people so that they can live here with God in their midst, an incarnation people. Luke/Acts puts this Pentecost some time after the Ascension. John puts it earlier, on Easter day evening when Jesus comes to the disciples and breathes his spirit upon them. According to John, Jesus had earlier, in the Farewell Discourses, given instructions to the disciples about how to carry on and promised to send the Spirit to be with them. However you want to parse these symbols from conflicting traditions, the point is that the personal Jesus is gone but God remains with us in his Spirit to fulfill our lives as we live them on Earth. Paul, in our Romans reading, said that as we were buried with Christ in baptism, so we are raised with him to new life. He surely believed in a resurrection after death. But his point in our passage is that we (or at least his readers) are *now* alive to God in Jesus Christ.

The night of the Easter Vigil is the midpoint in the story of the Incarnate Jesus raised to new life among us and for us. Suburban Bethany is the midpoint mediating between the expanse of wilderness on one hand and the disastrous City of David on the other, between Heaven above and ordinary life with the Incarnate God below.

Another dimension of this story around the Vigil needs attention. If the resurrection is understood in terms of the incarnation of the logos that was in the creation of the entire cosmos, what is the human place in all this? Paul in Romans is not concerned with the metaphysics of creation and the logos that might be incarnate in Jesus. Rather, he is preoccupied with human sinfulness, our deserving of death as punishment, and the astonishing love of God that causes Jesus to die in order to save us from God's own wrath. For Paul, the whole story is about us and our reconciliation with God.

I suspect that not many of us identify with a conception of God as a super-king who is torn between his need to execute justice and his feelings of mercy for his malfeasant citizens. In Paul's view, God's strategy is to send his innocent son to suffer death in place of his unjust people who themselves deserve it. This strategy is supposed to fulfill justice on the one hand and provide mercy on the other. The super-king's trick is that his son does not stay dead, and so everyone wins in the end except Satan. This was a prominent explanatory theme in Christianity from Paul through Luther and Calvin and their followers. For us, I fear this seems like a tawdry soap opera resulting from uncorrected anthropomorphic images of God. God cannot be conceived much as a king without exaggerating the importance of humanity in the sweep of cosmic history. To conceive of God as caught in a contradiction between having to be just and having to be merciful abases the freedom and total creativity of God. To acknowledge God's creative act as working through the logos that structures the entire cosmos means that we must downplay this anthropomorphized image of God as compromised king. To celebrate the incarnation of God with us is to require stretching our minds to conceive the vast created cosmos and our small place in it. The Easter Vigil pivots us from the vastness of nature to the heart of the City, from the heights of the logos to the plane of ordinary life.

Nevertheless, the plain truth is that we and our society are wretched in many respects and *this* is how we fit into the cosmic economy. Good Friday and Holy Saturday illustrate the wretchedness of human existence, with betrayal, injustice, undeserved death, grief, impotence, and despair. Each of us copes with pain, disease, and the prospect of death. We are fragmented in our lives, frustrated in our careers, and alienated from friends. Participating in movements of social justice, still we are lonely. Aiming to do good, still we are guilty. Without need of a king for a just conscience, we judge ourselves and fear the punishment we deserve. Part of the meaning of resurrection is that despite all these wretched ills, we are filled with the God who gives us existence in the first place, set within the cosmos on the third planet out from Sol at the edge of the Milky Way. So with the Easter Vigil we can overlay everyday wretchedness with everyday joy at renewed life and new possibilities, with healthy longing to be the best we can be, and with confidence that we live in the blessedness of the Creator even at the end of our days. Sometimes Paul had too small a view of salvation, namely that the aim is to win us a good place in Heaven later. But salvation is not leaving Earth for Heaven. The incarnational view of salvation is that God as Creator, exemplified in the perfect incarnation of the Word in Jesus, is present with us in all our days and in the days of the cosmos that are not ours. The pivot between vast wilderness and struggling city, between divine logos and the problems of tonight, is eternity. Amen.

Changes: Gen. 45:3–11, 15; Psalms. 92:1–4, 12–15; 1 Cor. 15:35–38, 42–50; Luke 6:27–38

Let me call your attention to our three scriptures for today: one about an incident in one of the world's most dysfunctional families, one about Paul's bizarre ideas about resurrection and immortality, and one about Luke's strange portion of his Sermon on the Plain.

The Genesis reading is part of the story of Jacob, the part where his son Joseph reunites his family. Jacob was the son of Isaac, the first schlemiel in recorded history, to my knowledge. Isaac as a boy was almost killed by his father to prove Abraham's faithfulness to God. As an old man, Isaac was tricked by his wife and Jacob into giving his blessing to the wrong son. Jacob as a young man was strong, if not particularly ethical, and did plot to secure his father's blessing that belonged in Esau. Isaac sent Jacob to his uncle Laban to get one of his daughters as a wife; the candidates were Jacob's first cousins, if you keep track of biblical family practice. He fell in love with Laban's younger daughter Rachel and served Laban seven years to pay for her. But on the wedding night Laban substituted the veiled older daughter, Leah, for Rachel and so Jacob was married to Leah. Wanting Rachel instead, or as well, Jacob worked for Laban another seven years and finally married Rachel too. The two wives constantly fought. Leah bore Jacob the sons Reuben, Simeon, Levi, and Judah. With a concubine, Bilhah, Jacob had Dan and Naphtali. With another concubine, Jacob had Gad and Asher. Leah became fertile again and bore Jacob sons Issachar and Zebulun. Then, last, Rachel bore Jacob his sons Joseph and Benjamin. You will note that the sons of Jacob were ancestors to the twelve tribes of Israel, Jacob's name won from his fight with the angel. With all those warring mothers, the sons of Jacob were hostile to one another, but especially to Joseph, the first son of Rachel, Jacob's favorite wife. You remember how they were offended by Joseph's coat of many colors and sold him to Midianites who took him to Egypt. In Egypt, Joseph worked his way up from slavery to friendship with the Pharaoh, who made him prime minister of the kingdom.

This is where our story today takes up. During a great famine, Jacob's other sons except for Benjamin came to Egypt to beg for grain. Joseph recognized them but they did not recognize him. He sent them back home with instructions to bring him Benjamin, which they did. And as you can see from our text, Joseph, after some trickery, reconciled himself with his brothers. They brought their father to Egypt, where Jacob enjoyed the greatest hospitality and reunion with Joseph. The good times of Jacob's family in Egypt lasted for generations until there was a pharaoh "that knew not Joseph." The moral of the story is that, at least for a few generations, the enmity within Jacob's family was overcome and they lived reconciled with one another and in the good graces of the Egyptians. What an extraordinary change! Everyone changed. In the time of famine the Egyptians became super generous and the household of Jacob was happy.

A moral of this story for us is that the enmity between nations, between parties, between families can indeed be overcome. Appearances to the contrary, those of us who have been aggrieved because of race, nationality, religion, or anything else can change to have the spirit of forgiveness, and forgiveness can bring about peace and happiness. Remember Joseph said that his brothers ought not think of themselves as guilty for doing something horrible to him, but that God used this to put Joseph in the high position where he could help them. Joseph not only effected the vast change of reconciliation in his family, he also changed his older brothers from being guilty to being instruments of great good.

Of course, we don't really know what happened in the Jacob story; even the part about Joseph being the prime minister of Israel does not have verification from any other source. We know only what the biblical sources say. The case with Paul's discussion of immortality in 1 Corinthians is very different. We know a lot about the range of opinions about that topic in Paul's day.

The basic Jewish view prior to the encounter with Greek thought was that death of the body and its decomposition meant the death of the person, with no separable soul that lasted long. Some people thought that the soul lasts a short time in Hades after death and then dissipates like smoke. In Jesus's time, the Greek-influenced Pharisee party that Jesus followed believed in the resurrection of the dead, not the dissipation of the person. The old-school Sadducees teased Jesus and the Pharisees about this; remember when they asked Jesus whose wife a woman would be in the resurrection if she had married several brothers. Some people believed that only the fortunate would be resurrected by God and that the others would just die. The few who would be resurrected had to be given a new embodiment either immediately upon death or at a later Last Judgment. Others believed that the human soul is separable from the body and is itself naturally immortal. For these natural immortalists, some people found a new life in Heaven, but if they didn't merit Heaven there had to be a hell for them to go to. Later Christians in medieval times elaborated the place for the next life to include limbo for unbaptized infants and purgatory for the purification of sinful souls that eventually would get to Heaven. No one in Jesus's time, however, would think about limbo and purgatory.

Paul accepted the natural cosmology of his day that said that the universe exists in layers with different physical properties for each layer or plane. On the plane of the Earth, people had physical bodies that die and decay. The higher levels had incorruptible physical properties, like layers of angels, all the way up to God. Planes lower than the Earth had tormented physical bodies where the demons were. Souls sometimes can traverse from one plane to another. Remember his hymn in Philippians where Christ lives at the top with God but then descends to Earth where he takes on a corruptible physical body as a slave. In Corinthians, Paul said that the afterlife consists in obtaining an incorruptible body and that Jesus assures that those who believe in him will be given an incorruptible body at the Last Judgment. Paul believed the Last Judgment would come within his lifetime, although some Christians had already died. The souls would exist bodiless from the time of death until that Last Judgment resurrection. Many Christians today believe this, but many other Christians also believe that people are raised with incorruptible bodies immediately after the death of their corruptible physical bodies. Either of those theories is a version of reincarnation that was almost universally assumed in South Asia and that came to Israel through Greece.

All of these opinions concern the afterlife as coming (or not) within time after the end of historical, temporal life. The authors of Ephesians and Colossians, whom scholars believe now to have been students of Paul, developed what scholars call a "realized eschatology." This is the belief that it's not the future but an eternal and present relation with God that counts. Christians are baptized into the death and resurrection with Christ and now already live rightly related to God. Therefore, those letters say, we should live with love and generosity now in this life, not worrying about any life to come. Eternity does not mean something that lasts forever, like two people and a ham (my wife told me to tell that joke). Eternity is rather the creative act that creates all moments as future, all as present, and all as past, all together, eternally together although temporally ordered and unfolding. Given what we know now about the dependence of the soul on the brain, body, health, and socialization, many of us now do not believe in life after death but rather in an eternal relation to God that we live out within the days of our temporal life. I myself believe that our day-to-day temporal life is but an abstract part of our real concrete life that is eternal within God's eternal creative act. The realization of this eternal identity transforms our temporal lives in mind-blowing ways. Acceptance of any of these views of immortal or eternal life, however, causes huge changes in how we live day-to-day. We come to live before God, not just within the world of our interests.

I don't know what you believe about these matters about which Paul wrote. All of them have biblical warrant, and they are all hard to believe. It is much easier to focus on Christianity as being about how to live now, which is the position of the part of Jesus's Sermon on the Plain in Luke. In keeping with our emphasis on comparative gospels, I urge you all to look up Matthew's Sermon on the Mount that encompasses three long chapters, five through seven. Read that against Luke's chapter six, beginning with verse 17, a terse rearrangement and reinterpretation of the earlier text Matthew and Luke have in common that is in neither Mark nor John. Matthew was writing for a mainly Jewish audience of Christians and so emphasized how Jesus sharpened Jewish law and attacked hypocrisy regarding Jewish practice. Luke was writing for Greek Christians and pretty much ignored Jewish law and interpreted that Jesus was saying simply how to live before God.

For Luke, the Christian life is not so much about obeying God's law in our heart as it is about being *like* God in what we do. Because God is kind to the ungrateful and wicked, so we should love our enemies, be good to everyone including sinners, and lend without expecting to be repaid. For Luke, Christian life is not so much about being good citizens of God's law-governed kingdom as it is about being "children of the most high." Children succeed by taking on their parents' work, and we should continue the work of God, who loves everyone, even the sinners. The Greek Christians can understand that without knowing much about the Kingdom of Israel. So can we.

Is it not shocking to learn that we should become children of God and heirs to God's work? What greater change can we be called to than to behave like the merciful creator who is kind to the ungrateful and wicked? The Bible of course had no conception of justice as the attempt to change social structures to eliminate poverty or prejudice. It even had nothing against the social institutions of slavery. Those insights did not arise until the modern era, and we late-modern Christians can add them as part of what we need to do to be just in the world. Luke would remind us that God loves the billionaires and racists, and loved the slave-owners, no matter how bad they are in a calculus of good and evil. A condition of us loving the wicked is that we forgive them, as we must do to be like God. What a change in the way we ordinarily think about justice!

Our three texts today are about changes. Joseph finishes the Jacob story by reconciling his family and turning his older brothers' guilt into God's instrument for reconciliation. Paul's understanding of Christian salvation is exchanging our perishable bodies for imperishable bodies so that we can rise with Jesus to the plane of God and enjoy fellowship with the divine. The journey upward through different planes of reality might not be how you think of a right relation to God, but there is surely a change from living in ordinary history to living in a history that is part of the eternal creation. Luke's understanding of true Christian life is not just to be good by worldly standards, nor even to be obedient to divine commands, but to become children of God acting like God in daily life. How different that is from the way we ordinarily live!

These three texts draw a distinction between the steady way things are and the constancy of change. Forget about the way things are. Pay attention to how they are changing. By the imitation of God, make changes for the better that lie within your means. Look for ways to make changes that you otherwise would not notice. See that in making these changes you are part of God creating with love, even for the ungrateful and wicked with whom we are intimately bound. Remember that we have two bodies, as Paul would say. Our historical body lives day to day with all the ambiguities of life, our successes and our failures. That historical body is only a part of our eternal body within which we are connected with all other things, including the past and future, within the eternal act of God's creation. When we realize that today's body is only a part of our eternal body, we can accept the fact that what we do today, obligated as it is to be just, cannot escape the love of God even if we do what we ought not. Who knows? Our best intentions today might be great evils that will be shown up in future generations. We can take comfort that even the worst of us is part of the eternity of God's creative act. Today we must act. In eternity we just rest in the bliss of God creating. Change exists in eternity.

Amen.

Have Courage: Isaiah 64: 1–9; 1 Corinthians 1:3–9; Mark 13:24–37

When I was a young adolescent, I thought the following was an outrageously funny joke. A man saw three holes in the ground and said, "Well, well, well." Nowadays, I suppose, nobody thinks of wells as holes in the ground, but it was very funny back then. Today in Advent I want to talk modestly about holes in our intellectual ground. I'm going to speak of these holes abstractly, but they are not only abstract. As Christians we recognize them as holes in the Trinity: the Son, the Spirit, and even the Father. Isn't it astonishing, however, to refer to the Trinitarian Persons as "holes"? After all, these Persons name the basic contours of the faith. All the other doctrines, stories, songs, and celebrations are elaborations of the Persons of the Son, the Spirit, and the Father. The usual order to list them is Father, Son, and Spirit. But I am going to change that for Advent to start with the Son, then with the Spirit as the animator of the religious community, and finally with the Father as the universal Creator acknowledged by many if not all communities. Instead of seeing these Persons as the most positive general doctrines of the faith, I confess with embarrassment to seeing them as holes. How astonishing! But consider.

Belief in Jesus as the Son of God is the most distinctive of Christian doctrines. Of course, it is extremely varied. The Gospel of Mark treats Jesus as adopted by God for a larger, salvific purpose. The Gospel does not even have a proper post-resurrection scene. The Gospel of Matthew was addressed to the Jews who surrounded Jesus and focuses mainly on how Jesus amended the Jewish teachings. It traces Jesus's ancestry back to Abraham. The Gospel of Luke was addressed to gentile followers of Jesus and traces his ancestry back to Seth, Adam, and God, with claims for Jesus's universality. The Gospel of John tells a very different story from the first three Gospels, beginning with a metaphysical sermon on the creation that claims that the Word or Logos that God spoke was itself incarnate in the person of Jesus, but then moving to a very personal account of Jesus's friendships and enemies, ending with a very long sermon, Jesus's crucifixion, and then his appearances first in Jerusalem and then at the Sea of Tiberias. Paul wrote about Jesus almost exclusively as a metaphysical antidote to the judgment of the Jews, the Second Man Adam responding to the First. He said almost nothing about the biographical details that interested the Gospels.

In post-testamental times, Jesus was interpreted in the terms of Greek thought with many variations in how he could be both God and man. Augustine recognized the difficulties of giving a straightforward interpretation of the scriptures and interpreted Jesus according to his own categories. Aquinas adopted many of these strategies of interpretation and embedded the highly interpreted Jesus in his dense fabric of ethics. Schleiermacher treated Jesus as the best example of a God-intoxicated person. Bultmann thought of Jesus as an historical figure who was given a highly sophisticated interpretation by the thinkers of his context. But in all of these, from the Gospellers to the twentieth century, Jesus was interpreted as the Son of God, whatever that might mean. Some of you longtime members of this church have heard my interpretations of Jesus over the years, drawing heavily on Tillich though set in a much wider context.

Without for a moment suggesting that a consistent story is true about Jesus, I want to make clear that I have a consistent story. It begins with John's Gospel, which swings from metaphysics to friendship and has nearly always two storylines: one that is for the masses and one for sophisticated Christians. I follow that through history to our own day. But is this not still only speculation? So I have an interpretive point of view, for which I can argue vigorously; is it still not merely an argument? Don't I recognize the power of many other interpretations, particularly more fundamentalistic ones? Don't I recognize that the finer my interpretations, the fewer people agree with me? Of course I do.

Moreover, the existential meaning of Jesus is itself speculative. How many people have believed that faith in Jesus will get them into Heaven? I don't even believe in Heaven as a place for afterlife experiences. How many people have believed that Jesus is the judgment of God, rewarding the good and punishing the evil? I believe that evil is to be endured but is not worth punishing. How many people have believed that everyone is saved in the end through faith in Jesus? I'm a little worried about salvation.

Now I'll bet a lot of you share my doubts about Jesus. In church, everything is fine because we know that the language of the liturgy, even of the preaching, is mainly metaphorical. But when pressed, how much can we affirm that Jesus is Son of God? Not much. And this is where the doctrine of Jesus as Son of God has holes in it. Your holes might be different from mine. Nevertheless, at some point, when pressed, or at night, or when faced with COVID-19, I bet you just get quiet and say someone else had better figure it out because you have good Christian work to do.

The doctrine of the Holy Spirit is equally full of holes. It began with the Gospel of John's introduction that took the form of a special midrashic sermon based on two texts. The primary text was the first part of Genesis that said that the universe was created by God speaking. This poses a question. Is God a person, unified whether speaking or not? Or is God whole only prior to speaking so that the speech is an addition? On this view the speech was divine but secondary, that through which all things were made. This latter was the view held by John and the Christians.

John's second text was the reference to Lady Wisdom in Ecclesiastes and the intertestamental writings as being neglected. Finally God made his speech or Logos incarnate in the person of Jesus who was himself treated very badly. But then John's text shifts to the biographical details of Jesus's life.

The Book of Acts records how on Pentecost day the Holy Spirit descended to the disciples in tongues of fire on their heads, giving them wisdom and the power to speak in all the languages represented in their audience. This marks the beginning of an association of the Holy Spirit with the Church that has come down to the present day. But Paul Tillich went so far as to say that the Church is not the real Church unless the Spirit is present. The holes in the Person of the Holy Spirit have lapped around the doctrine since its beginning. When we look to the Holy Spirit to give us a divine authority for anything we want to say, it surely is full of holes.

Backing off from the Son and the Holy Spirit, the Person of the Father is extremely general. The adoption of Greek thinking gave the Christians plenty of room to speculate on God as Creator. Aquinas defended the Neo-Platonic view that God is infinite and that the creation is finite and made from the infinite. Calvin too said that God is infinite. Schleiermacher and Tillich were somewhat vague about whether God is full or empty. West Asian religions have tried to carry over the personal characteristics of intentionality and wisdom to God, even when God is beyond real characters. South Asian religions instead have taken the intentionality line to be mistaken and have pushed for consciousness in some pure state to be the nature of God. The East Asians have given up just about all uses of the metaphor of the person for God and have talked about nature giving rise spontaneously to determinate things. The

Chinese have been naturalistic rather than theistic in their theology. All traditions have tried to claim that some line of finite characteristics remains with God, even when God is pushed to indeterminateness. At least, this is the way I read the intellectual progress of religions.

I don't know how far you want to go with me on this adventure of conceiving God. Most Christians want to hold on to some kind of intentionality in God and are reluctant to give up a vague claim that God acts with purpose or has hopes for us. But remember the intellectual pressures pushed to an extreme, remember the dark night, remember COVID-19.

Perhaps you would be willing to give up the view that God is a being, a thing, and consider God to be an act of creation. God as act is the original element of creation, not something prior. God is the creating of all the things. The things are the product of the act. The act is eternal because all time is created. Anything to be honored, prayed to, or located as present or absent is part of creation. God is God only because of creation. God as act is known only with the creation and not before the act.

To my mind, God is good only because the act creates determinate things, all of which are good, each in its own way. To be determinate, a thing is good just by itself. But no thing is just by itself; it is also with other things. God is the source of evil only because these goods inhibit one another and conflict. This is just the way determinate things are. Most of the goods and evils of human life are rather local and we do the best we can, although what we can do and fail at surely counts. But we count only proximately, not ultimately. Ultimately, we all are good in just the way we are.

Mine is a fairly extreme view. If you go with me, welcome. If not, I encourage your belief. But remember this is all just speculation, however sophisticated. It is the best that I can do. I presume on the basis of past experience that it is a hypothesis that will be superseded by a better hypothesis someday. From my standpoint, all previous hypotheses have fallen short and been superseded. Why not mine?

Surely there are holes in my hypothesis of the Father as the ultimate sheer act of creation, inseparable from the creation itself. I do not know what they are, but I fear them. By happy days I work on my hypothesis. But when pressed ultimately, in the ultimate dark, or even ultimately depressed by the virus, I am ultimately afraid. Of course, now it is daytime and light, and so I am only *referring* to my fears, not exhibiting them.

What did Jesus say about this situation? He said, "Take courage; I have conquered the world." According to John, he said this toward the end of his long speech at the last supper, a speech so complex and contradictory no one understood him. "Take courage; I have conquered the world." He said it after warning that his disciples would face persecution, as we all do whether we believe anything or nothing. "Take courage; I have conquered the world." He said it whether or not we believe in his later resurrection after crucifixion. "Take courage; I have conquered the world." He said it whether or not he *actually* said it, which he probably did not. "Take courage; I have conquered the world." He said it even if the whole story of his life, even if the rumors of the Holy Spirit, even if his belief in the Huge God beyond all reckoning is false. "Take courage; I have conquered the world." He said it even if there are holes in our best theories, even if there are holes in the roots of our life's determination, even if there are holes in the God beyond gods. "Take courage; I have conquered the world."

Even if there are holes in every theory we have thought, in every theory we now think, in every theory anyone shall ever think, Jesus says, "Take courage; I have conquered the world," which refers to the past, to what Jesus has done and endured. Whatever happens in his future, including crucifixion and resurrection and looking down from Heaven on his Church, counts as nothing because he has already conquered. "Take courage" refers to his disciples, to us, and to everyone from then on: it means that whatever happens comes from God and is good, and that we should anticipate it with joy. Even if the world is ultimately destroyed, we have had enough. Even if my ultimate hypothesis, according to which God is the act of creation and the creation is ultimately good, is mistaken, we have had enough. We have had enough in our local circumstance, even if we are locally evil, and we have had enough in ultimate perspective. Do not give up when things go bad. Have courage.

Well, well, well. Three holes in the ground. Three holes in our best understanding of what is ultimately real. So we should be modest in our claims as Christians. We should be strenuous in our attempts to do better. We should engage our local projects with determination but admitting our likely failure. We should engage our ultimate end with thanksgiving. "Have courage; I have conquered the world."

Amen.

Part One
Philosophy

Chapter 1

Being-Itself

Not a tiny trait,
Not a largest box,
Not a rushing stream,
Closer to us than ourselves,
Farther than unseen galaxies,
Here in every change.
The ontological creative act,
Maker of all things,
Nothing apart from them.
The world held together by this act,
Made possible because actual,
Possible surprise from actual creation

Being-Itself

Being-itself is strange. It is strange, surprising, and not what you would expect. But think. Being-itself is an *act*, not a thing. Ordinarily, we think of an act as performed by an actor. Yet here I think of an actor as the result of an act, not something prior. An actor that does not act is not an actor. Usually we think of an actor who has acted before, often, with many kinds of characters. In these circumstances, it is just fine to call him, her, or it an actor. But in the case of being-itself, there is just the singular act.

Being-itself is a *creative* act. Its product consists of every determinate thing. *Every* determinate thing.

So this creative act cannot be in time, not at all. It is not a first moment followed by others, or a present moment in which all times are included (a *totum simul*), nor a future possibility. Because of this, we call the creative act "eternal."

The creative act is also not in space, not in the north, not at the base of an upside down tree, not floating through empty space. Because of this, we call the creative act "immense" (literally, "unmeasurable," in Latin).

Because the creative act gives rise to *every* determinate thing, it contains no determinate characters apart from its products. Apart from what it creates, it is not Being, Existent, One, Good, True, Wise, Rational, or whatever you might have thought about God or the Ultimate. Apart from what it creates, the act is nothing. *Conceived* as apart from its product, it is indeterminate.

Because the creative act creates, its creatures are as necessary as the act that creates them. If there were no creatures, the act would not create them and therefore would not be the act. So the act and the created creatures together are necessary, given the contingent creation. This is ontological necessity.

Suppose there are determinate things or traits that would have to be true no matter what other things are created. These would be the true cosmological transcendentals, if you will. I believe there are four of these traits: form, components formed, existential location, and value. Take it on faith, for now, that there are these four. The point is that each of them needs the others and so they are cosmologically necessary. Whereas ontological necessity obtains between determinate things and the creative act, cosmological necessity obtains among determinate things.

The creative act is immediate. This is to say, it has no structure or process of creation. It just is, including the determinate things as its termini. Time itself is one of its products.

The creative act, including its determinate products, is radically contingent. There is no reason or cause for its existence because all reasons and causes are among its products. Perhaps the strangest element of the creative act is this: it is contingent. It is not contingent on anything. It just happens. It just is.

Nevertheless, the creative act is a movement from nothingness to the determinate things. So it is creation ex nihilo. That immediate movement, lacking steps, is the greatest mystery of all. Fortunately, it has indeed happened and so we all are relieved. The penultimate step in thinking about this is wonder, seeing how the creative act including its products has no necessity in itself. The ultimate step is surprise in realizing that it has happened and that we are in the midst of the determinate things and their creator.

The creative act is also ontological. I call it the *ontological creative act* in order to remind you of its strangeness (by the ugliness of its name) and also to call to mind its contact with being-itself. As the ontological creative act, being-itself is the act including its products, the determinate things. We might think of the determinate things themselves, by themselves and without the act. This is our ordinary way of thinking. We just think about the things, or some of the things, or some aspect of some of the things. But this is partial. The determinate things are created together, and this requires their ontological context of mutual togetherness. Their cosmological togetherness is constituted by their various relations, and those relations have their reality with the things related. But their ontological context of mutual togetherness includes their essential features that by definition are external to one another.

To say that being-itself is the ontological creative act is to remind you that it is implicit in any reference to any determinate thing. This ontological creative act is thus the "first object of the intellect," as the Western Medievals would say. Although mentioned only when doing metaphysics, it is implicit in every reference.

Genuinely to know being-itself is like aesthetic perceiving. Our usual knowledge is iconic in mapping the reality known. But being-itself as a whole does not have a structure to be mapped, only the determinate things do. So we have to come to perceive being-itself, and we can become better at this.

Is this not strange? Just about every claim I have made about being-itself is strange. If you don't think this is strange, sit back and think about it for a while. Then let me suggest some of the reasons for my claims.

Determinateness

Most of the metaphysical categories through which we attempt to understand the generic traits of existence (Dewey's phrase for the subject matter of metaphysics) are generalizations from more specific cosmological notions. For instance, from the cosmological observation that most things, if not everything, can be regarded either as acts of consciousness or objects of consciousness, South Asian philosophies developed metaphysical ideas such as atman and Brahman, emptiness, and Buddha-mind, all articulated in a variety of often competing ways. From the cosmological observation that things spontaneously expand and then recoup energy in interlocking dynamic harmonies, East Asian philosophies developed metaphysical ideas such as yang and yin, the Great Ultimate, Heaven and Earth, Principle and Material Force, all variously articulated. Plato observed that concrete things are always changing, always on the way to being something else, and developed his theory of forms to measure what things change from and to. Aristotle was more impressed with the identity of concrete things and developed a metaphysics of substance to explicate that identity. More recently, Whitehead developed his marvelously original metaphysical system by considering issues in scientific cosmology and worrying about what the sciences left out; he even called his metaphysics a "philosophical cosmology."

My proposal is to center metaphysics on the problem of determinateness as such. Appreciating that there are so many different cosmological intuitions and ways of imagining the world, still they are all determinate. If we can provide a metaphysics of determinateness, we can avoid having to choose among the cosmological visions, at least for a while. Of course, philosophical cosmology is extremely interesting on its own and we should work on developing the best cosmological theories, attentive to science, the arts, history, and all of the fields we call "philosophy of . . . ." But for purposes of metaphysics, there are things we can learn irrespective of the cosmological issues.

Heidegger is the philosopher who brought the metaphysical question of being-itself into focus in the twentieth century, with a focus much sharper than Whitehead's. The focus was achieved by his distinction between being-itself and beings. Beings are determinate things, and all determinate things are beings, for Heidegger. But he also wanted being-itself to have some kind of content, something that could appear or be revealed, something that the really ancient Greeks "got" and that the subsequent tradition lost or obscured. Still, Heidegger remained caught within the frame of transcendental philosophy, despite his best intentions. The ontology of being-itself had to be discussed in terms of the transcendental conditions of the self, or Dasein, to which being-itself might appear. Transcendental phenomenology, of the several sorts Heidegger tried, is a kind of cosmological filter or metaphoric system that prevented him from taking advantage of his liberating distinction between being-itself and beings and forced him to transform it into a distinction between being-itself and Dasein.

I propose to go straight to an analysis of determinateness as such, not determinate yin/yang vibrations, determinate consciousness, determinate change, determinate substances, or determinate transcendental conditions of subjectivity. Here goes.

To be determinate is to be this rather than that. Any determinate "this" can be determinate only in respect to some "thats" from which it is determinately different. If there were only one thing, it would not be determinate, and hence nothing rather than something. Any "this" needs some other "that" with respect to which it is determinate. Of course, we can imagine a false cosmological state of affairs in which there is only one actual determinate thing. But that thing could not be determinate unless there were other possible things it could have been and from which it differs. The metaphysics of determinateness is vague with respect to cosmological distinctions between actuality and possibility. But if anything is determinate at all, in any way, there must be a manifold of determinate things that are determinate with respect to one another. This is a conclusion the importance of which I shall stress in a moment.

To be determinate is to be internally complex, a harmony of multiple components. Determinateness requires two kinds of components, which I call "conditional" and "essential." The conditional components are those that register the other things with respect to which the complex harmony is determinate. The essential components are those that arrange all the components so that the thing has its own-being over against the other things with respect to which it is determinate; the essential components make the thing different.

If the thing had only conditional components, the thing would be nothing more than those other things. That is, it would not be a thing at all determinately different from those things with respect to which it is supposed to be determinate. If a thing had only essential components, it would have no relation to anything else and therefore could not be determinately different from them. Any determinate thing, therefore, must harmonize both conditional and essential components.

To be determinate, a thing must be both internally and externally related to the things with respect to which it is determinate. It is internally related to those things insofar as it has conditional components from them. The mutual conditioning of things constitutes a kind of matrix of things in relation. The kinds of conditioning relations are matters for cosmological reflection. But a thing must also be externally related to those other things with essential components of its own so as to be different from them. Things would not have different locations in a matrix of relations if they each did not have essential components over against what is contained in those other things. The matrix of determinate things in relation, being determinate with respect to one another, is what our philosophies' cosmological disputes are about. The context within which mutual conditionings take place is the ontological world of harmonies, however that is best described.

The question of being-itself can now be formulated with respect to this complex hypothesis about determinateness. The mutual conditionings of things that are determinate with respect to one another constitute their cosmological togetherness. But that cosmological togetherness would not be possible if the mutually determinate things were not also together in another sense. Each determinate thing is a harmony of its essential as well as its conditional components. Without both, it would not have standing to be related to other things as determinately different. The cosmological conditionings involve only the conditional components. The essential components are precisely what are not reduced to the matrix of conditional components.

So there must be a context in which the determinate things are together with their essential as well as conditional components. In this context, the determinate things have their being in relation to one another while also being distinct from one another. I call this the "ontological context of mutual relevance." Ontological togetherness is how things are in their being such that they can be cosmologically together.

To refer to an ontological "context" of mutual relevance is not an innocent phrase. The issue is that anything that is determinate has to be within the context, not the context itself. If the context itself were something determinate, then it would have to have essential components outside of the matrix of determinate things. This would require the context itself and the things within the context to be in yet a larger or deeper context. So the ontological context of mutual relevance cannot itself be determinate. This eliminates a variety of traditional suggestions about what the being-itself is of which determinate are beings. For instance, it could not be a property common to all beings, for the property would have to be determinate. It could not be a totalizing container, for that would also be determinate. It could not be a supernatural being like a God that creates all the determinate things, because that being would have to be determinate to be different from those things.

Rather, the ontological context of mutual relevance has to be an *act* that creates the determinate things together in their internal and external relations. Such an act is the most strange of the things mentioned above. The act can have no determinateness except in the determinate things it creates. The ontological creative act is not a thing with properties; that would make it a determinate thing. Rather, it is simply an act of making, the terminus of which is the determinate things of the world. Many people assume that the only thing that can explain something else is a determinate thing, as one determinate thing conditions another. But in the instance of the question of being-itself, it is determinateness itself that requires an account. The ontological creative act does not require an account.

If we conceptually prescind the ontological creative act from anything and everything determinate that it creates, it turns out to be nothing. It has no features and it does not do anything; it cannot even sensibly be called an act. It is not an act in the sense of an Aristotelian or Thomistic sense of actualization of potentiality, too parochial a cosmological notion. Some mystics ascend into the ontological act, virtually leaving the determinate world behind, and find it to be Nothingness; the journey of ascent, or descent into the abyss if you prefer, is what warrants an intelligible discussion of nothing.

If we conceptually prescind the determinate manifold from the ontological creative act, as harmonies mutually related but partially external to one another, we get the world, for which some cosmological account is relevant. The world, conceptually considered apart from the ontological creative act that is its ontological context of mutual relevance, is just the sum of determinate things, however one's cosmology articulates the summing up. The world, as a cosmological matrix of determinate things, includes the things but without reference to their being. The being-itself of beings is the unity of the ontological creative act and what it creates, its terminus as an act. Apart from the manifold of beings, being-itself is nothing. Apart from the ontological creative act that constitutes them as mutually relevant, the manifold of beings is the hollow abstraction of things that neglects, or obscures, the being-itself of beings as beings. The answer I propose to the question of being-itself is that the ontological creative act, inclusive of the determinate things it creates, is the unity of being-itself and the beings. Isn't this strange? Now I need to say more about the ontological creative act to make this answer persuasive.

The Ontological Creative Act

The ontological creative act gives itself the nature of being the creative act by creating the determinate things, whatever they are. Apart from the creation of determinate things, the act has no nature at all, which is to say that it is indeterminate if you could speak of it at all. This figure of an indeterminate ground giving rise to everything determinate is by no means a novel philosophical idea. Something like that is intended in the *Daodejing*'s theory of the Dao that cannot be named, Zhou Dunyi's theory of the Ultimate of Non-being giving rise to the Great Ultimate, the Hindu distinction between Brahman without qualities and Brahman with qualities, Madhyamika Buddhist interpretations of Emptiness, Neo-Platonic distinctions between the One and the Dyad (a distinction that is intelligible only from the standpoint of the Dyad), and Thomas Aquinas's theory of God as the pure Act of To Be. These and similar philosophical ideas are framed in terms of competing cosmologies and metaphoric systems. But they each in their own way reflect the basic conviction that anything with a determinate order needs to be explained or accounted for in terms of something that is not determinate. Determinateness is itself what needs explanation, as Peirce said.

A number of those theories of the indeterminate grounding the determinate hold that the indeterminate ground is itself a kind of fullness of being-itself and that determinate things are delimitations of infinitely full being-itself. Various Neo-Platonisms and Thomas Aquinas's theories say this. The operative supposition behind this is that all causation involves the deriving of the act in the effect from prior act in the cause. The cause must contain the act of the effect: "Out of nothing, nothing comes." My hypothesis about the ontological creative act says the opposite: the production of the determinate things is entirely novel, a genuine creation of that which had no reality apart from being created. The Western tradition has called this creation *ex nihilo*.

Analogies with human creativity lie behind the metaphoric resonances of the ontological creative act. Fullness of being-itself theories such as that of Aquinas stress that human creativity involves the rearrangement of antecedent resources in thought, intention, and appropriated realities; explanation of the created thing consists, for these theories, in tracing back the antecedent resources that show up in the product. For my hypothesis, on the contrary, human creativity is interpreted as the adding of something new to the antecedent resources, however small and minor. Novelty in itself, genuine spontaneity, is the hallmark of human creativity, despite the fact that novelty involves rearranging some antecedent resources and the novelty itself might not be very great. Working with these cosmological analogies, the ontological creative act is friendly to process cosmologies emphasizing novelty, such as Whitehead's. The difference, in the analogy, between human creativity on my interpretation and the ontological creative act is this: in the case of the former, the past resources are potentials for creative action and as such limit what can be done, whereas in the case of the latter, there are no antecedent resources, no potentials for creation, no limitations. The ontological creative act is total novelty with nothing given to it. Human creativity is mainly constrained by what is given and only a wee bit spontaneous.

Because everything whatsoever that is determinate has to be created in order to be determinate with respect to other things, the ontological creative act is immediate. It has no internal steps moving from absolute nothingness through infinitesimally more determinate stages to full-blown determinateness. In no way can the ontological creative act be likened to a process that can be understood by the formal stages through which it passes, as in Plato's cosmology.

With an important exception to be discussed shortly, not much can be said about the ontological creative act without some cosmology in mind interpreting the determinate world created. Without directly engaging philosophical cosmology, we can note that just about any plausible cosmology would want to account for things existing in the dimensionality of space and time, causing one another in some kind of temporal flow. Distinctions between temporal earlier and later, logical before and after, near and far, inside and outside, and the like are all determinate and hence are part of the created product. Cosmologies differ in how they interpret space-time dimensionality, for instance in asserting total determinism or partial indeterminism within temporal causation. The ontological creative act cannot be in any ordered or determinate relation to its terminus, the created world. The act cannot be at any time, even at a first moment if there is one. Nor can the act have an extensive dimensionality that might be filled in by determinate things.

The act rather is the being-itself of the determinate things, which is required by their ontological togetherness. Temporal things are determinately after some things and before yet others; this is part of their determinate nature. Therefore, they are together with those other things in a nontemporal context that makes possible their temporal relations, including perhaps creativity with novelty. That context is the ontological context of mutual relevance, namely, the ontological creative act. Although each temporal thing enjoys its being in its own time, if you will, the being-itself it enjoys is one with the being-itself of all the other beings. All process is within time; the ontological creation of time and temporal things is immediate, not a process.

A consequence of the thesis that everything determinate is created is that we have to look at the world to discover what the cosmos consists in. The hypothesis is vague with respect to whatever cosmology might be true. No findings of science, morals, or any other form of inquiry could contradict the hypothesis about the ontological creative act, so long as those findings are determinate. Some kinds of theism seek to gain cosmological predictability by asserting that the ontological creative act has some kind of antecedent character, such as being good, loving, or well-intentioned. Then the world must be the sort of thing a good, loving, or well-intentioned creator would create. But this gives rise to the intractable difficulties of theodicy. The hypothesis about being-itself as the ontological creative act of beings denies any such antecedent character or limitation to the act. From the human standpoint, the ontological creative act is gratuitous, arbitrary, surprising, and undeserved. Theisms that stress divine freedom over divine character are on the right track. Cosmologies can be entirely empirical, looking to see what determinate things there are.

A special qualification needs to be made to this point, however. No matter what things are created, to be described under whatever cosmology, they must be determinate. Therefore, if there are any traits characteristic of anything and everything determinate, they might be knowable apart from any particular empirical study. These transcendental traits of determinateness are created in the creating of anything determinate and therefore must obtain in any world created. In this sense, the created nature of the ontological creative act includes these traits as well as the adventitious properties of the actually created world.

We have already noticed certain transcendental traits of determinateness, namely, that to be determinate means to be an internally complex harmony with conditional and essential components, involved with other determinate harmonies in a matrix of mutual relations and enjoying being-itself because that involvement with others comes from the ontological context of mutual relevance that is the creative act. There are at least four other transcendental traits of harmony that can be mentioned here as following from what has already been said: form, components formed, existential location, and value-identity. To say much about these traits without supposing some plausible cosmology is difficult, but a sketch can be given.

Because any harmony is internally complex with a multitude of components, it has a pattern or form in which these components are together. The conditional components provide much of the material that must be formed together, and the essential components do the work of integrating them; the form is the result. We should be careful not to assume that form is static. If the world involves temporal dimensions—the unfolding of a symphony, or a personal life—then it involves diachronic form.

Because of its multitude of components, any harmony involves complex relations with its components. Every component is itself a determinate harmony in a matrix of relations with other harmonies. I have finessed, for now, the complications of harmonies containing harmonies containing harmonies, of overlapping matrices of conditions that make components partly inside and partly outside of containing harmonies. Harmonies on this account are not substances necessarily, and their components might have careers that begin outside them and continue on after them. The internal complexities of components provide the venue for discussing notions such as being in or out, earlier and later, and so forth.

Precisely because of careers of conditioning components, harmonies have existential location relative to the other harmonies with respect to which they are determinate. But in order to have existential location, harmonies need essential components to give them own-being relative to one another. The being of harmonious beings consists in their mutual relations that allow them to be related but also partly external with their own-being. Having existential location is a necessary part of being a determinate thing relative to other determinate things, and it constitutes a locus in a larger existential field. The metaphors of location conjure up images of space-time locations, but there might also be logical spaces, fictional spaces, and so forth. All these different structures of matrices constitute an integrated matrix to the extent that the harmonies involved are determinate with respect to one another.

Another transcendental trait of determinateness is that harmonies have the value-identity of getting their particular components together, in with their particular pattern in their particular existential location. This is the true identity of the determinate thing, not just its form, its parts, or its place relative to conditioning thing, but all these together. My hypothesis about this is that this identity has a value, but, without a more elaborate cosmology than can be articulated here, this thesis about value cannot be defended now. An analysis of value can follow in the line of Plato's *Philebus*, Leibniz, and Whitehead. If the thesis about value can be sustained, it would amount to saying that any created world would have value in its determinate things. It would have value because this is the nature of determinateness, not because there is some antecedent value in the ontological creative act.

My overall hypothesis is that the being-itself of beings is to be understood together with the beings through a theory of determinateness about its dependence on being created in an ontological creative act. Earlier I asked for temporary tolerance of my claims about the ontological creative act, which is not itself a determinate thing. Now I want to address some issues concerning why that is such a strange notion and seems counterintuitive to many people.

Knowing Being-Itself

Ordinarily we understand philosophical ideas to explain things by mapping them. In semiotic language, this means that we hope that our theories refer iconically in order to mirror what they are about. Because of the intelligibility of the theories, we can sort and resolve puzzles about their objects, organize our responses to the subject matter, and perhaps engage the world more wisely. Whitehead's criteria of consistency, coherence, applicability, and adequacy are a classical expression of the iconic mirroring that metaphysics hopes to attain.

The strangeness of the idea of an ontological creative act is that it does not have an internal shape or structure to be mirrored. Therefore, it cannot be referred to iconically, which is inconvenient with regard to our usual hope for metaphysical explanation. Philosophers have tried to remedy this by insisting that the ontological act must proceed from an ontological actor, an agent with a nature that might be mirrored, for instance as good, loving, and well-intentioned. Or philosophers have tried to say that the creative act itself is a process in time whose stages can be measured, giving intelligibility to the process, as Whitehead argued. But this will not work, because everything determinate is part of the resulting terminus of the creative act, not the creating itself. Charles Hartshorne thought that the business of metaphysics is to develop a set of first principles, the denial of which makes the world unintelligible. Those first principles themselves do not need explanation simply because they are first, he thought. But, to the contrary, they are determinate and they could not be such without being together in an ontological context of mutual relevance that is not just another determinate thing.

An alternative to iconic reference, as Peirce said, is indexical reference in which the object interpreted is pointed to so as to establish a real causal connection between the object and the interpreter. The interpreter is causally changed so as to encounter and take the object into the interpreter's own-being. The dialectical argument I have given here, coming at the topic of being-itself from so many different angles, is an elaborate index. Poetry is often indexical too, and in this respect metaphysical ontology is closer to poetry than to mathematical iconic explanation. But metaphysical indexical reference is filled with arguments, qualifications, criticisms of other views, and so forth to help make sure that we see where the finger is pointing.

Whereas the result of an iconically referential explanation is like having a map of the territory, the result of an indexically referential explanation is more like having a vision. Better, it is like actually grasping the thing explained, perceiving it, where perception means the modification of the perceiver to include the perceived. These are all metaphors, and the metaphors of vision have sometimes been overworked. But I want to stress that indexical metaphysics is the transformation of the metaphysician so as to get the object explained, in this case being-itself and the beings.

My thesis about being-itself and beings relative to the ontological act of creation claims to be knowledge in the form of something like perception. We can know not only what things are but also can feel that they are, that they are together as mutually implicated but also external, that they are as the mutually related termini of the ontological creative act. This brings us back to Heidegger's concern for the forgetfulness of being-itself. He was not complaining about a failure of knowledge of being-itself in an iconic sense. He was complaining that we lacked the feel of being-itself, the perception of it, the transformative incorporation of being-itself in beings, and hence ourselves are impoverished. Without apprehending and comporting ourselves toward the being-itself in beings we are inauthentic to them and to ourselves. We treat other things merely as useful or not and ourselves as fundamentally empty. I have argued dialectically that we could not even be our cosmological selves, perhaps as inauthentic, alienated jerks, unless we are created together in the ontological creative act. Heidegger dealt with this by postulating a lost golden age of being-perception in ancient Greece and a hunger revealing a deep ontological care in us that can be prompted into consciousness by the arbitrariness of existence shown in death. What I have argued here is that ontological metaphysics can provide a dialectical index that might help cultivate the apprehension of being-itself in beings. Intellectual seeing is thin stuff compared with mystical religious vision of the sort with which Heidegger flirted. Nevertheless, intellectual seeing involves the transformation of the soul so as to be more open to the being-itself of beings, which changes our comportment to other things, to ourselves, and to our common ground. We can be attuned to the gratifying shock of the ontological creative act.

All these aspects of strangeness will be explored further in the chapters of this book. Most of them will be even stranger. But for those of you who persevere, this strangeness will become a bit more kindly, more like the way things really are.

Chapter 2

Eternity

Eternity

Between past and present,
Between present and future,
Between past and future,
Past and present distinct,
Present and future distinct,
Past and future distinct,
Moving from past to present to future,
Moving from future to present to past,
Eternity is the context of time's flow.

The Eternity of Being-Itself

Eternity is one of the strangest traits of being-itself. Its "contrast" is with change. For change, the Chinese traditions of philosophy are famous, as well as the Platonic, in comparison with Aristotelian Western traditions. "Things" are construed as changes, not substances. Whatever is happening at any one time is on the way to becoming something else. Traditionally, this has been reflected in terms of contractions and expansions, or yin and yang. The classical models for understanding change are the hexagrams of the *Yijing* that express shapes through which processes pass while changing. This traditional philosophy of change has gotten all the subtler through the centuries of Daoist, Confucian, and Chinese Buddhist thought.

But the Chinese traditions have not been very much interested in *eternity*, a concept that has been so important in the West for understanding change. Of course, even in the West, eternity has fallen out of favor in deference to time. Kant defined existence as the occupying of a moment of time and a lot of people have come to believe him. Perhaps part of the current disfavor with which eternity is regarded comes from the popular religious association of it with some kind of transcendent realm above the things that happen in time. Eternity has sometimes meant this, but that is not the only common meaning of the term and not the dominant one in Western metaphysics. Eternity does not have to refer to any kind of transcendent realm that temporal things can get to, as in some popular conceptions of salvation as immortal, vastly improved life (such as Kant himself believed in). After developing a proper philosophical conception of eternity, I shall say more about what eternity is not.

I shall present here a strange argument that eternity is the context in which change is possible. Without eternity, the whole of the emphasis on change is a mere wind-egg. The same is true of Western conceptions of change. They all presuppose an eternal context that measures change. There are merely eighteen steps to my argument and they shall go quickly. You might think that any philosophical argument with more than half a dozen steps is no argument. But see whether you are not convinced after eighteen steps.

Change Supposes Eternity

The first step in the argument is to observe that change involves three modes of time: the future, the present, and the past. Whatever one's cosmology of change, if there is change, there is a future when part of the change has not taken place, a present when it is happening, and a past when the change has taken place and has become actual. For the moment, forget about the present for which there are many different theories of becoming; my own is a variant on Whitehead's. A change, or better, a chang*ing*, has a future that is ahead and a past that has been achieved.

The second step is to observe that, in a changing, what is past is always growing or being added to. Once part of the changing is finished, it cannot change any more; it is fixed. But it is always growing, more actuality being added to it moment by moment (please do not worry about what a "moment" is for the time being). While the *past* of the changing cannot change any more, its nature, meaning, and value continues to change as the change continues.

The third step of the argument is to observe that the future is constantly changing as its structures proximate to the present are resolved. The future consists of possibilities, and many philosophers, myself included, think that these possibilities contain internal alternatives. As possibilities are actualized, the alternatives are resolved down to just one form that is actualized. As Aristotle's admirals knew (extrapolating on Aristotle's example in *On Interpretation*, chap. nine, 19a30), on the morrow they could either engage the enemy fleet in battle or not, but as the night wears on they will have to make all the decisions that actualize the battle or sail away; at some point the next day, they will be fighting or not. The future is a kaleidoscope of shifting possibilities as present moments of actualization eliminate all the possibilities except those that are actualized. Every time something happens in the present, it alters the possibilities for the near and far future.

The fourth step of the argument is to observe that, in a changing, the future is conditioned by the past. The future possibilities are those that are open to the past things that have been actualized in the changing or before. In fact, without a past set of actual conditions for which to be the future, the future would be wholly indeterminate. The future would be pure unity or coherence but nothing to unify or make coherent. It would not be the future for anything. Only when it is the future for some actual past does it have determinate possibilities, which might contain alternatives. What the future is essentially and without any conditioning components is pure unity, or that which would unify whatever determinate actual plurality there is to unify. The future is a harmony of its essential unifying components and its conditioning components from the past that give it something to unify or be the future for.

The fifth step is to observe the same thing from the perspective of the past, namely that what is determinately actual in a changing conditions the future by giving it something to unify or make coherent in some possible way.

The sixth step is to observe that the actual past in a changing already has been conditioned by what had been future before it was actualized. The actual past is determinately formed by the possibility that had been actualized, and the past also has, as part of its determinate form, the exclusion of the alternative possibilities that were not actualized. We recognize this most readily by reflecting on the values of possibilities that we did not actualize, and thus lost. The past is a harmony or set of harmonies whose essential components are its fixedness and with conditioning components from the future and from the present. The future conditions the past by providing the possibilities that are actualized in the past and those excluded from it. The present conditions the past by adding new actual material moment by moment.

The seventh step is to observe that the present in a changing always adds something to the past actualized conditions. If the present contains only the past conditions, then it is not different from the past conditions, and there would be no change. Changing in the present always requires adding something to the past that looks spontaneous or novel from the perspective of the past. Whereas Aristotelians sometimes say that out of nothing, nothing comes, what should be said is that in any change something is always coming out of something in addition to the past, from something that was not actual until spontaneously emerging in the present. The present involves constant spontaneous input from something other than the past. The most powerful voice in recent philosophy to argue this wholesale rejection of total determinism has been Paul Weiss in his *Modes of Being*. Alfred North Whitehead, Weiss's dissertation director, also claimed that changing involves adding something to the actualized causes, the basis of his notion of creativity.

The eighth step is to observe that in any present moment of changing, the future alternatives that are relevant to the past in the change need to be resolved to singularity. That is, the present involves the changing of open possibilities to the actualization of just one. The future allows for alternatives and is vague with respect to which one will be actualized. The process of actualization moves from vagueness to singularity. Whatever is spontaneously added to what was past for that present moment is what does the selective actualization. So the spontaneity in a present moment of actualization adds a selection among open possibilities that was not present in the actual past, which was open to the possible alternatives. Thus the present moment of actualization in a changing is a harmony whose essential components are its spontaneity. That present harmony is conditioned by the future that presents alternatives among which the spontaneity selects; it is conditioned by the past that presents actual potentials to be reworked into something new by the spontaneous components according to what is possible. The present moment conditions the actual past by adding to it, and it conditions the future possibilities by eliminating the possible alternatives it does not selectively actualize, thus shifting the field of future possibilities.

The ninth step of the argument is to observe that a present moment is itself a constant changing of a somewhat open future into a singular fixed past. The present moment is the making of this change, however that is to be explained cosmologically. If there were no spontaneous input in the present making that change, the past actuality would stay what it is and the future possibilities would remain open. Change is only possible when the spontaneity essential to the present is added to the fixed past and to the future that by itself cannot change from possibility to actuality. Whitehead has a detailed theory in *Process and Reality* about how a present moment can change possibility into actuality.

The tenth step of the argument is to pose a dilemma. In a changing, are the past, present, and future as interacting modes of time equally real? Or is the present alone real, with the past and future being mere remembrance and anticipation within the present? Consider the latter view. Some people say the past is gone and the future is not yet, and so only the present is real. Whitehead's theory can be interpreted this way, as it is by John Cobb, who concludes that Whitehead was a Buddhist, believing that only present consciousness is real. But the past, once it is actualized, cannot change. It is a condition for change. It is what gets changed by being added to, but what you did this morning is ever after what you did last night and it cannot be changed into something else you did not do this morning, however often we wish we could change the past. The past has a real actual character whether or not it enters into a moment of present change. Similarly, the future has a real character of its own, not only as it enters into a moment of present change. The future is such that there is no way I can buy a Jaguar sedan, which I have always wanted, with the money I have in my pocket, including both cash and the spending limits on my credit cards. That is a fixed possibility in the future, what we would usually call an impossibility, given what is in my pocket now. The future has the reality of logical structure, just as the past has the reality of fixed, achieved actuality, and these realities are what they are in themselves, not merely as functions of the present. At this stage in the argument, the point is to show how past, present, and future can be together so that, in a changing, time flows. Are you still with me?

Eternity Made Plausible

The eleventh step is to point out that we sometimes think that our experience is focused on what is happening in present moments of change. Consciousness is always in some present moment of becoming conscious of first this and then that, or with a little practice in meditation, of being conscious of emptying our consciousness for a duration. So it is common for us to take our experience of present consciousness to be the hallmark and limitation of what is real. When the South Asian traditions of various Hinduisms and Buddhisms symbolize ultimate realty, they take the model of personal experience and exclude from it all senses of intentionality, will, longing, aesthetic responsiveness, and agency, paring it down to something like pure consciousness. They give radically different accounts of this pure consciousness, but it becomes a metaphor based on fairly easy meditative experience for what it means to exist: to be conscious alone and not to identify with the things of which one is conscious. For the Western tradition, existence has been identified most powerfully with present conscious existence. Descartes did not say exactly that denying that we exist is self-contradictory but rather that the thinking experience that we do not exist manifests the existence of thinking. Kant extended the point to say that existence is the filling of inner sense, which is conscious, present experience.

But sometimes our present experience is the intentional remembering of something past, and that memory is true or false about what the past really is. If the past were nothing but the present remembering, memory could not conceivably be mistaken. Similarly, we sometimes think about things that we regard as possible in the future, and we can be wrong about what is really possible. Such intentional cognitive judgments are themselves epistemological kinds of harmony that include the intentional elements of the thinker and the reality of what is thought about, plus their causal connections. To think about the past or the future is not to think about a present representation of the past or future but about the real past and future. The thinking is enabled by present representations that are better or worse as representations. So the past, the present, and the future are all equally real in the sense of being what they are and in the sense that we can be wrong about them.

The twelfth step in the argument is to observe that changing involves not only the actualization of possibilities in a present moment but also (1) adding to a real actual past and (2) changing the structure of the future by what is selected to be actualized. Changing makes a real difference to what is actualized and what is possible. The experience of changing might be focused largely on how the present reality feels, but changing itself involves a togetherness of the present moment with the past to which it adds and the future that it resolves. As phenomenologists of many stripes have shown, the experience of change, upon reflection, embraces the real past and real future along with present changing, "retention" and "protention," as Husserlians call them. In fact, the present changing includes the past and future with it as conditions. Temporality is a dynamic interaction involving changes in each. The changes in the past are growth as new things are actualized. The changes in the present are the spontaneous actualization of possibilities. The changes in the future are the shifting possibilities as the future has to relate to new actualities.

The thirteenth step is to point out that the togetherness of the past, present, and future in any process of change is not temporal. Changing things are temporal with earlier and later phases and changes that take place in present moments for which certain actualities are past and for which the future has logical shape. But the temporal modes of past, present, and future are not earlier or later than one another, and all temporal change takes place within their togetherness. The positive name for the nontemporal togetherness of the modes of time that make change possible is "eternity." Eternity in my philosophical sense does not mean everlastingness but rather that which is not a function of temporal changes or permanence through past, present, and future.

The fourteenth step in my argument is to observe that the past, present, and future as modes of time are both different from one another and related through mutual conditions. If they were not different, there would be no changings. If they were not related, there would be no changings. Change requires real multiplicity and interconnectedness in ways I have described. The interconnections can now be stated systematically. (1) The past conditions the future by giving it diverse structures to unify as possibilities. The past conditions the present by giving it actual things from which to compose a new actualization. The past is conditioned by the future because the past has the structure of what were once future possibilities, excluding the once future possibilities that were not actualized. The past is conditioned by the present by being continuously added to. (2) The present conditions the past by adding to it. The present conditions the future by shifting the shapes of the possibilities. The present is conditioned by the past by receiving actual things as potentials for being integrated into a new actualization. The present is conditioned by the future by the structure of the possibilities for actualization. (3) The future conditions the actual past by supplying its structures. The future conditions the present by supplying possibilities, perhaps indeterminate as to alternatives, for actualization. The future is conditioned by the actual past by having the structures actualized as the forms it has to unify in possibilities. The future is conditioned by the present that eliminates all but a singular possibility, thus shifting all the subsequent possibilities that were open to the alternatives. The structure of temporality is laid out by the kinds of interactions among the temporal modes, conditioning one another as time flows and changing happens.

The fifteenth step is to point out that the past, present, and future modes of time themselves are determinate harmonies, defined in terms of one another, but each integrated with its essential components. The essential components of the past are fixedness of actuality in actual things. Without actual fixedness, that past could not be formed by the possibilities the future offered nor could it provide real multiplicity of form for the future to take on determinateness by unifying. Without actual fixedness, the past could not grow because of present actualization, nor could it supply the present with actual potentials to be integrated in a new actualization. The past is a harmony of its essential components, which are not contained in the present and future (neither the present nor the future contains fixed actuality), with its conditioning and conditioned components. The essential components of the present are spontaneous creativity that does something new with the conditions given by the past under the conditions of possibility given by the future. Present spontaneous creativity adds to the determinate actual past and shifts the possibility structure of the future. The present is a harmony of its essential components of spontaneous creativity, which are contained neither in the fixed past nor the logical structure of future possibility, with its conditioning and conditioned components. The essential components of the future have to do with pure unity, whatever it is that would unify a plurality of different forms. Without unity, the multitude of actual past things could not be together in a new time. Without unity, present creative acts could not alter future possibilities by eliminating proximate ones. Without unity, the future could not have a logically consistent form integrating the multiplicity of forms. Without unity, the future would not offer the present a field of possibilities within which to actualize something. The future is a harmony of its essential components of unity or unifications, which are not in the multiplicity of past structures or in the spontaneity of present actualization, with its conditioning and conditioned components.

The sixteenth step is to point out that, as time flows and changes take place, the modes of time condition one another so as to constitute the structure of temporal change. Every time a change takes place, even the slightest difference, the past is added to, the present makes something new, and future possibilities are altered. Any change whatsoever, no matter how small, even infinitesimally small, involves such a dynamic temporal change, altering past, present, and future. The matrix of those alterations is temporality as the moments of the present slide on. But these involve only the ways in which the temporal modes condition one another and are conditioned. The essential components of the modes are outside the matrix, although the harmonies of which they are the essential components are determinately interacting with one another. What is the context, the ontological context, in which the essential features of past fixed actuality, present spontaneity, and future unity are together? They obviously are together, because the conditional and conditioning components of them are together making up the temporal flow of things. But the essential features of the modes of time do not change, only the harmonies of which they are the essential features. If there were no essential features defining fixed actuality, present spontaneity, and pure unity, there would be no temporal flow. The mutual conditionings would have nothing to condition. Therefore the modes of time must be together eternally so that temporal flow can happen. They cannot be together temporally, that is, as things that change. What can their eternal context of mutual relevance be?

The seventeenth step is a parenthesis in the argument to remind you to dissociate certain ideas commonly associated with eternity. Eternity does not mean some everlasting heaven, which would just be something temporal lasting without ending, as some forms of Daoism imagine liberated souls inhabiting. Eternity does not mean the creative act of a God, because that would be a temporal actualization within time, even if it means starting off the first moment, which would be a change from God alone to God plus the world. Eternity does not mean a First Cause that starts a temporal process of actualization rolling, because that would be just a temporal act in the past. Eternity does not mean a One that precedes the Two, as can be found in the *Daodejing*, because the evolution from One to Two is a change that needs a larger context that includes the One in the change, not as the ontological context for any change. Eternity does not mean an Aristotelian Final Cause ordering change, because that would just be a temporal act of the future. Eternity does not mean a *totum simul* vision of all times together, as Augustine thought, because that would be just a temporal act modeled on the present. Eternity does not mean static form, like Whitehead's eternal objects, because that would be only a structure of future possibilities. Forget eternity conceived in those ways.

The eighteenth step is to say that the only thing that can be the context in which the modes of time are together is an act that creates them to be together. That act is not in time but creates time with all its dates of past, present, and future. That act is not before the modes of time in any logical or ontological sense. It is rather with the modes as their being together. It is not itself a being but the making of the beings. This ontological creative act does not have any nature of its own, except that of giving rise to the world of temporal flow and spatial expanse. It has no potentialities for creating such that understanding the potentialities would give us a clue as to what the world might be: we have to look at the world created to see what it is, for instance, that it is temporal with the modes of time. Only things within the temporal world of change have potentialities or natures as creators within time. The creating or giving rise to the temporal world of change is not in time, not at a beginning, not now, and not in some consummation. It is a sheer act of making of what is totally new, there being nothing at all without the act making determinate somethings with temporal location and process. This is serious eternity, the ontological creative act. Is it not a familiar strangeness now?

Eternity and Ontology

The Confucian tradition has been very strong in emphasizing rootedness in time and place. Nowadays it also emphasizes the need to move from place to place and quickly develop new roots. Rootedness for us temporal creatures means that we have to understand our lives under the conditions of the present, rooted in the particular past of our time and special positions, and rooted also in the possibilities that are real for us, personally and together. We are rooted in the cosmos, and this begins with our rootedness in our local time and places. Confucianism is the best philosophical tradition for articulating and stressing the continuity of the proximate and local with the vast extent of the cosmos, with layers upon layers of personal, social, and natural depths. The relations with the distant are grievously mistaken if they are not mediated through individuated relations with the proximate. Confucians know that we human beings are cosmologically rooted in our world of changings.

Precisely because of our very specific rootedness in our temporal and spatial locations, we can become aware of another rootedness that I dare call ontological. We can be aware of the sheer contingent existence of the temporal processes of our time. We can be aware of the "thatness" of our changings. We can be aware of the radically contingent existence of change in our lives in which our movement through past, present, and future finds them internally related but also partly external to one another as time passes. This experience of the radical contingency of temporal happenings, not contingency on the past but on that which puts the flow of time together, has been widely noted in just about all civilizations, and here I have given an interpretation of it. We are rooted not only in the specifics of what the past gives us, the possibilities given by the future, and the spontaneous changes of our own present moment in time, but also in the unconditioned, wholly arbitrary, totally undeserved, and completely surprising fact of our temporal and spatial existence. To become aware of this ontological rooting is to surround our living with awe, wonder, and gratitude, despite any suffering or evil that attends our temporal rootedness.

A brilliant aspect of Chinese metaphysics is its realization that the complex cannot be explained by the equally or more complex but only by the less complex. Ultimately, the reason for determinate multiplicity, still or in motion, is that it is generated by that which is not multiple and not determinate. Call it the Ultimate of Non-being, as Zhou Dunyi did. What needs to be explained is order, and the only thing that can explain order is that which itself is not ordered, not determinate, not anything, but simply spontaneous generation. My argument is that the only explanation for why there is something rather than nothing is that there just is an act that makes determinate things together, mutual in their conditionings but separate in their essential components. This is true of time with its three modes and thus necessarily of all movement from nothing to determinate somethings. That cannot be a movement through time. It can only be spontaneous and immediate creation of all that is mediated. Remember that this is not a creation "at once," which would be in a temporal mode. It is the eternal creation of all time as it flows. It is not eternal in the sense of everlasting because that presupposes temporality. Of course, from the standpoint of things within time, they are being created within their own times, stretching through the three temporal modes.

As I said earlier, the fact that things are rooted in their own times means that they possess the existence of their times, which for things that change means that they have the existence of their past, present, and future moments in transformations. So, for human beings within time, the contingency of existence can be experienced as temporally located. We can experience the radical contingency of our past by extending our debt to ancestors. We can experience the radical contingency of our future and its duty by extending the mandate of Heaven. We can experience the radical contingency of our inner spontaneity of the changing now by intending our spontaneous existence in the moment with its astonishing novelty. Chinese poetry often emphasizes the radical contingency of life and nature, which is the appreciation of the ontological creativity in those things. Landscape paintings usually depict mountains, water, and persons at a still-point of turning. These are common experiences of eternity within change.

Simply put, change or temporal movement requires that some moments be earlier and hence outside of later moments. How can the later moments be together with the earlier ones so that time flows? Only by being in an eternal creative act that allows the movements from one to the other. To repeat, the eternal act is not in time: it creates time with all its dynamisms. Temporal things within time change, and the Chinese traditions in their various ways show how we temporal beings are rooted in that change.

Nevertheless, the eternal creation of temporality produces not only the dynamics of change among temporal things but also the dynamics of the three modes of time. The past always grows; the present always involves spontaneity; and the future is a constantly shifting kaleidoscope of possibilities. For philosophical and religious traditions that symbolize the ontological creative act with metaphors of personhood, that dynamical interplay of past, present, and future can be represented as the divine life. The divine life, for these traditions that affirm personified eternity, does not change, but is fully dynamic. The Chinese traditions do not employ the metaphors of personhood for the ontological creative act;

they restrict personhood metaphors to representations of the future as containing a mandate of Heaven. But most of the Chinese traditions do acknowledge that the Great Ultimate contains within itself the seeds of change in the movements of yang and yin. Until there is yang and yin succession, there is no temporal flow. Yet the Great Ultimate still contains that dynamic movement that, from the perspectives within time, is eternal dynamisms manifested in what is mothered here and now.

Another way to think about the eternal dynamics is to imagine that time flows through dates. Today is present, yesterday is past, and tomorrow is still future. Imagine a calendar of all dates. Relative to the modes of time, every date has a moment when it is present, in creative spontaneity of actualization. But that date had a gazillion moments when it was future, its shape shifted in each of those moments relative to the earlier dates that were in their present mode of time. Similarly, once actualized, that date has a gazillion moments when it is past, fitting in to an ever-growing actual past. As temporal beings, we are rooted in our time by the moments that are temporally present for us, and how they are located relative to what has just happened and its connection with the past, and how they are located relative to our proximate future that we are facing immanently and relative to the more remote futures. The more remote the past and the future dates are to our present moments, they less they seem like "our" past and present dates but are functions of much more continuous harmonies of ongoing nature.

But from the standpoint of eternity, every date is future, every date is present, and every date is past. Let me stress that every date is present within eternity as a now-happening spontaneously creative actualization. But every date also fits into its many places in past actuality and also has its real logical construction as a future possibility structure relative to other dates that are past and present. These are all together in the ontological context of mutual relevance that is the ontological creative act. They are not there simultaneously, for that just means being together at the same time, and those gazillions of dates are not together at the same time. They are not together "at once," for that is just simultaneity. Within the eternal reality of the ontological creative act, the moments of those dates with their three forms of dynamism, different at each date, are eternally in change. For people unaccustomed to thinking of the eternal rootedness of things with temporal rootedness, this might seem paradoxical. But this is only because it is difficult not to apply temporal metaphors to understand eternal matters. Thank goodness for metaphysics to push us beyond these temporalizing metaphors! Eternity needs to be understood on its own terms.

The Chinese traditions know this as well as any philosophically reflective or aesthetically perceptive tradition. Why have they not made more of it in metaphysical writings? Until the modern era it was a deep preoccupation of Western thought. The reason for the preoccupation in the West, I think, is that the personification metaphors carried over a connotation that there is a mind or rationality to God as the ontological creative act. This of course is an illegitimate carry over because the ontological act creates everything determinate and hence all senses of rationality. But if the rational metaphor is carried over, then for those claiming to know God's rationality or plan, something can be predicted about the world. This is important for those who believe that God intervenes in the world as an agent whose intentions would be useful to know. But there is nothing like this in the Chinese metaphorical system of spontaneous emergence. There is nothing to predict from. Hence, the ultimacy of eternity can be acknowledged but not used for much besides philosophic and aesthetic appreciation of eternal rootedness. Eternity has not been richly developed in Chinese thought, though I hope to have prompted more development here.

My argument has been that the temporality so appreciated is only possible within the eternity of an ontological act of creation. Appreciation of temporal rootedness needs to be contextualized in appreciation of eternal rootedness. For all, the more the eternity of existence is appreciated, the deeper the changes in life now can be grasped. How strange it is that an advance in the metaphysics of the ontological act of creation serves also to advance our appreciation of time and its deepest flow!

Chapter 3

Aesthetics

Out Comes Art

Art is mute without aesthetics.
Aesthetics is blind without philosophy.
Philosophy is wild without system.
System is dead without art.
Beauty is in everything,
Art in very little.
Beauty includes the bad within it,
Art is never perfect.
Artists strive to create,
Aestheticians strive to pin down,
Philosophers strive to imagine forever,
Eternity smiles in all.

Harmony

I mean here to sketch a twenty-first-century American philosophical aesthetic that involves both the broad and narrow senses that Walter Gulick marks out.[1] Broadly, aesthetics deals with all beauty and its perception; narrowly, with art and its appreciation. I accept and applaud Gulick's contextualization of American aesthetics and mean to work within that. My sketch will entertain five main hypotheses. First, we should understand everything determinate to be a harmony. Second, every harmony has goodness. Third, beauty is the goodness a harmony has in itself and is the mark of its existence, its primal trait. Fourth, we appreciate beauty by relating to the beautiful harmony in what I will define as an aesthetic "situation." Fifth, we can apply the theory arising from the first four hypotheses to the appreciation and criticism of art in ways that express American themes.

From this brief announcement of topics, you can see that I share the stretch for generality and abstractness in aesthetic theory that characterizes Wesley J. Wildman's chapter in *American Aesthetics*, "Axiological Landscape Theory: Uniting Aesthetics, Ethics, and Inquiry."[2] Like Wildman, I view aesthetics in art as part of aesthetics more generally, and that as a part of axiology that has the most abstract range. Wildman's development of axiology in terms of landscape theory is one I fully applaud and affirm as an account of one paradigm of the connections between goodness or value and its appreciation. His use of "affordances" and appeal to evolutionary theory is an important contribution to axiological philosophy.

In my judgment, however, his axiological landscape theory is not as abstract and general as he means and needs it to be. It does not account for *what* there is in the affordances of the environment and their valuations contoured to the landscapes that is valuable or good. It says only *that* things are valued in this way and that this valuation can be extended to all sorts of landscapes, including cultural and artistic ones. The tacit appeal to evolutionary success and individual continuance begs the question of what makes them good; existentialists have worried about why not to commit suicide, and Japanese aesthetics focuses on the exquisite beauty of death and decay. So I believe that true generality and abstractness of the sort Wildman seeks is to be found in the examination of determinateness and its axiological structures, the topics of the next two sections to follow.

My first general hypothesis is that to be a determinate thing is to be a harmony. This general Platonic-Edwardsian (in the sense of Jonathan Edwards)-Confucian hypothesis stands in contrast to the Aristotelian hypothesis that to be a determinate thing is to be a substance. Whereas goodness for a substance is its completeness, goodness for a harmony is its aesthetic properties of just fitting together (in ways to be explored here). A substance bears its properties in itself, as the subject of a sentence bears predicates. A harmony has properties only in relation to other things. Please forgive the abstract assertiveness of this hypothesis:

it will be built slowly in detail to become intelligible and illustrated to become plausible.

The analysis of harmony hangs on an analysis of determinateness. To be determinate is to be something rather than something else, and so every determinate thing is determinate with respect to something else. Therefore a determinate thing needs two kinds of components: (1) conditional ones by virtue of which it is related to those things with respect to which it is determinate and (2) essential components by virtue of which it integrates all its components and has its own-being over against the things that condition it. Thus, a determinate thing is a harmony of conditional and essential components. If it had only conditional components, it could not stand as a term in relation to other things and everything would be swallowed up in relations, with nothing to relate, something like Bradley's Absolute. If it had only essential components, it could have no relations with other things that could define it as different from them, as determinate with respect to them. As a harmony of conditional and essential components, a determinate thing is defined both relationally and in terms of its own existence as something in relation. A thing cannot be defined only in terms of other things, and it cannot be defined only in terms of some kind of internal atomic nature. It must be a harmony of both conditional and essential components.

The first level of aesthetic relevance of the hypothesis that any determinate thing is a harmony is that any harmony relates to all the things with respect to which it is determinate. Thus, nature is predominantly a tissue of relations relating harmonies. Because of the essential components, each harmony harmonizes its relational components from its own perspective. Nature is a togetherness of things *relating* to one another. The aesthetic principles that make things cohere or harmonize are manifest in the relations of things in nature.

That things are harmonies means that they all have four traits, according to my hypothesis, just by virtue of being determinate. Any harmony has (1) a form, (2) the components that are harmonized by that form, (3) a location in an existential field that is constituted by the ways the harmony relates to the things with respect to which it is determinate and vice versa, and (4) the goodness or value that is achieved by getting these components together with this form in this location relative to other things. The claim about goodness or value is what is most interesting to an aesthetic theory, and the next section will develop this claim at length.³

The form of a harmony is the pattern of how its components fit together. Some harmonies are static so that their form is how they are together at a moment. Most things in the world, however, are processes of change, so that their harmonies are dynamic and play out in time. Regarding art, a finished painting has a mainly static form, whereas a musical performance has a dynamic one. Remembering that the components of a harmony include all the other harmonies with respect to which it is determinate, the form of a harmony includes many things that are not obvious when we think of the thing as a substance. For instance, the form of a cherry blossom opening, flourishing, then dying and falling includes not only that trajectory, which can be celebrated in painting and poetry, but also the temperature of its duration and all the ecosystems that affect its nutritional and metabolic base. The way the form of the blossom composes the atmospheric and biospheric components likely happens by assigning them trivial or vague functions, reducing them to rather local conditions for its trajectory. Triviality, vagueness, narrowness, and width are terms I borrow from Whitehead and will define more technically in the next section. But those distant conditions are still components of the cherry blossom, and its form assigns them functions within the blossom's harmony. The components of the blossom that we notice most likely are assigned functions that Whitehead would have called narrowness and width. Narrowness is a function of components that have high contrast such as shape, color, odor, and so forth. Width is a function of components that integrate the many narrow components and hold them together, such as the physical structure of the blossom on the tree, its DNA, and the like.⁴

The components of a harmony include both the other harmonies in relation to which the harmony is determinate in some respect and the essential components by virtue of which the harmony composes itself. These essential components include the spontaneity in changing things according to which what is actualized is added to, moral decisions such as commitment to a course of action or a selection among alternative possibilities, and, in cases such as the cherry blossom, the DNA functioning both as essential for organization and as a condition to be integrated with, say, available nutrients. The components of an oil painting, for instance, would include not only the essential ones involving the artist's creativity but also perhaps the interests of the person commissioning the painting, the potential role of the painting in the artist's career, anticipations of the interests and abilities of the potential viewers, and the obvious paints, canvass, composition, and so forth. If any of those things were different, the harmony of the painting would be different. In understanding how a harmony composes its components, it is sometimes important to look at the components in their own integrity, not just according to the roles they play in the harmony itself.

Every harmony has a location in an existential field relating it to the other things with respect to which it is determinate. The ways in which a harmony internally relates itself to other things, and the ways in which those other things relate to one another and to the harmony in question, constitute an existential field of mutual relevance. This field is not an external container, such as a space-time box, but is constituted by the roles the harmonies play in each other. This does not make sense in a substance worldview where things have sharp boundaries and have what Whitehead called "simple location." The doctrine of simple location says that things are located only in their own proper place and can be in other things only by representation unless their proper place is contained within the proper place of the other things. The hypothesis of harmony says that a harmony includes other things within itself as components, while those things also have their own existence not reduced to their functions within the harmony. In addition, things can be represented within harmonies, but that is just a special way of including the other things as components. Within the formal perspective of a given harmony, other things are assigned functional roles in that harmony. But they also have their own natures to be appreciated as beautiful in their own way and perhaps deferred to. Landscape paintings, for instance, especially those of the American Hudson River School, can be appreciated for pointing to nature beyond what they present or represent.

The goodness of a harmony consists of the value achieved by getting its components together in the form that it has at its existential location with respect to other things. This sense of goodness, of course, is the root of beauty, and it is a complicated philosophical hypothesis to defend, the task of the next section. Beauty is that aspect of the goodness of a harmony that it has in itself. A harmony, of course, has many kinds of goodness insofar as it functions as a component in other harmonies. It also has value for what it does to or for things that function within it as components. For the sake of my hypothesis, I define beauty as the goodness that a thing has in itself in contrast to the kinds of goodness it has for other things. The "in itself" here should not be understood as the properties of a substance within its boundaries. "In itself" as I mean it here includes all the other harmonies with respect to which this one is determinate insofar as they are harmonized within the harmony's form. Those other harmonies have their own essence, existential locations, and goods that may not be part of the harmony in question.

With this sketch of a theory of harmony in hand, let me turn to goodness in harmony. Although I want to tie aesthetics to beauty, many of the aesthetic notions we associate with beauty apply throughout to goodness of other sorts. A drawback to the term "harmony" is that for some people it always has the connotation of being nice and helpful. When things are harmonious, "everyone gets along." Yet, in point of fact, although everything is good in itself and so is beautiful in itself, things can be very bad for other things that they affect. An aesthetically beautiful HIV virus is devastatingly wicked for those whom it affects; a perfect storm kills fishermen; a massive shift in tectonic plates is a beautiful geological phenomenon but destroys living forms all around; a beautiful supernova is a cascade of lost forms. Only with respect to its beauty, that is, the goodness it achieves in itself, is a harmony simply good. Given the relationality of the universe just sketched, no harmony is only in itself.

Goodness

We can begin with elaborating the hypothesis that every harmony has goodness. This argument has three steps, cumulatively making a case for Leibniz's idea that value consists in density of being. The first step deals with the ways in which the combinations of components within the hierarchy of a form lead to more reality than the components not combined. The second deals with the ways in which the combinations of components exhibit both complexity and simplicity, and the harmony of complexity and simplicity exhibits elegance. The third deals with the ways the pattern within a harmony, its form, composes the components in relations that exhibit narrowness, width, vagueness, and triviality. To understand that goodness or value consists in density of being requires all three levels of analysis. No one has ever said that strangeness lacks complexity.

The first level of analysis is fairly simple. The components of a harmony can be combined with one another is various ways that constitute new harmonies, and then recombined to constitute even more new harmonies, and so forth. The more harmonies that arise out of combination and recombination, the denser the being of the overall harmony.

The second level of analysis notes that the patterns of combination of components can have complexity in the sense that they contain many different kinds of components. They can also have simplicity in the sense that their components are not of different kinds but are homogeneous. Mere conjunction would be pure complexity and the total homogeneity would be pure simplicity. Neither of the pure extremes would be much of a harmony, and most harmonies have various elements of both complexity and simplicity. The combination of simplicity and complexity with which the components are patterned I call "elegance." A given baseline of components can be constituted with many different kinds and degrees of complexity and simplicity, thus with different kinds of elegance.

Elegance is the aesthetic trait of fitting things together with complexity and simplicity. Each harmony built on that baseline has its own kind of goodness, I want to argue, which is to say each has its own elegance. Each is elegant in its own way. Sometimes we want to say that one harmony is *more* elegant than another, and hence better. Somehow this has to do with optimizing both simplicity and complexity, although there might be variant ways of doing this. This is especially the case when faced with harmonizing a moral conflict, or when painters imagine first this composition with the three colors and then that they want to be able to identify the better or more elegant compositional pattern. Nevertheless, each harmony built upon that baseline has the value of getting its components together with its harmonic pattern or form, relative to the other things with respect to which it is determinate.

The third level of analysis is that of the compositional functions of narrowness, width, vagueness, and triviality. Narrowness is the focusing or concentrating of many components so as to have high contrast between two or more traits that just fit together and yet have depth of differences. Whitehead called narrowness "intensity of contrast." Width is the function of components in a harmony that put the narrow important foci together. In a painting, for instance, the compositional lines provide the width that arranges the narrow color contrasts together. Because harmonies can have many different places in a harmony, they can function as narrow foci in some places and in other places function to provide wide coherence of different focal points. The components in a harmony that we usually notice, and that are important in the sense that they determine how the harmony hangs together and how it behaves in a wider environment, are narrowness and width.

Nevertheless, components also can function vaguely so as to represent other components that therefore do not have to function with narrowness and width. So, for instance, we look into the sky that contains a gazillion (a very large number!) meteorological events, but we grasp them with the color blue that is vague with respect to all those meteorological events. When the mental image of the color blue vaguely stands for the gazillion meteorological events, those meteorological events function trivially within the person. That is, it is as if they were not there in forming the harmony of the person. They are still components, and if they should change in character, for instance lose their light, the mental image of blue would not contain them vaguely. The vague functioning of components is the way by which the infinite complexity of components of components of components is organized so that only a few focal and coherent elements determine the value of a harmony. Suppose the painting is an oil portrait of George Washington. Among its components are all the things that led to the production of the paints, canvass, and brushes, processes going back to the decomposition of dinosaurs to produce oil. But just having those paints in the tubes on the easel constitutes components that function vaguely to define the painter's situation and allow that long history to be trivialized and make almost no difference to what the painter does with the paints in that situation. A crucial part of the goodness of the harmony of the painting is that it is recognizably George Washington, and the artist takes this into account in creating the painting, anticipating how Washington will be recognized and the emotions and historical events that will be associated with him. The artist is likely to have a vague anticipation of the viewers, however trivializing the differences between the real possible viewers.

The more a harmony trivializes the components of components that play narrow and wide functions in it, the shallower it is. A rock is very shallow, vaguely repeating its earlier stages for the most part and trivially rejecting nearly all cosmic history. A human being, however, is likely to be very deep in bearing a DNA with an epochal history, living in a place with great complexity that makes a difference to human life, and having capacities of memory that allow for the vague symbolic encoding of many things that can function in the person's life through the vague symbols to determine narrowness and width.

Returning to our thought experiment, the discussion of the form of a harmony supposed that there are baseline components. These were treated as completely vague, having characters that are different from one another but neglecting all their own components of components as trivial for the sake of the discussion. The harmonies discussed there were shallow in that they were no deeper than the baseline. Going in the other direction, the more those harmonies exhibited narrowness and width of components that resulted in intensity of contrast, the more elegant they are—narrow things consisting of contrasts made coherent with the broad things that put them together in the harmony as a whole.

In reality, there is no baseline for any harmony save what we provide by how we focus attention, a topic for another time. No harmony is completely vague with regard to its components; in fact, it is a harmony because it has components that it composes with narrowness and width as well as vagueness and triviality. For any harmony, some of the roots are very deep and others trivial, some of the components are intense in narrowness and width and others are not. Each harmony is uniquely itself in the goodness it holds.

The density of being of a harmony is the unique goodness it achieves by its composition of components that can be fitted together with narrowness, width, vagueness, and triviality, achieving an elegance of its own. Harmonies have their own density of being in the larger environments, and they have components with their own densities of being. The "ten thousand things," to use the Confucian expressions for "world," are lumpy with densities of being, and each harmony itself has a density of being. This is what its goodness is, as getting these components together in this form in relation to the other things to which it is related.

This has been a complex argument developing a line of argument about aesthetic coherence as goodness that runs powerfully through Edwards. Now we need to ask why we identify this density of being with what we take to be good or valuable. This requires an examination of the experience of goodness because that is where my appeal must go: "See? Isn't this what you mean by goodness?" Before that, however, I need to identify beauty among the kinds of goods a harmony might have.

Beauty

For the purposes of my hypothesis, I heuristically define beauty as the kind of goodness a harmony has in itself, regardless of the other kinds of goods, or ills, the harmony might have for other things. Recall how complex a harmony is just "in itself" if the hypothesis about harmony here is close to correct: every harmony includes as components within "itself" all the things with respect to which it is determinate. This is so even when its form makes the vast majority of things in the world with respect to which it is determinate to be trivial in its own shape, perhaps not even vaguely represented. The crucial cosmological point to get here, however, is that the harmony composes those things within itself so as to have its own-being as a harmony. The essential components of the harmony work to make the harmony something in itself over and above the other harmonies that are its components. Without the essential components, the harmony would not be anything of which those other harmonies might be components: there would simply be the other harmonies. In their own turn, those other harmonies would not be determinately different from one another unless each had its own essential components so as to be itself over against the others. Unless harmonies have their own essential components, they would not have their own-being so as to be able to be determinate with respect to anything else. If things were not determinate with respect to anything else they could not be different, and so there would be only one thing. But being totally and in principle indeterminate, that one thing would be no different from nothing. Therefore, if there is something determinate, there must be a plurality of determinate things each with its essential components. That plurality of things might share all their mutually conditioning components. Each also needs its own essential components be itself in relation to the others.

A harmony "in itself" is its components, both conditional and essential, formed or configured in its own way, located in its own place in existential fields with other harmonies. Considered just so, the goodness it has is its beauty. To be sure, that beauty takes on other kinds of goodness when the harmony becomes a component in other things, including its multitude of relations that affect the things around it. That beauty also affects the goods of other things insofar as it modifies them or affects them and so has other kinds of goodness (or badness relative to the goods of other things). But what I mean by beauty is simply the goodness the harmony has in itself.

Beauty is thus the goodness the harmony bears just because it exists. Beauty is the good of existence itself. The existences of the plurality of determinate things complicate one another because they condition one another. Any harmony that comes to be achieves the beauty of its own existence. For any of its components, however, there is the existence of the component with its own beauty. Within the harmony, the component is integrated with some narrow, wide, vague, or trivial function in a form in which it fits with the other components. Within the harmony, the component contributes to some kind of elegance balancing complexity and simplicity, and to the density of being of the harmony. Yet the component not only plays functional roles within the harmony, it has its own in-itself nature, which is its existence. If within the harmony the component is modified, each of those modifications is itself a harmony with its own existence, and therefore its own essential components.

Although there are many kinds of essential components, for actual things in space/time they include spontaneous creativity that adds something to what was already actualized, and that resolves open alternate possibilities down to the singular possibility actualized. This spontaneity provides an ontological depth to existence. Earlier I characterized existential depth as the ways and degrees to which components in the past or distance are carried in to the makeup of a harmony, the elements below any artificially drawn baselines' representations. Now I call attention to the ontological depth of existence, namely that harmonies exist because they contain essential components that give them their own-being over against their conditioning components and allow them to receive and integrate those conditions into their own harmonies. Not only does a harmony have the ontological depth of its own-being coming from its own essential components, but each of its components has that ontological depth on its own terms.

Now the "density of being" takes on a new dimension of meaning. It refers not only to the complexity and simplicity of a harmony resulting in its elegance. It refers also to the ontological depth of the harmony and of each of its own components. Suppose we would say, as Edwards did, that because each thing is a creature of God, its existential createdness consists in its beauty that is its goodness as simply existing in itself. To be a thing is to be a beautiful creature, and to be a creature is to be a beautiful thing, for Edwards. I will not defend his or any other theory of ontological creation here. Nevertheless, with this theory of harmonies as good, and with the goodness of beauty insofar as they have goodness in themselves in their sheer existence relative to other things, harmonies can be understood in an Edwardsian way to exist as they are beautiful.

I have made some strange philosophical claims here that make aesthetics more abstract and complicated than many people hope it would be. The abstractness of the theory of goodness so that it applies to everything determinate stands in its favor. So does its coherence, if in fact it turns out to be coherent on further examination. But how does it stand when illustrated by experience? Don't you have moments when you focus on something in nature, a bird, or a branch, or light shining on a rock, and become transfixed by its beauty, by its existence just as it is in the moment? Don't you have moments with friends when time seems to stand still and you focus just on the existence of the moment as something it itself that you might call beautiful? Steve Odin has written a remarkable book mentioned earlier about Japanese aesthetic sensibilities and Whitehead's theory of tragic beauty: it is when something perishes that our attention is called to the beauty of its existence, now contrasted with its fading or nonexistence. Sister Mary Corita Kent, the American artist famous for the painted gas storage tank in Boston, had a lesson for her art students in which she gave them sheets of paper with a rectangle cut out in the center. With these "finders," they would set boundaries on things in nature, the classroom, or magazines to see elements isolated for the moment, "harmonized" momentarily by the finders. This was supposed to show both the sheer existence of the isolated view through the rectangle and a beauty that would not have been noticed otherwise. Many moments occur in common experience in which attention is suddenly called to something isolated to be experienced "in itself," and that experience notes its beauty and its sheer existence, which are the same thing.

To be sure, this naive appeal to experience only carries so much weight until we have a theory of the experience of aesthetic objects, things regarded as to their beauty, which is the next topic.

Appreciation

I have spoken of beauty as a goodness proper to beautiful things, and the argument for this has to come down to getting you to agree that this is how we see things to be beautiful. The experience of something as beautiful is very different from the beauty in the thing experienced, however (although the experience of something beautiful might be beautiful as an experience too). Experience is always interpretive, mediated by signs. We can experience the beauty in a thing only in terms of the signs we have to interpret it. Because we never interpret a thing in all respects, only in the respects for which we have signs and that fall within our interpreting purposes and habits, we never grasp the whole beauty of something. Our aesthetic experience is always partial to our own perspective. Nevertheless, we commonly revise our aesthetic judgments on learning something new about the aesthetic object or changing our perspective. Therefore, it is something in the object that constitutes it as beautiful and about which we might be wrong in our interpretation. This requires greater explanation.

The house where my wife and I live in Milton, Massachusetts, is on a rocky hill and faces west. Our good neighbors across the street and slightly uphill, Tim and Tony, have a beautiful house with a side yard surrounded by a yew hedge and containing flowering shrubs and small trees. Directly in front of our view, Tim and Tony have a classically shaped hemlock in which birds like to nest, but it is not so tall that we can't see over and around it. Blessedly often, we are treated to beautiful sunsets, moving swiftly with torquing shapes and tumbling colors before the prevailing northwest wind. For over a quarter of a century, incrementally we have built up a sunset viewing terrace with a small fountain and four reasonably comfortable chairs where we can relax with some wine (white for her, red for me), delight in the sunset, and watch the birds go to roost as evening falls. That's the time of day for neighbors to stroll by, stopping to talk and sometimes joining us for wine; our sunset terrace has a definite social location in the habits of our neighborhood and in the punctuation of our lives.

In what does the beauty of the sunset consist? It is a harmony, of course, the beautiful sunset, and it is located within a vast global, solar-system wide, indeed galaxy wide, existential field of a gazillion harmonies with all sorts of causal properties. Most of these cosmic harmonies are trivial in the beautiful sunset. Unlike most of our daily lives in which the rotation of the Earth is vaguely dismissed by attention to the clock time of night and day, the beautiful sunset includes observation of that moving rotation while not always acknowledging the astrophysics of it.

The beautiful sunset itself is a harmony of a kind I call a "situation" that includes at least the meteorological events on the horizon and the intentional observations of us viewers. That situation also includes the physical geography that allows the viewing angle from our sunset terrace to the meteorological events in the sky above the horizon, as well as the intervening atmosphere that allows us to see that far (our area too often is fogged in, which makes the beautiful sunset an impossible harmony insofar as we are concerned). The meteorological events include the winds blowing the clouds as well as the angle of the setting sun to our horizon. The situation in which there is a beautiful sunset in addition includes viewers with the optical capacities to see the colors in the sky, to see the shapes and movements of the clouds, and with the kind of attention to watch something happening on the horizon.

The situation of the beautiful sunset has another characteristic of its harmony, namely the perspective and intentionality of the viewers to enjoy sunsets, including this one. Indeed, by "situation" I mean the kind of harmony that takes its form and limitations from the intentionality structure, broadly interpreted, of the experiencers. Without the intentionality structure of the experiencers, there could be many elements in the connections between the meteorological events and the people on the sunset terrace, but these would not make up the beautiful sunset. In the language used earlier, the beautiful sunset has two points of narrow importance, the meteorological events and the intentionalities of the viewers intent on viewing. The components that are important for the situation are those that serve the viewers in their experience of the beautiful sunset. The rest of the components are only vaguely relevant, or to be dismissed as trivial.

Part of the intentionality structure of the viewers is the capacity to represent the meteorological events in the colors, shapes, and movements of human experience. The earthworm at the base of our fountain would not appreciate the sunset. Up close, the meteorological events would not be so colored or shaped. Only from the angle of vision structured by the horizon, the terrace, and many things in between can the sunset be seen in the sunset's terms. The human signs and viewing habits are necessary for there to be a beautiful sunset. As I have described it, many sunsets are seen with the auxiliary symbolic associations with the pleasures of relaxing with wine, conversing with neighbors, and exercising an important rhythmic structure of our lives. The beauty of the sunset often includes many of these associations that are not merely functions of the meteorological events and our ocular structures. My wife often compares the sunset at hand with paintings by Thomas Cole and Frederick Church, Hudson River School painters, or to her own painting. When that happens the experience of the sunset is all the richer. So the situation of the beautiful sunset includes not only the physical properties of the elements in the connections between the meteorological events and the acts of vision but also the cultural and semiotic apparatus we bring to what we experience, often with elaborate interpretations.

The radicalness of this aesthetic observation and the theory with which I am interpreting it becomes clear when we distinguish between three kinds of harmonies that are at play. One kind is the human harmonies that are my wife's and my lives. Among the components of our lives are the sunsets we have experienced. These components are integrated into our larger lives.

A second kind of harmony is the situation within which we experience the beautiful sunset. This harmony is not just a property of our own subjective experience, as many philosophers would say. Rather, it is a harmony in which the real meteorological events, our real observations, our experiences and social lives, and all the connecting causal harmonies are integrated into the harmony of the situation. Experience in this sense is not something within a subject to which the events on the horizon are a kind of external world, but it is a kind of harmonic interaction or engagement between the human intentionalities and the meteorological events, something Dewey called the interaction of organism and environment, the words Whitehead also used to name his chapter on narrowness, width, vagueness, and triviality. In this harmony of the situation, the human intentional structures, including the social activities, are components. The beauty of the situation is that all the components harmonize so that the meteorological events are seen as a beautiful sunset. This is not just internal to the viewers but embraces all the nature and culture involved.

A third kind of harmony is what happens in the meteorological events themselves, which might not be a beautiful sunset at all. Those events would be what they are whether are not there is anyone in the right place to see them as beautiful. The beautiful sunset itself is the harmony of the situation in which the meteorological events and the viewers with their intentionality structures, plus many mediating circumstances as "width" functions, come together just so.

Given the angle of vision on the horizon and the intentionality to enjoy beautiful sunsets, there can be a beautiful sunset situation only if the meteorological events are just right. If there are no clouds or if the sun is in eclipse, there is no beautiful sunset. That is why we say that the beauty is in the sunset, not in the sunset terrace or in our imaginations or capacities to see colors, shapes, and so forth. Many days, there are no beautiful sunsets. This is the sense in which beauty is "realistic," that is, characteristic of the object interpreted in the situation. Also, there is no beautiful sunset if there is no vantage point from which it could be seen by viewers with our visual and interpretive apparatus. But if there is that vantage point, and there are such viewers, there is a beautiful sunset.

Some people will object that there is no beautiful sunset if there are no actual viewers. But I say that there is a beautiful sunset if all the conditions are right except for the fact that my wife and I are preoccupied inside and do not notice it. There is a beautiful sunset but we missed it; neighbors comment on it next day and we are sorry we missed it. The sunset is beautiful *if it could be seen* as beautiful from our vantage point. What makes the sunset beautiful or not is the meteorological events related to our vantage point so that it could be interpreted as beautiful by viewers if they are there. This point reflects a deep philosophic dispute between nominalists, who would deny the beautiful sunset if it is not observed, and realists such as the pragmatists, among whom I am, who say that the general conditions are real whether or not they are being actualized at the moment. I say that the sunset is beautiful *if it could be seen* as such in the right situation.

We human beings are in many situations where we appreciate the beauty of various things. The appreciation is in the harmonic structures of those situations, not merely in some kind of private experience. The situations of appreciation require the conditions of our intentionality structures as well as the forms of those harmonies that we appreciate as beautiful. Those situations of appreciation in turn are components of our lives, and we interpret them in terms of many kinds of interests. Because of the mutual conditioning of situations of appreciating beauty with the formation of human experience, such that each is a kind of condition in the other, human life is filled with beauty, as well as all sorts of other things that are not so good. This leads me to narrow our focus to art.

Art

Art is humanly produced beauty. Just about all that I have said about harmonies and their goodness, and beauty as the goodness of harmonies considered in themselves, applies to art. I also want to say some things that are specific to art. First, I gratefully follow John Dewey in saying that art arises out of what people appreciate for the intrinsic appeal of it, beginning with what they do for the fun of it.

> Human experience in the large, in its coarse and conspicuous features, has for one of its most striking features preoccupation with direct enjoyment: feasting and festivities, ornamentation, dance, song, dramatic pantomime, telling yarns and enacting stories. . . . The body is decked before it is clothed. While homes were still hovels, temples and palaces are embellished. Luxuries prevail over necessities except when necessities can be festally celebrated. . . . Useful labor is, whenever possible, transformed by ceremonial and ritual accompaniments, subordinated to art that yields immediate enjoyment. . . . Most sources of direct enjoyment for the masses are not art to the cultivated, but perverted art, an unworthy indulgence. Thus we miss his point. A passion of anger, a dream, relaxation of the limbs after effort, swapping of jokes, horse-play, beating of drums, blowing of tin whistles, explosion of firecrackers and walking on stilts, have the same quality of immediate and absorbing finality that is possessed by things and acts dignified by the title of aesthetic.[5]

Dewey says that people sing when doing drudge work because it makes the work less odious and because singing is fun in itself. He says we deck ourselves before we clothe ourselves. We have religious festivals to appease the gods or to make it rain, but mainly because of the beauty and fun in celebrating stuff. Art begins with these common and perhaps "primitive" things that we seek, repeat, stabilize, and perform because they are intrinsically enjoyable and make our lives better. Art is more serious when we distinguish the better singers from the worse and encourage them, finally professionalizing training in music and investing in the institutions of music of all sorts. Dewey rightly advises against drawing any sharp distinction between common arts and "fine" arts.

Second, works of art, including performances, can have all sorts of goods that are not themselves artful beauty. For instance, professional artists and performers sometimes make a living out of selling or performing. They earn monetary value because people think their artwork is good, but that commercial value is not part of the value of the work as art unless it affects how the artist harmonizes the components in the work, considered in itself. A season of performance by a symphony orchestra has the value of helping pay the rent on the concert hall but is not part of the artful beauty of the music played, unless some of it is composed just for spaces such as the hall. Many symphonies indeed are composed with sounds that are expected to be heard in large halls.

Third, the beauty of a work of art is the good it has in itself considered as a harmony. As a harmony, however, it contains all its components in a composition that exhibits the functions of narrowness, width, vagueness, and triviality. If one of the components of a work, for instance a painting, is to memorialize a donor or decorate a space in a house, then that component is taken into consideration in the composition of the painting.

Fourth, the components of a work of art include much more than the materials of the artwork, more than the paints and canvasses, the moves of the dancers, or the surface storyline of a novel. The paints, for instance, have among their components the history of their being made from oil and color pigments, perhaps from plants or ground-colored minerals. The paints' origins are trivial for the painting, and all that matters is that they are vaguely captured in the paints that the artists uses. If the artist avoids certain colors because they are too expensive, then something in the past of the paint tube is relevant to the artwork's harmonic structure. But if there is a portrait, more is relevant in the person posing than the look of the person posing; the painting might aim to commemorate an important person or portray a certain character. All those things function as relevant components.

Fifth, one of the things that distinguish art works from natural things of beauty, besides being made by human beings, is that art works focus very sharply on the narrow and wide compositional elements, distinguishing these elements from the trivial components that make hardly any difference and the vague components that can be pretty much taken for granted. Artwork has a high focus that often compels our attention. Things of natural beauty, by contrast, are usually deeply embedded in their ecologies, and this is noticed in their beauty.

Sixth, when artwork is done deliberately, not absentmindedly humming while hoeing, the prospective audience is taken into account in the composition of the work. A painter composes with some sense for what a viewer would see, what kinds of signs the viewers would bring, distinguishing how different cultures might see a painting. Music is composed and performed within music traditions, and composers and musicians work within what can be interpreted. Good artists often are creative with what people can recognize and create surprises, but this supposes expectations, or at least a repertoire of aesthetic expectations.

Seventh, all art is appreciated only in situations, as described above, in which the appreciators have signs that allow interpretation. This means that art is always embedded in a culture that involves much more than the art at hand. Because art often plays all sorts of nonartistic roles in many societies, such as producing income for artists, soothing the savage beast, structuring industries such as oil paint makers, piano tuners, and publishing houses, the culture within which its artistically relevant signs and symbols exist is interwoven with many other cultural parts of society. Nevertheless, certain arts can develop ingroups of interpretation to which much of society's culture is indifferent.

Eighth, the appreciation of a work of art on the one hand is immediate. That is, we grasp its harmony as hanging together in itself. This is so whether we are looking at a static statue, walking through the Taj Mahal sequentially appreciating it, or listening to a performance where the harmony comes to be through time. Appreciation is the aesthetic grasp of the artwork's components as related together according to its form in its existential relation to other things with respect to which it is determinate, all as interpreted.

Ninth, on the other hand, any given appreciation of an artwork is fallible and we frequently have the experience of finding new components, new compositional elements, new symbolic references, and so forth as we see the sculpture again and again, live with the painting on the wall, hear the song over and over. This sense of many levels of sophistication in aesthetic appreciation of an artwork is magnified in the face of sophisticated art criticism. Such criticism can bring to appreciation a sense of context, of the historical place of the work, and of the elements of artist's own life. One of the great joys of art in our contemporary cultures is that it gets better and better the more we enrich the harmony of the situation of appreciation.

Tenth, however, sometimes it works the other way. The more we come to perceive in an artwork by more sophisticated interpretation, we see that the aesthetic harmonies, functions of narrowness, width, vagueness, and triviality, do not in fact come together as it seemed at first. The apparent beauty on first look was kitsch, or a cheap trick, or too derivative to be part of the whole integration. In literary criticism, we learn how to read a novel appreciating the truly great "densities of being" in the writing, the lesser lumps, the incoherent parts, and all the rest. Appreciating a work of art is not to see it as a surface quality with no depth but as the contrast of all the elements composed with narrowness, width, vagueness, and triviality, at least to the degree of the appreciator with cultural signs.

Eleventh, whereas natural things of beauty simply have what beauty they have in their own natures, works of art need to embody an ideal beauty. Art as art aims to be good art (even when it fails), so we say that the composition does have striking points of narrow focus, compositional coherence wide enough to encompass the whole, and all the rest. So we say novels are more or less good, most somewhat flawed. Performances have high points and low points. Most paintings are not great, employing stereotyped elements, incoherence compositions, and the like. It helps to see, read, or listen to some bad art to appreciate just how complicated and wonderful great art is. This is not to say that medium-good art (even kitsch) is not a source of beauty in people's lives, in amateur music, theater, painting, and so forth.

Twelfth, because art is appreciated always through interpretation, Wildman's point about the axiological landscape is relevant to art too. Each individual always has a personal history of what can be appreciated, what is desirable in art, what is of artistic interest. In this sense, beauty is in the eye of the beholder. However, this is only because artistic beauty requires a situation to be appreciated and the situation requires the intentionality structure of the appreciator. Different intentionality structures give rise to different appreciations and assessments. The artwork is the same in different situations in which it might be appreciated. "Classics," as David Tracy would call them, can be appreciated for widely different things in different cultures and by different individuals within a single culture.[6]

Thirteenth, in creating a work of art, even in performing a previously composed score or script, the artist engages in a kind of creative dialectic between an imagined ideal for the work intended and the materials at hand, perhaps changing the ideal as much as the material. Before putting paint to canvass, the artist might have a vague imagined composition with imagined colors, or perhaps a quick sketch. Working on the painting, the artist modifies the imagined ideal upon seeing what some actualization looks like. Rarely would an artist have a completely determinate vision of what the painting should be; rather the vision of the ideal or goal for the work becomes more determinate as the creative process progresses, sometimes altering radically.

Fourteenth, the other side of that dialectic is that the artist comes to know the materials better and sees new possibilities in them. Much of creativity comes in seeing such new possibilities in the materials with which an experienced artist is at home, not only in thinking of new compositional patterns. Artistic creativity is not just finding a way to harmonized a paint-box full of colors on a canvass, but finding new ways to combine them to produce new kinds of harmonies that add up to great intensity and depth in appreciability.

Fifteenth, kinds of works of art are almost infinitely various, and the boundaries of kinds are constantly shifting. There are songs and stories, storytelling and novels, choreography and dance, plays and performance, music of many sorts: Dewey's quaint celebration is the art of walking on stilts at American Fourth of July celebrations.

Sixteenth, ways of appreciating art are also various, usually taking time, walking around a static thing, returning to a painting, participating in a performance whose harmony form takes time and space to play out, and so forth.

Seventeenth, in all cases of artwork, I suggest, what makes it art is the beauty of its harmony in itself and as that is appreciable. In contrast to natural beauty, which need not be appreciated in order to be beautiful, art is intended to be appreciated for its beauty.

I have swept through an American aesthetic philosophy quickly and on many levels. I have presented mind-numbing abstractions about what it means to exist as a harmony, applications to beauty in art, an epistemology of appreciation of beauty in nature and art, and an array of points about art and its differences from beauty in nature (though that is not a sharp distinction), all of which illustrate some of the more general points. As an American aesthetic philosophy, it has elaborated existential points from Jonathan Edwards, aesthetic points from Ralph Waldo Emerson, semiotic points from Charles Peirce, artistic points from John Dewey, and a classificatory point from David Tracy. As a typical American philosopher, I integrate approaches from outside the Western tradition, something that Emerson began in a big way. With the sense of accountability of a systematic philosopher, however, I do not take this aesthetic philosophy to be a good example of American exceptionalism but a hypothesis worth discussing in the global philosophical conversation.

Chapter 4

Experience

Fancy Meditation?

Fancy meditation? Close your eyes and concentrate!
Worried that your choices are all self-centered? Well, worry!
Concerned to choose to make you a good self? Think about that!
Interest piqued by things that don't affect you? Pursue that interest!
Fearful that your life lacks meaning? Forget it and laugh!
Small starts lift up the hidden Ultimates.
Meditation is mere play unless the Ultimate allures.
Self-centeredness is no worry without the Ultimate center.
Integrity is no concern without Ultimate identity.
The world of other interests makes no claim without Ultimate breadth.
Life's meaning is a game without Ultimate destiny.
Small starts lift up the hidden Ultimates.
Beyond all our questing the Ultimates exist.
Whether known by us or no one,
The Ultimates are conditions for any existence.
What luck we live to quest them, no matter how wrong we are!
Glimpses we get, but what glimpses!
Small starts lift up the hidden Ultimates.

The focus in this chapter is on human experience in religion, specifically the experience of transcendence. By human transcendence I do not mean simply learning and doing more than was possible before, although I am in favor of that. Transcendence does mean the acquisition of new capacities to engage reality in aspects that hitherto were not accessible for engagement. The development of bigger muscles allows people to engage heavier weights for bench pressing. The acquisition of language allows transcendence of communication otherwise limited to gesturing. The development of better theories allows transcendence of what previously could be understood. I want to focus on religious transcendence, however, which means the engagement of aspects of Ultimacy that hitherto were not accessible for engagement. I define as religious any human activity that engages whatever is Ultimate.

To be sure, in one sense, only one Ultimate Reality exists, the ontological creative act. That act would not exist without the world existing. In fact, the determinate things of the world are precisely the termini of the creative act. Their ontological reality is as parts of the creative act itself. The world is the creature of the creative act. The creative act exists only in creating. So whatever is ultimate in the world of determinate things is also co-prior with the ontological creative act. Call them the cosmological Ultimates, if you will.

Thus five related Ultimates exist. These five are the ontologically Ultimate and the four cosmological Ultimates. The cosmological Ultimates are form as a trait of anything in the world that is determinate, a multiplicity of components for any determinate thing harmonized in its form, existential location of anything determinate relative to the other things with respect to which it is determinate, and the value-identity achieved by getting these components harmonized by this form in this location relative to other things. The ontological creative act is real only insofar as it actually creates a world of determinate things; therefore it is contingent upon the existence it gives the determinate created things. The determinate things, whatever they are, have to be harmonies with form, components, existential location, and value-identity; therefore, they are contingent upon those created Ultimates. Without the ontological creative act, there would be nothing. With the ontological creative act and the harmonies it creates, there are the necessary implications of the five Ultimates for each other. The necessities of co-implications and the various kinds of causation in the world are radically contingent upon the ontological creative act, and there is no reason for there to be such an act. It just is. The issue of human transcendence regarding Ultimates is about transcending what we already engage to new dimensions of engagement.

We human beings can engage only those aspects of the Ultimates from our own perspectives within the world and only insofar as we can interpret them. Interpretation is limited by semiotic resources, which include the physical (especially neurological) structures of human beings, our habits of quotidian engagements of our natural and social environments, our semiotic systems of signs, and our interpretive interests and purposes.

Where we stand with regard to interpretive engagements of the five Ultimates is a matter of our biological and cultural evolutions as well as more individual aspects of engagement. In what follows I shall comment on the evolution of transcendence with regard to five universal religious problematics for engaging the Ultimates, one for each Ultimate. Many other religious problematics for engaging Ultimates exist, and these interact and condition one another in multiple ways. But five problematics will tax your patience enough. These five problematics are (1) the mystical engagement of the radical contingency of the ontological creative act, (2) the issues of righteousness in interpreting and acting upon the different values in possibilities for human life, (3) the issues of integrating the components of a human life so as to make a self, (4) the issues of engaging other things in the world, especially people but also nature and institutions, that are located elsewhere from us, and (5) the issues of finding meaning or value in life. All developed religions have ways of addressing these problematics.

Mystical Engagement

The experience of transcending our engagements of the ultimate creative act is usually called mysticism. At least four basic forms of mysticism are widespread as ways of engaging what I call the radical contingency of the world on the ontological creative act, which is the same as experiencing the act itself including what it creates.

Meditation

The first, which I call "meditation," is the attempt to grasp the world as a whole being created in a unity that relativizes internal differences and perspectives. Often associated with samadhi—seeing everything together—this meditative engagement depends on signs we might have for the whole. Of course, many such signs exist, and they range from signs that run things together, as in much nature mysticism, to signs that convey blank undifferentiated unity.

The Axial Age was a time of radical transcendence of previous ways of imagining everything as created together. In fact, prior to the Axial Age, few if any serious signs existed for imagining "everything." So it was difficult if not impossible to imagine any aboriginal creation of everything, and this kind of mysticism was itself largely unformed. Nevertheless, the Axial Age introduced many ways of conceiving of everything. The Chinese developed a cosmology around notions of Heaven, Earth, and Dao. The South Asians developed signs of pure consciousness as the source of things of experience and elaborated this in different ways. For one line of elaboration, personal consciousness was interpreted as atman, which in turn was interpreted as Brahman both with and without qualities. For another line, personal consciousness was interpreted as wholly empty with only the contents of consciousness arising and ceasing to be acknowledged as real. West Asian religions developed notions of a monotheistic God creating a wholly dependent world, or notions of contesting creator gods of good and evil. What a merry chase these divergent ways of transcending old signs for everything have led religious thinkers and meditators since the Axial Age!

Now, however, we have another revolution in signs for everything that can allow us to transcend old forms of meditation. On the one hand are signs of the extensiveness of the cosmos, over thirteen trillion years in the past and trillions of years into the future, with innumerable galaxies and distances imagined as exceeding the speed of light. On the other hand are signs of the intensiveness of things, for instance how your own body has layers of evolved organs relating on many levels to environments, the organs harmonizing many levels of chemical interactions that themselves are built of kinds of change that were prominent in the first moments of the big bang. Signs of many kinds point to these extensive and intensive dimensions of everything and can be employed in focused meditation transcending what mysticism could engage before.

Contemplation

A second form of mysticism for engaging the ontological creative act and the world as its terminus is what I call "contemplation," although I admit that distinguishing meditation and contemplation is somewhat arbitrary in my use of words. Contemplation does not try to embrace everything but focuses on the particularity of some focal things. Most branches of Buddhism cultivate the contemplation of the arising and ceasing of dharmas in consciousness, however much they interpret this differently. Whereas meditation attends to the togetherness of the things in contingent creation, contemplation attends to the suchness of particular things. The things of the world have "pied beauty," to use Gerard Manley Hopkins's phrase. Most religions have techniques for developing "one pointed" intentional foci.

I see that our time has evolved much that is new in the mystical contemplation of suchness. We now know much more than we did a century ago about the neurophysiology of contemplation. Practiced contemplators, such as Tibetan Buddhist monks, have been studied by scientific means. Many scholars and religious practitioners think of contemplation as a technique that can be learned rather than as the achievement of a certain kind of vision. Moreover, we have radically improved scientific understanding of the interior depths of the things that are such as they are, the harmonies within harmonies within harmonies. These can prompt new signs by which to grasp suchness.

Love's Path

A third form of mysticism for engaging the radically contingent world in the ontological creative act is what I call the "path of love." Fundamentally, the path of love is the cultivated capacities to appreciate the goodness in things within creation and to grasp this as gratuitous and contingent on the ontological creative act. Experience is permeated by our appreciations of the positive and negative values of things in their various relationships, and these appreciations need not have anything to do with mysticism. They are mystical engagements, however, to the extent they interpret what they appreciate as radically contingent on the ontological creative act, however that act is symbolized. There need not be a world with valuable things in it, but here it is. To call this the path of "love" is metaphorically to stretch some of the meanings of human love.

The mystical path of love involves two such directions. The first is to identify love with the ontological creative act making good things. To love something is to appreciate and improve it, and in basic instances to make things with value for the sake of their value. To imagine a creative monotheistic God as a loving creator is easier than to imagine the Dao that cannot be named as a lover; nevertheless, even the Dao can be imagined as the mother of all things that bear value, and all harmonies do have value-identity. The second direction in which the mystical metaphor of love is developed is in imagining ourselves, the mystics, as loving the creation we encounter as radically contingent. We become lovers of the creation as such, whether we focus on a small part of it, imagine everything together, or find the ontological act creating interior to ourselves. We become ontological lovers in engaging the world, or some part of it, in the ontological creative act. In well-cultivated cases, we achieve the capacity to love the world in its worst circumstances, when it causes untold suffering and kills us. An adept in the mystical path of love can bless the world without him or her. A mystic on the path of love engages the ontological creative act in the world as a lover.

In the historical evolution of the mystical path of love, the modern period has been significantly retrograde. Instead of allowing people to transcend previous forms of mystical engagement in love, modern science has taught many people that the world is just a bunch of facts and that all valuation is mere human projection. In terms of experience, the so-called fact/value distinction is just plain false. We apprehend things as good or bad, in this way or that, all the time, and we are conscious of how our valuations of things might be false to the values things really have. Nevertheless, the authority of science based on an ideology of just getting at the facts, and employing ideas, procedures, and peer review processes that reinforce this ideology, makes it difficult to count experiences that appreciate the vast intermix of values in human affairs as knowledge. Hence, for many people, the mystical way of love is more difficult because they cannot take seriously the reality of the goodnesses in creation nor the appreciation of the ontological creative act as the creator of those goodnesses.

Freedom's Path

The fourth form of mysticism I call the way of "freedom." The logic of this way has two moves. The first shares with the way of love the semiotic reversal of experiencing the world from the standpoint of the act creating it. Of course, this is done only partially and through the use of symbols that put us in the position of the creator creating us as objects of creation, the termini of the creative act. These have mainly to do with the experience of spontaneous making, which we have rarely in big ways but perhaps pervasively in small ways. The second move in the way of freedom is to appreciate the fact that the ontological creative act is immediate, that it has no antecedent potentialities or possibilities, that it has no antecedent nature that constrains what it creates. The ontological act has no determinate structure of its own, only the structure of its terminus, its products, the things that are determinate. So viewed by analogy with processes within time, the ontological act has no past and its creative activity is the total production of what is new. It is totally free, totally arbitrary, totally gratuitous, and is not constrained by anything to create at all, not for any good or purpose. The closer the mystical way of freedom comes to identifying with this absolutely free creative act, the closer we attain to ontological divine freedom. If the mystical way of love seems to be failing because of diminished senses of real value, the mystical way of freedom is unaffected by this. Whatever is created, valuable or not, is freely created. Creation is absolutely wild.

Most of the metaphorical cultures of East and South Asia have generally held to this notion of ontological freedom. The only thing that does not need explanation from some prior cause is nothing, and nothing is the free source of any something. West Asian monotheisms often have wanted to attribute a mind or nature to God in order to be able to predict what will happen or what purposes are in order. But even the Neo-Platonists and Thomists, who believe that God is the fullness of being and that determinate things are bounded negations of the being as such, claim no determinate process of creation, moving immediately from the One to the Dyad, or from an identity of essence and existence to a delimited separation of them. The creation is a mystery that is absolutely free from prior determination. Nowadays we are seeing a growing consciousness of the absolutely surprising fact of existence. The late Stephen Hawking asked why there is a world to which his explanatory hypotheses might apply. Tyler Tritten has written a splendid book called *The Contingency of Necessity* that traces the emergence of a realism regarding this point out of postmodern Continental philosophy. People are appreciating anew what Tillich called the ontological shock of existence as such. So I see significant progress in transcending common ways of domesticating the mysticism of the way of freedom to better ways of radicalizing it. A philosophical group once gave me a T-shirt quoting my *Ultimates* that says "God Is Wild." That's a transcendent move.

Ultimate Obligation

Having form is an Ultimate condition that is necessary for anything to be determinate. We human beings of course have form and relate to form in the world in many ways. One of the most important, especially in religious matters, is that we face the future regarding our lives and choices as having forms of many different possibilities. Many possibilities contain alternatives, and the alternative forms have different ways of bearing value. We make choices among alternatives of different value. Sometimes the values in the options are between clearly better and worse, and we view these choices as moral in a narrow sense of morality. Other times the values are merely different, as in choosing to read a philosophy book for an afternoon rather than watching a football game.

The matter of choosing among alternatives with different values is double-sided. On one side, it contributes to determining which future possibilities get actualized and which ones are excluded from actualization. This determines the shape and value of the world that gets actualized, insofar as this is subject to human influence. On the other side, choosing also determines the value of the chooser as chooser. To choose something evil rather than good makes the chooser evil to the extent that this particular choice affects character. To choose to read philosophy on an afternoon rather than watch football reinforces the chooser's philosophical rather than sports-fan character, although the opposite choice can be taken on some other afternoon. Human beings develop their characters through countless choices large and small. I define "being under obligation" as the ultimate human condition in which choices determine the value character of the chooser. We are obligated to choose well by the fact that our choices determine our own value as choosers. Although all people lie under obligation, cultures have many different ways of dealing these issues. The choices people make concern a vast array of possibilities, some shared in common and others local to geography, particular histories, and social and personal circumstances.

Nevertheless at least four main kinds of obligations have bearing in every rich context of choice: obligations to truth, morality, rightness, and virtue. Permit me to describe these very briefly and comment on transcendence in their regard.

The obligation to truth is to make our interpretations of the world as true as possible. Interpretations allow us to parse the possibilities of our situation, evaluate them, work with others, and choose well or poorly. The obligation to truth is betrayed by habits of stubbornness, denial of what we do not like, closing off evidence, abusing those from whom we could learn, and confusing what we would like reality to be with what it is. The obligation to truth means we should cultivate a rather constant state of inquiry, making ourselves vulnerable to correction. The pursuit of power, wealth, and adulation often have set roadblocks to inquiry and have led to failure of our obligation to truth. We can see as never before the religious Ultimacy of our obligation to the truth.

The obligation to morality I define broadly as the obligation to make good choices. To do this requires more or less true interpretations of what the choices and their consequences are. But choosing well also means learning how to act, not merely to will to act but to act effectively. This involves both personal and social cultivation of skills of acting on the basis of choice. We know now, more than we did before the rise of modern science, about what goes into choosing. Recently the science of big data has allowed us to understand and follow through on choices that have great social and natural depth as well as temporal extent. Although we might not have transcended old senses of having the integrity to act well on the basis of choices, we now know better the contours of what shape choices might take. Whereas St. Francis might have been well-intentioned in bringing the people together in the cathedral to pray about the plague, we know now that his choice helped spread the disease by the sharing of fleas. Our current knowledge of environmental matters such as climate change gives us new and transcendent ways of choosing well. I do not mean only that we know more about consequences but that we can learn how to choose consistently over time to deal with climate change. The rejection of such new ways of acting consistently through time is an evil failure of moral obligation. The good news is that transcendent social responsibility is now more possible.

I define the obligation to rightness as the obligation to comport the shape of our lives overall to the contours of the world in which we live. This conformation does not mean that we should seek to fit in, because sometimes we need to oppose certain aspects of our personal, social, and natural environments. Rather, we should take regard for how to shape our lives so as to be responsive to the values (and disvalues) of the world in which we live. The obligation to be right in relation to the world has large dimensions, such as devising lives that are responsible to our natural environment; we should devise lives that are responsible to our historical and political environments, as well as to the contours of our communities, families, friends, and personal careers. This obligation has less to do with making specific choices for the future day by day than with shaping our lives overall to be in appropriate normative conformation to the relevant contours of the world. Many cultures have been shaped by an excessive individualism that supposes a kind of opposition between individual persons and the demands of their environment, suggesting that the environment is there for our chosen actions. I believe that contrary to this we are developing a consciousness of the deep relationality of the interior personal life with all aspects of existence, as shaped by causal environing contours. The obligation to rightness is a somewhat fresh perspective on what it means to be relational beings, fresh at least for the Western modern world. The Daoists and Confucians have been way ahead for centuries. This is a special kind of contemporary transcendence.

The obligation to virtue I define as the obligation to live as a good person in the world given our time and place. This includes the obligations to truth, morality, and rightness. But it includes also the obligation to attain as much value as possible in life, including what we embody in ourselves and contribute to the world. What it means to be virtuous differs for each of us because we are in different situations. Virtuous people who flourish in one situation might be disastrous in another. Nevertheless, whatever a good self would be in a situation is what a virtuous person should attain. Perhaps the thing most affected by a person's choices through life is the creation of that person's own self. It should be as good as it can be.

Is there any recent transcendence in the attainment of virtue? My guess is that the most important advance is the growing recognition that the goodness of a person is relative to the life situation in which a good self might grow. Therefore many different kinds or styles of virtue exist. Because relating to other people is among the most important things a person should be good at, internalizing a sense of the vastly different kinds of virtuous persons is important, transcending the old sense that virtue is only one thing.

Selfhood

All of the senses of Ultimate obligation, including obligation to truth, morality, rightness, and virtue, are involved in the quest for wholeness of self. But they are not the only factors. Becoming a self requires integrating all the factors that are components of personal identity. Personal identity necessarily has a de facto pattern, even when it is terrible, miserable, disorganized, consisting in a heap of failures, perpetuating further decline, and harmful to people, social situations, and the natural environment. Persons necessarily are harmonies and they can be extremely wretched harmonies. Better selves are harmonies of their components that respect the values in those components, that combine the components to achieve greater value, that enhance the person's relations with other things in the world, that give access to even better components, that allow for a person to develop with some excellence through the stages of life, that strengthen the person's capacities to fulfill obligations regarding choice, to engage the other things in the world with better integrity, and that address the issues of the meaning of life with more enhanced balances of achievement, acceptance, and probity. Among the components that are common to most if not all people are a genetic inheritance; biological and social circumstances that affect genetic expressions; families of origin and accidental placement; local communities at different stages of life; local educational, political, economic, and judicial systems with which the persons interact through life; the climate and geography of the person's habitats; larger historical and social developments within which the person lives; and perhaps all the ways in which these kinds of components can be broken in the individual's case or conflicting with one another so that the person and surrounding people suffer. Then more idiosyncratic components exist such as particular friends and foes, opportunities, accidents of social and natural life, and choices of careers and habitats. The quest for wholeness of self aims to integrate all sorts of components such as these, enhancing them, or at least positioning them, to achieve some kind of optimum personal value.

Different cultures have radically different ways of modeling the quest for achieving a good self. Let me illustrate this with some wildly speculative characterizations of different styles of personal integration. Most prominent in the West is the style of self-building by doing something about it, by exercising agency. Perhaps this comes from the West's tendency to think of the ontological creative act in terms of divine agency. More prominent in South Asian cultures, for instance Buddhist and Hindu, is the approach to selfhood by separating deep consciousness from what arises and ceases in consciousness, renouncing many of the metaphors of agency as the kinds of clinging that lead to bondage, confusion, and suffering. Of course, the Buddhists and Hindus live daily life, with all its decisions, components, engagements, and meanings. But they promote the self as enhanced with subtle disconnection from that. Most Hindus believe the deeper self is like consciousness and is a deeper reality, such as Brahman. Most Buddhists believe that the continuities of consciousness are themselves an illusion and that enlightenment consists in merely attending to what arises and ceases. This kind of self-building, involving much meditation, is quite different in style from the Western style of achieving a self through action. Both differ from East Asian styles of self-building that emphasize harmonization, flowing relationships, and connections with circles upon circles of personal, social, and natural environments, all configurations on the spectrum of nature. Such differences in styles of self-building are vastly more complex than I have indicated here. But the obligations to truth, morality, rightness, and virtue are found equally, though in different forms in all. Individuals move from birth to senility, sometimes never reaching the capacities for obligation, in which cases they are not fully human. But most do.

I believe we are in a period of great potential transcendence of older practices in the quest for wholeness of selfhood because of one of the blessings of globalization. Without difficulty, persons now can draw upon a great many styles, potentially combining many models of good selves. A person whose self is fragile because of anxiety can take action to intervene with an anti-anxiety drug, can practice any of a number of forms of calming meditation for liberation from psychological bondage, and can find many modes of harmonization in appropriate ways with personal, social, and natural environments. Ours is a time of exciting creativity in the envisionment of the goods of selfhood and the means of achieving and integrating them.

Engaging Others

Another ultimate condition of human life, in addition to living under obligation and needing to build a self, is the fact we live in existential fields with many other things, each of which has its own value and valuable relationships. Obviously many of these things become significant components of our lives and should be dealt with accordingly. Obviously, how we engage them depends on how we choose under obligation. Nevertheless, how things become components of our lives and are affected by our choices does not exhaust their own realities. Each of those things to which we are related in our existential fields is a harmony of its own, with an internal composition of its nature most likely changing through time. Each has elements that have little or no bearing on us and our situations. To engage those things truthfully, morally, rightly, and virtuously requires both learning to appreciate them in their own existential locations and acting appropriately so as to respect their values, for better or worse. To engage other things well is to engage them according to how they deserve to be engaged.

Lines defining "otherness" have many and shifting loci. For instance, a person engages family members according to the ways kinship relations are part of the person's own components. Yet all the family members have lives of their own that are not reducible to their kinship relations and thus need to be respected as others apart from how they are components in the person as such. Families have a harmonic integrity to which other families in the community are "others." Small cultural groups are ingroups with respect to which neighboring groups are outgroups and need to be respected as others when the tendency might be to reduce them to how they affect one's ingroup. Cultures, cities, nations, and civilizations relate to one another as outgroups and ingroups, and most civilizations have advanced modes of engagement that are versions of the Golden Rule.

But now we have recognized the otherness of nature in its many environments and understand that we should not merely exploit it for our personal or our ingroup's advantage. Because of greatly enhanced scientific knowledge, we know, for instance, that what we do with fossil fuels that affects climate change is also going to have enormous effects on our waters, forests, fields, and mountains. Moreover it is also going to have effects on people far from us in space and generations distant in time. Therefore our engagements with things affected by the use of fossil fuels are systematically related with how we need to respect the personal, social, and natural harmonies that hitherto had seemed merely "other."

I believe we are in a period of significant transcendence of our old ways of relating to others, for instance, supposing other people to be like us and supposing nature to be worth nothing unless it is worth something to us. Now we can formulate much more accurately the kinds of ecologies of harmonies that exist in nature, the diversities of cultural life, and the different kinds of values things can have in distant parts of our existential fields. We are able now, if we follow our obligations, to engage things far more appreciatively and appropriately.

Value-Identity

The question of value-identity has many venues. One is the reach of the cosmos: What is the value of the cosmos itself? If my metaphysics is correct, every determinate thing has value in itself. But how do things relate to and affect the values of other things? We have such a small sample, being rather limited to the density of value we can see in our world on Earth, that we cannot know much about the values of things in far-off space, whether they are thin or dense. Some people like to see the cosmos as the achievement of a divine purpose. The ontological creative act has no purposes in itself, although the cosmos might be ordered in ways that reflect an overarching purpose for everything together. But we simply do not have evidence to answer that question. We can transcend the hopes of purpose-oriented theists by leaving the overall design and value-achievement of the cosmos as an open question.

Another venue for the value-identity question is asking what our own individual lives add up to. Have we achieved something of value in life? Of course. Have we achieved all we should have achieved? Surely not. Our lives are of mixed value, and most of what we do and become is ambiguous. Nevertheless our identities consist of two different kinds of thing. A person's subjective identity is the harmony a person creates through a lifetime of living, something like the self I discussed previously as being built through agency, enlightened liberation, and harmonization with the world. Although much of life is given to us, what we do with what we are given is most important for the value of our selves. We are responsible for how we harmonize the components of ourselves.

The other kind of thing that is part of our identity is how we impact other things. We each have a metabolic footprint. We each are and do things that are taken up in the lives of others. As a teacher I was responsible for teaching well in all sorts of senses, but I am not responsible for what my students do with my teachings. That is their responsibility, even though it is part of my identity. Think of all the people for whom we are significant figures, playing roles in their identity; those influences are part of our identity. Think of all the institutions in society and human relations that we affect; we are not responsible for how they take us up, but how they do so is part of our identity. I call this our objective identity, our identity for others but still *our* identity. No finite perspective exists that constitutes a harmony of our subjective and objective identities, unless it be the ontological creative act itself, which is not a perspective in any ordinary sense. So it is extremely puzzling what we mean by our own value-identity. It is almost impossible to sum up, let alone appreciate. Yet it is an ultimate condition of human life.

I believe we are in a position now to relate to the ultimate condition of having a value-identity in three ways that transcend many traditional ways of engaging it. Religious cultures, to be sure, have many different ways of so engaging. Some believe the meaning of life is to attain immortality. Others believe it is to cut off finite existence and cease to exist once and for all. Still others believe that the value-identity we have in life is only what we contribute to the good harmonization of things. The following three ways seem opportune now to transcend all this.

The first is to admit that our value-identity is just a mystery, that it cannot be added up, and that there is nothing conclusive to understand here. No single standpoint exists from which to assess or evaluate our value-identity.

The second is to admit that, even with all the bad things, all the wrongs we have done, the ambiguities of what we have achieved, and the final mystery of our value-identity, everything is good, satisfactory, and to be accepted with gratitude. This is to transcend the ultimate quest to achieve a good value-identity and recognize that what counts is the creation. It's not about us, it's about the ontological creative act and its products. Even where some things are bad for other things, each is good in its own way of harmony, and we can accept being acceptable. This is surely strange, but it follows from all that has been said.

The third element of transcendence is to come back home to the recognition that the ideal meaning of the lives of us all is to live life as well as we can. We should strive to do our best under the circumstances of our lives, varied as they are. To the extent we fail to do our best, we are acceptable nevertheless. I believe we can transcend our struggles to be saved in ultimate perspective, transcend the struggles for salvation or successful value-identity, and enjoy our existence no matter what.

Chapter 5

Emergence

Like a Flowing Stream

Mind emerges from matter
Like a rushing stream?
Mind begins with matter
Like a gushing fountain?
No, flowing comes from eternity,
With no abstractions.
Humans are marvels
To catch this.
The mind uncovers novelty,
The mind relates this to fact,
The mind says "Aha!"
Eternity smiles.

The Problem of Emergence

Our colleague Terrence Deacon has made a signal contribution to the vastly interesting and important conversation about emergence, and in this he is as strange as I am. In his *Incomplete Nature*, he speaks as a scientist when he points out that some of the most obvious elements of human life, such as having purposes, cognitive and emotional intentionality, and being able to make judgments about truth claims, in principle cannot be explained or understood on the methodological and metaphysical assumptions of modern science.[1] Those assumptions are that the explanations of anything can appeal only to causes that are actually present at the time of the causation. Old-fashioned mechanism is an obvious example of such assumptions, but new-fashioned causal conceptions, for instance appealing to statistical laws, have the same vague property, namely that only the actual can explain what happens.

This language comes into our sensibility from Aristotle's metaphysics, which said that all change is the reduction of potentiality to act and that the potentiality exists only in something actualized. Potentiality can be a property only of what is actual. This assumption is often expressed in the adage that "nothing can come out of nothing." It sounds more profound in Latin: *ex nihilo nihil fit*. From it, Thomas Aquinas concluded that God has to be the pure Act of To Be, because any finite actuality has to derive from a cause that has at least as much actuality as itself. Because Thomas thought there is no limit in principle to what might become actual, God, the first cause, must be infinite or pure act. Most contemporary scientists are very far from being Aristotelians, Aristotle's science being so out of date. They associate Aristotle with teleological explanation, which they reject, and they usually do not study ancient philosophy either. But those scientists are materialists in the sense that they appeal only to actual material in their explanations, even when that material is stuff of which Aristotle could not conceive, such as quarks and neural transmitters, all understood basically in terms of mass and/or energy that needs to be present in order to act.

Deacon, however, is an uncommon scientist in recognizing that so much of experience, as well as consciousness, is determined by what is absent, not by what is actually present. Moreover, what is absent has material consequences that need to be explained. What we do so often has its most important intelligibility in the causal effects of unfulfilled purposes, for instance, when we act to fulfill them. The very plausibility of a scientific hypothesis depends on the possible discovery of evidence that is absent and needs to be found precisely in the form of evidence. Deacon's own work is to develop cognitive science in ways that do make appropriate appeal to what is absent in this sense. (To be sure, the causal determination of what actually happens by what is absent is what Aristotle meant by teleology, but we will gloss over that.)

Deacon's program in this regard is important for science because of its radical questioning of the received scientific assumptions. Descartes, on whom all bad things are usually blamed, said body and mind can be conceived entirely separately and that each is what it is entirely without the other. Modern science picked up on his notion of body and has developed that in extraordinary ways; sure enough, those ways do not allow mind to be conceived as part of body. Most philosophers in the Continental tradition pick up on the mind part of Descartes's metaphysics, associating it with consciousness, and worry about how a material world outside of mind can correctly be known within mind. Most Continental philosophy, though not all, takes a negative view of the claims of modern science. Postmodern philosophers often distance themselves from it by associating science with colonialism.

Other philosophers, particularly in the American tradition, are themselves naturalists who take science to be a central source of knowledge, even if it has flawed metaphysical assumptions. But they recognize that the intentionality of human life and perhaps much more needs to be shown to evolve out of nature, or rather within nature. This calls for a reconception of nature, rejecting the view that only what is actual, material, or present can have significant causal consequences. Over a hundred years ago, Charles Peirce, the founder of pragmatism, developed a theory of the reality of habits to explain mental activity. A habit can have an instance of habitual behavior actualized at a particular time, but as a habit, a tendency, it is never exhausted in any particular time or sum of particular times. Peirce's own philosophical cosmology claimed that habits are a part of nature all the way down to the most elementary causes, not just in highly evolved mental states. He also was deeply concerned about how to develop habits of good thinking, of controlling thoughts so as to be able to conduct inquiry. Alfred North Whitehead wrote after the great transformations in physical theory at the beginning of the twentieth century. He developed a truly astonishing philosophical cosmology that escaped not only Aristotle's principle of actualization deriving only from the already actual but also the whole theory of substance. Deacon recognizes Whitehead's contribution but backs away from it in large part because its concepts are too far from those used in natural science, especially post-Whiteheadian biological science, to be of much use in reforming that science.

I write as a metaphysician, however, and so am going to address the question of emergence and relate that to religion, with regard to its metaphysical underpinnings. Much as I like Peirce and Whitehead, I think their theories are not adequate to what needs to be done and so will present my own theory.

Determinateness

Most metaphysical theories are based on generalizing what philosophers take to be the basic traits of the world they experience. So, Plato thought the world is a rush of processes passing through the temporary shapes of static forms; Aristotle thought the world consists of substances; Peirce thought it is an evolving harmonization of Firstness, Secondness, and Thirdness; Whitehead thought it is creativity and actual occasions whose relations mirrored the mathematics of the physical sciences. None of these is sufficiently general or abstract enough to tolerate much significant change in what we think the world to be. The same goes for the yin-yang metaphysics of East Asia and the consciousness metaphysics of South Asia.

So I propose that metaphysics focus on the nature of determinateness as such. To be determinate is to be something rather than something else or nothing at all. A determinate thing has to be determinate with respect to some other determinate things if it is to be itself rather than them. It might also be indeterminate with respect to some other things, but not with respect to all things; otherwise it would not be itself rather than something else. A central focus in metaphysics, I propose, is to give an account of determinateness.

Notice how utterly abstract this account must be. It is applicable to any possible theory of the world, because any such theory must represent the world as being some way or other. Plato's, Aristotle's, Peirce's, and Whitehead's theories all illustrate the metaphysical account of determinateness, each in its own way. The same is true with the theories from any civilization, and from the ancient or contemporary worlds. So the metaphysics of determinateness is a hypothesis of the most vague logical scope, vague in the strict sense of tolerating, as an illustration, any more specific determinate view of the world, no matter how much those more specific theories contradict one another. For our purposes here, the metaphysical hypothesis about determinateness is tolerant of anything contemporary science might suggest, of any line of plausible scientific inquiry, of any set of theoretical constructs and standards of good judgment or, as in the case of our colleague Deacon, any criticism and redirection of a scientific program.

Here is my hypothesis about determinateness. To be determinate with respect to some other determinate things requires anything to have two kinds of components. One kind is *conditional* components that register the other things to which the thing is determinate. We can imagine these as effects or conditionings by those other things, although there are many conflicting theories about how such causation takes place. A determinate thing has to have conditional components from all the other things with respect to which it is determinate. The other kind of component is *essential*, by which I mean that it functions within the thing to integrate the conditional components, to give those conditions something to condition, to provide, in conjunction with the conditional components, an own-being of the thing.

Let me offer a brief negative argument for the necessity of both conditional and essential components. If a thing were to have no conditional components, it would not have the determinateness of being related to the other things so as to be different from them. Without conditional components, a thing would be a pure atom without the capacity even to be in a field with other things or in the void relative to other things. Isn't it good to be rid of all atomistic theories? If a thing had no essential components, it would reduce to the conditional components alone. But if there were nothing for the conditional components to condition jointly, there would be no conditioning at all. The situation would be just whatever the other things are relative to each other without conditioning the determinate thing at hand. Both conditional and essential components are necessary.

This is all very abstract, but we do conclude two things from it. Any determinate world must consist in a multiplicity of things so that each determinate thing can be determinate with respect to something else. A world of only one determinate thing is impossible. Also, any determinate thing is internally complex, containing a multiplicity of components, some conditional and some essential. Any determinate thing is a harmony of conditional and essential components whose conditional components are due to other things with respect to which it is determinate. Now we are rid of any metaphysics of pure monism.

What else do we know from this analysis? One more thing we know is that the tissue of conditional components relating determinate things to one another is a cosmological togetherness or field of mutual conditioning. The field in this abstract metaphysical sense has no characteristics of its own except for the mutual conditionings of determinate things. To call it a field is merely to refer to the networks of mutual conditionings. In this sense of cosmological togetherness, any determinate thing relates to the other determinate things with regard to their conditional components alone: relating means conditioning.

But those other things cannot be only their conditioning components because they too must have their own essential components. They could not themselves be real "other things" with respect to which the thing at hand is determinate if they were not themselves harmonies with essential as well as conditioning features. Therefore, there must be a more basic context in which mutually related determinate things can be together with their essential components external to one another while their conditional components are internally related. I call this the *ontological context of mutual relevance*, "ontological" because it refers to the whole being of different things that are determinate in part with respect to one another. If there were no ontological context of mutual relevance, the mutual conditioning of things in their cosmological togetherness would be impossible.

What can this ontological context of mutual relevance be? Philosophers have tried a number of hypotheses, for instance, an underlying trait such as being-itself, an overarching principle that contains the things as a totality, or a principle such as Whitehead's creativity that makes any plurality into a new unity. But all these hypotheses suggest that the ontological context of mutual relevance is something determinate, which is precisely what it cannot be. If it were determinate in any sense whatsoever, it could relate to the other determinate things it is supposed to contextualize only by means of a yet deeper ontological context of mutual relevance. So the ontological context must itself be indeterminate.

I propose that the only "thing" that could be the ontological context of mutual relevance is an act of creation that simply makes the determinate things in their mutual relations, determining each other with their own essential features, giving them own-being. The act of creation has no nature or any other kind of existence, such as potentiality, apart from creating. Its nature comes from the things created as they are created together. Togetherness in this ontological sense is singular and eternal. It is singular in the sense that, no matter how far apart in space, time, or any other cosmological relation things might be, if they are determinately different, they are created together. It is eternal in the sense that temporal distinctions of past, present, and future, any form of earlier and later or nearer and farther, are all determinate and hence elements of the created product of the ontological act of creation. The act of creation is not in time at all. It is not in the beginning as Thomas Aquinas thought. It is not some kind of specious present time in which the whole temporal array is present at once, as Augustine thought. It is not some kind of ideal pulling from the future as some Platonists and Whiteheadians have thought. It is creative of all those things and not one of them because all of them are determinate and therefore created. The ontological creative act is singular and eternal.

(In case you missed it, that was a proof for God, in Western terms, conceived as transcending all determinateness and creative of all that can be imagined, a classic position.)

The eternity of an ontological act of creation that makes temporality and spatiality possible is not an ordinary way to think nowadays. We are deeply conditioned to think that only things in space and time are real, and indeed the eternal act of creation is not a determinate thing. For the most part, the eternal act of creation is not of much interest to the sciences because they inquire into the structures of things within space-time and how they arise and change. The singular eternity of the ontological act of creation is of very great interest to religion, however, and in many respects. I shall return to some of these religious interests shortly because I think religion loses its soul if it cannot deal with eternity.

Science and Emergence

As for science, however, there is one topic with respect to which the not-in-time-or-space ontological act of creation is very relevant, namely the topic of emergence. Let me shift the level of my metaphysical abstractions from the very highest that deals with determinateness as such to that of a temporal world that has flow and causality. This still is quite vague because so many different theories exist about how space-time flow and causation works; I will not try to sort these here.

Let us assume for the sake of argument, however, that temporal flow involves the past, the present, and the future. The past is actual and fixed; it provides potentialities for what might happen. The future is a field of possibilities of what might happen, given what has already been actualized. As time passes and more things are actualized, the possibility structure of the future changes to keep up. The present is the temporal mode in which possibilities are transformed into actuality. The actualities in the past are the potentials for being made into the newly actualizing present moment. The future possibilities for the integration of past actualities in a new present moment might allow alternative actualizations. In this case, the present is not only transformative but selective among alternative possibilities.

Given that the past is fixed and fully actual, the present must add something to the past that it does not already contain. If nothing new were added, the present moment would already be actual and past, and temporal flow would be impossible. Perhaps what the present moment adds is little or nothing more than a new actual space-time instance of what was before. Perhaps it adds a new rearrangement of past things that can be described on a set of trajectories through a duration. Thinkers in the early nineteenth century imagined that the course of the world was like a deterministic picture in which every change is "sufficiently" caused by the antecedents and that it would be possible to reverse the direction of time and move either forward or backward. But that imagination was only of a possible world. It did not take into account what it would mean to be *at* a particular date within that world and would have to move from that date to the next. That movement would require a transition from the past, actualized date to the next, hitherto unactualized date so that something would have to be added, over and above the mere possibility for the next, to the past in order to actualize the next and not leave it as a mere possibility. The metaphysical way to regard this is that any kind of temporal movement at all needs to have something added to the past to get something new, even if what is new could be predicted entirely from the potentials from past actualities. In this minimal sense, whenever there is temporal movement, there is the emergence of something new, not contained within the past. If it were contained within the past, nothing new would ever happen and there would be no temporal flow.

This something new is the location within time of a bit of the ontological creative act that creates the whole temporal flow. Such ubiquitous emergence seems to be trivial and rightly ignored by those who seek to understand what happens and why. But it illustrates the important metaphysical point that the flow of time is impossible if something absent from the already actualized past does not have causal consequences in actualizing something new. Relative to the past, this something new is spontaneous.

The interesting question that prompts emergence theory, however, is whether new structures emerge so that there are new kinds of things not previous contained within the past. This requires being more specific than looking merely at the cosmology of temporal flow. We have learned from evolutionary thinking that it is not enough to have just any old new kind of thing. The important new kinds of thing are those that can survive and be sustained in the environment of old kinds of things and in turn create new environments within which even newer kinds of things can survive. This is the point at which science needs to discover what novel structures in the organism-in-environment need to emerge and be sustained for the really interesting structures, such as purposive behavior, musement, or the love of God, to emerge. Philosophers can say "how mind emerged from matter" in terms of a naturalistic cosmology and with a full-blown account of the intentionality that emerges. But cognitive scientists need now to be able to work in detail, from reformed conceptions of matter in neurobiology and human ecological interactions to explanations of how scientists can write intelligible grant proposals that meet the expectations of funding agencies and at the same time further the scientists' own agendas.

Emergence and Religion

I am required now to shift my focus to emergence within religion, not cognitive science. Let me begin with a heuristic definition of religion, namely human symbolic engagement with Ultimate realities in cognitive, existential, and practical ways. Please accept this as a hypothesis for now. Religion is an engagement with Ultimate realities, whatever that turns out to be. Three general ways exist for that engagement, although engagements are so dense and thick that all of them might follow all three paths. The first path is cognition, which is what we shall deal with mainly here. This ranges from abstract metaphysics to primitive myths. The second path is existential content, and this means the things in reference to which people define themselves at the most basic levels. The third path is the practices, mainly in public, by which individuals and communities act out their relations with Ultimate realities.

Fortunately, you already know about one Ultimate reality, according to my metaphysics, the ontological creative act that creates everything determinate. You also know about four more that are necessary traits of any determinate thing that is a harmony of a plurality of components. They are the *form* in which the components are arranged, the *components* themselves as playing roles within that form, the *existential location* of the harmony relative to other things with respect to which it is determinate, and the *value* of getting these components together in this location with this form. Form, components, existential location, and value.

In the human scale of the world, form is ultimately important as the possibilities among which people have to choose when the possibilities have different values, giving rise to the religious problematic of lying under obligation. This problematic includes issues of discerning what the possibilities really are and what they are worth, determining the moral character of the choosers by the choices made, and dealing with moral failure of righteousness and what to do about that. The components are ultimately important because they are so hard to integrate and themselves are often broken. All religions have problematics of attaining personal wholeness, dealing with suffering, problems of integrity, and peace of mind. Existential location is ultimately important for people because they necessarily engage other people in different social locations, some of whom are within one's ingroup and others outside. The values of those other people, and the natural environment as well I might add, deserve respect from the standpoint of the whole of creation, and all the Axial Age religions say people should be universally compassionate and just. The value of life, what it adds up to, is ultimately important and gives rise to religious problematics of seeking meaning or justification.

Like any determinate world, a world within which human beings can live has form, components, location, and value and these are ultimate boundary conditions for human life. Any human culture has to engage these just as it has to engage the weather and geography of its place. The symbols guiding these various cultural engagements, and the practices guided by them, have emerged in ways historians of religion can describe and perhaps explain if they have detailed enough accounts of what is required of new structures in order to arise and be sustainable for a while.

With this little sketch of a theory of religions, it is easy to see how there have been significant emergences in religion's history. The Axial Age illustrates striking emergence in all five problematics.

In the Axial Age were the first clear formulations of the awareness and dedication to some unifying source or ground for all the multiplicity of the world, also conceiving the world as a whole for the first time. Some cultures elaborated personifying metaphors for the ontological act of creation, and in the great monotheisms tribal gods were replaced, or made merely finite components of a complex world, by notions of a single creator. This is illustrated in the shift in the Hebrew Bible from conceiving of Yahweh in the Ten Commandments so as "to have no other gods before me" to being the transcendent source of everything. Other cultures elaborated metaphors of deeper and deeper levels of "consciousness" to develop concepts of Brahman and Buddha-mind as symbols of the ontological act. In this shift, the multitude of gods were clearly relegated to being subject to karma except when they in turn are symbolic of indeterminate Brahman. In other cultures, the concept of a highest god, for instance Shangdi in China, was not transmuted into a monotheism but rather dropped out almost entirely in favor of metaphors of spontaneous emergence, the Dao, or the Great Ultimate of Non-being whence the Great Ultimate arises. These parallel shifts were a striking emergence of related new ways of thinking about what I call in metaphysical terms the *ontological creative act* and with corresponding new ways of devotion. Historically, there were many points of cultural interaction during the Axial Age.

Similarly, with regard to the ultimate boundary condition of obligation, there was a massive shift from tribal morals of protecting the ingroup while readying hostility toward outgroups to some sense or other of universal compassion and justice, or regarding all people as one's ingroup under heaven or all people as children of God. With regard to the ultimate boundary condition of the quest for wholeness, the Axial Age religions came to orient that quest around devotion or commitment to the ontological act of creation, in whatever unifying symbols they had for it, rather than appeals for magical help from various agencies. With regard to the ultimate boundary condition of engaging others, the Axial Age religions came to appreciate all things, including all people, as in some sense having a common standing within the created order. With regard to the boundary conditions of value-identity and the meaning of life, the Axial Age subtly began the shift from finding ultimate meaning in one's place in a tribal structure and history to finding it in reference to the ontologically ultimate ground of the world, however symbolized. The Axial Age religions did not do away with the us-versus-them or ingroup versus outgroup distinctions. It only relativized them and made them important but proximate concerns. The Ultimate, that is, truly religious elements, became focused according to the Axial Age ideals of Ultimacy in thought and practice that emerged with astonishing universality. We are still working out the implications of the Axial Age emergences.

How can there be significant emergence regarding religious communities? Surely, new forms of community life have evolved through history, including those that bear and institutionalize the various Axial Age emergences. But I would be slow to call them religious emergences. Whereas those newly emergent forms of community life became vehicles for some for sharing and transmitting the new forms of Axial Age conception and devotion, they also had their own social and political dynamics. Politics and social life are important in their own right and are not to be reduced to the ways in which they facilitate people engaging Ultimacy in religion. Many people can participate in the emergent social and political forms without being much engaged with Ultimacy at all.

Sometimes, of course, that social or political dynamic itself is an emergent condition that in turn provides the environment for genuinely religious emergence shaping engagements of Ultimacy. For instance, the political emergence of great empires in China, India, and around the Mediterranean during the Axial Age forced tribes together, with some peace, rather than as outgroups hostile to one another. It relativized tribal languages and imposed common languages; it brought people wider conceptions of the world and revealed the arbitrariness of tribal sacred things. All these emergences are to be understood in terms of politics and cultural interactions, not engagements of Ultimacy. But they did provide environmental conditions for the possibility of the Axial Age religious emergences regarding the ultimate boundary conditions of human life. So also nowadays new forms of communal life might make possible newly emergent forms for the engagement of Ultimacy.

Religion in its Ultimate engagements is fundamentally an inward matter. Both William James and Alfred North Whitehead said that religion is what one does with solitariness; the latter said that whoever is never truly alone is never truly religious. Both recognized that culture, tradition, and community are necessary environments for religion, without which we would have no symbols for symbolic engagement or the livelihood to do much of anything; without them, we could not share religious engagements. But it is in the inward parts that religion can emerge with new forms beyond the ordinary.

I'm thinking here, of course, of the great heroes of spirituality, those whose emergent genius lies in restructuring the self to attain and be able to sustain for a while some new union with the ontological creative act, symbolized perhaps as God, the ground of consciousness, or the abyss of non-being whence all determinate things come. There are many kinds of religious creators of emergent connections with Ultimacy, to be sure, including heroes of righteousness, masters of inner harmony, saints of compassion, geniuses who penetrate to new meaning for existence, and those we often refer to as mystics. I have in mind here especially the last, those who find emergent ways for engaging the creative act of existence itself, or the determinate world *as* the product of the ontological act. In the pragmatic epistemology that lies behind the notion of symbolic engagement, "union" with the object means that the object is carried across into the interpreter in the respects in which the symbols can interpret it. For mystics with emergent transformative realizations, this means the transformation of the self to be able to bear yet one more dimension of the ontological act creating the world.

The study of this inward kind of religious emergence is extremely complicated, not to say contentious. We know about only those mystics historically important enough to be written about or who write about their own experience with understanding. We are rightly suspicious of self-presentations. No matter how inward, such religious emergent creations are always in the symbols of some tradition or other or build upon such culturally located symbols. No fair understanding of this kind of spiritual emergence can fail to triangulate in with some independence on the Ultimate reality engaged, and hence it involves normative theology through metaphysics, comparative theologies, or techniques of spiritual discernment, all of which make religious studies scholars nervous.

Nevertheless, it is in these emergent achievements of the inward heart, either directly in mystical devotion to the ontological act or in mediations through obligation, personal wholeness, engagement with others, or the search for meaning, that religion consists as the symbolic engagement of Ultimacy. Insofar as these inward achievements employ or build on the symbolic terms of a cultural tradition, that tradition can be called religious. But others can participate in that tradition without the serious engagement of Ultimacy, employing the symbols as part of culture but not through personal engagement of Ultimacy. Hence, "history of religions" can be a misnamed discipline. Tracing the evolution of historical culture can be as much about the historical circumstances of the culture as it is about whether it is actually employed as the symbolic vehicle for actual religion that engages Ultimacy, which in fact might be missing. Only when there is actual engagement of ultimacy does that cultural history have a religious dimension. The study of religious communities and their new emergent forms is really a political study; only when individuals within those communities actually engage Ultimacy do the communities have a religious dimension, and they can very well lack such.

I suggest that we take traditions, communities, psychological structures, and many other aspects of life as evolutionary conditions for the symbolic engagement of Ultimacy rather than as religious as such. They can be studied on their own. Also their study needs to be internalized to the study of religion. Innovations in culture, politics, and the rest might become new environmental conditions for the emergence of new religious forms. This needs to be understood in terms of the *possible* religious dimensions of tradition, politics, and much else. But what makes these other fields of life religious is their bearing as environing conditions for the inward engagement of Ultimacy and their roles in the sharing of this inward religiosity so far as it can be shared. To confuse the traditions and religious communities with the ultimate engagements themselves is easy. It leads to according those traditions and religious communities' falsely ultimate status and devotion, which in some circumstances is harmless.

But as often as not, emergent new engagements with Ultimacy result in radical breaks with tradition, even while building on it. Religious emergence often disrupts communities, contrary to Durkheim. Religious emergence transforms structures of the self so as to engage the Ultimate in new respects and so is more than psychology in any form to which the religious emergent might be explained reductively. Genuine religious Ultimacy has many experiential components that can function to contribute to religion but that are really subject to their own structures and can fall away from serving religion.

Conversely, emergent religious structures can function as environing conditions for emergence changes in tradition and community. Politics can be influenced by religion as much as the other way around.

This chapter has approached its topic from the top down: first a metaphysics of determinateness, next a cosmology of determinateness relative to science, then a treatment of emergence within science, then religion in light of science, and finally a treatment of religion as carefully discriminated from other domains of experience that can but need not be parts of religion. This reverses the bottom-up approach of the previous chapter.

Chapter 6

Indeterminacy

What Implies What?

Creator and created co-imply each other.
Each is contingent on the other.
Neither is contingent on anything else.
The creator makes possible and existent things together.
Nothing is determinate without being created.
The creator is indeterminate except for its creatures.
Determinate things have form, integration, locality, and value.
Some of these are conditional and some essential.
Determinate things are harmonies of all these.
Through conditional elements things are together and
    mutually influencing.
Through essential elements things are apart in their own-being.
Harmonies are partly together and partly apart.
The creator creates harmonies together and apart.
The creator is an act of creation
Whose terminus is all determinate harmonies.
The creative act is immediate.
It does not exist unless its terminal harmonies are created.
The creative act with its determinate products is a total
    surprise.
We would not be surprised without some determinate
    intelligibility.
Intelligibility means the surprise has happened.

Happy we are to be surprised!
No reason exists for the creator and created, no reason external or internal.
Not even eternal space-time awaiting something.
Nothing.

Cosmological versus Ontological Indeterminacy

Two broad problematics of indeterminacy obtain in both China and the West. The first is what I call "cosmological" because it has to do with indeterminacy in how the processes of nature, institutions, and personal life play out. In Plato's *Republic* and many other dialogues, the characters debated how to balance or harmonize the many natural, social, and personal factors in play, supposing that it was not absolutely determinate what was going to happen in advance of developing good judgment and choice. Aristotle discussed the indeterminacy of the future when a group of admirals debated whether to go to battle on the morrow (in *On Interpretation*, chap. nine). Set against this cosmology of partial indeterminacy was the principle articulated by Aristotle and winning favor through much Western (and Muslim) medieval philosophy that all the actuality in an effect must be contained in its antecedent causes with nothing new: *ex nihil, nihil fit*. Although many interpretations of this arose, the principle basically said that the present, where choices might be made, and the future are determined by the past; no indeterminacy. With the rise of early modern science, Aristotle's complicating formal, final, and material causes were eliminated from scientific consideration and efficient causes alone were allowed to explain, resulting in rigid "determinism." Kant went so far as to say, in the *Critique of Pure Reason*, especially the "Second Analogy," that determinism must be presupposed by science so as to distinguish between the objective order and the subjective order of representations. This scientific determinism was qualified in the nineteenth century with the rise of statistical causal explanations: a population (say, of gas molecules) is determined even though its members (the individual molecules) are not. I shall shortly trace down the Chinese alternatives to this Western story of indeterminacy.

The other problematic of indeterminacy I call "ontological" because it has to do with how a determinate, or at least partly determinate and partly indeterminate, cosmos arises from a simple, undifferentiated, indeterminate ground. Plato said in the *Republic* that the Form of the Good gives rise to or creates everything knowable in any sense and all kinds of knowing in any determinate sense. But he did not elaborate that point. In the *Parmenides* he showed just how complicated this notion is when run through the changes of the problem of the one and the many. Aristotle said little or nothing about this. But Plotinus in the *Enneads* said that the One or Being is beyond all determination and overflows to give rise to it. The One in itself is indeterminate and it gives rise to the Dyad, and hence to all else, which is where determinateness of any sort lies. Versions of this "infinite fullness of being contracting itself to intelligibility or determinateness" developed in Pagan, Christian, Jewish, and Muslim Neo-Platonic philosophy. Though influenced by Neo-Platonism, Thomas Aquinas went on a slightly different tack to modify Aristotle's idea of "being in act," as in finite actualities and actualizations, into the idea of God as the pure Act of To Be, infinite and simple. Aquinas's God creates finite things by putting limitations on the infinite, that is, indeterminate, Act of To Be. However, those things are separate in the created world, are indistinguishable within the divine essence, which is pure Act with no potentialities or delimitations. The Neo-Platonic and Thomistic conceptions construe God as an infinite fullness that is somehow contracted or delimited in the creation of the determinate world, moving from ontological indetermination to the ontological being of cosmological determinateness. These positions called themselves creation *ex nihilo*, meaning creation from no determinate thing.

In contrast, Descartes denied the fullness of being interpretation of the indeterminate and said that all creation of determinate things, including intelligibility, is positive creation of something from absolutely no thing, not even fullness. Finite things for Descartes are wholly positive realities that can be known (with the proper method) by the natural light of reason. The positive realities are entirely novel, not made from antecedent actuality, infinite or finite. Descartes's general position was followed by Paul Tillich (and me), among others. For all these ontological positions and their variants, any determinacy is grounded in, created by, or caused by the indeterminate. Another way of saying this is that the complex arises from and is to be explained by the simple, somehow or another. These positions of creation ex nihilo stand in contrast with positions that say the most fundamental source of finite things is itself determinate and rational, such as Aristotle's Thought Thinking Itself, Leibniz's God finding the best harmony of compossibilities in order to have sufficient reason for creating, and Hartshorne's God of necessary metaphysical first principles. I shall discuss some Chinese alternatives to these strategies for explaining how the determinate arises from the indeterminate.

Cosmology

The aboriginal Chinese sensibility about the cosmos is that it consists of changes. To find anything like the notion of things as substances is difficult in Chinese philosophy, literature, or art. The cosmos is composed of a universal stuff, *qi*, that has different scales of changes, from the rough changes of mountains that seem very solid and extremely slow to change, through the swifter and more complicated changes of biological nature, to the extremely subtle changes of highly complex and interactive changes of human thinking, even the most speedy or tranquil thinking of the sages. Mind-body dualism is almost impossible to imagine in the Chinese philosophical sensibility. The closest is a problematic of inner personal development versus outer action in the world, but even here the dominant positions have stressed the continuity between thought and action. Wang Yang-ming is famous for emphasizing the continuity of inner impulses with outer actions.

The fundamental units of changes in *qi* are yin and yang. Yang is a movement of extension or expansion. When it reaches its limits or end of its resources, it stops and begins to contract. Yin is a movement of contraction, consolidation, returning to a matrix of resources. No such thing as a static yin-yang state of affairs exists in Chinese thinking; rather there are only increasing and decreasing yang and increasing and decreasing yin. The concepts of yin and yang have great metaphoric reach. Originally yin meant the north side of the mountain, which in China's northern hemisphere location was associated with winter, cold water, and women who dominate when most of life is indoors. Yang meant the south side of the mountain, summer, warmth, and men who dominate during times of outdoor labor. But the calendar is always changing, moving through the stages of winter into spring, summer, autumn, and winter again. Each day brings a new shifting of the proportions of yin and yang.

Yin-yang changes can be visualized as wave patterns. Waves vary in amplitude and frequency and they limit what each other can do. Like a piece of music the various amplitudes and frequencies of sound harmonize with one another; when they do not harmonize, discord happens. The body contains thousands of yin-yang harmonic transformations, often working together and enabling one another during times of health. But in sick conditions, the various harmonies do not harmonize with one another and medicines need to be introduced to heat up or cool down some organ system. Chinese traditional medicine is based on the arts or rebalancing yin-yang transformation that get out of harmony. The cosmos of *qi* is a vast maelstrom of yin-yang transformations going into and out of harmony. This is explicitly brought to attention in *taijiquan*, the exercise and martial art that consists in intertwining different yin-yang patterns of *qi* energy.

Nature, society, and personal and interpersonal life depend on the changes of yin and yang holding to patterns of structure. These patterns include slow-changing mountain patterns, stability of natural and social environments so that human life can go on, stability of the human body so that it can do the things it must do in the day's round, and stability of culture and thought so that people can lead intentional, communicative, and artful lives. So the interweaving of mutually supportive and limiting yin-yang movements must have some pattern. This is the problem Plato meant to solve by saying that concrete things are always in a state of becoming, not being, passing from one form to another. Whitehead agreed with Plato and the Chinese that concrete reality is in constant flux and said that static forms "ingress" into the flux to give it temporary passing shape. In Chinese thought the earliest attempt to understand structure was with the hexagrams of the *Yijing*. In the hexagrams, six lines symbolize phases of yin or yang through which a movement passes. Broken lines are yin and solid lines are yang. The sixty-four hexagrams represent all possible combinations of yin and yang phases. Used for many purposes, from divination to esoteric numerology, the sixty-four hexagrams give an exhaustive set of descriptions of possible movements. But of course many movements have fewer or more than six phases. Moreover, alongside, within, and inclusive of any given movement are other movements. Therefore, the organic connections of movements within movements are very difficult to identify.

In application to human affairs, for instance conducting a war, raising a crop, or dealing with a recalcitrant child, some hexagraphic pattern is unfolding, the Chinese tradition supposes. Suppose you have gone through a yielding yin phase, an assertive yang phase, and now another yin phase. Perhaps it is possible to decide to act with another yin phase of retreat or a yang phase of advance. Whichever you choose, as king, farmer, or parent, will determine which the fourth line or phase will be, for disaster or success. Sometimes the inertial forces of the pattern in play at first prevent any choice. But at other times you can make a difference to which hexagraphic pattern will emerge. In thinking about your situation in hexagraphic terms, the earlier phases might be quite indeterminate with regard to the later phases of the emerging pattern. Not only is there room for choice, sometimes there is also room for accident, as when your enemy in battle finds a sudden new ally, an unusual drought occurs, or your child is suddenly disabled.

Yin-yang thinking in the *Yijing* is not really practicable for science or guiding affairs, except that it calls attention to all the ways in which yin and yang movements can interrelate and affect one another. Another model for the grounds for order amidst change was the notion of Heaven that flourished by the time of Confucius and Laozi; Heaven was also discussed in the *Yijing*, beginning with the very first hexagram. Much earlier the Chinese had believed in a high God, Shangdi, who was a storm God similar to Yahweh or Zeus in the West. But by around 1000 BCE, the literate elements of Chinese culture subordinated the personal characteristics of such a god to impersonal Heaven. Heaven was associated with the night sky, with fixed and moving stars, an impersonal but very awesome display of regular and irregular movement. As the notion of Heaven developed in diverse ways, the Chinese conceived it as the source of pattern within the cosmic changes of *qi*. Different interpretations of how Heaven is the source of patterns developed, and by the time of the rise of Neo-Confucianism in the tenth and eleventh centuries Heaven was conceived as *li*, Principle, or Coherence. Under the slogan "*Li* is one, its manifestations many," *li* was generally thought not to be a super-pattern itself but rather the principle of coherence that made various pluralities of processes cohere in a pattern. A given plurality of changes could be made to cohere with the pattern of a mountain, another plurality with a coherent social structure, another with the patterns of an individual's life set in a family, neighborhood, topological setting, and country. However much a given patterned harmony was changing, with its components themselves changing and its environment changing, to the extent the changes held to pattern, then harmony had *li*, a given local manifestation of coherence. The result was a conception of the cosmos as consisting of layers upon layers, intertwinings upon intertwinings, of coherences as manifestations of *li*.

These changes exhibiting *li* are all yin-yang changes with their ecological complexities. A fundamental sensibility from early to late in Chinese thought was the recognition that a lot of things just do not cohere. Not everything can be made coherent. The feistiness of *qi* does not take pattern or coherence easily. The reason for this is that yang can increase until it reaches its limit, but that limit might be wholly beyond the bounds of previously prevailing harmonies. Devastating floods can wash out an entire economy; barbarian hordes can overwhelm and destroy a society; a cancer can kill a body that no amount of counterbalancing can help. Similarly on the yin side, a biological ecosystem can lose its integrity and collapse into constituent parts that cannot sustain themselves in isolation; a government can attempt to mollify the barbarians and collapse completely; the integrating vital forces in a person can retreat to death. Medical models can make it seem that the various movements of yang and yin in a person's life are in balance, and that advance in yang is balanced by retreat in yin. But it does not work that way; no balanced harmony exists. This is precisely why medical procedures are needed: to push back against the unbalancing forces of nature. The *Daodejing* says that "Heaven and Earth are not humane (*jen*). They regard all things as straw dogs," referring to ritual dogs made of straw that are thrown into the fire after the ceremony.

Daoists and Confucians have stereotypically different responses to the forces of nature, society, and human life that threaten the more or less balanced ecologies, economies, and social and psychological organizations needed for human habitations. The Daoists identify with the forces that bend and duck, the tree that blows flat in the wind rather than the sturdy oak that is cracked in half, the water that flows down and around rather than the attempts to contain it. The Daoists see nature as fearsome and seek elixirs to transcend it, spiritual practices to leave or transform the body, hermitages that avoid the big battles. The Confucians attempt to build resources to protect the parameters of human habitation, dikes to control flooding, granaries to tide over years of bad crops, armies to oppose the barbarians, social structures built upon rituals to sustain stability and flexibility through change. The Confucians especially see the education of sage-like qualities to be able to identify what the underlying patterns of coherence and incoherence are, to shore up the desirable coherences, to build new structures of coherence that unite things otherwise at odds, and to seek out the coherent structures that themselves contribute to making other desirable coherences impossible, for instance flourishing cancers. Daoists and Confucians agree that the human condition is fragile in the extreme, with the coherent conditions for human life under constant threat and with a constant need for people to do something about that.

I need to introduce another aspect of the cultural concept of Heaven here. Just as Heaven is that which makes determinate things coherent with their patterns of changes, Heaven makes the heart of human nature to be an aesthetic capacity to appreciate the coherence of things and to respond in an aesthetically appropriate way. The ancient classic, *The Doctrine of the Mean* (Zhongyong), begins "What Heaven (*T'ien*, Nature) imparts to man is called human nature. To follow our nature is called the Way (Tao). Cultivating the Way is called education."[1] The Confucian conception of the self is radically different from all the models in the West. A person is a continuum of elements reaching from the center of human nature to the world, "the ten thousand things." Among the elements are the person's body and physical environment in its various interactions, such as metabolism and growth through time; social elements such as elementary rituals including language; institutions such as families, neighborhoods, economic relations, and the like; and the personal educational processes. Without any of the mediating elements that differentiate people, human nature is the same in each person, the capacity to appreciate and respond aesthetically according to what coheres but with nothing to appreciate or respond to. The world of the ten thousand things is public and available to anyone, but only according to the individuating ways of their different bodies and physical environments, their different semiotically defined social elements, and their different developments in education.

The goal of a sage is to be able to see the things of the world without distortion, to grasp their coherence or value, and to be able to respond appropriately all the way through. Under ordinary circumstance, however, people's bodies need development and their physical environments need to be arranged so that they can perceive accurately, grasp the realities of their semiotic and social environments, and perfect their skills at acting effectively. Most of the time they are deceived by selfish physical and social structures and are incompetent actors. Education is super important for Confucians so that the continuum between the things in the world and each person's Heaven-bestowed nature is transparent, which the Chinese call "sincerity" (*cheng*). When the continuum of human embeddedness in the world is sincere or transparent, people can appreciate the true coherences or goods of things and respond effectively and appropriately to the things according to their worths. Confucians differ significantly in their interpretations of what causes the blockages in personal engagement of the world and what to do about it in matters of education. But they conceive the world to be filled with things of value, in constant change, that people usually misperceive and with respect to which they respond with biased and incompetent ways. Human virtue is to follow the Dao by becoming educated to perceive and respond to things more appropriately, especially noting what is and is not coherent and knowing what to do about that.

To summarize this already overly summary account of indeterminacy in natural process and what human beings can do about it, the Chinese philosophical tradition (and the cultures it has influenced over two millennia) sees nature as constant changes consisting in movements of yang and yin, all modulations of *qi*. These changes clump into larger patterns of coherence that make up the things in the world to which we relate, always under conditions of change. The world of *qi* is a vast maelstrom of changes, some of which cohere with *li*, some of which do not. *Qi* does not take on coherent pattern easily and it loses it all too easily. The human place in the world is to struggle with the forces of change that threaten the human habitat. But human beings have an inbuilt aesthetic capacity to recognize coherence where it exists and incoherence where it does not exist and might be valuable for life. Human beings also have an inbuilt aesthetic capacity to make appropriate responses to the values of things in the world, although that capacity has to be developed through education.

Determinateness in the world, to return to the Western question, thus consists in the patterns that happen to hold sway in the maelstrom of changes. Some of these are well reinforced by the patterns of change around them and others are undermined by both internal and environing changes. Much of nature is indeterminate, in the Chinese view, save for the expected coming of change. The opportunities for human intervention to determine things for the better are ubiquitous, although human powers for intervention might not be strong enough to make a difference for human life. The Daoists tend to look to small, immediate opportunities for spontaneous intervention whereas the Confucians tend to look to opportunities to build human institutions that might have the capacities to contain the forces of nature and transform them into high civilization. The Daoists want to "go with the flow" but be ready to duck when the flow will kill you. The Confucians want to reinforce those patterns that make for a flexible and stable human habitat, being constantly vigilant, thinking about deep structures of coherence and incoherence, looking ahead, and reconciled with a tragic sense that sometimes nothing can be done to protect or advance what is humanly good. With this sensibility, Chinese philosophers have had little occasion to imagine that the course of things is determined completely or partially by the unfolding of actuality or by rigid laws of nature.

Chinese Ontology

Ontological indeterminacy is the view that the determinate world, perhaps including some indeterminacy within it, is grounded in something that is not determinate. On the Western side, this might be a Neo-Platonic One, or a Thomistic Act of To Be, or a Cartesian creator-God who creates positive, new things. On the Chinese side, the dominant tradition has been to ignore the question of how or why there is anything at all, the ontological question. The interest in Chinese traditions, Daoist, Confucian, and Buddhist, has been mainly on what to do in our contexts of change. Nevertheless, a tradition has existed in China since the *Daodejing* that does hold to the claim that the world of process arises from something indeterminate. I shall explore this tradition shortly.

First, however, let me observe that a special reason exists for interest in the ontological question in the West. Most Western symbols for the ground of being develop from conceptions of persons as agents. To the extent people can know the intentions of the gods, or of God, they can know a lot about what to expect in the world and what is valuable. To be sure, many levels of transcendence in conceptions of God exist. In the more anthropomorphic ones, God can be conceived as an agent acting in history on the side of his or her favorite, as in the preference of Yahweh for the Israelites over the Canaanites or the preference of Zeus for the Greeks over the Trojans. More transcendent images of God as creator might attribute benevolence or rationality to God, so that the created world would be expected to be fundamentally good or rational. The goodness of God as a person gives rise to puzzles about theodicy, and the rationality of God has been seen as the ground of the scientific faith in the ultimate knowability of nature. To be sure,

Neo-Platonic, Thomistic, and Cartesian conceptions of God, strictly speaking, do not allow for rational complexity or ordered intention within a divine mind; none of those allows for divine potentiality that might create something for a reason. But theologians and other religious people have associated those highly transcendent conceptions of God as beyond any determinateness with biblical images of God as a good, just creator whose mind can be known through the divine Word. Thomas Aquinas had an elaborate theory of analogy that allowed him to make those associations. He claimed that goodness and rationality are positive virtues, and their opposites are corrupted with non-being. The infinite act in God must be infinite in goodness, rationality, and any of the other positive virtues such as love, even though within the divine nature they were not determinately different from one another. If the world is created by a good and rational creator, it would be good to know that. If the world is created by a biased and irrational creator, it would be even better to know that. Hence, Western thought has had a strong motivation to be interested in the agency, mind, and intent of the ground of the world's being.

Chinese thought has very little if any commitment to understanding the ground of being on the analogy of a person. Rather, the Chinese metaphors for the ground of being are like spontaneous emergence—a spring of water bursting from the ground or buds opening as winter turns to spring. I will analyze cases shortly. South Asian metaphors for the ground of being, like the West Asian ones, begin with the notion of the person. But whereas the West emphasizes the person as an intentional agent with determinate ideas and plans, South Asia thinks those are precisely the traits of persons that cause trouble—attachment, clinging, desires to possess the fruits of actions rather than only the actions themselves, as the Bhagavad Gita says. South Asian metaphors press personhood to mere consciousness, purifying the mind of reasoning and intentions, as in the emptiness of the Buddha-mind or Nirguna Brahman. The intent in South Asian religions is to identify with the indeterminate purity of the ground or with its indeterminate emptiness.

The thesis that indeterminacy gives rise to the determinate world has not been the dominant tradition in Chinese thought, which has mainly ignored the "ontological question." I will give attention to three cases, however, in which that thesis has been expressed, from the *Daodejing*, from Wang Bi, and from Zhou Dunyi.

The *Daodejing* begins by distinguishing the Dao that can be named from the Dao that cannot. A straightforward reading of this is that the Dao that can be named or told of is the Dao of natural process with temporal change (including human beings and their social institutions). It is the "mother of all things" in the sense that current happenings flow from the antecedent movements of the Dao. This Dao is nameable in the sense that it has determinate features that can be described, as most of the rest of the *Daodejing* proceeds to do. By contrast, the eternal Dao is itself the origin of the nameable Dao and it itself is indeterminate in the sense that it cannot be named. Anything that can be named, because determinate in some sense, requires being originated by the eternal Dao.

The eternal Dao can be indicated (named?—surely an irony exists here) only by its function as the origin of the Dao of process. On the one hand, the eternal Dao is non-being in the sense that it has no character of its own save that it originates the process Dao. On the other hand, the eternal Dao is being in the sense that it is the origin of the determinate Dao of process. The Dao of process is not separate from the eternal Dao but is simply the terminus of the originating act. If the eternal Dao did not produce anything, it would be nothing, non-being. But after they are produced, the originating and terminating Daos can be distinguished, despite the fact that the two are the same. Another way to put this is that an eternal ontological fecundity exists that grounds any movement of processive or cosmological antecedent fecundity. The eternal Dao is an ontological ground of the cosmological Dao at every moment but is not antecedent to any moment. The being of the Dao includes its ontological arising from non-being. The eternal ontological indeterminate Dao is not a separate being or agent transcendent of the cosmological Dao but rather is the ontological dependence of the cosmological Dao on its indeterminate, nameless origin.

Cases

This passage can be read in many ways, of course, and it can be assimilated to the dominant Chinese tradition that says everything is temporal and that nothing is eternal. But Wing-tsit Chan's translation, quoted in chapter two, is moderate and middle of the road. It is a plausible interpretive translation at the very least.[2]

Wang Bi (226–249 CE) was a contemporary of Plotinus, living only twenty-three years in the middle of the Western philosopher's life. He was the brilliant originator of some of the most important ideas of later Confucianism and Neo-Confucianism but is most famous for his commentaries on the *Daodejing* and *Yijing*. It would seem that Wang Bi claims there is or was a time before a first temporal creation, and his work can be read this way. But for him, the cosmological Dao that is the mother of all things is subsequent to their origin in some sense of subsequent, "develops them, nourishes them, and places them in peace and order." This is to say, the temporal ordering and mutual relating of determinate things is caused by the cosmological Dao subsequent, in some sense, to their origin. This is compatible with the interpretation I gave of the *Daodejing*.

Wang Bi reinforces my interpretation when he writes, "All beings in the world come from being, and the origin of being is based on non-being. In order to have being in total, it is necessary to return to non-being."[3] This is Wang Bi's commentary on chapter forty of the *Daodejing*: "Reversion is the action of Tao. Weakness is the function of Tao. All things in the world come from being. And being comes from non-being."[4] It is possible to interpret this to mean that first in time there was non-being and then being with its myriad things arises. This would contrast with my interpretation that the eternal Dao is not in time, not before determinate things and their changes but eternally related to it, their eternal depth dimension. But my interpretation is straightforward and has been an undercurrent tradition in Chinese thought.

Zhou Dunyi (1017–1073 CE) addresses this ambiguity directly. Zhou was one of the most important founders of Neo-Confucianism and brought the influence of Daoist and Buddhist metaphysics into that movement. Without the alternation of yang and yin, there is no temporal succession, no time. The originating of yang and yin from the Great Ultimate is not temporal; it is their ground in every one of their temporal manifestations. In the sequence of ontological progressions Zhou traces, there is not a temporal sequence but rather an ontological sequence present in all times or changes. Real temporal flow requires everything up through the Five Agents.

Controversy has surrounded the Chinese word translated by Wing-tsit Chan "and also" in the first line of the *Explanation of the Diagram of the Great Ultimate*. It can also mean "in turn" and "and then." If it is the last, it suggests that the Ultimate of Non-being and the Great Ultimate are two things. This would give a transcendent existence to the Ultimate of Non-being. I suspect that the Ultimate of Non-being and the Great Ultimate are two ways of looking at the same thing, as in the *Daodejing*, but with an ontological order. The whole sequence of things Zhou mentioned builds up to a statement about the materially changing world, with each step a complication of what came before. Without anything having form, there would be nothing, the Ultimate of Non-being. But once the progression to complex, changing things begins, the Ultimate of Non-being is seen as the Great Ultimate from which yang and yin arise. The ontological creative act is regarded as the Great Ultimate insofar as it is fecund with the cosmological Dao. Considered as if nothing came from it, the Great Ultimate is the Ultimate of Non-being. Underlying the entire cosmological Dao of changes is this ontological structure of completely indeterminate Ultimate of Non-being giving rise in its very act to the Great Ultimate from which yang and yin arise, finally giving rise to the complicated determinate structures of the temporal Five Agents.

The claim in this line of Chinese thought is that what explains is simpler than what it explains. The complex or ordered is what needs explanation. The only thing that does not need explanation is that which has no nature to be explained, that is, the Ultimate of Non-being. This bespeaks an astonishing (to Western-cultured people) appreciation of creativity in the sense of making novel things. To be sure, there is a recognition of spontaneity in the present in which something is added to the past to get the next phase of actualization, a horizontal kind of creativity as it were, as I explained concerning cosmological indeterminacy. More profoundly, however, is the appreciation of the fact that the material-rushing complexity of the present movements of things rests on existential spurts of creativity through which the world emerges from nothing, vertically, as it were. *What* things are is determined by the Mothering of the cosmological Dao. However, *that* they are is built on the ontological productivity of the indeterminate, layer by layer, down to the aboriginal ontological creative act.

An epistemological side of this point about the simple giving rise to the complex, the indeterminate to the determinate, has to do with intelligibility. What is ultimately intelligible? A set of first principles in terms of which things can be understood? Or the existential acts by which complex things come to be? I think the latter is surely the case for the Chinese ontological tradition I have described and that it is true. In the long run, in the depths, to understand something is to have a kind of aesthetic perception of it being made. Because most things are temporal, intrinsically temporal, time itself is being made in the things whose existence we come to perceive with understanding. The Chinese are right, I think, to say there is something "subtle and mysterious" about the being of things in the Dao and that the grasp of this is more intellectually satisfying than seeing how the principles of things can be used to describe their order.

The language of indeterminacy and determinateness arises out of the history of Western thinking. I hope to have shown here that similar issues are native to the history of Chinese thinking, and I have expressed the issues in the thematic ways of Chinese thought. The places for indeterminate openings for human intervention and for nature's own spontaneity are thematically dominant in China. Here is the place for cosmological indeterminacy. The recognition of ontological indeterminacy and its spontaneous creativity is a subtheme in Chinese thought, but surely present.

In our present situation, we should not think as Western philosophers or Chinese philosophers but as global philosophers. The erudition for global philosophy needs to include comparative philosophy. The stance of global philosophy, however, is to be erudite in all the philosophical traditions so as to craft our ideas with wisdom and perceptions from all. Just as Western philosophers have learned to think with Greek, Roman, medieval, French, German, Iberian, and English ideas, so Chinese philosophers have learned to think with Daoist, Confucian, Buddhist, and Neo-Confucian ideas. We need to think with ideas from all of them, and from South Asian philosophies too.

Chapter 7

Wisdom

Like a Shortstop

Like a shortstop,
Catching a grounder and throwing to first:
One motion, catching and throwing.
Receiving and responding.
No receiving without responding.
Empty self to purify vision and
Full self to engage the throw.
A wise one is like this.

Philosophy and Wisdom

As Peter Jonkers says in "Philosophy and Wisdom," wisdom is greatly prized in all cultures of the world.[1] Chinese culture is no exception to this. As in all traditions, wisdom means a variety of things, usually brought into relation by close family resemblances. The Chinese tradition is no different from the Western in this respect. But where the Western tradition has been in a discussion among many of its points about wisdom, this discussion has not until very recently considered the Chinese perspectives. Therefore, I shall introduce the Chinese tradition as a whole, taking certain points as peculiar to it and then at the end introducing some comparisons.

Let me begin with a quotation from Mengzi (Mencius):

When I say that all men have the mind which cannot bear to see the suffering of others, my meaning may be illustrated thus: Now when men suddenly see a child about to fall into a well, they all have a feeling of alarm and distress, not to gain friendship with the child's parents, not to seek the praise of their neighbors and friends, not because they dislike the reputation [of lack of humanity if they did not rescue the child]. From such a case, we see that a man without the feeling of commiseration is not a man, a man without the feeling of shame and dislike is not a man; a man without the feeling of deference and compliance is not a man; and a man without the feeling of right and wrong is not a man. The feeling of commiseration is the beginning of humanity; the feeling of shame and dislike is the beginning of righteousness; the feeling of deference and compliance is the beginning of propriety; and the feeling of right and wrong is the beginning of wisdom. Men have these Four Beginnings, but saying that they cannot develop them is to destroy themselves. When they say that their ruler cannot develop them, they are destroying their ruler. If anyone with these Four Beginnings in him knows how to give them the fullest extension and development, the result will be like fire beginning to burn or a spring beginning to shoot forth. When they are fully developed, they will be sufficient to protect all people within the four seas (the world). If they are not developed they will not be sufficient even to serve one's parents.[2]

Wisdom (*zhi*) is presented here with three other cardinal virtues: humanity (*ren*), righteousness (*yi*), and propriety (*li*).

Wisdom is also presented as the result of a process. Wisdom and the other virtues derive somehow from the feeling of right and wrong, humanity from the feeling of commiseration, righteousness from the feeling of shame and dislike, and ritual propriety from the feeling of deference and compliance. Notice that these beginnings are all feelings. Their start is not from knowledge. Moreover, the knowledge in the fourth, wisdom, is practical reason, not knowledge in any abstract sense.

The feelings are all innate in some sense. Seeing a child playing on the lip of a well, the people all feel alarm and distress, at least for a moment. It is as if they all skip a heartbeat, have a premature ventricular contraction. Of course, they do not all rush to save the child. They might in fact stop their response because of unfriendliness to the parents, because no neighbors are around to witness their actions, or because they like the "bad reputation" they might achieve. They might even enjoy the bad taste the well will have for several months! But they all will have the momentary feeling of alarm and distress. Mengzi believes, and the whole Chinese culture agrees, that this feeling of alarm and distress contains the seeds of commiseration, shame and dislike, deference and compliance, and right and wrong.

Although the relations among these four are extremely complex, and will be fought over throughout China's history, somehow they come together. They show up in flashes of responsiveness in everyone. No matter how quickly they are suppressed, distorted, or never developed beyond their primitive stages, they are present in all people: commiseration, shame and dislike, deference and compliance, and right and wrong. Wisdom is the development of feelings of right and wrong.

The Shortstop, Mengzi, and Xunzi

Mengzi believed that the development of wisdom from feelings of right and wrong is natural unless something interferes. To understand this, a genuinely fundamental conception to Chinese philosophy needs to be developed first. This stands in some opposition to most Western notions. The *Zhong Yong*, a text a little earlier than Mengzi probably, says that Heaven bestows the original of human nature. This means that each person has part of human nature in his heart/mind. But human nature is the same for all people, and the inner heart/mind must be the same also. Part of human nature, the most interesting part in many respects, comes from the person's relations with the world. The Chinese term for world is the "ten thousand things," and literally everything in the world is in the ten thousand things.

This part of human nature is the *relations* with the ten thousand things. These relations include both each of the things to which the person is related and the innermost heart/mind. We are all alike in our innermost heart/mind, but we differ greatly in the ways we relate to things. Perhaps most obviously we differ in our initial positions: you are there and I am here. Or rather, each of us is in a different place relative to one another. Also each of us was born at a different time and place.

Each of us relates to things differently. For instance, there might be a distant thing that we relate to differently according to our knowledge, differently again according to our emotions, differently again according to our relations of relations of relations. Each of us has a densely packed world with thousands of different relations among the things in it. We differ by our worlds.

Nevertheless, included in our world are all sorts of public, shared things. We all learn a language, and gestures, and ways of moving from a family. We all live in common societies and have common histories. We all learn differences that we express in common ways. Because these common elements are parts of the relations we have with things, we are intrinsically public beings. We have built in to our very selves many things we share with others, especially rituals. We do not have an inner self that is private that we express publicly. Rather we are common down to our core relatedness. This is immensely important for Chinese ethics.

Furthermore, the Chinese believe that things are processes of unfolding harmonies or, in fact, of unfolding disharmonies. The things to which we relate are always changing, interacting, and moving. So we react to things as changes, not as steady persevering things. Of course, some things change so slowly that we relate to them practically as substances. But not for long. Even our mountains change, however slowly.

Now what is the inner core that we receive from Heaven, or have built into us from the very beginning? It is a peculiar kind of change. It begins with receiving input from the ten thousand things. It registers that input and responds in ways that are supposed to be appropriate to the ten thousand things. This is the heart/mind: to register and respond appropriately. Perhaps a figure from contemporary baseball will make the point. A shortstop fields a ground ball and throws to first base: a Westerner would see that as two moves, catching first and then throwing; a Chinese person would see it as one, catching-throwing. Or it is like the afferent-efferent response of the nervous system. A Westerner would see those as two different things, with one set of nerves bringing in the information and another sending out a response. A Chinese person would see that as one change. Now, it is obvious from these examples that both can be faulted. The shortstop has to judge the trajectory of the ball from the hitter to their glove, calculating the wind, perhaps the bounces on the grass, and so forth. A five-year-old would have a great deal of difficulty, perhaps not even moving in the right direction to make the catch; a ten-year-old makes the moves but is likely to miss the catch; a twenty-year-old would be much better, and a trained player would be quite good; a real star would make unexpected catches. In neurology, the pathways of response include integrating the sight of the ball, its sound, and the complex senses of the shortstop's body moving, and all might be inadequate to make the catch. All these are Western ways of making the catch. But a Chinese baseball player would have to make the catch, somehow, and throw it to first base, somehow. The five-year-old would probably have to stop and think about where to throw it if they did make the catch; the ten-year-old would stand up straight and throw it, perhaps missing first base; the twenty-year-old would catch their balance and throw it rather accurately; the trained shortstop would be far more accurate; and the star would leap into the air, make the catch, and get off the throw to first before their feet returned to Earth. In neurological terms, the afferent and efferent nerves would have the job of integrating better and better.

The existence of the shortstop is paradigmatic in integrating the catch and throw, in the player's afferent and efferent nerves coming together. Their heart/mind is in the integration. Of course, the player thinks about the ball, the first baseman, and the rest, but their heart/mind is in getting the ball caught and the runner thrown out. No matter how small the interval is between the catch and the throw, no matter how infinitesimal, the heart/mind is there. To locate the heart/mind as it comes from Heaven would be to find something that would be indistinguishable from the heart/mind of the first baseman and the runner, although they have very different jobs to do. But the heart/mind of the shortstop is never by itself. It is always making the catch and throw. Although the baseball game involves the three players, each is in a different space doing different things. They all have afferent nerves to detect what is going on and efferent nerves to contribute their parts, but those nerves are different. They are three individual players relating to one another in a common game with different parts to play. Each is individual but also is related to the others and to the whole baseball field at once. And, of course, the continuity of the shortstop comes from not just this play but all the plays leading up to it and all the reflexes exhibited throughout, indeed from all the activities of receiving and responding since birth. We are amazingly intricate and multifaceted creatures!

Where does the value in the actions to be perceived and responded to come from? Some Western thinkers believe it comes from the heart/mind itself, or at least from some close inner workings of the heart/

mind. Therefore, one should begin with the roots of the Four Beginnings and carefully exfoliate them to their flowers of humanity, righteousness, propriety, and wisdom. Sometimes Mengzi has been read this way. But I believe that it comes more from the structures of the ten thousand things. By age ten, the shortstop probably understands the importance of throwing out the runner. A non-selfish and well-poised observer of the child at the well naturally springs to his rescue, accurately grasping what is at stake. But an economics minister deciding on a tax rate needs to have studied a lot of economics and understand the situation before making a decision; most people would not even know what things are important to consider in economics. An economist would have to be well-trained in economics and experienced in the situation to be able to choose well; if all those conditions were met and there were no misunderstandings, then the heart/mind of the economist could instantly make that decision. But rarely are those conditions known well, and decisions are just well-educated guesses. Especially, it is important to keep one's knowledge, feelings, and practices free from selfishness in all forms in order to be "spontaneous" in decisions. This is the case in all matters, and it means constant attention to one's own media of reception and reactions. But knowledge of what to do comes from understanding, or misunderstanding, the situation.

Mengzi believed that the flow of moral progress moves from the innermost heart/mind toward the full-fledged virtues of humanity, righteousness, propriety, and wisdom. For this reason he thought of human beings as fundamentally happy. Always, despite the corruptions of selfishness, there is an impulse that is good and appropriate. Society can intervene at any point to teach misperceptions and distortions in actions. Selfishness is easy to acquire and societies need to be especially watchful in preventing them. In fact, they usually do not prevent them. They always fight against the learned, selfish impulses at the heart of a person.

Xunzi, however, believed that the heart/mind and the ten thousand things need to be supplemented by Humanity to get things right. Heaven and Earth, together constituting nature in his mind, provide all the natural resources but do not make up the right connections. Babies face the ten thousand things and have the beginnings of a good heart/mind, namely physical, emotional, and cognitive capacities. They do not have the teachings of their parents, however, to do the right thing, to attach emotions to the right things, and to know the right things. They need to learn these connections from parents first, and then slowly from the rest of society. Babies behave with straightforward selfishness, looking to their own immediate, and sometimes very false, pleasures; they are "evil" when judged by the norms of sages. And so they need to grow up under the tutelage of parents and others, especially with regard to learning the right rituals. Far more than Mengzi, Xunzi emphasized the important of learning the right rituals to connect individuals with others. Xunzi pointed out that there never are human beings without having human ancestors, no matter how primitive one's origins.

If one follows Mengzi, then people would naturally grow to have the full-fledged virtues, if only we keep the corrupting influences of society away. If one follows Xunzi, then society is not only capable of corruption but also far more important to learning the virtues in the first place. People are evil without society to teach them the good connections that obviously must be known in order to rule the economy, to play baseball well, and even to see what is going on when a child is on the lip of a well. It is easy to see why Xunzi would pay far more attention that Mengzi to the building up of a functional society, measuring its good and bad elements. Suddenly, the public, shared aspects of an individual's life are of far greater importance on Xunzi's theory because they are objectifiable in ethics.

The Unity of the Virtues

Whether one sides with Mengzi or Xunzi on the Four Beginnings, neither one makes the relations between them of great importance. Mengzi lays them out in sequence: commiseration/humanity, shame and dislike/righteousness, deference and compliance/propriety, feelings of right and wrong/wisdom. Are these all equal in importance? They obviously sum up other virtues in various ways and are extremely complicated beyond these discussions. But are they coequal?

Zhu Xi, one of the most important of the medieval Neo-Confucians (1130–1200), chose four among the many writings of the ancients to be the four books on which examinations would be based. These were the *Analects of Confucius*, Mengzi's writings, *The Great Learning*, and the *Doctrine of the Mean*. He left out Xunzi. Zhu Xi greatly favored the ordering of the virtues so that humanity was the strongest and the others were expressions or explications of humanity. Because we now possess the *Mengzi* in Zhu Xi's edition, with his commentary that gives priority to humanity, most scholars read Mengzi as holding to that priority despite the text's neutrality.

Zhu Xi had benefited from over a thousand years of deliberation about humanity, or *ren*. He even wrote a cosmological treatise on *ren* in which he says:

> The moral qualities of the mind of Heaven and Earth are four: origination, flourish, advantages, and firmness. And the principle of origination unites and controls them all. In their operation they constitute the course of the four seasons, and the vital force of spring permeates them all. Therefore in the mind of man there are also four moral qualities—namely, *jen* [*ren*], righteousness, propriety, and wisdom—and *jen* embraces them all. In their emanation and function, they constitute the feeling of love, respect, being right, and discrimination between wrote and wrong—and the feeling of commiseration pervades them all.[3]

This is an evolutionary account of happenings and an evolutionary interpretation of the operations of the virtues.

The West has a strong tradition of giving love the most important place among the virtues. Therefore, Westerners would agree with Zhu Xi. Nevertheless, there are important reasons within China for keeping the door open for the equality of these virtues. After all, they come from different sources. Humanity comes from commiseration, righteousness from shame and dislike, propriety from deference and compliance, and wisdom from feelings of right and wrong. These are by no means the same. Commiseration means identifying with the other person, taking up at least some of their positions, and feeling things the ways they do. Shame and dislike here mean something self-reflexive, referring to one's own posture. Westerners are unlikely to have strong feelings of deference and compliance; indeed they are taught that deference is something that the other needs to earn and that compliance is in some kind of competition with self-assertion. But the Chinese would say that they are immediate feelings that come from feeling oneself as part of a group and acknowledging the group's importance. For the Chinese, these feelings are more natural and immediate, perhaps needing human structuring, than feelings of self-assertion that arise only when the Four Beginnings are more advanced. At any rate, the feelings of right and wrong are *about* something. They require at least elementary knowledge and should involve more secure knowledge. Whereas Westerners are more or less wise just on their own, Chinese believe wisdom is knowledge *about* something, knowledge of the value of a baby's life when crawling to the edge of a well, knowledge of what to do in baseball, knowledge of how the economy should be run. These four separate origins suggest the separation of the virtues.

Zhu Zi suggested an evolution of the virtues. Commiseration/*ren* or human heartedness is the first feeling, and upon its relative success the other virtues come. One would have no shame if one had not first regarded the other from the other's standpoint. One would not have a deferential relation with the others if the relation were not first established. One would not be able to describe this deferential relation and see what is right or wrong unless one were already aware of deference and compliance. But the order could also run in opposite ways. A strong sense of shame might awaken one to the need to engage the other on the other's terms. A strong sense of wisdom might stimulate one to greater deference and compliance, even to the point of identifying with them. And so forth.

In practice, the Chinese, especially the Confucian, ideal is the sage, the one who knows what to do. The Daoist is suspicious of too much ordering, of regulations, knowledge, social relations, and the like. Daoism does not reject the Confucian ways so much as worry about them too much. But the Confucian sage does worry that the richness of human life will be distorted or broken by inadequate love, righteousness, propriety, and wisdom. There are very few sages in the world, and of those most of them stand out in only one or another of the virtues.

Wisdom among the Others

Wisdom is the only one of the four primary virtues to consist in knowledge. In the long run, for the Confucians all knowledge is practical knowledge. It determines, or at least illuminates, how we behave toward the issue. Of course, all sorts of knowledge contribute to the long-standing practice. A five-year-old has a lot to think about concerning baseball and showing off for parents and friends; they are likely to be mainly wrong about baseball but rather shrewd about what their parents and friends like. A ten-year-old is probably pretty sharp about the exact rules of baseball and also about how their play affects parents and friends, and deeper in both of those relations than the five-year-old. A twenty-year-old knows most of the rules of baseball, especially if they are a trained player, and has a much wider and more sophisticated knowledge of how their play is regarded. A true star might approach sagacity in wisdom about the game but is not going to be a likely star in respect to knowledge of the game. In all these stages, the player's "knowledge" is likely to be somewhat wrong or selfishly distorted. Only a highly trained player, or someone deeply devoted to family and friends, would have much true knowledge approaching wisdom.

A person seeing a child about to tip into a well is likely to act to save the child, although many people would inhibit their reactions because of other considerations. Knowledge is not to be much of an issue unless the person is trained, perhaps as a medic or a police officer. On the other hand, perhaps the person is wise in lots of things and immediately flashes those things before their mind in doing something about the child. Perhaps the person knows to call to a closer person, or to let the child fall while the person gathers some equipment to rescue the child. The speed with which something must be done, or left undone, suggests that wisdom is not likely to be a much help.

The economist, however, needs a lot of speculative and practical knowledge even to see that there is a problem for which their reaction is important. The economist needs to know the situation that gives them the authority to act and to understand how others in the bureaucracy must cooperate for the decision about the tax rate to be effective. This includes knowing where the opposition is and understanding what to do to oppose it. More than any other example, the economist needs to understand and appreciate economic theory to make accurate predictions, assessing how accurate that knowledge is. This includes grasping the large-scale economic situation, its relation to other factors, and its contested long-term history. A sage in the position to make wise decisions about the tax rate needs to know a great deal indeed, most of it rather far from personal experience. Even with such enormously diverse and relevant knowledge, a sage might be mistaken, unaware of some relation of theory to practice, ignorant of some important factor, or partly oblivious to some element of their role. Perhaps economics is just not a field where much sagacity can be inspired.

Confucians tend to distinguish sage-wannabees from experts-in-training. Experts know clearly what their goals are. Well-trained, experts know when their knowledge is appropriate and is a good judge of competence. Experts are not wise but smart, or in training to become smarter. A realm of expertise has a fairly set range of relevant elements, and experts receive training here, sometimes even exceeding training with fairly radical learning. Sages, by contrast, generally set their expertise within a larger framework and appreciate factors that lie outside the expert range. The wiser the economist, the more likely they are to switch to some other portfolio, for example statecraft or the arts. Of course, given the complexities of contemporary society, economists rather than diplomats need to deal with the economy. There is no such thing as a generally useful person. The fine art of being a scholar-official requires depth of education in some one field. Neighboring fields are also close, nevertheless, and a person might move to another and quickly gain erudition. Other fields would be more distant. A good government would have many wise amateurs who specialize in individual fields and move from one across another. A large bureaucracy would consist of many experts dealing with special fields whose goals are set by more amateurish people who can work out the larger settings with wisdom.

Wisdom and the Wise

Earlier I said that wisdom is self-reflexive, referring back to the wise person. I quickly corrected this by an emphasis on learning the real situation, including learning expertise in an area of limited definition. The wise person aims beyond this to learn the special weights other specialties gain in the neighborhood of specialties, and then more broadly surrounding the larger whole. What kind of person is wise?

The Confucians always stress change, not static classifications. So a person committed to being or becoming a sage is always trying to become wiser. "Confucius said, 'At fifteen my mind was set on learning. At thirty my character had been formed. At forty I had no more perplexities. At fifty I knew the Mandate of Heaven. At sixty I was at ease with whatever I heard. At seventy I could follow my heart's desires without transgressing moral principles.'"[4] This very famous passage from the *Analects* has many interpretations of its stages. But it makes the point that what matters for Confucius is his growth. He himself never claimed to have reached the status of being a sage, only approaching it. But to have his mind set on learning at fifteen was already to be wise in its way; that later would be interpreted as making a commitment to becoming a sage. At thirty his character had been formed, which meant that he had participated in enough human engagements, especially those of a ritual sort, to have learned the character that is appropriate. At forty he had no more perplexities, which meant that he had resolved the large questions and merely had to apply his answers. At fifty he knew the Mandate of Heaven, which at the very least meant that he understood his place in the world. At sixty he could no longer be shocked by anything he heard but knew how to respond. At seventy his moral sensibilities were so refined that he naturally desired them.

However you think the Chinese might have weighed the four primary virtues, Humanity and Wisdom are complementary opposites for Confucius. "Confucius said, 'The man of wisdom delights in water; the man of humanity delights in mountains. The man of wisdom is active; the man of humanity is tranquil. The man of wisdom enjoys happiness; the man of humanity enjoys long life.'"[5] Probably a sage needs both of these virtues. Every person will want to be both active (with wisdom) and tranquil (with humanity), although with differing circumstances that need each. Perhaps wisdom is more important in the middle years when one is active, and tranquility is more important in later years, although circumstances can certainly change.

Nevertheless, wisdom is always required for activity, and one is always at least a little bit responsive to things of the world. This raises a question of interpretation about Confucian ethics from the Western standpoint. Westerners are quick to point out that ethics means mainly working on the soul of the ethical-wannabee. So improvement in wisdom is making oneself wiser. But this can easily be misleading. Wisdom means mainly engaging the world to find out about what to like and dislike. This is the importance of education, and it requires acting in the world to learn what the world holds, and how to appreciate it. This learning is not turning attention to oneself usually, but rather to the child at the well, the game of baseball, the economy of the state. To be sure, this engagement has its effect on the persons engaged, and this is an increase, or at least a change, in wisdom. But the difference in wisdom is made by the real relations and connections discovered or learned. This requires a lifetime of exploration of the world, by oneself sometimes but more importantly along with others. Therefore, the pursuit of wisdom is not merely a personal matter but also a group one. Playing rituals, like baseball, and more complicated matters, like wisdom in economics, require cultivating a whole array of fellow seekers after wisdom. To become a wise person without being in a wise society—a society cooperating more or less to acquire common wisdom—is very difficult.

Confucius, by reputation at least, was in a peculiar situation. He generally wandered around outside his home surroundings, talking with people. And even when he stayed at home, his recorded sayings were noted by his disciples. So it is natural that he felt a little isolated: nothing like having only students to make oneself feel wise in contrast. But for the most part, Confucians have been involved in government at higher and lower levels. Here it is important to live in a community where everyone, at whatever stage through which they are passing, is searching for wisdom. As I say, most of us are merely expecting expertise, but the challenge of wisdom around the edges is tantalizing. For those of us who are genuinely seeking wisdom, engaging the world more broadly is surely important.

What can we say about wisdom in summary in the context of Confucianism?

The first thing to say is that the whole of Confucianism, both in its theory and in its practice, needs to be taken into account. Of course, the "whole" is a silly ideal. No one, in a paper or even a three-volume work, could take into account the whole within which Confucian concepts of wisdom rest. Nevertheless, it is important to note that wisdom means something subtly different in the Chinese Confucian context than in the Western.

Second, the present context studies wisdom in Confucianism already from a comparative perspective. Few of the other approaches to wisdom do this, taking the Western perspective to be sufficient. The other papers do not ask what wisdom is in Confucianism and then seek to understand it by contrast in Western terms. They generally take wisdom to be a "natural" category in Western terms.

Third, I am a Westerner who is doing the comparative work. No matter how much I study Confucian ethics on my own, even "Confucian ethics" is a Western category. Tu Weiming, Cheng Chung-ying, Shen Kwong-loi, Li Chenyang, or a variety of other Chinese-born writers in English could have written it with more faithfulness to the Chinese side in the comparison. This is not to disparage my own contribution, only to call attention to its peculiarities.

Fourth, I have focused on wisdom in Confucianism's earliest or classical forms, with minor comparative work down the line. Most of my discussion has taken off from the story of the observer seeing the child on the lip of the well, which is only Mengzi's statement. This statement is very important in Chinese history, and nearly every other thinker has referred back to it. It has many more conflicting interpretations than I have mentioned. True, I have interpreted it from Xunzi's as well as Mengzi's point of view, and that distinction is one that echoes down through history. Xunzi and Mengzi were nearly contemporaries. I have also indicated Zhu Xi's much later emendation of the Mengzi passage, emphasizing its unity and the subordination of three of the virtues to humanity, pointing out that most of us now read Mengzi as saying this. But this is a small detail in a much larger history. If I were to have told the whole story, there would be as much variation in Chinese history as there is in Western history.

Fifth, serious comparative work from the Western perspective has been going since the mid-nineteenth century, if not from the sixteenth century with Mateo Ricci. Since the mid-twentieth century until the beginning of the twenty-first, Confucianism, including its ethics, has been generally banished in official China. Its main Confucian expositors have lived in Taiwan, North America, and elsewhere, not in China. In the twenty-first century the Chinese government has reversed itself on Confucianism and now is developing its version as China's great contribution to world culture. Meanwhile, many Western-born experts in Confucianism have taken up Western virtue-ethics as a connection point with Confucian ethics, a position that I have rejected in my exposition here.[6] All this is a background for my presentation.

Sixth, I have stressed the Chinese notion of progress or change in the conception of wisdom. To be sure, people in all cultures stress that wisdom is an ideal that we approximate. But in China this rests within a conception of what it is to be a thing, and that conception is that a thing is a harmony always in process of becoming something else. This is very different from the conception of a substance undergoing changes of features. The entire Chinese conception is different. From the Chinese perspective, Plato in the West looks to be a fellow believer in basic change, with only forms remaining the same; nevertheless, Aristotle's substance philosophy is usually read back into Plato. In China, the conception of change is much more basic. The innermost core of a person is the heart/mind, which is a change consisting in receiving and responding to given data. Wisdom is a feature of this transformation, marking both selfless reception and selfless action. Of course, there are thousands of transformations going on all at once, and only the most basic ones with identifiable language are marked as wise. Wisdom is not even a candidate in the great mass of perceptions and reactions to the world. But in those few instances in which wisdom is a candidate, it consists in action-reactions.

Seventh, the line between wisdom and humanity is one that crosses the heart/mind. If one emphasizes action, then it describes how the wise person is able to perceive accurately, with all the education that involves, and then acts clearly, with all the education that involves. If one emphasizes tranquility, then that describes how one relates to others, standing in their stead and responding to them as they deserve. This dual crossover reflects on oneself and provides a sense of righteousness, taking pleasure in the perceptions and reactions. It also takes the external form of propriety in dealing with others, receiving the hits and throwing out the runner. Wisdom is the knowledge that guides this heart/mind. Or, to the extent the heart/mind fails to perceive accurately and to act well in response, wisdom is lacking.

Wisdom, of course, is always on the way in all traditions, always generally lacking but also always an ideal. The most important point here is that wisdom in the Confucian tradition is not alone. In fact, it requires some general recognition and acceptance of the process cosmology and the heart/mind. Without the heart/mind, wisdom is not relevant.

Chapter 8

Shallow Roots

Confucians Have Shallow Roots

Confucians have shallow roots.
Confucius kept leaving home
Zhou wouldn't mow his grass
Wang generaled in the south.
Now we move all over.
Some of us never see China
Others descend from John Calvin.
Where does our heritage matter?
What matters is our shallow roots,
Quickly put down where we land,
Intertwined with roots of others,
Recalling roots we had before.

Mobility

Confucians today and for the foreseeable future can expect to move around a lot. Ours is not a period in many places on the globe when peasants and gentry stay in one place for generations and plan the same for their grandchildren and great grandchildren. The Confucian emphasis on education is likely to promote success in meritocratic societies that often entails enhanced mobility. Many societies, including China's, are moving populations from rural to urban areas, from cities to suburbs, and from one geographical condition to another. The great migrations out of the Middle East are filling many lands with relatively rootless migrants, or people whose traditional roots are elsewhere. The imminent effects of climate change also promise to increase uprootedness. If Confucianism is to flourish as a global philosophic culture, it cannot count on deep roots remaining in place.

Speaking beyond individual Confucian lives, Confucianism itself as a philosophically shaped way of life that both critiques and constructs the personal and social structures of its place has long ago gone to places other than China. Korea, Japan, Vietnam, and Taiwan might not be all that different from China, but they are still different, and Confucianism had to put down different kinds of roots in different kinds of soil in those places. Confucianism in Amsterdam, Boston, Sydney, and Mexico City has to have very different kinds of roots in different kinds of natural and social soil. Because Confucianism does have to be firmly rooted in the places where it is lived, it needs new, quick-growing, and adaptive roots. This is my thesis.

Much as we like to think of Confucianism as deep-rooted, as my friend Cheng Chung-ying argues, Confucius himself did not stay at home. For at least some of his life, Confucius taught his disciples on the road, and the China he traversed was very big with diverse places. For the last century, many of the leading China-born Confucian intellectuals have been educated and employed in the diaspora, including my friend Chung-ying, surely one of the original Boston Confucians. My friend Tu Weiming, born in Kunming, China, who legitimated the school of Boston Confucianism during his long career at Harvard, returned to Beijing to teach and has retired to Berkeley, having been educated in Taiwan and at Harvard and having taught at Berkeley and Princeton as well as Harvard. That is a lot of places to sink Confucian roots. Geography does not tell the whole story, of course. Weiming, like just about all the rest of us, is rooted in the soils of academic cultures that increase the connectivity between the world's academies. Nevertheless, even considering only academic Confucians, we know that Confucianism insists on being rooted in its local living and working situations for family and friends. Therefore, Confucians need to put down salient and nourishing roots quickly and in soils never imagined by Confucius. If the roots get too deep, moving will seem too much like loss, though it is always that, and Confucians will turn curmudgeonly when instead we need to dig in to its new places in the world.

To back up this claim, I am going to say some things about what is continuous and important to Confucianism and how this Confucian core needs to grow new, if shallow, roots, in its new places. Then I shall say something about how those roots might grow in new places.

Continuity

Frequently and with good reason, Confucianism throughout its long history has been associated with the cultivation of the personal virtues of the sage or the "exemplary person," as my friend Roger Ames translates *junzi*.[1] John Makeham's edited volume *Dao Companion to Neo-Confucian Philosophy* contains nineteen chapters, sixteen of which, by my count, are about moral character, even when several of them relate this to the metaphysics of Principle.[2] Remember that the Neo-Confucians are generally regarded as introducing metaphysics, perhaps from Buddhism and Daoism, into the Confucian traditions that earlier had been even more focused on personal virtue. Vincent Shen's edited volume *Dao Companion to Classical Confucian Philosophy* has sixteen chapters all about personal experience and morals, if you count essays on music and poetry in that camp.[3] Shen's volume has a forty-four page essay by the late Antonio Cua called "Early Confucian Virtue Ethics: The Virtues of Junzi."[4] Cua treats the virtues of humaneness (*ren*), righteousness (*yi*), and propriety (*li*) as the cardinal virtues of the *junzi*, but also treats filiality (*xiao*), magnanimity (*kuan*), trustworthiness (*xin*), courage (*yong*), wisdom (*zhi*), respectfulness (*gong*), loyalty (*zhong*), reverence (*jing*), consideration of others (*shu*), self-control (*keji*), and many others. Roger T. Ames's *Confucian Role Ethics: A Vocabulary*, also analyzes these and other ethical terms.[5] Confucianism has frequently been brought into conversation with Western virtue ethicists.[6] Surely it is the case that Confucianism requires continuity with the emphasis on the cultivation of the virtues of the exemplary person and of the sage.

Nevertheless, Roger Ames calls attention to another aspect of core Confucianism with the title of his book, *Confucian Role Ethics*. Personal cultivation is not just the virtue of a person as a self or subject. For Confucianism, Ames says, it is the cultivation of skills, capacities, and the arts of playing roles relative to other people. The Confucian exemplary person does not have humaneness, righteousness, and propriety in general but always as involved in roles, such as those of filiality, husband or wife, neighborliness in economic and social life, responsibility and subordination in political life, and roles of friend to friend. The limitation of Western virtue ethics is that it locates the venue of morality in personal character, whereas Confucian role ethics locates that venue in role-defined relations among people. Within Western virtue ethics today lurks a holdover from Kant's attempt to define morality in terms of the autonomous character of the individual subject without having to make heteronomous judgments about what is good or bad in the environment of choice and action. For Confucianism, from Master Kung to professors Ames and Cheng, the self, and hence ethics, is never independently autonomous but intrinsically relational.

I would go farther than Ames, though perhaps not from his intent, to stress that roles are themselves defined within ritual systems, often with many different kinds of roles interlocked, often with different ritual systems interplaying with one another. A person plays roles in ritual systems with a mother, in different ritual systems with a father, and in varied ritual systems with siblings. These ritual systems can be aggregated as family rituals, but they are constantly changing, improving relations with a brother while coping with alienation from a parent or in-law. A person has ritualized relations with the people in the neighborhood, with those at work, and those in the larger society. The playing of the ritual systems is what constitutes the having of a family, successful or unsuccessful economic productivity, social life with its tensions of friendships and enmity, the cultivation of arts and entertainment, the celebration of a calendar of changes, institutions of education, and the very intricacies of government at various levels. Most ritual systems depend on the more or less successful playing of other ritual systems, and the weaknesses of society come often from some ritual systems not being adequate to support other ritual systems on which they depend. To say, as I have, that contemporary Confucianism needs to be rooted in the specific places to which it has moved is to stress the importance of those rituals that are appropriate to the situation at hand, for instance, how to behave on a crowded city bus or how to bring up small children when all the adults in the family work outside the home.

Balance

Let me step back and express my appreciation of Xunzi's rebalancing of Mengzi's attempt to ground exemplary virtue in the sprouts of the heart.

Mengzi probably would like Ames's claim that what sprouts is action and emotion directed at roles. But Xunzi would say that nothing sprouts at all, except a baby's selfish cries (which are mere Heaven and Earth minus the Human), without learned habits giving specific, culturally constructed meaning to action and emotion. A baby cannot stand up and toddle without learning ritualized ways of interacting with gravity; as it turns out, East Asian babies learn to stand and toddle with their feet rather parallel, whereas Western babies point their toes outward. Learned rituals are not only among human beings but also among human beings and nature: toddler and gravity. Our economic rituals involve ritualized relations with the soil, the climate, and the waste that we dump somewhere, however much they also involve interpersonal roles in production. Rituals obtain not only in human relations with nature and with one another but also in our relations with institutions as such. Institutions are themselves ritual systems that function in various ways in societies. Confucians have long called attention to the need to minister to the institutions as well as to the people interacting in institutional ways, as exemplified in the virtuous role of the scholar-official. Rituals of care or neglect for institutions permeate life. There are family rituals, to be sure, but there are also rituals of caring for the family as such, or ritualized habits of neglecting or harming family institutions. The same is true for how individuals relate to all the institutions within which they also have specific roles. The different places of Confucian life, both as a socially and personally effective philosophy and as the practices of Confucian individuals, differ according to different contours of nature, different institutions of social life, and different kinds of people with whom ritualized life is carried out.

My most important contention here is that the cultivation of Confucian virtues such as humaneness, righteousness, and propriety takes place within, and only within, the playing of roles in the rituals that make up an individual's contextual life. A person is a process of playing in thousands of rituals at once that make up the person in relation. A person operates out of a rich matrix of roles, balancing the playing of them like a logger trying to stay atop a log shooting through rapids on a river. To be an exemplary person requires extraordinary poise, to be humane, righteous, and properly deferential to people, institutions, and nature at all the levels operating at once. The rituals so often demand competitive or contradictory responses; to play them skillfully requires discerning what comes first, distinguishing root rituals from branch rituals in the particularities of the situation. To be a person is always to be in action amidst changes. Rituals themselves, considered as social constructs in part but also as structures for physical interactions with nature and others in society, are like vaguely defined dance steps. They need to be individuated. Maturation means, among other things, the individuating of the important ritual roles of one's life. More, it means cultivation of the arts of knowing how to individuate each of the ritual plays in the matrix of rituals defining one's contexts. I am amused that Roger Ames and our late friend David Hall make this very important Confucian point by translating it into Latin, *ars contextualis*.[7] Confucian virtue, with which contemporary mobile Confucianism must be in continuity, is cultivated *ars contextualis* where the context is a vast and shifting set of ritual systems particular to each place in which Confucianism might be lived.

One more point about Confucian continuity needs to be made here. Ritual role playing, even exemplary role playing, can become almost unconscious or habitual when everything is going right. But hardly ever does everything go right for very long. Rituals get misplaced for the situation, the players don't play well, or the rituals habituate evil and destructive social patterns as in the oppression of women and sexual minorities. Therefore, Confucian virtue requires constant discernment and attention to just what rituals are in play and how they are working. The Neo-Confucian theme of Principle (*li*) is about discerning what things cohere and what things do not in the ongoing processes of personal and social life. When are social or personal ritual habits destructive, or in jeopardy? What background rituals or specific actions might be deployed to make things better, or stave off disaster? The Confucian exemplary person, especially the sage, has the specially cultivated virtues of discernment and habits of attention and analysis. This involves mastering the institutionalized educational disciplines of social analysis and also aesthetic discrimination. Because high civilization and sagely personal life depend on rituals working, and working well together, and because conditions are always changing, the playing of rituals in an exemplary fashion involves changing and improving the rituals themselves.

Rootedness

My final remarks are about how contemporary Confucians, among whom I count myself, should think about being rooted. One sense of rootedness is the continuity of what is important in Confucianism, which I have analyzed here in terms of ritual embeddedness and the cultivation of virtues in playing the rituals well and balancing them out artfully. This continuous tradition includes cultivating attention to what the rituals are and who other people are as ritual players. It also includes critical analysis of the rituals and steady efforts to improve them. This is not the sense of rootedness connected to *place*, however. Confucians should cultivate their roots in the continuity of the core of their tradition but spend equal energy cultivating the branching of these roots into new situations.

Concerning the sense of rootedness connected to *place*, there is a grave danger that deep roots will lead to fixation on the rituals and personal skills at playing them that are embedded in the actual conditions of a lost past. Either we have moved away from that past, from China to America, Africa, Europe, or some Mid-Pacific Island, or the social and physical conditions of the same place have changed very radically. Confucians look very conservative when we hang on to ways that were virtuously embodied in some other place but are not virtuously embodied in where we are moving now.

Confucianism betrays the tradition with which it should be continuous when it resists change, keeping people in ritual roles that are oppressive in the current circumstance and hiding its eyes from what is coming down the road. The entire Confucian tradition is embedded in a metaphysics of change. The *Yijing* could never have been named The Book of Substances; it is not about things that are what they are but about things that are on the way to becoming something else. It is misleading, on Confucian terms, to think of persons as *having* virtuous characters, cultivated over time, as a virtue ethicist might think. The better Confucian frame is to think of persons as playing—actively playing and living out—a multitude of ritual roles regarding the changing natural and social settings and regarding other persons also playing ritual roles.

There is mobility in moving from place to place, and I began by calling attention to the geographic spread of Confucianism today. But even a singular place defined by geographic coordinates changes over long years. The rituals that Confucius thought embedded him and his students in their situation in Shandong province would not work to embed his successors today in that place. Today, Confucians need the ability to discern what the conditions of their situation are, inquire into and discern what rituals are appropriate for humanizing those conditions with righteousness and propriety (and all the other virtues), and then sink the roots of ritualized behavior into the soil of that place. The natural language of Confucianism in Boston is English, not Chinese. By "soil" I mean the natural, institutional, and interpersonal conditions at hand. Confucian rootedness means not only learning about those conditions but engaging them so that they become the conditions of highly civilized human life. Confucian rootedness needs to go just so deep as to resource the ongoing and shifting rituals that constitute flourishing civilized life.

I have warned about Confucian rootedness that is too deep in a place so that they cannot be pulled up and moved to a new place, new conditions. The result is a static commitment to conditions that no longer exist, with ritual structures that often are counterproductive. I want to express sympathy, however, for those who take their old ritual roots with them and use them to order life in new circumstances. The roots do not sink in to the new soil very much, and the Confucians live like resident aliens for a generation. But Confucianism aims to be rooted, embedded, particular, and moving with concrete changes to improve the future. The second generation needs to learn the new language, engage the new economic forms, and deal with the opportunities and conflicts on the ground. If Confucianism were to flourish in sub-Saharan Africa, it would need to deal with ritualized tribal conflicts only lightly covered over by universalistic religions such as Islam and Christianity. That is not the problem for Confucianism in Boston, Beijing, or Brisbane. They have other soils, with other conditions and other civilizing ritual needs.

In between roots that are too deep and roots that are only habits from some other place or time that do not sink in are the quick-growing shallow roots I advocate for contemporary Confucianism and Confucians. *Ars contextualis* means first finding out what the context is and how it differs from the contexts of our inherited ritual practices and virtuous arts of ritual playing. Bear in mind that our ritual habits of discernment and analysis themselves need to be under constant attention and modification to new conditions. Then in the new situation Confucians need to discern just how ritually to engage the natural environment, the social institutions, and the people with whom we interact. Roots should be sunk deep enough to effect that engagement so that the rich texture of civilized life can flourish as best as possible.

Let me close by acknowledging an important difference between the sensibilities of Mengzi and those of Xunzi. I think it is fair to say that for Mengzi, society should be structured to facilitate and not hinder or distort the cultivated unfolding of personal virtues. Tu Weiming, a follower of Mengzi, once said that ritual is for the external expression of the inner sagely virtues.[8] The point is for people to be virtuous. For Xunzi, the point is to have a high civilization where the arts, the economy, neighborliness, government, and other forms of excellence can flourish under specific and concrete conditions. To achieve and sustain this, the exemplary, sagely virtues need to be cultivated so that individuals can play in their matrices of rituals with individuation and artful poise. The point of Confucian roots is to embed in the soil the dynamic civilized structure within which artful individuals can flourish, not to embed virtuous behavior for its own sake. I confess to be on Xunzi's side here and acknowledge that my argument will look superficial from the perspective of the people of Mengzi. I look to them for correction. For the moment, however, I look to Xunzi for the way forward with shallow roots.

Chapter 9

Pragmatism and Confucianism

Pragmatism at its coarsest means getting what you want.
With philosophic savvy, pragmatism means getting what
   you want
With more uumph to what you want.
Peirce turned pragmatism on its head (Pragmaticism)
By claiming it is the search for what is worth wanting.
Value is what is really Ultimate.
True pragmatism finds what is most worth wanting in the
Obligation to be of service.
Wide as cosmic dust blown free,
Deep as duty one to one,
Continuous from world to world
Ten thousand steps lie in between,
You attend to all,
Moved by shifting stars,
Earnestly Earth-bound,
Sweeping the twigs in the garden.

The American pragmatic tradition that I espouse and work to extend regards human experience as interactions of persons with their environments. Pragmatism took its initial shape in the works of Charles Sanders Peirce, William James, and John Dewey. It had American antecedents in Jonathan Edwards and Ralph Waldo Emerson and close neighbors in Josiah Royce, who called himself an "absolute pragmatist"; George Santayana, a fellow naturalist; and Alfred North Whitehead, who called his epistemology "pragmatic." Since the latter part of the twentieth century pragmatism has seen a revival in several directions, usually called "neo-pragmatism," including analytic pragmatism associated with Richard Rorty, Donald Davidson, and Robert Brandom and African American ethical-theological work associated with Cornel West, Victor Anderson, and Eddie Glaude. I sometimes call myself a "paleo-pragmatist" to distinguish myself from the neo-pragmatists. Mine is a fundamentally different frame for experience than the transcendental frame common in most forms of European phenomenology, as will become clear in what follows. It can rather neatly be mapped onto many themes in Confucian approaches to experience.

Value in Interpretation

For the pragmatists, experiential interactions are interpretive in the sense that they employ signs to grasp the environmental elements in certain respects. The word "interaction" was popularized by John Dewey, who also sometimes used the word "transaction." I often use the word "engagement" to stress the explicit or implicit intentionality in interpretive interactions. The interpretations are always triadic, taking the signs to represent the objects interpreted in the respects as interpreted by the interpreter. As Peirce said, the basic form of interpretation is that the interpretation takes the object to be as represented by the sign in a certain respect, as in interpreting a barn to be red in respect of color and 1912 in respect of the date it was built.

The selection of the respect in which to interpret the environment is always a function of valuation, taking that respect to be the relevantly important one. The valuation might be significantly biological, as in the quick flight that interprets a rustling in the bush with the sign of danger: the interpretive flight precedes analysis of the sound or even consciousness of the potentially dangerous situation. Such biological valuations have evolutionary adaptive value: persons who flee first and inquire second stand a better chance of living to pass on their timorous genes than those who look first to see whether the noise was made by a tiger and don't live to pass on any genes.

Most human experience is guided also by values built into the culture and made habits of daily life, indicating what is important to notice and respond to in typical environments, shaping the quotidian day. These include interactions that are more responsive as well as those that are more active and directed. Some of these come to consciousness but most do not unless the interactions are misguided by the habitual signs. For instance, we usually do not notice the furniture when walking through a familiar room unless something is out of place and we bump it.

Much of human experience is guided by values that involve explicit purposes that are more or less conscious. Sometimes we greet friends not only out of habit but with sincere interest; sometimes we purposely seek for a strategy to act in order to deal with a difficult person or situation. Sometimes we sit down to write papers and organize our hours around intellectual inquiry. Sometimes we move vigorously in order to get exercise. Most of the time, we are making many interpretations all at once, with shifting phases of conscious attention. A short time ago on my morning walk I was reflecting with good, nostalgic feelings about being on a panel with my old friends Ed and Chung-ying (I also was thinking about Linyu but she is not old!); these reflections were interspersed with wonderings about what I should say and what they were likely to say, a kind of easy musement that shifted among the intellectual and personal elements. Then I got to the big hill and suddenly became aware of my heavy breathing and concentrated on raising my heart rate. Until then, the interpretive habits of my walking engagements of the environment were pretty much unnoticed. All through the walk I was taking appreciative stock of the beautiful neighborhood near my home, admiring the trees and many of the houses, and nodding to an occasional neighbor. Simultaneously, I was interpreting the aesthetic qualities of my neighborhood, walking for the sake of exercise, attending to my body's needs and habits, thinking about philosophical issues, reflecting on the different paths my friends and I have taken, and delighting in the memories of friendship.

Different values, and values of different sorts, guide the multiplicity of congruent interactions involved in my walk. Among the most important are those that parse the "environment" into foreground and background elements. The foreground elements are the objects of an interpretive engagement, but objects always as set within backgrounds. Each of the interpretive interactions on my walk identifies my environment differently regarding foreground and background. Moreover, the configurations of foreground and background are constantly changing. Sometimes the changes are caused by arising attractions and repulsions. Often, however, they are caused by interruptions, something that Peirce called Secondness, a kind of brute opposition that interrupts the continuous operations of habits, and that will be described below. Conscious attention is highly sensitive to interruptions.

On this pragmatic model of experience as multileveled and dynamic interpretive interactions and engagements, it is plain that value is involved in the environments as well as in the interpreters. On the side of the interpreter, value is involved in the selection of respects of interpretation. At the same time these personal valuations are good or bad insofar as they recognize what is important in the environment. The real value resides in the environment in correlation with what human beings can apprehend and respond to. A tiger rustling in the bush is really bad for the slow-to-flee interpreters and their potential progeny. An environmental disaster would make my walk through town horrific. The structure of the environment is what contains the values we more or less relevantly learn to recognize, and our experience is shaped by signs that are more or less in accordance with the "affordances" of the environment to fit our valuing habits. "Affordances" means the ways by which environments are structured that afford being interpreted with the resources and interests of an interpreter's semiotic system. The walker in the jungle interprets the whole situation of noise in the bush at once. The value in the interpreter's intentional sign-filled interpretation is matched more or less by the structure of the environment. People, of course, want to develop value-laden interpretive structures that pick up on what is important in the environment.

This pragmatic valuational experiential model is different from the dominant model of phenomenology in Continental philosophy, from which both Cheng and Casey pick their major cues. Broadly speaking, the Continental tradition follows Kant in supposing that experience is what is in consciousness and its subconscious layers and that this makes possible the project of describing consciousness. Phenomenology is description of experience for this tradition, description deep and multilayered.

My pragmatic trajectory, rather, says that experience is not especially a matter of consciousness but of interpretive interaction. Peirce argued, conclusively to my mind, that there is no such thing as intuitive consciousness but rather that what we think we see and hear in consciousness is a matter of inference. He showed that our sense of the seemingly continuous visual field fills in inferentially all the spots that don't register where the optic nerves enter the eyes and no rods and cones can pick up anything. Nothing is simply *given*, only selectively *taken* in a complex environment of multilayered interpretations with a lot of corrective interruptions or Secondness thrown in.

Because consciousness is a vagrant and often ephemeral aspect of experience, pragmatic phenomenology cannot be something controlled by ideals of description. Hegelian phenomenology described the appearances of the rational advance of consciousness through the dialectic of Spirit (*Geist*). Value or importance, for Hegel, is defined by the place in the dialectic. Husserlian phenomenology bracketed claims to say what is real and important in order to describe accurately the forms of consciousness. If things appear in consciousness as carrying one value or another, this is just a matter of their form and indicates nothing about what is really important. Later phenomenologists such as Maurice Merleau-Ponty recognized the limitation of the consciousness model and worked hard to articulate experience through the body. The point about perceptual experience through the body places these phenomenologists close to William James. But whereas James held to a metaphysical "neutral monism" according to which the neutral experience stuff can be organized either according to subjective selves or according to logical structures in the environment, with the result that the self is just as much a contingent construct as a mountain viewed from many angles, Merleau-Ponty treats the body as a medium for a self to engage objects of appreciative perception. Heidegger was aware of transcendental philosophy's hidden commitment to construing the world as a function of the self's synthesizing activities and struggled to define phenomenology as the world "coming across the open" to us (Dasein). But he never escaped the priority of Dasein as the subjective condition for experience.

My pragmatic model of valuationally ordered interpretive and interactive engagement is radically different. The self and its first-person perspective is just as much a *product* of ongoing interpretive interactions as any representation of the world engaged, not the a priori or transcendental condition for the interpretive interactions. On this pragmatic model, phenomenology, in Peirce's use of the term, is not description but rather the classification of things engaged or interacted with, including the "interactors," according to basic categories.

Peirce argued that all things encountered or supposed in any way can be classified in one or several of three categories.

For Peirce, all things have an immediate character, perhaps as experienced but always as simply being what they are. The immediacy of qualities is included here. This is Firstness. Because the Firstness of things is "in itself" or immediate, qualities or things as Firsts do not differ comparatively from one another because they cannot be compared. We can never interpret something as a First without mediating it. Secondness is the oppositional quality of things, their in-itselfness and resistance to being absorbed into others. One of Peirce's examples is the feeling of someone pushing against you on the other side of a door; interpreting this as opposition is more than Secondness, but the opposition itself is a Second. Secondness is the source of reality's correction of our bad signs and habits. Thirdness is the mediation of things so that they are brought together in some respects, related while maintaining their differences. All signs are Thirds, for Peirce. They have their own-being, Firstness, and their oppositional differences from other things, Secondness. But their Thirdness consists in their mediating functions. Only things that are Thirds can be interpreted. Indeed, only things that are Thirds can be determinately what they are and different from other determinate things in some respect. There can be no Firsts alone, or Seconds alone, or Firsts and Seconds together, although Peirce speculated that an evolutionary metaphysics might move from Firsts to Seconds to Thirds. If there is anything determinate, it is a Third that is what it is (its Firstness) over against something different (its Secondness) in some respect (its Thirdness). Experience as interpretive interaction is primarily a function of Thirdness, although the realities interpreted have their corrective Secondness and all experience has the qualitative immediacy of Firstness.

With reference to Casey the Continental phenomenologist and Cheng the Chinese philosopher, I want to say that Confucianism supposes experience to be much the way the paleo-pragmatists affirm. Human life is interactive and responsive, grasping things as having value and responding valuationally, appreciative in positive and negative senses and struggling to improve interpretive reactions. I have focused my discussion so far on Peirce because he had an explicit "phenomenology," to which I will return shortly. But James and Dewey have even more detail about experience that resonates with the Confucian tradition. Moreover, Whitehead too can be counted as a pragmatist and he leads to even more comparative connections with Confucianism. Buddhism, with its many approaches to interpreting consciousness, is much closer to Husserlian phenomenology and I am willing to give Buddhism over to the Continental phenomenologists as a friendly conversation partner. When we get to issues of ordering life, where the millennium-old debates between Buddhists and Neo-Confucians take shape, we would need to look at the approaches to morals that relate Continental and pragmatic approaches, which is another topic. For the present, let me note the similarity between pragmatism and phenomenology, except that pragmatism limits consciousness to what is only a small part of experience.

Ritual

Now, however, I want to pick up on a specific kind of interpretive interaction that is most profitably understood in terms of the Confucian tradition of ritual analysis. Although ancient beyond accounting and anticipated articulately in Confucius's *Analects*, Confucianism understands ritual in a fundamental ontological sense to supplement the material forces of nature (*qi*) and the ordering principles of Heaven (*li*). The classical slogan hails the ontological "trinity" of Heaven, Earth, and the Human. Xunzi pointed out that people have bodies with many material capacities and also emotional and intellectual capacities deriving from the source of coherence and intelligence. Moreover, we have a psychophysical governing capacity that can take control of our actions. But neither the material forces of physical properties nor the naturally given capacities for emotional response can tell us what is worth hating and loving, emulating or fleeing, fearing or trusting. The biological capacity to control our actions does not by itself, without education, tell us what to control and for what purpose. In addition to Heaven and Earth, Xunzi gave metaphysical primacy to Humanity, by which he meant the development of conventional ritualized meaning with cogent signs. These conventional interpretive rituals are habits, as the pragmatists say, and include, among many other things, learned ways of standing and moving, gesturing meaningfully, talking in the semiotic structure of some language, habits of family and personal interactions, and, more obviously, ceremonial rituals

Not all rituals are plays among people. Some of our rituals focus mainly on the natural environment exclusive of human beings and social institutions. When gravity causes us to fall, that by itself is not a ritualized interaction with nature. But as soon as an infant learns to interpret the pull of gravity and develops habits of throwing his toys high and attempting to stand, the interactions with gravity are ritualized. Most rituals are learned with some kind of imitation. Infants imitate their elders' ways of standing. When a cancer starts growing in us without being noticed, that is a non-ritualized interaction with nature. But when we interpret how we feel as sickness and go to a doctor, thus discovering the cancer, the interaction with the cancer is ritualized. Cultures differ in the ways they ritualize illness. When the tiger in the bush did not make a telltale sound and simply pounced on us for dinner, we were not ritually interacting with the tiger. But the tiger perhaps was hunting with ritualized habits; perhaps tigers in different families ritually hunt in different ways. If we were walking by the bush on the alert for tigers, and failing to escape because our rituals for jungle-walking don't pick up on wholly silent tigers, we still were ritually engaged with the tiger.

A great many of our interactions inclusive of people and social institutions are ritually shaped for better or worse. Among the most important things in our natural environment are other people and all the social institutions and organizations of our lives. The Confucian tradition has always seen human individuals and social realities as interacting parts of the environment, specifications of nature while also being of human composition. What is especially striking in the Confucian understanding of ritual is that nearly everything we do is made possible by learned, that is, ritualized behavior. Talking with friends, we are already engaging in rituals of balance against the force of gravity, rituals of greeting, rituals of language speaking, and rituals of conversational interaction, all at once. That we speak in a common language does not tell us exactly what to say, though we might also have rituals that direct the conversation to certain topics. The rituals that are explicit ceremonies, say in politics or religion, themselves are made possible only by the vast web of rituals in which the ceremonies take place. Confucians focus on being in healthy ritual interactions with other people at all levels of civilization.

In contrast to most of Western modernity and postmodernity, both pragmatism and Chinese philosophy see individual human action and interaction to be interpenetrated by ritualized institutions and all other forms of causal interaction. Nature, institutions, and individual agents are not three distinct spheres but overlapping and interpenetrating layers of different kinds of natural processes.

Rituals of all sorts are somewhat vague forms that need to be made specific in order actually to be played. This is somewhat like the distinction prominent in Continental semiotics between a language and actually speaking in the language, which would be like the distinction between a ritual as a complex of habit-potentials and actually playing the ritual. Rituals are like dance steps: they are vague patterns and within each pattern there are many different specific ways they can be played. The vagueness of the steps means that they can be specified in different ways, perhaps even contradictory ways, by different players or even by the same player on different occasions. A person learning a ritual, like one learning a dance, can play or dance the ritual many different ways at first, perhaps not even noting how different the specifications are from one another. As a dancer becomes more expert, however, the difference specifications within the pattern become less random and more individuated. In time, the dancing becomes this individual's way of dancing the pattern, distinct from and likely recognizable in contrast to the ways other dancers do the steps. Likewise with rituals. Though the ritual can be played by any individual in many ways, as they mature individuals individuate themselves more and more. The mature individuating of ritual playing is a large part of how we become individual selves. A small child can learn some large set of role-plays for treating mother and father. But by late adolescence most people can play those ritual roles to relate to their own specific mother and father, and do so to express their own individuated ways of playing those roles that might be played quite differently by siblings.

A significant part of the human self, although not the only part, is the individuating of role playing. A mature individual is involved in playing a gazillion ritual roles all at once. Each self is a matrix of ritual intersections and also the extensions of activity to play rituals overlapping within that matrix that individually reach out to interactions perhaps far distant from other rituals within the matrix. The rituals for relating to colleagues at work overlap those for relating to family members, but they also extend out in nonoverlapping ways.

One of the most important things to recognize about rituals such as these is that when people play together in rituals, they can relate to both others and themselves as equally role players. Instead of the modern Western primacy of self-and-other, the basic Confucian sense of self is to be related to other players of ritual roles as one among the many selves playing. We can regard ourselves as being one among many players in any given ritual. Or to put it differently, the concrete reality is the rituals being played and ready at hand for play. Human beings conceive of themselves as ritual players among and with others if they are alert to the rituals as such. We can conceive of the other players as themselves matrices of multitudes of rituals, just like us, but unique in their own bevy of rituals and playing reciprocal roles to ours in the ritual at hand. We see the others as working through the individuations of their ritual play just as we are, becoming more mature. From the perspective of the ritual play itself, not the conscious perspective of any subject-self within, all the players are viewed as players, including ourselves with the others. The fundamental frame is not me facing the others but rather all of us playing together. This is the first part of the sense of self that I want to stress.

Responsiveness

A second basic pragmatic-Confucian part of the self comes from the observation that each of us has at our core a capacity to perceive and respond to the value-laden things around us, to the ten thousand things, as Confucians call the world. Each individual is a continuum from the inner elements of response through bodily functions, postures, and actions to being able to perceive and act across space and time to connect with the other things. Those abilities require the individual to develop language and other sets of symbols for parsing out the objects in the foreground of their environmental background, as well as interpretive knowledge, skills at moving through the natural and social environments, and many other things. Pragmatists and Confucians emphasize the great importance of learning so as to be able to perceive distant things through helpful theories and practical habits, and to act willfully. Sometimes Western phenomenologists think that the perceived world is simply given, "there" in consciousness or in experience to be analyzed. Think of how anyone from any culture can listen to Bach and find it interesting, perhaps pleasurable. But someone from the Chinese musical tradition would find it less comprehensible than a Westerner who recognizes its harmonies. Someone with a highly refined musical responsiveness in Bach would hear much more than those of us whose musical education is at the entertainment level. It is not that the musicologist hears the same thing as us amateurs and can analyze it better. The musicologist actually hears things we amateurs miss. Perception is an achievement that requires learning. In many ways, becoming a mature self so as to relate well and responsibly to the ten thousand things is like becoming a martial artist, learning to sense and bear the eddies in the *qi*.

The importance of ritual here is that my own personal self includes all the rituals I learn to play. Because the rituals, including speaking my language, intrinsically include the other people and things who reciprocally play them, the others are parts of my own individual self. I am all sorts of rituals shared with others: in many places in my life, I am we. All the things playing ritual roles with me are in various senses components of my personal continua of connections with the things of the world. So the general Western ideal for the individual, to be a subjective self over, against, and in relation to objective Others and the world, is hard to register on my pragmatic-Confucian model. Western sociologists and anthropologists often think that East Asians put the group or community ahead of the individual. But that simply is to misread the Confucian metaphysics of selfhood.

Yet another part of the Confucian responsive self is what the tradition calls "sincerity" or *cheng*, and I adopt it to pragmatism. Sincerity is the educational ideal of becoming transparent through all the layers of the continuum each person has with the things of the world. It means eliminating selfishness that might distort perception and response. But it also means untangling our emotions that hide our motives from others and ourselves. It means practicing ritual play that relates properly to the ritual components and situation. It means learning how to be "present" to others in ritual play and elsewhere.

The English word "sincerity" often has the connotation of expressing oneself honestly, not holding back our feelings, "letting it all hang out," to use a phrase that for some signifies a virtue. The Chinese word *cheng* has a slightly different structure. It means first having developed the skills to appreciate other people for who they are, our institutions for the good they make possible, and surrounding nature for its many worths. Then it means clearing up the continua of interactions that connect us with those others so that we can respond appropriately. Confucian sincerity is a clarity or transparency between the ten thousand things and our inner heart with its natural openness to appropriate response. Becoming sincere means working on oneself, but the ground for this is not oneself but rather the nature and values of other things with which we interact. Sincerity in the Confucian sense is not expressing oneself without disguise but rather making oneself appropriately responsive to the things in the world whose nature and value need to be discovered and appreciated.

One of the great advantages of many rituals is that they allow people who have directly conflicting interests and who hate one another to cooperate in the ritual dance to get something done, for instance run an economy or a household. You don't have to like your ritual partners in order to play the ritual that accomplishes something.

Sincerity is the deepest existential virtue for us pragmatic Confucians because it is so hard to attain and failure in it is a form of existential self-contradiction. The ancient fault of Confucianism, for which it has been criticized by Daoists from the beginning, is that the emphasis on ritual can degenerate into mere formalism. When sincerity is lacking, that is what happens. An insincere person can even individuate much role playing, or at least develop an individuated style. Sometimes such phonies can deceive many people, though we usually can detect a bad smell.

Confucian rituals historically have been criticized for being oppressive, men degrading women, the rich oppressing the poor, mothers-in-law enslaving their daughters-in-law. This should be impossible if the men, the rich, and the mothers-in-law were truly sincere as they played the rituals with their potential victims. In each of these instances, sincerity requires true respect and appreciation of the others involved in the ritual, and ritual play that cannot be played sincerely ought not be played. But who can completely purge selfishness, straighten out their emotions, play rituals rightly, always be humanly attentive, or afford a proper wardrobe? We can always make progress; the Confucians say this potential for progress lies even in "small people." But almost inevitably, failure blunts responsiveness.

Confucians, including pragmatic Confucians, thus have a deep sensibility of tragedy. Partly this is because sincerity is so hard to attain and even then seems to be a vagrant and ephemeral trait. This is only part of the reason for the Confucian tragic view, however.

The other part is that many of the rituals we play are corrupt and bad. Many of the traditional Confucian household rituals have such unevenness of power that women simply cannot be respected sincerely, the poor cannot be related to by the rich with sincerity, and mothers-in-law cannot run their daughters-in-law's family with true sincerity. Those rituals need to be changed. In our own time, think of all the rituals that carry on racism, or worsen a dysfunctional family, or sabotage a social institution, or promote war, or desecrate an environment, or keep certain people in oppressive poverty. In so many places there is an obvious need to change the rituals we have. Confucius and Xunzi were right that without appropriate rituals, children cannot be reared, family life is impossible, and the body politic is a chaos of the strong against the weak. So Confucius said we need to recover the rituals of the sage emperors on antiquity that made high civilization possible in the first place. But having some rituals does not guarantee that they are the right rituals. The right rituals are those than can be played with sincerity. Sincerity is the touchstone for judging rituals. We need to remember that sincerity requires learned appreciation of the ten thousand things, particularly other people, and the cultivation of one's own sagehood of transparent appropriate behavior in the environment.

The need to change our rituals for the sake of sincere deference for all involved is at the heart of Confucian morals. To be sure, Confucian ethics includes learning some moral virtues in order to be sincere. But I believe that even more important than these well-recognized themes of Confucian morals is the imperative for active ritual analysis and the correction of bad rituals. Better than most cultures, Confucianism is sensitive to ritual and can point out how our lives operate by rituals that need to be understood as such. Whereas many cultures think social relations, including power relations and class distinctions, are "natural," we should understand them as being ritualized all the way through, although of course not reduced to rituals alone as some "social constructivists" are likely to say. So we can learn from Confucianism to put great emphasis on analyzing and reconceiving our global societies in terms of their ritual structures and judiciously criticizing them from the standpoint of their justice. For this, Confucians need to lighten up on their attention to the past, recovering a great history after a century of suppression. Instead we need to look outward and to the future to facilitate an appreciation of our institutionalized rituals with an eye to changing them, a trait typical of pragmatists.

But changing rituals is very difficult. We late-moderns hope that changing laws will do it. But the experience in America of changing the civil rights laws shows that this has helped the African American middle class but has done little for the underclass who are still in bondage to rituals of self-hate, economic self-destructiveness, and dysfunctional civic life. It is those deeper rituals that need to be changed. Whereas Confucius thought in his own time that presenting the rituals of the sage kings could help the problem, most scholars today believe he just made them up, his protestations of merely passing on traditions notwithstanding. Through much of Chinese history it was believed that emulation of a wise emperor, or a good grandfather, could develop improved rituals. Sometimes it seems that the most helpful models to emulate are athletes. Can we not do better? The great Confucian contribution for our time needs to be the invention and deployment of rituals that make for peace, freedom, resolution of conflict between genuinely contradictory interests, and human flourishing. Strange, this sounds like John Dewey, does it not?

Pragmatic-Confucian phenomenology of Peirce's sort is not a descriptive examination of consciousness but rather an analytical classification of the kinds of things that need to be harmonized for high civilization. The value of those classes is that they point out some of the tasks of ritual formation, as well as the difficulties of harmonizing what we simply cannot imagine how to fit together. Nevertheless, some things can be fixed. The Confucian approach to tragedy, like the pragmatist, is to feel it in the heart as sincerely as possible, lament what has happened, and then get on and try to do better next time. Pragmatic Confucians do not expect victory, only the opportunity to do the best we can on our watch, educated to appreciate both the vast and deep values and the pervasive injustices in our environment. Philosophy is not just for description but for learning to appreciate and renovate.

Notice that this is an ideal, defined relative to the real situation in the world. The real situation is that the world's many cultures are interacting on countless levels. This interaction is guided by the many forms of thought for prioritizing and appreciating things. It is also guided by the even more numerous way each culture betrays its philosophies. Even more complicated, each culture in this mix does not have one philosophy as its guide, but many, often in competition. Beyond this, each tradition within a culture has a history that is changing and has interacted at different periods with other traditions within the culture in different ways.

Among contemporary Confucian scholars has been a controversy about whether Confucianism is a religion. Those who say *no* do so because their definition of a religion is theistic. They believe that a religion needs to believe in a God or Gods who are personal in some sense. Those who say *yes* do so because their definition of religion is broader than that. They say that religion is the possession of beliefs about what is Ultimate, convictions about what to do to relate existentially to what is Ultimate, and practices that are shaped by how they understand Ultimacy. I find that Chinese culture including the history of Confucianism, which is generally nontheistic, has much to say concerning beliefs about Ultimacy, existential determination by ultimate matters, and practices shaped by Ultimacy, and so I fall within the *yes* camp.

The differences between the first and second definitions have to do mainly with theism versus Ultimacy. I hold that religion really is about

Ultimacy and that those who mean theism in some personal sense are too limited. Personal theism falls under Ultimacy but is not the only form of Ultimacy, and not the Chinese. The Confucians dealt with the questions of Ultimacy in naturalistic ways, not in ways of personal theism.

The East Asian traditions generally reject all models of persons for referring to the ontological creative act and instead lift up instances of pure spontaneity. Confucianism in various ways says that the Great Ultimate gives rise to the movements of yang and yin that make for the changing world. But the Great Ultimate itself has no inner foundation and simply is the result of what some call the Ultimate of Non-Being, *wuji*. Many lines of interpretation have developed this notion, some separating Non-Being from the Great Ultimate, others combining them in various ways. But they all have the great power of recognizing that only Nothing has nothing to be explained. They all recognize that determinate existence, however interpreted, can only be explained as coming (in some sense of "coming") from what has no determinate existence except the power actually exercised to make determinate things.

Confucianism has an important contribution to make in this regard. Specifically, it offers a cosmology or ontology within which only that which itself is without features is the ultimate explanation. The movement of yin and yang is not what contemporary physics teaches. But it is close enough that we can adopt it as a starting point for ontology. Only when the Great Ultimate is actually doing something do we have the phenomenon of creation. But once this is there, we see that the creation is from the Ultimate of Non-Being, which would not be apparent without the Great Ultimate. This point about the creation taking place once the creation is in order, and that it comes from absolutely nothing in itself, is very important for the Confucian tradition and a great contribution today.

Confucianism is a religion because it has from early on had concepts and symbols about what is Ultimate, existential demands that determine who individuals are in ultimate perspective, and practices of life, albeit various, for living relative to Ultimacy. But Confucianism has rarely been organized according to Protestant models of religion, namely congregational life. (Most religions have had many forms of organization, although many tend these days to institutionalize themselves on the congregational model.) Confucianism was taught in families and academies, not churches, and it was practiced through the roles of scholar-officials in the institutions and adventures of life. Some people have thought that

Confucianism beyond Asia needs to be organized like a church, with congregations. Perhaps that is appropriate for some situations. But not for all. Nowadays, for most Confucians, congregations are not so likely to be the places of Confucian education but rather families, schools, and colleges.

Continuities and Changes

From ancient times, Chinese thought has understood the cosmos to be all of one stuff, variously ordered by a single source of order. The cosmos extends from the farthest stars to each inmost human heart. Some of it is ordered as brute physical nature, some as social relations, some as subtle thought, and some as personal individuation. Nevertheless there are only gradations among these realms, with myriad kinds of causation that move from one to the other. Social groups are constituted by geography and the sharing of microbes as much as by conventions and authority structures. An individual's heart is moved by the cosmic gasses as well as by the attractiveness or repulsiveness of another person. The cosmos is conceived as a vast, hugely complex harmony of harmonies of harmonies, with many kinds of harmonies made possible by other kinds of harmonies.

Furthermore, the harmonies are mainly changes, with some changing so slowly that they seem relatively unchanging. The traditional Chinese way of putting this is that every harmony is some collocation of changes to more or less yin and to more or less yang, more or less balancing each other out in regions of relative stability but often overwhelming and transforming relatively stable harmonies. The yin-yang symbol of traditional Chinese cosmology suggests a coordination of more or less yin and yang, maintaining stability. This is particularly important in Chinese medicine where individual balance is sought. Nevertheless, nothing in the Chinese cosmology suggests that yin and yang will automatically be in balance. In fact, nature is not very well scaled to the steadiness required for human habitation.

Daoists and Confucians have emphasized different strategies to deal with this. The Daoists have recommended bending and hiding. They want simple settlements that can easily be rebuilt. They recommend cultivation of medicines and skills that allow a person to escape some of the horrors of nature, aiming at an existence beyond the non-humanly scaled forces of nature. The Confucians advocate organizing societies to build dikes against the floods and granaries against the drought; fund militias and standing armies against the invading barbarians and internal disruptors of the peace; organize communities from the family to the empire to have authority structures to keep mending the unruly forces of nature. Although some forces of nature are simply destructive of human habitats, no matter what is done, many of those forces can be tamed and dealt with by a highly organized society with specially prepared leaders.

Chinese images of the cosmos, social organizations, and individual lives have changed greatly over the last three millennia. Contemporary Confucian philosophy needs to deal with the world as we now understand it. Confucians need to rearticulate the theme of cosmic continuity in terms of what we know from modern science and the lessons of recent history. Our contemporary images of the cosmos are vastly older and broader than most of the Confucian traditions have thought, and we understand the microscopic far better.

Nevertheless, contemporary Confucians outside of as well as inside of China need to understand the contemporary science that has developed mainly with cosmologies of discontinuity, not continuity. Early modern materialists could not understand how the mind of the scientists could be harmonious versions of the same stuff of mountains and balls dropped from the Leaning Tower of Pisa. Contemporary scientists are better at this but still carry a legacy of fundamental discontinuity for which Confucians must correct in the current discussion.

Another aspect of Confucian continuity is that the patterns that order the yin-yang changes, or matter/anti-matter exchanges, yield value in the harmonies they organize, as we have noted with regard to interpretation. This has two faces, articulated with many different Confucian theories. One face is that everything in the cosmos has value in its harmony of changes. Thus human beings need to be cultivated to appreciate this value. The other face, already mentioned, is that the values of things in the human habitat are generally under threat of dissolution or are unjust and in need of rectification. So there is a constant need for moral action with regard to the natural and social environments for life. Because of the causal connections of harmonies within harmonies, from the standpoint of human beings the "moral orientation" to the cosmos is indeed cosmic in scope.

These Confucian points of aesthetic and moral continuities are greatly needed in the contemporary global philosophical discussions.

Modern science has thought itself to be value-free, looking simply at the structures and changes of things. Despite the fact that this runs contrary to the familiar value-ladenness of experience in nearly every culture of the world, it needs to be brought to the fore in the global philosophic discussions.

This Confucian sense of what self-cultivation means is an important alternative within the contemporary global discussion because it works with an unusual sense of the self. You and I "are one body" in that we all speak and read English. We are one body because we approach the institutions of publishing from different angles while still interacting. We are one body because we have different physical bodies while still engaging the world together from different positions. Our human physical bodies share many traits but are also relatably different in structure as well as material. We probably all share some of the microbes within our bodies and on our skins but also differ in other microbes because of our different places and times. The continuities of the world mean that we share one body. But the differences in perspectives that you and I bring to the affairs within which we interact mean that we are different beings. This is radically different from the Western vision within which our differences in being mean differences in the material across which we interact, your material versus my material. For the Confucian, there is no part of my inner body or thinking, feeling mind that is alien to others. An ocular physician knows my eyes better than I do myself. A psychiatrist knows my feelings better than I do. Those doctors, however, have a different perspective on my inner workings than I do. All this is possible to acknowledge because everything is always relational, even my eyes and my inner feelings. Confucians understand this point well: the self is a relation of many things, from the innermost eye to things distantly seen and from the innermost feelings to the distant objects felt. Whereas most Western philosophers would see a substantial difference between people, Confucians see different perspectives on shared relational material.

I want to recommend one more theme of continuity and change from Confucianism, namely the important role of being a scholar-official (*shi-zi*). This role combines the Confucian scholar's cultivated knowledge and accomplishments with responsibilities toward ministering to the institutions of life. Being a scholar-official is an ideal for just about every Confucian person. To be sure, many people are too young and can only look forward to a properly mature state of life. Also, many people are too old and hopefully can look back on earlier careers as scholar-officials; those who missed out can only be sorry. Many different ways of self-cultivation have existed and many different "offices" exist to serve on countless levels of social organization. In the days of the Chinese empire, most of the scholar-officials were assumed to be men, well-born and highly educated. Now that is far less true, both in China and in Western societies. Probably what is most important in Western societies is the breadth of officialdom. Confucians need to look at many more jobs within the intimacies of neighborhood and family life to find ways of being scholar-officials.

The point of the scholar-official ideal is that every person has a responsibility to serve in what the West would call "public life." Civilizations have so many interlocking institutions needing administration in some sense or other that it is impossible now to mark out particular role models of scholar-officials. Some are governmental or religious, and hence somehow obvious. But superintendence or ministry is needed for businesses large and small, sports, entertainment, schools and educational institutions, and economic activities from artificial intelligence and computer science to farming and cleaning beaches. Some scholar-officials are very good at their work, others not so good, and most people are good at some things and bad at others. A Confucian's "official" role does not have to be publicly important or honorific. Heading up the garbage detail in a military camp or household might not seem important, but it is, even when the official is the only one on the job.

The main delineations of human environments are through the complex webs and matrices of ritual life involving nature, institutions, and personal interactions. Much of the work of people as scholar-officials has to do with maintaining, correcting, and improving the complex harmonies of rituals, especially as these are identified in institutions. Ritual-maintenance is an important part of Confucian ethics.

To be a scholar-official requires education, not just in personal virtues but also in knowing how one's environment works. Conceived on a global scale, Confucianism calls for education for everyone, focusing on learning what one might do in a properly interpreted nest of environments. Although education for everyone is becoming accepted in nearly every society today, the Confucian ideal of the scholar-official gives education a new dimension, namely relevance for making things better. This is usually, but not always, compatible with education for the sake of learning what one enjoys, making a good living, and so forth.

It is education for making the environments better as environments for life, not just for oneself or even one's personal virtue. No matter what one's status in social life, or placement within the shifting of civilizations, one can always become a little bit better at the work of being a scholar-official.

Recall the Confucian emphasis on continuities and changes. Not only is nearly everything related to everything else, but everything is changing. Hence the relations among the harmonies of the world are constantly changing. We like to think that we are shoring up institutions under threat or building new institutions in an otherwise stable environment. But in fact we are always only dealing with changes that differ in relative speeds and at various levels of shifting hierarchies of interactions.

Chapter 10

Philosophy

Philosophical Studies

Only philosophy studies everything,
From philosophers' puzzles to scientific wonders,
From eternity to glimpses in passing,
From life's meaning to moral blunders.
Philosophy's greatest gift is speculation
Beyond the human, social, and natural.
It analyzes as it goes and
Critiques its guesses.
Philosophy ends with guilty suggestions:
Looking for a hidden challenge,
Looking for a better vision,
Looking for the next philosophy.

Philosophers

Confucius and Laozi, the Buddha and the Bhagavad Gita, Plato and Aristotle, all had predecessors. They also had successors who mixed them up and combined them with philosophers from Africa, the Islamic world, and the Americas. By the middle of the Han dynasty, about the same time as the rule of Aspavarma in India, around the year 1, these groups of philosophers likely would have known of each other. Gore Vidal's novel *Creation* is a barely fictionalized account of philosophy in fifth- and sixth-century Greece (young Socrates), India (the Buddha), and China

(Confucius and Laozi). Plato wrote about the Africans. Islam joined the conversation from the Straits of Morocco to the Straits of Molucca by the end of the Common Era's seventh century. The descendants of Cahokia, Tenochtitlan, and Cuzco joined the conversation by the end of the sixteenth century. The conversation waxed and waned again and again and was brilliantly broad.

Of course, most of the people involved in this philosophy would not be counted as philosophers today, only Plato and Aristotle, their Greek forebears, and their European and North American successors, with Asians coming in mainly with Western schools. But what about the long and continuous traditions of China bearing not only the Confucians and Daoists but also the Chinese Buddhists of many kinds, and the deviant and sometimes short-lived schools? Matteo Ricci learned Chinese in the beginnings of the seventeenth century and had long discussions with the Confucians and Daoists. Why do we know only the Western side of those discussions? Why do we know only the Western visions of the nineteenth and twentieth century Chinese philosophers and not their continual revisions of the Chinese side? Scholars of Buddhism know the Dialogues of King Malinda and trace its developments in India and China but rarely point out, and far less trace in Western contexts, the fact that King Malinda's name was really King Menander, one of Alexander's generals. The Buddha lived in the mountains just south of what is now Tibet, and his gospel spread in Hinayana and Mahayana forms south into India. But it also went north throughout Tibet with elaborate philosophical forms and is best represented in the world now by the deposed Dalai Lama. Al-Kindi, al-Razi, Jabir, Averoes, Avicenna, and many others are well-known to scholars of medieval thought, but only in the West and because of their connections with Western medieval philosophers. Baghdad was halfway across the Muslim Empire when it stretched to the Straits of Molucca, and yet who today would count the Asian Islamic philosophers such as Liu Zhi or Hamzah Fansuri as philosophers until the British arrived?

Today the academic world is somewhat embarrassed to deal with mainly successors to Plato and Aristotle alone. Philosophy departments scurry clumsily to include the suddenly relevant Muslim philosophers and all the rest. Often philosophy is best found outside of philosophy departments when it comes to non-Western and Muslim kinds. Over the next fifty years, in their reorganizations, philosophy and other academic departments will struggle to find their way to global philosophy, whatever it is called. Some areas of consolidation will move faster than others, and some might just drop out of the conversation entirely. In fifty years, philosophers will know a bit about all modes of philosophy, specializing in some in combination or perhaps not specializing at all. Nowadays just about all Western philosophers know enough of Plato and Aristotle, Anselm and Aquinas, Descartes, Leibniz, Spinoza, Kant, Hegel, and even Whitehead to at least associate some doctrines with them all. In fifty years, nearly all philosophers will be acquainted with African, Muslim, pre-Columbian American, South Asian, East Asian, and West Asian philosophy that these separate origins will be unimportant except for history. Whatever they call this discipline, I just call it philosophy.

Philosophers write for a field, and "philosophy" names the field, not the conclusions. Philosophy is a little like music, where Bach, Beethoven, Brahms, and Bartok write their best for an unknown audience and all are equally good; the audience appreciates them all despite how they hear differently. Philosophers do contribute to philosophy like composers. Most philosophers appreciate each other and themselves as composers.

But more than composers, philosophers want their work to be right. Even if ultimately different and irreconcilable, like composers, they will want their work to be right. I recognize my own philosophy to be uniquely trajectoried and idiosyncratic, thus like a musical composition, or a series of compositions. But for all this, I still want it to be right. And I hope you want your own philosophy to be right, however different it is, and like a musical composition. We all are inventive and are working hard to overcome the localism that has held us back from global philosophical discussions. In many fields, local work is reaching out to engage other local works.

But metaphysics, philosophical theology, the study of what is Ultimate, is a universal problem with local contributions from just about everyone. It would seem that philosophical theology is an ideal candidate for globalism, with universal reaches and local contributors. The call for metaphysics or philosophical theology at the outset leads us to recognize that each of the world traditions has many levels, from the various forms of popular religion, step by step, up to discussions that legitimately can be called philosophical theology. Popular religions are extremely concrete and are widely practiced, although with different structures of practice. Fundamentalisms, variously interpreted or uninterpreted, are popular religions and they can be oriented to aspects of nature, such as seasons, or society, such as relevance to only certain kinds of people. Moreover, they can accommodate more than one "religion," or none, as in many Indian festivals. With more interpretation, they can take on "mythic" proportions and be celebrated with the knowledge that reality is not really like that. How many Christian services use the rites of worship of God as king without taking the kingship very seriously?

The West Asian religions assume nearly everyone in a family belongs to the religion and that only some elite people in elite families rise to the level of philosophical theology. Usually this has been men, but with recent education of women, women are coming to speak for the elite. Hinduism organizes itself into clannish groups with separate Gods put in charge of each group. A God like Krishna appears differently in different groups. Only sophisticated people see the Gods to be connected by more than the stories about them. Buddhism's popular religions are a lot like those of Hinduism, and the Western appreciation of Buddhism starts out fairly high up in the membership. Nevertheless, the weddings and funerals of Buddhism evoke many Gods. Daoism in China is a kind of universal religion with many beliefs held for everyone, in one or another senses of holding. But its popular forms are very much involved with magic and its sophisticated forms go far beyond popular beliefs in souls that can outreach the body. Confucianism is a religion mainly for literate men, with women only recently coming to hold serious Confucian beliefs. The Confucian emphasis on rituals was expected to be followed by people in all social classes, but only the literate were supposed to be able to understand them. Then, understanding of the rituals could be limited to what they are and do, or it could be expanded to the role of rituals in making civilization possible.

In any society, according to any religion, membership and the ability to think philosophically about ultimate matters are related but different. Whatever the roles of hierarchy are in the various religions, at least one role is differences in the levels of thinking and the exclusive preoccupation of theology with the upper stands of certain kinds of thinking about Ultimate matters. Philosophical theology is limited to this upper atmosphere.

Cultures

So my purpose here is to raise the question of Ultimate reality in ways that acknowledge that it might be far from the Western paradigms. I shall begin by discussing three paradigms for God, arising from West Asia, South Asia, and East Asia, stressing the latter two more than the first. To begin with these traditions of Asia—the Western, Southern, and Eastern—is itself striking. Partly I do it to balance the Christian orientation of the prologue. More largely I do it to emphasize the unity of the Asian traditions, despite the differences. The flip side of this motive is the recognition that academic scholars of religion know a lot more about the first tradition than they do about the second and third unless they are specialists in the latter. Philosophers are even worse than scholars of religion unless they start out as South Asian or East Asian philosophers. That I write in English is an obvious clue to where I'm coming from. To be sure, many religions of Africa and the Americas exist that I'll simply not mention; I'm doing well enough to deal with Paganism, Christianity, Judaism, Islam, Hinduisms, Buddhisms, Daoism, and Confucianism.

The metaphoric systems of West Asian theology generally take the form of emphasizing the agential character of persons. By this I mean the intentionality, will, desire, rationality, and creative effort to do something. The various main religions of the West push these notions of personhood toward very high levels of abstraction, but the route of the metaphoric systems allows them to employ high levels of abstraction of these characteristics. Plato, for instance, played with various Gods in dealing with personalities but opted for something like the Form of the Good for his Ultimate. To be sure, the Form of the Good could not have agential characteristics, but its metaphoric train did and the religions resulting from this carried them too. Aristotle's God was a substance that was pure act thinking itself and also had leftover personal characteristics, as showed up in Thomas Aquinas's conception. Plotinus was probably the purest conception to develop from Greek paganism with his conception of the One beyond Being; Contraction to finite modes of being and goodness were made by the One (which was One only after the fact). The same is true for Augustine's and Aquinas's conceptions of God, and for Calvin's, Schleiermacher's, and Tillich's. Among the vast array of Western conceptions of God are surely many variants. But most of them point toward a conception that is beyond all characters and yet that carries on some version of agency. The problem with philosophical theology is that it talks about an Ultimate that it has to represent as a being or process even though it knows Ultimacy is beyond that. The being thus inherits personalistic shades of the metaphoric origins.

The West Asian religious traditions begin with some popular understandings of human beings and make them greater and greater until they approach indeterminacy. Nevertheless, the people taken to be god-like are intentional and deliberate when acting. Ares, Hermes, and Zeus are like men, and Artemes, Aphrodite, and Hera are like women. They have superpowers and affairs that break human rules but still have deliberation and intentions. By the time of the great philosophers, these figures were taken to be mythological and used that way by several of the philosophers (e.g., Plato).

This tradition of great paganism reached its climax in Plotinus who ranked the deities as the One, the Dyad, and the Triad. The Triad was the world soul that contemplated all that could be contemplated. The Dyad was the intelligible where one thing differed from the other in some respect. The One was the source of all else but was known as the One only because it transcended the rest. It was First because there was a Second and Third, the Beautiful because it created beautiful things, the Good because all goods flowed from it. It was the fullness of being because all determinate beings came from it, in order. Plotinus's One was preeminent in priority. It was the Fullness of Being in a very real sense and hence was the most real thing. It was not sheer emptiness that created finite being from nothing. The One is necessary in itself.

Plotinus's view of the One has few followers today, but it was remarkably effective in modifying the three great religions of The Book. Judaism began as a sky-god religion whose God moved about with the wandering tribe. By the time of the writing of the Bible, this was taken to be rather mythological. The second creation story has God walking about in the garden. The first creation story, however, raised a deeper question. When God speaks the word to bring order to the chaos or to create the world, is his speech something in addition to God or just God in action? If the former, then Sophia is divine, however related to creation. If the latter, she is not anything created at all but simply God acting. The former theory was legitimate for Jews through the Jerusalem Talmud and was the orthodox position for Christians who treated the Logos incarnate in Christ as divine. The latter theory was the orthodox position for the Babylonian Talmud, which thereby distinguished ancient Judaism from Christianity. The Muslim tradition began with a staunch monotheism, which meant it rejected Christianity as anything but a late prophecy. One branch of Islam, however, believed that the Qur'an preexisted its being spoken to Mohammed and was eternal in the mind of God, which made Islam a bit like Christianity.

All three of these Western religions, of course, grew in sophistication and developed religions for the elite. Interestingly, all three took on more and more of the Neo-Platonism of Plotinus. Judaism became religiously mystical in Kabbalism but received its sophisticated center in Maimonides. Christianity became rather like Plotinus in Augustine but was desperate to keep its connection with the Bible. Pseudo-Dionysius was more like Plotinus in holding to a hierarchy of levels of reality. Thomas Aquinas was deeply interested in Augustine and Pseudo-Dionysius but gave an Aristotelian interpretation of God as the One. Ibn al-'Arabi was a Neo-Platonist fairly straightforwardly, as was Jabir ibn Hayyan before him. All of these people said that God transcends (most) distinctions and is the One for the world.

From an historical perspective, the paths these figures of the West took toward the indeterminate was heavily laden with their scriptures. Plotinus was least of all bothered by scriptures, although his path of the soul toward God moved along through the levels of determinateness. Pseudo-Dionysius, however, was extremely scriptural and institutional. Augustine had a philosophical interpretation of God that lay behind his distinction of literal versus symbolic interpretations of scripture. Aquinas said that God in himself is the pure Act of To Be, which was complete, indeterminate, and unrelatable to the creation, but when it came to ethics, his God was as loving as the Bible said and strongly opposed to evil.

Like the religions of West Asia, those of South Asia begin their conceptions of the Ultimate with persons. Nevertheless, whereas West Asian religions emphasize agency, South Asian ones emphasize consciousness. Like West Asian religions, South Asian philosophical theologians do not limit themselves to any recognizable "person" at the end. Whereas West Asian theologians move toward a "simple" being, or perhaps non-being, but carry along some of the personal agential connotations of personhood, South Asian theologians carry along consciousness, made purer and purer. Whereas West Asian theologians believe that the agential aspects of personhood are the most valuable to carry along in more or less purified form, South Asian theologians believe the agential aspects are precisely what need to be left behind. They are the very aspects of personhood that cause trouble when ascribed to the Ultimate. Whereas

South Asian theologians take consciousness, made purer and purer, to be the path toward a supernatural Ultimate, West Asian theologians consider consciousness to be too weak and ineffectual to be the Ultimate.

My own position is that either way is appropriate, and that West Asian and South Asian theologies come out of their respective traditions. Moreover, there are many, many traditions in both West and South Asia, many forms of Judaism, Christianity, Paganism, Islam, Buddhism, and Hinduism, each with its own variety of the main metaphoric systems. Religious people, including theologians, have membership in only one or a few of these, even changing through a lifetime. As a philosophical theologian, I think beginning with any one of these is just right, although what must be given up or modified or taken to be legendary in each differs radically from the rest. So I am not choosing among these now.

The South Asian traditions divide between those, particularly Buddhists, who believe that the Ultimate state of affairs is that there is no Ultimate and those, particularly Hindus, who believe that the deeper you go, the closer you come to the purest form of consciousness. I shall take a representative of each to make my case about Ultimacy, recognizing that a full case would require a complete survey.

For Buddhism, I shall discuss briefly the views of Nagarjuna (second century), a Madhyamika thinker. The Madhyamikas generally hold that ultimate reality is completely empty whereas the Yogacharins believe that the base reality is that of representations. The Yogacharins and Madhyamikas together constitute the Mahayana schools and stand in contrast to the Theravadins who believe that all things are in constant change. Nagarjuna is famous because of his view that all things are real, nothing is real, all things are both real and non-real, and all things are neither real nor non-real. His *Mulamadhyamikakarikas* is a long essay that works through many issues with this as a theme. Because all things are changing, nothing is real; according to this thinking, to be changing is to be on the way from something to something else. This is true even of consciousness. So we begin with *samsara*, ordinary consciousness in life, and realize that it is false. This leaves us with *nirvana*, the consciousness of enlightenment. But that nirvana is that nothing is real, so nirvana is samsara. The result is that we take life as it comes, knowing that it is nothing more than what it seems to be. This is Nagarjuna's general picture.

What is the role of meditation in this? It certainly is a lot of work! Officially, of course, it cannot be anything. But it is the Buddhist way of making progress in recognizing that nirvana is samsara and so it is the move from notional to real knowledge. The real life of samsara is filled with all sorts of confusions and pains of soteriological import, and these are false. They need to be given up, and to give them up means attaining release from all desires that come from believing in real, unchanging things. This is extremely difficult to do and comes, in the end, to be the abandonment of all consciousness. If even we find that consciousness has a real object that does not change, then the whole scheme of Nagarjuna's Buddhism fails. But Nagarjuna shows that the reality of an object of consciousness is not real. Everyone knows that human beings are powerful agents, the more human, the more powerful they are. But the contemplative side of human nature was a surprise and it needed protection. The West Asian religions made their gods like superheroes. The Southern Asian religions treated agency as a distraction and often as the source of religious imperfection. Instead they took meditation, contemplation, retirement to the interior of the self, to be what is truly most human.

Buddhism, as we know, is older than Hinduism, and Hinduism is a very late term for the six orthodox schools and for many other developments. Both Buddhism and Hinduism arose out of a long development from many sources that reflected a kind of proto-South Asian culture. In 3000 BCE the Indus Valley culture even had indoor plumbing and toilets with running water!

Early Buddhism had a great many gods, mainly the gods of the earlier time. The Buddha himself, however, did not find the Ultimate in worshipping a God or Goddess. To be sure, many popular Buddhists did. For instance even down to this day, devout Buddhists worship Avalokiteshvara, or, in China, Guan Yin, the God(dess) of healing. Buddhism in China today is a distinguished religious denomination, and many people follow its ceremonies for weddings and funerals. What the Buddha actually said and did, we do not exactly know. He spoke a language of northern India or Nepal that we do not recognize, and his words comes to us in Sanskrit and Prakrit translations.

One of the basic themes of South Asia, from before Buddha's life, is the law of karma. Human beings are in a series of lives, one after another, that are usually determined in their level of existence by the moral consequences of previous lives. Fairly enlightened human beings know about this and seek release from the cycle of rebirth. But not all lives are human ones. Beasts, birds, insects, and microorganisms are also in this path of rebirth and are among the ancestors of us all. Although both East Asians and West Asians sometimes believe in rebirth, it is not a main theme for them as it is for the South Asians. Life for most of the South Asians is extremely painful. For the Buddhists, it is painful in all its aspects, and Buddhists have spent 2,500 years exploring just how this is so. Therefore, after mastering living well in the noble Eightfold Path, with right views, intentions, speech, action, livelihood, effort, mindfulness, and concentration, Buddhists want to end the cycle of life and die. Nirvana is being dead. What a contrast this is to East Asians who hope to be remembered after death! Or to West Asians who generally hope to live again! The hope for "salvation" differs radically among these major traditions.

For sophisticated Buddhists, the cause of suffering is wrongful craving or passionate commitment to the things of this life. The more sophisticated the Buddhist, the more detailed and non-obvious the forms of craving. The cessation of suffering consists in enlightenment of some kind, the more sophisticated the better. The kinds of enlightenment are many. Some, focused more on merely being mendicants with specialized knowledge, characterize the Theravada school. The Mahayana schools are more ontological in their outlook. Of them, the Yogacara school is called "consciousness-only" because it believes in the existence only of conscious things, with belief in the reality of those conscious things being a step toward craving. The Madhyamika school believes that all realities are mere illusory dharmas or things. True enlightenment consists in realization that all things are merely illusions, or in fact delusions.

There are thus two truths, for Buddhists. The truth of ordinary life is the belief in the things of the world as being what they seem to be, and life lived in this truth is indeed full of cravings and desires. But the truth of enlightenment is the realization that this truth of ordinary life is only illusion and that its cravings themselves are not really real. In fact, in the Mahayana schools, the search for enlightenment needs itself to be abandoned. The life of nirvana, where the flame of craving is blown out (nirvana means that the flame is blown out), is just the life of samsara, where one lives ordinary life but without the commitment to anything except what one is committed to. In fact, the person who has attained nirvana, according to some schools, looks just like the ordinary person, with the ordinary person's concerns, but without the craving. To be fully enlightened is to realize that one will not be reborn. For some schools, this is compatible with living one's last life. Perhaps it is just the realization that one never has the rebirth of lives. For other schools, it is necessary to die in order to reach full enlightenment. Enlightenment itself is death.

Nevertheless, what if the Buddhists are mistaken about the unreality of (un)real things? What if there are real, solid dharmas? What if there are ontologically real things? The Buddhists' beliefs are based on ontological considerations. They might want to say that, with Nagarjuna, one falls into contradiction if one thinks hard about them, but this is itself an ontological commitment. Although Buddhism is aimed to deal with the soul and not ontology, its theory of the soul is based on ontology. Ontology is where sophisticated Buddhists think.

The arising of Buddhism in the sixth century BCE was the occasion for the formulation of the six orthodox schools of Hinduism, as they came to be known later. These are Nyaya, Vaisesika, Samkhya, Yoga, Purva Mimamsa, and Vedanta of several kinds. The six orthodox schools are philosophies whose "truth" consists in a kind of action. These schools themselves are reorganizations of society after the impact of Buddhism (and Jainism and Carvaka) that denied the separation of castes. The schools also wrote in Sanskrit, which was an artificial language invented to fix up the earlier proto-Sanskrit of the Vedas and some of the Upanishads. The Vedas and earliest Upanishads also provided a background for the Bhagavad Gita and its much larger poem, the Mahabharata. The Mahabharata has many parts, written over a thousand years most likely.

The Bhagavad Gita is largely a theistic work consisting of a long conversation between Arjuna, the leader of the Pandeva army, and Krishna, who is his charioteer. In the climax of the discussion of raja yoga, the royal way of understanding, Krishna is transformed into Vishnu, the super-transcendent God who is both Brahman and Ishvara, Absolute and God. This is the famous "light of a thousand suns" passage in which Vishnu becomes transcendent of all finite things, eternal and infinite. All Arjuna's enemies, all the divine and demonic beings, all the gods and goddesses, everything in the universe, and all non-being is assumed into the transcendent one who is beyond them all. While this remains a theism of sorts, it is a very transcendent theism.

In the early schools of Hinduism, one of the most basic roots was Samkhya philosophy. Samkhya distinguished nature from consciousness. Nature, prakriti, consists of three main forces: sattva, rajas, and tamas. Sattva is intelligibility, rajas is activity, and tamas is resistance to activity. Consciousness, purusha, is the self, which consists of two sorts of consciousness. It is likened to two birds sitting in a tree. One bird watches around for bugs on the tree and attaches itself to objects of consciousness. The other watches the first bird. The first bird is aware of nature, and the second of consciousness itself. The practical point of this ancient philosophy is to retreat to the position of the second bird, being aware of nothing but the consciousness of nature and other objects. This thought pattern underlies much of Hinduism.

Now, return to the idea of person involved in people and the gods. There is a line of persons, such as Agni, Indra, Brahma, and Ishvara, who are gods who create and have deliberate intentions, which itself aims at indeterminateness. Different peoples of India and in different time periods have their own lines. But they all add up, if followed far enough, to a kind of Brahman-without-Qualities. This kind of line has, as its penultimate stage, Brahman-with-Qualities, which identifies it in a series. Something like this is true of all these lines.

Somewhere toward the far end of these lines the notion of person is purified. The active elements, the deliberation and intentionality, get left behind and the valuable part of personality, namely consciousness, remains. Everyone can notice ordinary consciousness. Many forms of Hinduism develop practices of meditation that purify it. There is much diversity in the kinds of purity to be obtained. Much of it consists, as in Buddhism, of rejecting the reality of the objects of consciousness. But there are also ways of simply emptying consciousness of all objects. What is left is merely consciousness itself. This differs from Buddhism: instead of finding nothing in consciousness, Hinduisms find the pure reality of consciousness itself, or something like it.

I do not want to make these forms of Hinduism seem similar. They are radically different in their popular extensions. They have different names, and often they are recognized as different gods, each with its purpose. Many people stop their reflections somewhere at these points on the line. Others continue them but keep their differentiations as well. Hinduisms are perhaps most distinctive in this last mode, acknowledging the great diversity of gods and their roles while also acknowledging higher levels of reality, approaching consciousness. This differs from East Asian modes of naturalism that have sharp breaks between the eternal and the temporal Daos. It also differs from West Asian modes of theism that have sharp breaks in kinds of Neo-Platonic levels. The South Asians love to worship and can worship Gods on many different levels, all at once, as it were.

Consider the case of Abhinavagupta, who lived around a thousand years into the common era in Kashmir. He was perhaps the greatest genius of Kashmir Shaivism. He was a great tantric master in religion and wrote many works on religion, philosophy, art criticisms, and other topics of his time. He would have thought himself to be a theist of the highest sort, particularly because of his tantricism. Paul Eduardo Muller-Ortega says of him:

> But his theology centered on the heart of Shiva, which he construed as a vibrating union of Shiva's heart and Devi or Shakti's creative expression. The Heart is the Ultimate (attunttara) which is both utterly transcendent to (visvottirna) and yet totally immanent in (visvamaya) all created things. It is the ultimate essence (sara). Thus, the Heart embodies the paradoxical nature of Siva and is therefore a place of astonishment (camatkara), sheer wonder (vismaya), and ineffable mystery. The Heart is the fullness and unboundedness of Siva (Purnatva), the plenum of being that overflows continuously into manifestations. At the same time, it is also an inconceivable emptiness (Sunyatisunya). The Heart is the unbounded and universal Self (purnahanta).[1]

To be sure, the Heart of Siva is a self and thus is to be understood to be in a line of abstractions from the notion of a human self. But it has left behind all the deliberation and intentionality of the self, except when it manifests as an ordinary self.

The Heart of Siva has two sides. One is the feminine side that consists in manifestations of "groups." All the things of the world are such groups or harmonies. They fit together in larger and larger groupings. They are also constantly changing, moving, as it were, from one group to another. The usual objects of our consciousness are these groups. They are the real things of the world. This feminine side, Deva or Shakti, is where we meet the world. So the god we meet ordinarily is feminine. This draws in a long line of gods and goddesses, and it also manifests itself in the practices of tantrism.

The other side of the Heart is pure consciousness without an object, Siva. Siva is unbounded by space or time. It has no characteristics at all and is literally infinite. But Siva has no reality except in conjunction with Shakti. If there were no pulsing expressions to produce the manifestations, there would be no Siva as well as no Shakti. Nevertheless, there are manifestations, there is Shakti, and there is Siva.

Why could we not stop with Shakti alone and eliminate Siva? The answer is that Abhinavagupta's philosophy is a radical creationism. The creation does not arise from some already present spouting forth of things but from nothing. The "already present spouting forth of things" would be a complex that needs a source. That source is nothing. The nothing by itself would be nonsense. But the nothing as the ground of the spouting forth is sufficient. The vibrating manifests Siva as well as Shakti.

All this is to say that absolute contingency applies here too. The manifestations of groups, in Abhinavagupta's theory, is contingent upon the nothing, Siva, from which it arises, and that "nothing" is real in the vibrating contingency. There is no necessity to Siva alone that would make Him [sic] create; he does not. But there is the Ultimate contingency in the Heart of Siva that makes Siva create with the Shakti that is combined with him contingently.

Where does this leave our argument? As said, Abhinavagupta was fully tantric, and the stories of how he achieved the tantric vision of the Heart of Siva are legendary. One legend is that at the age of seventy-five he walked off to a cave with twelve hundred disciples and simply disappeared, Abhinavagupta plus the disciples. Another is that he was always learning and took up learning about all cultures that came his way. Other legends have to do with his learning from many masters whom he venerated highly. So he was surely religious. And he surely worshipped on many levels, including devotion to statues of Siva and Shakti.

Nevertheless, the personal god he worshipped at the highest was the god of pure consciousness, not the god of theistic intentionality and deliberate creation. The god Siva was pure consciousness, requiring the goddess Shakti that manifested itself in objects of consciousness. Shakti was like Brahman-with-Qualities. Siva was like Brahmin without Qualities. Abhinavagupta was a theist in the sense of believing that persons can lack all but the manifestations of consciousness.

Now let me suggest how the Western and Southern Asian religions are to be compared. Both take images from personhood and develop them into conceptions of god or goddesses that are non-personal. But each carries on some aspects of their different aspects of personhood. The Western theological traditions press forward with images that suggest that God has a mind, intentions, and actions. The Southern traditions press forward with images that deny explicitly those agential notions and instead produce consciousness that is not individual consciousness. What is being prepared are separate trajectories that might aim at the same thing but that are radically diverse.

The Chinese trajectory is quite different. Early in the Zhou dynasty, their philosophical theologians abandoned personal models of gods and adopted Heaven as the image of stars in the sky. Shangdi, the Sky God of the prior dynasties, was set aside. Sometimes, Heaven was viewed as having something like intentions for human beings but not in any literal sense. Confucius himself dismissed concerns for Heaven as an agent and focused on the ultimate in human life. Four generations later, Xunzi explicitly talked about Heaven, Earth, and the Human and had qualified worshipfulness for Heaven. The Ultimate in Chinese thought was not as important as it was in West and South Asian thought. But it was still the object of philosophical theology in East Asia, starting out in philosophical Daoism. In order to make this case, let us review the following.

Laozi, the Daoist, was most explicit about Ultimacy. The *Daodejing* begins:

> The Tao (Way) that can be told of is not the eternal Tao;
> The name that can be named is not the eternal name.
> The Nameless is the origin of Heaven and Earth;
> The Named is the mother of all things.[2]

The Dao that can be named is the temporal Dao in which each moment arises out of its predecessors. The Dao that cannot be named is that which is the source of the Dao that can be named. How to interpret this has long been a source of debate, but in any case, this is a theory of the Ultimate. My own suspicion is that the Dao that cannot be named is the eternal source of temporality, which is evident only in the temporal. The eternal Dao that cannot be named is related to each moment of the Dao that can be named but is not temporal itself. Rather, it is the eternal depths of temporality.

Zhuangzi had a related notion of Ultimacy. "In the great beginning, there was non-being. It had neither being nor name. The One originated from it; it has oneness but not yet physical form. . . . That which is formless is divided [into yin and yang], and from the very beginning going on without interruption is called destiny. Through movement and rest it produces all things."³ This suggests a temporal evolutionary theory going back to the earliest time. But the Chinese do not hold exactly to that. Rather, non-being is at the root of anything that happens in an eternal way. You can get from now to the eternal source just as you can from the past. Indeed, you can get from the unrealized future to the depth as well.

Wang Bi (226–249) wrote briefly but brilliantly. In his commentary on the *Daodejing*, beginning, he said: "All being originated from non-being. The time before physical forms and names appeared was the beginning of the myriad things. After forms and names appear, Tao (the Way) develops them, nourishes them, and places them in peace and order; that is, becomes their Mother. This means that Tao produces and completes things with the formless and nameless. Thus they are produced and completed but do not know why. Indeed it is the mystery of mysteries."⁴ He said, "All things in the world come from being, and the origin of being is based on non-being. In order to have being in total, it is necessary to return to non-being."⁵ This is a clear statement of the Chinese principle that only the less complex (e.g., non-being) can explain the more complex.

Perhaps the most complete statement of the general Chinese position on Ultimate reality comes from Zhou Dunyi:

> The Ultimate of Non-being and also the Great Ultimate (*T'ai-chi*)! The Great Ultimate through movement generates yang. When its activity reaches its limit, it becomes tranquil. Through tranquillity the Great Ultimate generates yin. When tranquillity reaches its limit, activity begins again. So movement and tranquillity alternate and become the root of each other, giving rise to the distinction of yin and yang, and the two modes are thus established. By the transformation of yang and its union with yin, the Five Agents of Water, Fire, Wood, Metal, and Earth arise. When these give material forces are distributed in harmonious order, the four seasons run their course. The five agents constitute one system of yin and yang and yin and yang constitute one Great Ultimate. The Great Ultimate is fundamentally the Non-ultimate.⁶

Here is a sophisticated evolutionary account of the origin of all things from the Ultimate of Non-Being. The evolution is not temporal, however, in starting with an earliest time and moving forward. Rather it is eternal in that at any time within the temporal flow one can go down to that which does not move, the Great Ultimate. Without the Great Ultimate, we would not be able to say that there is the Ultimate of Non-Being; with the Great Ultimate, it is possible to say that being arises from non-being. This is an important statement of ultimacy. Only with the positivity of the Great Ultimate is it possible to say anything about the Ultimate of Non-Being. but with that positivity, the Ultimate of Non-Being is seen to give rise to everything that finally issues in the determinate world.

Whereas the Western and Southern Asian trajectories of metaphors are those of persons, the East Asian ones are those of spontaneous emergence. Popular religion in China, so long as it is not influenced by West and South Asia, takes its rise from water fountains arising out of the ground or the blossoming of bare roots in the springtime. Sometimes there are deities associated with nature, but by and large this association goes back to nature. The more Chinese religions are pushed toward sophistication, the more they tend to the nature of Non-being. Western scholars, in fact, are so wedded to notions of personhood that they have sometimes declared Daoism and Confucianism to be non-religions, something else entirely. The East Asian traditions, vaguely speaking, take the cosmos to be elements of process that are structured by yin and yang formations. Perhaps the founding document in East Asia is the *Yijing*, which is a commentary on hexagrams of dotted and undotted lines, the former standing for yin and the latter for yang. In various ways, all the Chinese schools and traditions adopt and relate to the *Yijing*, not only Confucianism and Daoism but also Mohism, the school of yin/yang, and many others. Popular religion in China has been some variation or other on shamanism combined with other religions.

The metaphors surrounding the creation of the world of yin-yang passages are all naturalistic, things like the burgeoning of flowers and trees, the sudden emergence of springs of water from the ground. Because all determinate things are themselves changes, their ground must be indeterminate. The vastness of spontaneous emergence far overwhelms human persons. Persons, for the Chinese, themselves have both agency and contemplation, but they are by no means called nothing, and by far the greatest bulk of Chinese philosophy is devoted to their proper formation. Agency and contemplation are the rare achievements of truly great human beings, not some aboriginal elements that might be brought to consciousness.

Scales and Trajectories

It is necessary to look more closely at the sliding scale from popular to sophisticated religion.

This scale differs with the religious traditions at hand. In East Asian societies, there seems to be a difference in social class. For Daoists, popular religion seems to be located mainly in popular classes where temples to the Daoist gods crowd the streets. Daoists who pursue philosophical Daoism tend to be more reserved and associated these days with colleges and universities. Scholars of Daoism such as Livia Kohn tend to view popular Daoism as a basic form but give it highly metaphorical interpretations when pressed. Confucians always were a separated group of people, even when the distinctions among social classes were murky. For the Confucians, popular religion could be Confucian in the sense of following out rituals and some ceremonies, but they also sometimes did not care what religions other people were. Chinese were famous for being Confucians in their sophisticated thinking: Buddhists in their attention to other ceremonies and Daoists (and shamanists) in women's daily lives. Nowadays, after strong criticism of Confucianism by Marxists, and the recovery of Confucianism as a basic Chinese contribution to culture, the situation is very mixed. The non-Han peoples of China carry on with their native traditions, now blessed with Communist oversight. The previously Confucian segments of the population seem to be reviving in part, especially in recovering rituals; for instance, yearly travel to one's family burial ground is increasing now, especially for those whose parents have died. But the sophisticated Confucians are now somewhat divided between those who stayed at home (and their children and grandchildren) and those who left for Taiwan, Singapore, America, and other places where Confucianism flourished continuously. There are also now many Confucians of non–East Asian extraction. Those Confucians interested in Ultimate matters now find their work to be intimately involved with non-Confucian sources.

West Asian religions have a very different pattern, namely one of a gradual continuity from the most popular to the most sophisticated, not a difference so much of social class. The most telling element of this is churches, temples, and mosques. These institutions are for everyone, not only those of specific social classes. Perhaps evangelical institutions stray from this generalization because they reject others who disagree, but even here there are sophisticated people who are not limited to belief in the infallibility of scriptures. Mainline denominations of Jews, Christians, and Muslims display a range of theological options regarding Ultimacy, however much they share an equal range of ritual symbols. In all three branches, there are those on the sophisticated end who view themselves as coming out of those traditions, no longer attending services or belonging to those communities. Nevertheless, these people acknowledge their roots and even share them with members of the other communities. Some even claim an equal sharing of all roots and sometimes reject membership in one or several of them, claiming to be wholly unreligious. These last still have a trajectory of their religion, however, that gives them a sense of identity.

What is the case with the South Asian traditions, particularly Buddhism and Hinduisms?

Buddhism from the beginning downplayed caste distinctions. The earliest texts began with the Buddha's male disciples who followed him personally, but then took in the Buddha's sister and her disciples. The Buddha, according to legend, founded monasteries and then also, at his sister's request, nunneries. These monasteries and nunneries institutionalized sophisticated learning; they also allowed temporary membership for laypeople who wanted more sophistication. And then there were vast hordes of people who did not hope for enlightenment in this life but looked to live in ways that would help them in future lives. After about a thousand years, Buddhism died out in India only to return in recent years as a religion of the Dalits, the people on the bottom of the reconstituted caste system. Buddhism flourished in Tibet, China, Korea, Japan, Southeast Asia, and more recently in the West.

These days, however, the more sophisticated Buddhists are not limited to monasteries and nunneries but also live in modern communities that pretty much ignore those institutions. If religion is defined as membership in denominations, these modern Buddhists are not exactly religious. But they recognize their trajectories through their various societies and think in those terms. Sophisticated modern Buddhists treat their pantheon of gods as legends and do not worship them as such. Rather they see consciousness as the Ultimate and take their various approaches to consciousness as atheistic. This approach to consciousness as declining deliberation and intentionality, and acting as finite or infinite beings within the world, is what makes these sophisticated approaches Buddhistic.

The Hindu approach slides through its break on the principle that persons with deliberation and action are subject to the law of karma and therefore cannot be ultimate. This slide through might be more gradual than happens in Buddhism. It might also never be complete. But then examples such as Abhinavagupta make a good case that the break is final. Of course, Advaita Vedanta Hindus such as Shankara do as well. Shankara believed that only males of the Brahmin class could find enlightenment and advocated waiting through many lives to find that one. Or at least it is said that he believed this. But then in the end, for representatives of this life, this current birth is the last. Shankara of course believed in experience, not just notional knowledge. But if the experience of enlightenment in this life is as empty of ontological commitment as he said, why could not anyone who happened upon that experience also find release? With regard to the quality of his experience, Shankara's seems at the opposite end of the pole from that of Abhinavagupta's tantric experience. But do they not amount to the same in the end?

Today sophisticated Buddhists and Hindus are in the situation I have described. A very few, I suppose (I have met none), completely forget the paths that brought them to where they are, and where they are is meditative serenity in the nothingness of no-consciousness or the fullness of being in pure consciousness, a debatable difference. They live their lives in the ordinary world and it makes little difference what path is followed in the ordinary world, nor in what nations or social classes one lives. Most of the sophisticated people, however, enjoy that serenity but hold it in continuity with their paths. The most sophisticated of these, upon reflection, acknowledge that all paths might be equal, or at least several other larger ones than their own (and their own might not seem as good in fulfilled enlightenment as a new one). Most of the rest of them would hold to their own paths and take them to the fulfilled state of enlightenment. They would call themselves Buddhists or Hindus of some sort or other. But they are likely to take themselves to be in close communication with members of other paths.

To be sure, all of these people are characterized as somewhere along their paths, not only at the end. A follower of Abhinavagupta might feel enlightened and committed at the age of thirty but continue to grow for another forty years. Nagarjuna might have had his basic insights at the age of thirty but continued to work on the experience of the world with them for decades longer. The distinction between notional knowledge and experiential knowledge that I have employed here is by no means fixed. There are all sorts of connections between them that might be followed directly and indirectly, with much backsliding. Here are some of the variable tensions between the popular and sophisticated.

First, the most obvious is the conceptual polarity between the popular and the sophisticated in reflection. This is the one I have relied upon in this chapter because it refers most obviously to texts that illustrate its movements. Whereas Christians, Jews, and Muslims might have some overlapping belief systems, taking a semi-popular theology for worship services and a much more rigorous sophisticated theology for philosophical discussions, the representatives of South Asia do this far more solidly. They occupy diverse points on this scale of polarity as equally important. Sometimes they even might pay much more attention, and give greater value to, the less sophisticated. Much depends on how much they remain involved in denominational worship life.

A second scale for religious faith is that between intimacy and transcendence. Ordinarily, we would think of intimacy as related to popular religion with gods on the street corner as intimate and the sophisticated theories as transcendent. But it might work the other way, with the popular religious worship sights being abstractly transcendent while the more sophisticated meditations become far more intimate. Both Buddhisms and Hinduisms claim that the most sophisticated is also the most intimate. Nevertheless, in the experience of most people, the intimacy of personal experience is associated with the end intentions of religious reflections. For the people of multigenerational tantric paths, the intimacy of the tantric outcome is what draws the serious reflection.

Yet a third scale is that from widespread worship to private meditation. The widespread worship can be from popular assemblies and mere vacations to private devotions of intimate or popular forms. Abhinavagupta's legend of departing with twelve hundred disciples certainly seems like a sophisticated version of his religion. But likely he himself was more devoted to sophisticated versions of private meditation.

This is closely related to a fourth scale, that of personal practice oriented to that of a widespread faith community and to that of relative isolation. Personal practice differs from worship and perhaps is different from the previous scale. Whereas one might worship promiscuously, one's personal practice is more important and one's location on this continuum requires confidence in that community's integrity. It still is possible to worship in a more or less popular way but to insist that one's personal integrity is more sophisticated.

Yet a fifth scale ranges around the extent of one's community. One can assume a community of very wide scale, where the religious practices and beliefs affect everything in life. At the opposite end is where the religion makes no difference at all to how one lives publicly and is almost entirely private. Most people lie between these two poles and even shift their positions depending on whom one is with. Some people "pray" before they eat, others have no entirely connections between eating and religion.

A final scale is the intensity of commitment to the religious practices, no matter at what level of practices one might be. Sometimes the intensity is completely lacking and one is not aware of any particular religious element in life. Sometimes it is merely inherited from parents, is involved in rejecting one's parents' religion, or is rather frivolous. Other times it is very important indeed, perhaps giving order to the whole of one's life, or at least a part of it, sometimes taking over the whole of it. In classical Buddhism and Hinduism, it is customary to think of the late stages of life, those beyond the householder's responsibilities, as devoted rather much, if not wholly, to religion. These distinctions might still be observed today in some places, but one's work has taken over from householder's responsibilities for defining one's life. Retirement might be the equivalent of the forest wanderer stage of life and might focus to a very great extent on religion.

These scales, or something like them, or some alternatives, characterize the life lived relative to thoughtful reflection and experiential reflection. They lead from popular religion to more sophisticated religion: between popular and sophisticated reflection, intimacy and transcendence, widespread worship and private meditation, widespread personal practice and private meditation, the extent of one's community from widespread to personal private use, and the intensity of taking religions seriously, from nonexistent to overwhelming all of life. Each of these can be studied far more. But here my point is that they mix around in an individual Buddhist or Hindu's life, shifting among themselves and changing throughout life. By no means do I intend that one naturally progresses toward greater intensity of religiousness. One might end up with nothing at all.

Mixtures

It is remarkable to Western comparativists that the Chinese do not make more of their theories of Ultimacy than they do. Compare the treatment of Ultimacy as an agential god in Western Asian religions with the treatment of Ultimacy in South and East Asia. I believe it is because there is a hint of leftover intentionality in West Asian religions that people are concerned to be looked at favorably by God, even though officially that is impossible. Aquinas's God is pure Act of To Be who has no mind to change, being already always fulfilled in actuality with no potentialities. Yet Aquinas's God has all sorts of intentionality, will, and intelligence when looked at across the Summas. All this is justified on the grounds that the pure act has to have all the finite acts within it.

God on the model of pure consciousness, however, has no intentionality. It is the sheer registration of objects of consciousness, about which a clear consciousness simply registers. The nature of "registration" is itself a complicated debate. God as pure consciousness has the attractiveness of complete quiescence and so it can be an ideal for human persons, but only for sheer union, not for union in will, desire, or other agency.

The Ultimate as the spontaneous emergence of being or non-being has no intentionality at all. The model of spontaneous emergence, as in China, is not itself a model for human worship. Rather, worship for the Chinese elite Confucians is to assume the right relation to the Ultimate, not to try to be it. The right Confucian relation is perhaps to gesture in awe to the deep underpinnings of things in non-being. To be sure, many Chinese worship gods and ancestors in various senses. The same people might worship Daoist deities, Buddhist spirits, and Confucian gods such as the gods of the kitchen. The Chinese philosophical theologians, however, rise above these things and attend to the spontaneous emergence of the Dao in various forms, which are not human, might even be non-being, and are known only in knowing the Dao that can be named, the Mother of things.

In the way I have told the story, our comparison has proceeded in the following way. We begin with West Asian models, all assuming agential realities. Then we move to having both the individual monotheisms and the pluralistic paganisms united with notions of Plotinus's One beyond Being and the like. With the Indian notions of divinity, we see that the divinity in the Gods is more like consciousness and less like agency. The great gods do not act so much as rule, something like Aquinas's God. But then the gods are all subject to karma insofar as they involve agency, and thus they are not Ultimate. The great gods cease to be many and are more like pure consciousness.

But what about Chinese images of the Ultimate? The personal images of the Sky God with a mandate lurk in the distant background. But the naturalistic images of spontaneous emergence are solidly affirmed.

The Dao is not like any kind of god. The emergence of the world from the Ultimate of Non-being and from the Great Ultimate have no connections with persons. Persons are organized way down the line, with yin and yang and a consciousness of the Dao emerging only late.

All this comparison has been moving East from starting in the Western religious traditions. What if we began with the East and moved West? Then we would see philosophical theology as being at home first with nature and relating the human to Ultimacy as a part of nature. Ultimacy would be understood as the ground of nature that includes the human. Ethics might be related to the Dao, or Non-being, or the Great Ultimate, as objects of awe. But it would not be oriented to becoming that ground. A comparative philosophy that begins in the East and moves West to South Asia discovers something profound about personhood that makes consciousness a model for the Ultimate. And then it moves farther West to discover the agent in personhood that can function as a model for the ultimate, something contrary to the South Asian model. These personhood models also must be taken into account to develop an adequate comparative category of Ultimacy.

I take it myself that the model of the Ultimate that allows for both naturalism and the two divergent senses of personhood is one of pure creation. All natural or personal traits are created, as well as all other determinate traits. Prescinding from everything created, the pure creation is simply an act that has the world as its product. That act is indeterminate and even to call it an act is to refer to its created creation. Were there no creation, there would be no act. Sheer nothingness. Not even nothingness, which gets its meaning from the erasure of all things. But because there obviously is a creation, we can speak of the creative act. Every other characterization depends on how we characterize creation, and the characters of the natural Dao, the pure consciousness, and the pure agent are candidates. In fact, they are so obviously candidates that the characterization of creation must allow for them. The category of the Ultimate must be vague enough to allow for all three cosmologies, and others as well.

It is important to emphasize once again the dynamic nature of the religions and philosophical theologies mentioned. All of the religions run the gamut from the most popular manifestations through alternative philosophical theologies and toward some kind of basic unity. The unity in East Asia is something like that of non-being behind or within the Great Ultimate. The unity in South Asia is something like pure consciousness as we glimpse this. The unity in West Asia is something like that of infinite actuality with no potentialities to limit it. Of course, there are variants within each major tradition, and the traditions borrow from one another. But most generally their unities are something like this. The most daring philosophical theologians in the South and West Asian traditions point beyond the view that the Ultimate is a thing, a substance. Those in the East Asian traditions point beyond a process. But one of the things we learn from global philosophical theology is that these traditions are trajectories, not positions. When we are pursuing philosophical theology, we are not to stop with any one position and say that this is "the tradition." The tradition is the trajectory with many philosophical theologians arrayed along the way. We must think toward the end of the trajectory.

I have put forward my hypothesis about the category of the Ultimate, namely that it is an ontological act of creation with all determinate things being products of the act. Of course, it needs to be proved in countless other ways. It would need to be made intelligible with some account of determinateness that would apply to all possible cosmologies. It would need to be proved with application to our own cosmology, about which there are still many debates. Especially, it would have to be proved with regard to any possible trajectory of cosmologies that might come from future generations of scientists. Furthermore, it would have to be proved to be applicable to all generations and races of religious people, assuming that my definition of religion above is generally helpful. It is, after all, only a hypothesis, and the fallibilist epistemology upon which I am relying here suggests that any hypothesis is subject to revision or downright rejection. But hypotheses should not be revised or rejected until there is reason to do so, and reasons have not shown up to criticize the hypothesis I have put forward for the category of the Ultimate.

Objections can be made to my category, of course. Anywhere along any of the trajectories a person can say simply, "Stop here! Common sense, tradition, or revelation says this is as far as we should go looking for the Ultimate." Commands like this shut off appeal to reason, however, and appeal instead to the will to shut off. They are fine so long as there is no reason to look beyond the cutoff point. But as soon as there is such reason, philosophical theology must go beyond. Subtler objections of this sort can also be made. For instance, it can be argued that only a certain spot on the trajectory, usually rather far ahead, is intelligible and that the alternatives are not, justifying that initial spot. It can be argued, for instance, that the idea of something coming from nothing is unintelligible because only a cause with as much reality as the effect can explain something. But then there would be no real creation. Or it might be argued that a naturalism is unintelligible because only consciousness is intelligible. But then there would be no objects of consciousness, such as this alleged mistake. Or it might be argued that anything other than agential being is unintelligible because any creation requires actual will. But then the agent's will would be differentiated and not pure. It seems to me, from my perspective, that the idea of an ontological creative act of the sort defined here is intelligible.

But before pursuing the question of the nature of religion as such at greater length, let us switch to the level of philosophical sophistication and consider, in a preliminary fashion, Ultimate reality as such. This first consideration of Ultimacy is at once a continuation of what various religions have thought about Ultimacy, and it is also my own philosophical theology. It is not only sophisticated comparative or history of religions but rather metaphysics.

Ultimacy

What is Ultimate? This is the most important and central metaphysical question, as well as the most important religious one. I believe, for reasons that will be apparent throughout this volume, that the argument for this metaphysics begins with finding the basic question. So let us ask whether the Ultimate is something determinate or indeterminate.

If it is determinate, it is either a smallest something, a largest something, or a process. If it is smallest, like a property that attends all the things that have being, and it is determinate, then it adds one more thing to the many and needs a larger category to encompass them all. If it is largest, and determinate, it is like a box that contains all things and is different from the things it contains, therefore needing yet a larger category. If it is a process, and determinate, it must also be indeterminate because it is always on the way to becoming something different. Therefore, the Ultimate is not itself determinate and must be indeterminate. This is a huge conclusion just by itself.

What kind of Ultimate could be indeterminate? The only relevant hypothesis I know of is that it is an ontological creative act with no nature of its own apart from what it creates but that it has the nature of what it creates. This is an extraordinary hypothesis. The act creates only completely novel products; everything determinate is created. The act "before" creation has no potentialities; it has no features such as goodness or wisdom. In fact, there is no "before" the existence of determinate things. Because all temporal distinctions are determinate, the act must be eternal; because all spatial distinctions are determinate, the act is immense or unmeasurable. Prior to creation of anything, in any sense of "prior" you might want, there is nothing, no act, just nothing. Eternity and immensity are features of the act that come from its product. The ontological creative act exists only given the creation of determinate things.

The determinate things are harmonies integrating the other things to which they are related. Each is a one for the many of the others. But the others also are ones for their manys. Each of the many has its own essential conditions whereby it is external to the others. The essential features of each harmony are external to the ways they are related, external to all the ways other harmonies function in any one harmony.

The context of *cosmological* togetherness consists of all the ways harmonies function in other harmonies, all the ways they are related to one another. Strictly speaking, all these relations are constituted by conditional components of one or another of the determinate things. Determinate things have both essential and conditional components because they are related but also independent.

The *ontological context of mutual relevance* is all the many determinate things existing together, in whatever patterns of harmony they have. The ontological creative act creates all the many to be together in the context of mutual relevance. The creative act is nothing other than all the many existing together. But they would not do so on their own because they have their own individual essential components. Therefore they are created to be together as the collective termini of the ontological creative act. Whatever kinds of temporal or spatial relations there might be, they are modes of togetherness and are possible only because of the creative act. There exists a multitude of determinate things. Therefore the Ultimate is the ontological creative act.

A determinate thing is a harmony of its essential and conditional components. The conditional components constitute its relations and the essential ones determine how the relations come together in each determinate thing. Each determinate harmony has its own essential way of uniting its components and therefore its own cosmological relations.

This is true for us, although we see so many overlapping harmonies that we apprehend most things together and in overlapping cosmological ways.

I have spoken here of each determinate thing and its relations. We can also speak of the field of determinate things, or rather, of two fields. The first field is that consisting of all the relations and the things related. I call this the cosmological field of mutual relevance. The determinate things are the perspectives on this field, and there are many of them. But there is also the field of the things considered absolutely, with their essential as well as conditional features. This is the field in which the determinate things exist together as external and internally related. I call this the ontological context of mutual relevance. This ontological context embraces all determinate things in their various relations. Strange? Right!

Why mention the ontological creative act at all? Why not just stay put with the ontological context of mutual relevance? Because that ontological context is itself an abstraction from the ontological act. By themselves, the determinate things could not be together. They need to be made together. This ontological making is the ontological creative act that includes the made products as its termini. Precisely because each determinate thing is external to the others, it is alone, not connected. Nevertheless it is determinate and therefore also connected. So each determinate thing exists by virtue of being made with the other things.

The determinate things are made together with whatever diverse patterns the things in fact exhibit. These patterns are mainly empirical matters to be discovered. Given the creation, the ontological creative act has all the patterns in its termini. Apart from its termini, the act is indeterminate. This is the sense in which the Ultimate is indeterminate. But we can ask what the ontological act is apart from its products only because our minds exist and we can ask about these things. *Really* apart from its products, the ontological creative act would not exist, would have no features, would not be. That would be absolutely nothing, something not even conceivable. Thus the Ultimate is radically contingent. The Ultimate is not contingent upon anything; this is why it is called Ultimate. It just has happened, and we should be happy it has.

If you do not understand this argument, or do not see it as an argument, or think I have just gone crazy, don't worry. Just accept it as a place-marker about metaphysics. From the standpoint of the history of metaphysics, the theory of the ontological creative act is just one Ultimate metaphysics among a great many. Suppose you take as true Zhou Dunyi's argument that the Ultimate is Non-being that is real only when the Great Ultimate is real. Or suppose you look at Abhinavagupta's philosophy and find Siva always to be accompanied by Shakti who creates the world, and vice versa. Or look at Plotinus's theory of the One, Dyad, and Triad; or Aquinas's theory of the Act of To Be; or Descartes's theory of the God prior to any determination; or Spinoza's theory of God as natura naturata and naturans; or Leibniz's theory of God who cannot create without a sufficient reason. These are all alternative metaphysical theories to my own, some more distinct than others. If I were doing philosophy of metaphysical culture, I would have to relate them all and a great many others. Nevertheless, I intend here only that my theory is true and promise many arguments. You will discover more arguments in the following chapters. For now I ask only that, for the moment, you accept it as true for the sake of my argument.

What is the implication of a successfully defended category of the Ultimate for global philosophy? In one sense, the success is only a matter of comparative philosophy. One can say that all it shows is how the various trajectories of religions point toward a rather empty category. They all find themselves well represented there—that is the advantage of a fair category. But they might all be mistaken. The *real* notion of Ultimacy is something quite different that has never been thought about. Nevertheless, this total missing-of-the-mark is extremely unlikely. The very meaning of "the category of the Ultimate" comes from its long and elaborate discussions in the various world religions and philosophies. How could anyone define the topic without reference to the traditions, the more the better?

The real importance of a successful category of the Ultimate is its contribution to a world philosophy. Its rising up through comparisons can be subordinated to its functions in world philosophic systems. The category of the Ultimate has a standing on its own and must function as true within any system, or be shown to require revision or even rejection. Of course, considering it in a system that highlights ecosystemic philosophy, or philosophy of the person, or institutions, is likely to make those changes. Any implication of the category of the Ultimate in any system adds to its meaning and force, sometimes altering those. Or, to put the matter more generally, global philosophical theology is merely a part of global philosophy systematically considered. It is characteristic of any system that to alter one part is to alter the others also, sometimes in dramatic ways.

I hope in this chapter to have accomplished several goals. First, I want to make sure that you understand that I am really a philosopher and not just a preacher, although I am a preaching philosopher. Second, I want to indicate that the field of philosophy embraces the whole of world cultures, or at least those of South and East Asia as well as West Asia. Third, I want to treat my own philosophy as one among many, and yet as true. Fourth, I want to present my own philosophy as arising out of the trajectories of any (or at least three) of the great world traditions so that those traditions give weight to my own. Fifth, I mean these remarks to be only introductory and summary, some to be followed up in other chapters.

Part Two
Philosophers

Chapter Eleven

On Josiah Royce

Moral choosing is a penultimate goal.
Morals concerns the shape of the world insofar as we might affect it.
We should attend to the outermost imagined
As well as to the most precious intimacies.
But it is still penultimate.
Righteousness is to make ourselves moral.
It aims to make us good choosers.
We tend to ourselves mainly in the closely imagined future
And neglect the cultivation of distant righteousness.
Righteousness treats our personal identity insofar as we can treat it.
Wholeness is what we seek in the context of others.
We are not responsible for their righteousness,
But we are for setting the context in which become whole while they become whole.
The best we can do is community-building.
But no perspective exists from which we can imagine the wholeness of many wholes.
Others are a mystery to us.
We interact in many ways, we make them parts of ourselves, and we become parts of them.
We regard them in our morality
And defend against them in our righteousness.

> But we are irrelevant to them in their inner selves.
> Only the creative act treats all things together.
> The creative act is indeterminate and has no perspective.
> The creatures are together but also apart and have no perspective.
> Life has no meaning
> Except to love all the creatures as the creator does.

Royce's Angles of Analysis

Josiah Royce (1855–1916), a great American philosopher from its Golden Age, did not separate philosophy of religion from his philosophical orientation as a pragmatist and his approach to ethics. In this chapter I shall focus on Royce from the standpoint of religion, however, and this will determine the outline of my critical argument. Royce himself had many views of religion, depending on the angle of analysis at hand.

In his early (1885) *The Religious Aspect of Philosophy: A Critique of the Bases of Conduct and of Faith*, Royce entitled the first chapter "Religion as a Moral Code and as a Theory."[1] The association of religion with morality, not only morality but mostly morality, stayed with Royce until the late (1918) *The Problem of Christianity*.[2] Dwayne A. Tunstall subtitled his 2009 book *Yes, But Not Quite: Encountering Josiah Royce's Ethico-Religious Insight*.[3] I like Tunstall's naming of Royce's philosophical project "ethico-religious insight." Royce's 1912 *Sources of Religious Insight* bears the association with morals even though its primary focus is epistemological.[4]

Part of Royce's association of religion with morals comes from his pragmatism. Randall E. Auxier, in *Time, Will, and Purpose*, has argued persuasively that Royce's pragmatic doctrines and temper were present from the beginning of his philosophical career, before the label was invented and long before Royce turned to adopt Charles Peirce seriously in *The Problem of Christianity*.[5] This pragmatism says that the import of ideas is the difference they make to practice. Like William James, Royce was always on the lookout for the practical upshot of ideas, especially religious or theological doctrines. Not all practical consequences of ideas have to do with moral practices, however, and Royce also associated religion with morality in a narrower sense. For Royce, the central moral issue was the formation of the moral will that unifies the self and gives it Ultimate, that is, religious, significance.[6] This was made explicit in different ways in the two volumes of his Gifford Lectures, *The World and the Individual,* published in 1899 and 1901, respectively, and in *The Philosophy of Loyalty* (1908), but it was a powerful theme from *The Religious Aspect of Philosophy* to *The Problem of Christianity*.[7]

In very different ways, Royce always said that the formation of the moral will requires or presupposes a relation to the Absolute, interpreted as a kind of personal theism in his early career and increasingly as a community of interpretation in his later writings. So morality always has a religious dimension, where that means some connection with the Absolute as a Whole, a temporally spread out whole.

Yet another angle of analysis of religion for Royce was his steady interest in German idealism, as evinced in *The Spirit of Modern Philosophy, Lectures on Modern Idealism,* and *The Sources of Religious Insight,* as well as many passing references elsewhere.[8] This aspect of Royce might be of great interest to European colleagues for whom German idealism is a defining tradition. But I agree with Auxier that the connection with American pragmatism and its milieu was really more important for Royce and that he was part of that from early on. The decisive pull of German idealism for Royce was that it was a philosophical religion, a philosophical way of engaging Ultimacy or the Absolute, or God, in real life. Royce broke with the conservative evangelicalism of his parents early in his life and, like James, was interested in religious ideas and practices without much actual participation in a denominational church. Charles Peirce, by contrast, was a rather faithful churchgoing Episcopalian. Royce was deeply concerned about the practical effects in daily life of religious ideas, not so much in how church practices gave rise to or required justification from religious ideas or theology.

Yet another angle of approach to religion for Royce was that he was part of the great American enthusiasm for non-European religions exemplified in the previous generation by Ralph Waldo Emerson and focused, for most Americans, with the great 1893 Parliament of World Religions. Who thinks of Royce these days as a Sanskritist? Royce was a Sanskrit scholar from his youth, however, who read Hindu and Buddhist texts in the original. His knowledge of Buddhism was extensive for his time. Although it would be an exaggeration to liken him to a contemporary scholar of the history of religions, he did see Christianity as one religion among others and not as superior to the others as Hegel had thought. I think he wrote his magnum opus *The Problem of Christianity* more because his readers and neighbors would be interested in that religion's problem than because he thought that Christianity could be the world's religion. He did believe that the form of Christianity's atonement theory was required for the construction of a salvific religion.

My Theory of Religion

My aim here is to sketch a systematic critical appraisal of Royce's philosophy as it bears upon religion. I will not try to construct for Royce an official "philosophy of religion." Suffice it to say that Royce joined the German idealists in thinking that philosophy of religion has to deal with the first-order questions of theology. I will employ the categories of my own philosophy of religion or philosophical theology to structure the systematic critical appraisal.[9] To begin, I define religion heuristically as the human, symbolically shaped engagement with Ultimacy in cognitive, existential, and practical ways. Royce would surely be happy with this. The definition here does not identify religion with any or all religions, except insofar as they are venues for engaging Ultimacy or what he would call the Absolute, or the quest for the Absolute.

The first philosophical task around this definition of religion is to say what Ultimacy is. I say it is five things, five Ultimate Realities that provide problematics for religion to engage. Nearly all religions engage them, though sometimes in radically different ways.

The first Ultimate is the ontological Ultimate of an ontological creative act that creates everything determinate. The heart of my analysis here is an argument that for there to be anything determinate at all, it has to be within a plurality of other determinate things with respect to which it is determinate. The ontological creative act cannot itself be determinate in any way except as being the creator of all determinate things. The determinate things of the world are the termini of that creative act and so the act is determinate in the sense that the result of creation is the determinate (and partly indeterminate) world. An ontological creative act is required because a plurality of determinate things needs an ontological context in which they can be relevant to one another and also somewhat external to one another so as not to collapse in just one thing. The ontological creative act is that ontological context of mutual relevance in which things can be together, not itself determinate because then it would be in the context requiring a yet deeper ontological context. I call this radical contingency of any and all determinate things on an ontological creative act the *ontological ultimate*.

Note that there could be no ontological creative act without its creating of something, and so the determinate things of the world are just as ultimate in their boundary conditions as the ontological creative act. Given determinate things, we have a cosmos, and so I call the ultimate conditions of determinateness *cosmological Ultimates*. A determinate thing, I argue, is a harmony with four Ultimate conditions: form, integrity with reference to its components, existential location with respect to the other determinate things, and the achieved value-identity of getting these components together with this form or pattern in this existential location. This analysis would hold for any world whatsoever as long as it is determinate in some way.

For the interest of religion we need to look to the world as habitat for human beings. What do the ontological and cosmological Ultimates look like within human life, such that engaging them in one way or another constitutes religion? People engage the ontological creative act as they hit upon the radical contingency of the world—why there is something rather than nothing—face death as the big surprise in life, or respond to life as gratuitous, arbitrary, surprising, and undeserved, even when things within life are bound by bundles of causes and consequences.

People engage the cosmological Ultimate of form mainly as the structure of the future that sometimes contains alternate possibilities among which they personally and jointly choose. This is the ultimate problematic of righteousness, moral choice, discernment of what the values are that would be actualized in the possibilities chosen, issues of moral mistakes, guilt, punishment, atonement, and the like. All religions have ways of addressing this complex problematic of righteousness.

People engage the cosmological Ultimate of integrity as the problematic of the personal quest for wholeness as they come to terms with the various components of their lives: their families, their bodies at various stages of aging, their friends and social situations, and the various ways in which they suffer. Some religions, for instance Buddhism, place the greatest priority on suffering; Confucianism places the greatest priority on relating to family and developing sagely skills. Some religious people, including Royce, place great emphasis on strenuous agency for integrating the self, whereas others sit and meditate.

People engage the cosmological Ultimate of existential location as the religious problematic of engaging others, other people but also other institutions and nature in the ecological sense. It may be hard to engage people within one's ingroup and one's local place. But it is far harder to deal with strangers, enemies, and people and places far from familiar contact with oneself but that require being appreciated for what they are in the existential field relating everything. Engagement of others is an ultimate boundary condition and hence is a religious problematic.

People engage the Ultimate cosmological condition of value-identity by asking about the meaning of life, and the practical consequences of life's meaning, or failure to have meaning in any human sense. These ultimate boundary conditions are part of reality, and every culture has to address them one way or another, such as every culture has to address its climates.

I am now going to discuss Royce's philosophy as it bears upon these five Ultimates scaled to human life: radical contingency, righteousness regarding choice, the quest for wholeness, engaging others, and life's meaning.

Ontological Contingency

The ontological Ultimate reality, I claim, is that all determinate things must be created together with their mutual conditions by an ontological creative act that itself is indeterminate save in what it creates. People have had many different ideas of what the world consists in and have many symbols for how that can be contingent. But there is not much religious power in referring to an otherwise indeterminate creative act. The world's civilized cultures therefore have elaborated three main families of symbols for that upon which their world is radically contingent. These symbol-families take ordinary things in the world and transform their symbolic meanings so that they approach the transcendence needed to refer to the ontological creative act, though they carry finite connotations that give them religious interest. East Asian thinking transforms the notion of spontaneous emergence, resulting in symbols of the Dao that cannot be named, or the Ultimate of Non-Being. South Asian thinking transforms the notion of consciousness, resulting in symbols of Saguna and Nirguna Brahman and the Emptiness of Buddha-mind. Roughly speaking, for South Asian cultures, what needs to be purged from ordinary kinds of consciousness are will, desire, intentionality, creativity, and commitment to agency, although there are many forms of this transcendence. West

Asian religions, including Christianity, transform the notion of person into symbols of a creator God, or several such, who manifests precisely the elements of intentionality purged from the South Asian families of symbolic systems. The symbol of a person as a creator is transformed into a high God who is the source of everything that is finite.

Of course, fueled by the dialectic of overcoming idolatry, Western thinkers push the notion of person to the point of indeterminateness or pure simplicity, as in the Neo-Platonic One beyond all determination and the Thomistic pure Act of To Be. Only mystics take religious comfort in the One beyond Being or beyond the pure Act of Esse. But there is a trajectory of transformation of the symbol of a personal agent that carries religious weight, allowing for the at least temporary supposition that God is a person with personality, rationality, will, and deliberate creativity. The advantages of this supposition are many, including the hope that if we can know the mind of God the Creator, we can know something about what to expect of ultimate significance in life.

A decisive philosophical question thus is whether rationality, as it might be found in God, is contingent upon creation or is itself a necessary condition for creation. The ontological creative act, on my hypothesis, and the Neo-Platonic One and Thomas's Act of To Be insist that rationality itself is fundamentally contingent on determinateness: A is not non-A only in reference to determinate things. But most Western theists, especially Protestants, have identified God the Creator as essentially rational and necessitated to create rationally. The Absolute Idealists, to speak roughly, took rationality or pure knowing as the hallmark of God, in one way or another.

Insofar as Royce was such an idealist, he too identified God as the rationality that measures our own finite and error-filled thinking. His early argument for the Absolute on the basis of the possibility of error was a stroke of genius.[10] His deep commitment to temporality, however, as Auxier has pointed out, did not let him rest with such a conception of the Absolute and he moved increasingly to a conception of God as an ideal end for human rationality and also human morality.[11] This was not much like a personal God, and in fact is remarkably close to the theology of John Dewey in *A Common Faith*. In *The Problem of Christianity*, neither the word "God" nor the word "Absolute" appears in the index. The same is true for *The Philosophy of Loyalty*.

The result was that Royce was very far from having a robust theory of divine creation that could acknowledge the radical contingency of the cosmos. Royce was much concerned about the intelligibility of the cosmos and, like Peirce, James, and Dewey, was careful not to deny the absurdities of ordinary life. I think he moved from the supposition that there is a real ground of rationality to the supposition that there is the actual possibility that we might make things rational in the infinite long run through the interpretive community. But so far as I understand him, Royce did not wonder about the contingency of determinate being itself. There is no place in his theory for wonder and awe at the gratuity and arbitrariness of the fact that there is something rather than nothing, or even that there is intelligibility. The word "creation" does not occur in the indices of *The Philosophy of Loyalty* and *The Problem of Christianity*.

Royce, of course, would not take this as a criticism. How could an act of creation that does not have an internal reason or rationale explain anything, he would ask. I would answer that "explanation" is inappropriate to the question; what we need is "understanding" of how determinate things are possible, and a dialectical analysis of determinateness gives the answer, by being created together. This debate aside, Royce has cut himself off from the religious problematic of engaging the radical contingency of the world, something very important in most of the world's religions because of the real contingency of the world (on my analysis). His theology is not vague enough to allow for that possibility. In fact, he was deeply concerned to eliminate vagueness in favor of engaging the perfectly specific and concrete, a point made most decisively in *The World and the Individual* but also in his very long essay "The Absolute and the Individual" in *The Conception of God*.

Righteousness

The first of the cosmological Ultimates to be explored in reference to Royce is form: any determinate thing has form, and the form expresses the value of getting the components of the thing together with that pattern. For human beings, the most important engagement of form is in the choices that we make personally and collectively regarding which future possibilities to actualize, to the degree and in the ways we control what we can do. The possibilities among which we must choose are alternate ways of arranging what is actualized, and thus bear alternate values. Each choice we make determines us to be the chooser of that value, and cumulatively our choices go a long way to determine the value we have as persons. Some choices are between moral and immoral alternatives, and so we build our moral character that way. The values we bear as persons in large part come from the values of what we inherit in our lives, but often the most interesting thing about us is what we do with what is given to us regarding possibilities.

Royce is one of the clearest and most thorough philosophers of the modern era in analyzing how the value-character we have as persons, especially our moral character, stems from the complexity of our choices among possibilities. We might complain, as I shall, that Royce overemphasizes morality to the neglect of other problematics of religion. But we learn enormously from him with regard to the ultimate significance of character formation, personally and collectively.

Yet a peculiar blind spot disfigures Royce's moral theory. The field of future possibilities, including alternative possibilities, is what bears the values of what might be actualized. The values are in the possibilities, and the possibilities that get actualized give the value-character to the actual world. Royce recognized this on many levels. And yet the analysis he gives of choosing well, for instance in *The Philosophy of Loyalty*, is based almost entirely on considerations about willing itself, the integrity of a unified will, the integration of one person's will with the wills of others, and so forth. Here he is strangely Kantian, grounding morality in the nature of the subjective or transcendental will rather than in choosing among the better and worse possibilities in the possibility field of the future. Kant, of course, thought that a will determined by its object would be heteronomous, not autonomous and therefore not an expression of a categorical imperative, only a hypothetical imperative. Buying into a strict fact-value distinction regarding knowable nature, Kant wanted to avoid making choices on the basis of things' values. So he turned the problematic of morality away from the engagement of possibilities in nature and society into the problematic of personal wholeness. For Kant, morality is a matter of making us better persons, not making a better world. Royce wanted a better world, not just better choosers. Because of Royce's theory of how choice among value-laden alternatives determines moral character, he did not have to say that categorically imperative choices are determined solely by the character of the act of will. He could have said that good and bad choices are measured by the values in the alternative possibilities among which choices are made. The fact that choices among value-differentiated possibilities determines, in part, the value-identity of the chooser is what determines the categorical imperative in those instances in which the value-differences are between better and worse rather than simply among different kinds of value. Royce recognized this point in many ways. And yet in *The Philosophy of Loyalty*, when it came to giving content to morality Royce did not enter into an analysis of possibility fields but rather retreated in Kant's direction to his intriguing version of a universal will, the loyalty to loyalty as such. From the standpoint of religion, concerned with the ultimacy of possibilities and the obligation they place upon us, this deflection of attention from the content of possibilities is a blind spot.

A negative result of this is a skewing of the process of the discernment or analysis of the values in alternate possibilities. We know the possible future by means of the signs we have for understanding it. Given Royce's concern for will, and for the form of a community of willers or interpreters, those aspects of will, with individual and collective willers, are the things that stand out in his philosophy for the appreciation of future possibilities. To be sure, he recognized that the field of possibilities included structures of social institutions of many sorts and of the natural environment. His way of seeing the world of possibilities was not like those Personalists who thought that only persons are fully real; he saw the moral importance of social and environmental issues. But he was skewed from seeing that these issues have religious importance because they are ways of engaging the ultimacy of form. The religiously important possibilities, in his view, are those bearing on human will, particularly a community of wills.

One more aspect of the religious problematic of righteousness is what to do with moral failure, with guilt. On this point Royce was convinced of the importance of atonement, the main plot of *The Problem of Christianity*. Given the nigh universality of guilt or sin, the Beloved Community was to be a community of sinners for whom atonement had been made. A sinner can be accepted into the Beloved Community by the community because atonement has been made universally for sinners. I will avoid the complexity of Royce's Christology here, and his interpretation of St. Paul's views on the importance of the church. I will also avoid the complexity of his theory that sin consists at bottom in action contrary to loyalty and that atonement is the restoration of loyalty to loyalty, although I recommend the book by Mathew A. Foust *Loyalty to Loyalty: Josiah Royce and the Genuine Moral Life*.[12] But let me ask whether atonement depends on actual acceptance by a real community. I think not. Repentance and forgiveness can take place in the absence of any actual community, although the signs for understanding and effecting this come from relevant traditions. Let me also ask whether the need for atonement is the only way to understand moral failure. I think not. In many cases the proper response by morally failing persons and by their surrounding society is simply reeducation and the attempt to make amends. Royce's preoccupation with atonement resulted from his consideration that matters of the form of the will trump misjudgments and bad choices. Sometimes moral failure comes from not paying attention to the possibilities and not doing the right things about them, not from an ill-formed will.

Wholeness

The cosmological Ultimate of integrity in a determinate thing for human beings is mainly the problematic of wholeness or the quest for the integrity of the self. By virtue of its form, any determinate thing has the unity its formal pattern provides; for temporal things, this means unity through time as well as synchronically. The quest for wholeness is more and means that the components of human life need to be present, working, and mutually reinforcing so that the important values can flourish. A person's wholeness is threatened by all kinds of suffering, physical, emotional, and situational. Positively put, health is important. So is relating to one's family, friends and enemies, and social situation. Among the many choices a person makes in the field of possibilities are those that pertain to the person's own quest for wholeness, although that is by no means the only kind of choice. Religious cultures have taken many different views on what constitutes the wholeness or integrity of the self, with many Buddhists going so far as to say that there is no own-being to a self at all. Some believe that the quest for wholeness is achieved by abandoning the quest itself and getting out of the life of choices. Western religious cultures have usually emphasized the aspects of the self that center on intentional agency, will, and the skills and capacities for acting, often in creative ways. With good biblical warrant, Western religious thinkers have often said that human beings are made ideally in the image of God, who is imagined to be personal in the way of a creative agent. Suffering in body and mind is largely construed as an impediment to good agency; the cultivation and education of the self requires mastering the knowledge and skills required for agency.

Josiah Royce made two outstanding contributions to a contemporary philosophy of the self as an ultimately important, and therefore religious, project. John E. Smith has argued that Royce's theory of the self is his most important contribution to philosophy.[13] The first contribution is Royce's interpretation of the self mainly in terms of will, and the second, his theory that an individual's will requires essential participation in community.

Royce's emphasis on will, especially cognitively shaped will, was a theme throughout his career but received special attention in *The World and the Individual*. It provides the main plot of *The Philosophy of Loyalty*, which stresses the importance of unifying many things willed into a unified or consistent will. Emphasis on will underlies that argument of *The Problem of Christianity*, which advocates the perfecting of the will to interpret. One of Royce's main arguments is that the will is the source of individuation. He was resolute in his individualism. He did not think that human beings are merged into some larger whole of society or God. He was suspicious of mysticism for obscuring the concrete thisness of each person. He was a strong advocate of treating individual will as the means of participation in a community, which he analyzed formally as a community of interpreters, citing Charles Peirce's semiotic theory of interpretation. Like Peirce before and Dewey after, though not so much like William James, Royce taught that community provides the ontological setting for the development of individuality. Royce is astonishingly helpful in understanding will and community. He combined these themes to provide a practical theory for finding a cause to which one can devote oneself wholeheartedly and in company with similar devotees.

The limitation of Royce's view of the self is that it obscures other elements of the quest for wholeness that might be equally important. Looked at broadly, the theme of will in self-making is diametrically opposed to the theme of the aesthetic that might evoke our interest. Just as his theory of morality detracts from the task of learning to look at possibilities on their own terms, so his theory of the will, especially in an ongoing interpreting community, detracts from those aspects of the self that are improved by just appreciating the main goods and evils of life. Is not part of the quest for selfhood in wholeness the achievement of a kind of resignation regarding one's health and agency? While it is ultimately important, that is religious, for people to act under the obligations of choosing well, it is only proximately important that they make good choices and win. We are all losers, and in several sense we need to be resigned to that. Both Buddhism and many Hinduisms say that the goal of life is to get out of it, though with different ways of conceiving this. Royce's Christianity aims to build the Kingdom of Heaven on Earth, and he says that we already proleptically can undertake willing about quotidian affairs as if we were in that Kingdom. But are not practices of meditation and the cultivation of mystical self-transcendence also valid aspects of coming to wholeness, at least for some people? In some important religious senses, the quest for wholeness involves a kind of deconstruction of the self. We act in daily affairs because there are good and bad things to be addressed. But is there not a moment in which we simply have to accept who we are in ultimate perspective and not expect the quality of our will, personally and in community, to do much to save us. I am not saying that Royce is wrong in his analysis of the will and community, only that he did not integrate this with other elements of selfhood that he should have been able to appreciate. His frequently expressed unhappiness with mysticism indicates that the contours of his voluntarism made it impossible to appreciate the gratuitous, aesthetic appreciation of life.[14]

Others

The Ultimate cosmological reality that every determinate thing has an existential location relative to the other things with respect to which it is determinate gives rise in the human world to the religious problematic of relating to others. The problematic is complex. It is easy to relate to other persons in our ingroup; well, it is not all that easy. But to relate to people outside our ingroup is far more difficult, especially if those outgroups are our enemies, challenging our right to exist and to have the culture we want. The Axial Age religions in one way or another said that other human beings have a right to be respected, appreciated from their own standpoint, and cared for just because they are human, and sometimes this compassion works at cross purposes to the interests of our ingroup. In our time, many of us have come to believe that we need to respect the environment on its own terms, not just in the ways it supports or impedes us. I would say that every determinate thing in our environment deserves to be respected and appreciated on its own terms, even when for other reasons it may be more important to alter or destroy it.

Royce addressed this problematic with his evolving theory of community, as we all know. For him, an actual community is constituted by mutual interpretation and shared possibilities. The norms for the Beloved Community include welcoming sinners for atonement, giving everyone the right to be interpreted and to interpret, and having some unity of a common cause universally acknowledged. Royce's way to treat those others who are outside of our community, or the Beloved Community, was to invite them in. Our own common causes, uniting our wills relative to our existential location, are imperfect if they cannot accommodate or transform the wills of the outsiders. Royce was by no means naive about the actuality of this universally welcoming Beloved Community; we do not have an actual community of this sort, only the actual possibility for such a community to develop. Communities that approximate his ideals for the Beloved Community are highly desirable.

But there is a fundamental metaphysical flaw in Royce's notion of community, I believe. He had a monistic streak according to which differences between things should be overcome with some kind of unity. Differences among people should be overcome by integrating them as individuals within a larger community. But why not let them be what they are, so long as they are not too destructive? The metaphysical mistake is that for anything to be determinate it has to be determinate with respect to other things—this and not that. Thus there must be a plurality of things and, although things enter into each other for mutual conditioning, each thing must have its own essential components that give it a partial externality. Genuine plurality requires that there be no inclusive determinate thing that internalizes all the other things as its proper parts. This is one reason the ontological creative act cannot itself be determinate except in the determinate things it creates. On the human level, this means that others should be respected even when they do not fit into our community. The reason they should be respected is that they have value in their own identity, even if that does not include being part of our community. For all of his stress on how individuals individuate themselves by participating in some cause within their community, there remains a totalitarian underside to Royce's Beloved Community. People are not primarily valuable because they belong together in a more or less unified community. They are primarily valuable because they have the natures they were created to have, natures to be lived out in ways inclusive of some communities and exclusive of others. Some people are only marginally communal.

Nearly every cultural tradition has places for hermits, for retirement in the forest, for the ideals of Mount Athos.

Let me stress the creative originality of Royce's monistic metaphysics of Being. As he put it in defining the Fourth Conception of Being (in *The World and the Individual*), to be is to be individual, and individuality is what would satisfy the purpose involved in our now too general ideas.[15] For us as separate individuals, our very being depends on the integrated unity of our various purposes in the individuality of our singular life. Our finite grasp of this individuality of self is always somewhat general or vague. Therefore, if we are really individual in this finite state, then we must be already the fulfillment of some divine purpose, and reflection on this bends Royce to Absolute Idealism. Because we interact with other finite things, there must be a comprehensive Absolute purpose that is fulfilled or satisfied at each stage in the course of the world. This was Royce's bent early on. Nevertheless, there is a sense in which our finite lives are indeed not yet fully individual because they do not completely satisfy the purposes they embody in perfectly individuated ways. Reflecting on this, Royce emphasized the temporal futurity of being, the importance of will working out its purposes, the cooperative sociality of social causes, the imperative of loyalty to loyalty in social process, and the normative unifying of social conflict in the absolute possibility of future interpretation. This bent Royce to sack the rhetoric of Absolute Idealism for that of the Beloved Community of interpretation and declare his explicit allegiance to Peirce in his later philosophy. *The World and the Individual* exhibits Royce bending in both metaphysical directions, a tension hidden by the strategy of making metaphysical arguments almost exclusively through epistemological considerations. Royce struggled from the monism of the Absolute to the monism of the Beloved Community.

The Meaning of Life

Royce's monism was decisive for the ways he thought about the question of the meaning of life, our fourth cosmological Ultimate determinant of human existence. What value is achieved in our lives, personally and collectively? What value does the universe have, if any? What values have we failed to achieve, and what is the significance of this, if any? Does it matter that we die? Does it matter that we exist at all?

Royce's answer to this question, at root, is that the meaning of life is the fulfillment of purpose embodied in will. In the venue of individuals, this means that the meaning of one's life is to have some integrating purpose that makes for a singular life. Life's meaning is frustrated to the extent its purposes are not fulfilled, dying too young as it were. Life's meaning is even more frustrated by not being able to make our many purposes coherent, by living at cross purposes to ourselves. Because we live together, we need common purposes in which we can play cooperative roles. Hence we need loyalty to loyalty and participation in an ever possible self-interpreting community. Lacking coherence of personal purpose, lacking participation in a possibly coherent community with an integrated purpose, individuals are cut off from the possibility of life having meaning, for Royce. Atonement is necessary to bring outsiders back in to the community because there is no meaning outside. This is worse than having or participating in the purpose but leaving it unfulfilled. I think that for Royce's bent toward Absolute Idealism, what looks like an unfulfilled purpose from our standpoint is fulfilled in Absolute perspective. For Royce's bent toward the temporality of the infinite Beloved Community, the finite failure to fulfill one's part of the larger purpose is still meaningful participation. For Royce, the question of the meaning of life is decisively monistic: to be on the trajectory of the fulfillment of a complex but singular purpose.

This can at best be a partial and biased theory of the meaning of life, however. I have many different kinds of purposes, some having to do with my family, some with my teaching, some with my thinking and writing, some with pursuing friendships, some with my health, and a host of others. These do not cohere in an overarching plan at all. My best hope is that the pursuit of any one of them does not interfere with the separate pursuits with the others—my wife, my students, and my friends would not think I neglected them in favor of the others and the dean, that I neglected my committees. These are all good purposes and it would be silly and hurtful for me to force them into some overarching plan or super-purpose. Royce would probably like Kierkegaard's saying that "the purity of the heart is to will one thing," but I say that the richness of heart is to engage many things, willing, enjoying, hating, and ducking. Purity is for those who are afraid of life's messiness. That fear is to be honored in its place, and so the search for purity and a cohesive plan of life is also meaningful. Honor also goes to those with the aesthetic delight in simply passing on the task of getting it all together.

A person's achieved value-identity as life goes on to the end has two parts. One is the identity I have as a subject, responding myself to what is given me and integrating that with many purposes or, if Royce is right, with the ambition of a single complex purpose. These are the things over which I have some subjective control and responsibility. The other part of my identity is how I objectively affect other things, other people, the institutions of my society, and my footprint in the natural environment. As a teacher I have affected students for many years, some of them significantly but most trivially. I have little or no control over my influences within them. What they do with my influences is their responsibility. What nature does with my metabolic cost is a matter within nature's processes, not with me. My identity is just as much my objective effects on things as it is my subjective persona. Perhaps the effects of my life will be felt centuries hence, for better or worse. If I have contributed to climate change, I will affect people I've never met and who will come generations later. All this is who I am and the meaning of my life in the cosmos.

No finite point exists within the world, especially within my subjective life, from which my achieved value-identity can be appreciated. I can get some feedback from the ways others condition me about how I might have conditioned them, but I do not get very far into them; this is especially true once the mutual conditionings get mediated at greater and greater distances. Only by assuming the perspective of the ontological creative act can I imagine all things that I might influence, and that is with the great metaphysical abstractions of thinking about all determinate things being created together with the ontological creative act as the ontological context of mutual relevance. In this sense, I cannot really know myself, let alone others. In this sense, the meaning of life is that it is a mystery from any finite standpoint.

Now if the early Royce and many other theists are right that the ontological creative act is itself a person with intentions and that God could look out on the world and synthesize a perspective to know the world in which all things have their own-being and also their mutual conditionings, then from that divine perspective there would be a real truth, a representation of meaningfulness, for the meaning of life. But then this God would be conditioned by the world and thus finite, and thus in need of a deeper ontological context of mutual relevance for being together with the world. It is better to say, I think, that the ontological creative act is the singular creating of all determinate things in all their relations, such as temporality. The creation need not have any overall unity, only the various patches of order as things relate as determinate with respect to one another. Especially, the world need not have any kind of overall unity in the form of a purpose and the trajectories of its fulfillment. That would be just too much anthropomorphizing. I think the meaning of life is just to let things be, including ourselves.

Perhaps my critical assessment of Royce's philosophy of religion has been unfair because it has employed an alien conception of religion to judge him, namely my own. Royceans might prefer that I work from his own categories outward. But I agree with Royce that the aim of philosophy is to devise ideas adequate to the full panoply of what might be experienced concretely. And so my critical assessment is that his theory of reality blinds us to the religious importance of creation or radical contingency, that his emphasis on morality blinds us to those possibilities that have value but perhaps not much to do with human character and to the obligatory character of the aesthetic, that his emphasis on unity of will blinds us to the religious importance of integrity as the acceptance of disunity, that his emphasis on community biases our ability to accept the independence and nonconformity of others to our sociality, and that his emphasis on a monism of meaning for individuals and the world hides from view the glories of a pluralism needed to articulate a plurality of determinate things in creation.

Chapter 12

On Alfred North Whitehead

Astonishing Genius

Rebellious son of a rural pastor,
Cambridge student of only math,
Learning philosophy from only talk,
Becoming a mind of astonishing genius.
Not since Plato thinking more rightly,
Even Taylor was not his equal.
Always growing, engaging wonders,
Yet ever keeping his ancient collar.
We can fill our life retracing his,
Every reading a novel revelation,
But visiting Grantchester sets us free
To be original, free, a genius.

Creation

Whitehead is famous for thinking poorly of the Christian doctrine of creation *ex nihilo* and in fact of most doctrines of divine creation. In *Religion in the Making*, he said there are three "simple renderings" of the concept of God. One, which he called the "Eastern Asiatic," is of an impersonal and wholly immanent order to which the world conforms, not an external order imposed but an internal order. A second, which he called "the Semitic concept of a definite personal individual entity," is of God as "the one ultimate metaphysical fact, absolute and underivative, and who decreed and ordered the derivative existence which we call the actual world. This Semitic concept is the rationalization of the tribal gods of the earlier communal religions." The third, which he called "Pantheistic," is like the second in that it affirms God as a single individual but treats the world as a phase within the reality of God, an extreme monistic conception.[1] One thinks of Hegel's Absolute in this regard, though Whitehead cited Persian Islam instead. Note that none of these straightforwardly affirms God as creator. The first explicitly excludes that and the third allows it only in the sense that earlier or more primitive phases of the monotheistic God give rise to the phase of God that is the world. Describing the Semitic concept, Whitehead said God "decreed and ordered" the world and that the world is "derivative" from this. But never did he say outright that God made the world, either out of himself or out of nothing. Christianity, Whitehead said, did not opt clearly for any one of these.

In his later *Process and Reality*, Whitehead developed his own concept of God that drew from the Semitic conception the claim that God is a "definite, personal, individual entity" and gave his own rendering of the Semitic notion of God as the source of all order, by means of the subjective aim at the initial phase of every concrescent entity. But he rejected the Semitic notion that God is the "ultimate metaphysical fact, absolute and underivative," saying instead that God is one among many and ultimately relational and derivative from all other facts. Whitehead drew from the Eastern Asiatic concept the notion that there is a universal order immanent in all things, affirming that all things, including his finite God, are subject to the metaphysical categories. Whitehead denied the Eastern Asiatic notion that this order is God, saying rather that God is one among many entities embracing that order and subject to the order, even if unique in a divine way. Whitehead's own concept of God radicalizes the third, Pantheistic, concept by saying that anything in the world becomes a phase in God and God too becomes a phase in everything else. His lyrical description of God in part five of *Process and Reality* sings the parallel inter-relationalities between God and the actual entities in the world. This parallel is no monism, however, but rather a strict pluralistic democracy of actual entities, one of which, God, is the perfect Boston citizen who votes early and often.

Whitehead vehemently rejects any conception of God for which God can be construed as the actual creator of the world, himself metaphysically absolute, imposing order on the world externally, and unresponsive to the worldly things as phases within divinity as much as divinity is a phase in each other thing. He thought this was the conception of a tyrant with bad moral consequences. So he rejected all the kingship and lordship metaphors for God in religious life in favor of the "fellow-sufferer who understands."

Judaism and Christianity, and later Islam, all held, contrary to what Whitehead would have liked, that God creates the world in some sense or other. Genesis 1 can be read as saying that alongside God there is a formless chaos that God brings to order by the divine Word; many contemporary process philosophers like this reading. Whether God's creative Word is wholly internal to a monistic God or something alongside was a matter of much controversy in the Hellenistic period. Lady Wisdom in Proverbs and Sirach, and the divine Logos in John's Gospel who was with God, who was divine and was that through which all created things are made, were candidates for this second divinity. The author of John's Gospel and letters, Philo, and many rabbis up to the time of the Jerusalem Talmud thought that the High God and the Logos are two things, however related.

In the first and second centuries, when popular Aristotelianism was becoming the philosophical common sense in the Mediterranean area, its doctrine of hylomorphism, or form and matter physics, reshaped the creation question. Is God the source of both matter and form or of form only? Justin Martyr and subsequent Christian theologians said God creates both matter and form. But just what does creating mean? There were many models of creation, but most assumed that God the Creator is extraordinarily transcendent, transcendent of most things or anything, but still is determinate. The view that God is some kind of very large being, perhaps even an infinite being, was subject to criticism for idolatry. Any description of God as a being (e.g., sitting on a throne in the highest heaven), was construed to be at best metaphorical, however helpful for liturgical practices. So we can borrow Tillich's term for God, "Ground of Being," for the background supposition of the extreme transcendence of the creator. There are two rough classes of Ground of Being conceptions of the creator.

The most common is that the Ground of Being creates out of its fullness of Being-itself its own reality, or substance, or whatever stuff the Ground is made of. So in Plotinus and subsequent Neo-Platonists, the High God is the One that is the absolute fullness of Being-itself, so uncontainable by anything outside that it constantly overflows. To overflow, it needs to create difference from itself, which Plotinus called the Dyad, or distinction as such, or pure intelligibility. Itself super-abundant Being, the Dyad must overflow into the Triad, or the World-Soul, which in turn must overflow into finite selves, which overflow into materially embodied persons with soul, which continues the overflow level by level downward. The lower levels are always one (if haphazardly), good (if also bad), and beautiful (if also disfigured). Because every level of being is made originally of overflowed Being-itself of the One, every level is good in its way; each way is distinguished as a privation of some good on a higher level. This Neo-Platonism is good for incarnational theology because it is the One all the way down; however each level is a contraction of its superior. But this sense of creation by the One as the Ground of Being-itself is not free. It all happens by necessity. God creates *a se*, out of its own nature as soon as it gets a nature, and that nature is and acts by necessity.

A second fullness of being-itself version of the Ground of Being-itself is Thomas Aquinas's conception of God as the pure Act of To Be. God is pure, simple, infinite actuality with no potentialities or internal complexity at all. The created world consists of things that are bits of the divine actuality delimited by their essences. In God there are no distinct essences, but in the created world there are. So, perhaps paradoxically, for Thomas God creates by making "nothings," delimitations, that can mark out separate created things. There is no ontological novelty in Thomas's creation theory, strictly speaking, only the separation of finite things from the infinite God by the divine introduction of negations, of delimitation that constitute finite essences. "All determination is by negation," Thomas and many others believed. God, being pure Act, has no potentialities to create things. God in a literal sense cannot do anything that is not already done within the infinite divine reality. Thomas was motivated by the Aristotelian principle that nothing comes out of nothing but only out of some prior or superior actuality. If nothing can come from nothing, only from something else with as much actuality as the effect, there can be no real novelty. In a strict sense, for both Plotinus and Thomas, creation is at best the unfolding of what is already enfolded in God (to use the Neo-Platonic term). In neither Neo-Platonism nor Thomas is God construed to be a being because beings have to have essences according to which they can be fit under some genus. Neither the One nor the Act of To Be has an essence that fits somewhere.

Sometimes it is said that the essence and existence of God are one and not distinct. But they have no character in themselves.

Creation ex nihilo belongs to another kind of Ground of Being conception. The first theologian to defend that concept explicitly was Theophilus of Antioch who wrote in the 180s CE. He wrote addressing a friend, "For first He created you out of nothing, and brought you into existence."[2] But he was not very explicit and wrote mainly to defend God as the source of all things, only once saying that things are created out of nothing rather than out of God. His emphasis was mainly on God doing the creating, not where the creation comes from.

Creation ex nihilo came into its own with Augustine. That immensely complicated and many-sided thinker argued that time and space (in the sense of positions outside of one another) are contingent upon being created and that therefore God cannot be a being located anywhere or in any time. Augustine in part used the metaphors of Neo-Platonism with its levels of reality and conceptions of infinite goodness and beauty in the One divine. But he was skittish about the Aristotelian substance metaphors that clung to the Neo-Platonic notion of the One overflowing or unfolding what was enfolded. Rather, Augustine identified God with the act of loving from which all good and beautiful things come. Loving and creating are the same thing, for Augustine. God is not so much a thing with properties (e.g., infinite oneness, goodness, beauty, etc.) as an act that does things (e.g., lovingly create or creatively love). God's creating of the world is not necessitated by anything in an antecedent divine nature, so Augustine could say that the creation of the world is absolutely free. But if it is free, and if one is blinkered by the Aristotelian view that to be a thing is to be a substance with properties, then God's free creation has to be preceded by whatever reality God has that would be what it is if God does not create. And so Augustine worried about God's aseity apart from creating. He wanted to say that God is love. But love at the ontological or divine level is not a disposition of a being waiting for some occasion to love or for something to love. Love is the act of loving, which ontologically means, for Augustine, the act of creating. So Augustine's theory of creation ex nihilo is left with tensions.

The greatest tension in all these Christian theologians mentioned, however, is how to reconcile the biblical depictions of God with the philosophical ones. Not only is God often depicted in the Bible as a finite agent interacting with things and people within a larger setting of world/ heavens/hells. In many of those depictions, God is a nasty piece of work. Marcion and the Gnostics thought the main biblical God was so nasty that the true loving God had to be a different being. For most other Christians, however, the solution was to find ways of treating the nasty passages as symbolic of something else consistent with the claim that God is good and loving, demanding the same of people. Augustine's world of pagans, Manicheans, and Christians was aswirl with different strategies of giving symbolic, nonliteral interpretations of scripture, and Augustine had his own approach. Thomas Aquinas famously had his doctrine of analogy. Whatever the approach in the great Christian theological tradition through the Medieval period, all had some combination of a conception of God as Ground of Being-itself transcendent of all determination and a conception of God as an agent in history, particularly involved with judgment and redemption. The images of God as a just king and loving father, obviously not literally true of the One, the Creator ex nihilo, or the Act of To Be, were far more powerful in the religious imaginations of various Christian groups than the honest anti-idolatry metaphysics of the philosophical theologians. It is the imaginative association of these personifying symbols with the metaphysical conceptions that allowed Whitehead and some of his followers to be offended by the image of God as tyrant or patriarch.

For the first millennium and a half of Christian theology in the West, the interpretation of the Bible and its images of God was under the control of the philosophical conceptions of God. Because God is good, either in the divine substance or in the divine creative act, the story of God commanding the genocide of the tribe of Agag must mean something other than what it seems to. But with the Protestant Reformation and the rise of widespread biblical literacy, that relation reversed itself. The language of the Bible became the language of theology for Protestants and philosophy became secondary. Calvin's magnificent attempt to build a consistent biblical theology, however much a failure, has continued in many forms down to the work of Karl Barth. The Roman Catholic Counter-Reformation intensified the subjectivity of faith, experience, and devotion to keep up with Protestant subjectivity but shunted theology to the cottage industry of defending versions of Thomism, from Cajetan and Bellarmine down to Mercier, Lonergan, and Rahner. The Eastern Orthodox subordinated theology to liturgical thinking.

The relative isolation of Protestant, Catholic, and Orthodox theology from the intellectual excitement of modern science had the strange effect of moving the real theological action during the modern period from church theology to the philosophy that found its public in the scientific arena. Descartes, Locke, Hobbes, Spinoza, Leibniz, Berkeley, Hume, Kant, and Hegel are usually thought of as philosophers, not theologians, although each had brilliant concepts of God, or at least of the problem of God, worked out to deal with the new world revealed by science and not much encumbered with biblical thinking. Descartes, for instance, was an ardent defender of creation ex nihilo, claiming that A is not non-A because God makes it so.

The astonishing theological importance of Whitehead is that, after half a millennium of the separation of church theology from philosophical theology, he, an heir to the modern philosophic tradition, has inspired a vigorous church theology. Most process theologians, as in the Claremont group, have been Protestants. Joe Bracken (SJ), is a systematic Roman Catholic process philosopher, along with James Felt (SJ), Joseph Grange, Joseph Hallman, and Elizabeth Kraus, among others. Whitehead's metaphysics also is growing in importance as an interpretive philosophic base for religions and religious cultures other than Christianity.

Mistakes

I myself celebrate Whitehead's game-changing metaphysics. But I think its theology is fundamentally flawed and that he would have done far better to have embraced the issues surrounding creation ex nihilo. Now let me make some points as an opponent of Whitehead.

First, he does not offer a suggestion about why there is a world rather than nothing at all. To be sure, that never was his intent. He meant the "philosophical cosmology" in *Process and Reality* to be a description of our cosmic epoch, not a metaphysical interpretation of how or why the cosmos is. But the radical contingency of the world is a thematic question in all the world's religions, albeit expressed in many different ways. Process theology either ignores that basic theological question or argues that the world is not contingent. If process philosophy ignores it, we cannot. If the world is not contingent, how can it be necessary if necessity itself is contingent?

Second, Whitehead did not address the problem of the one and the many. That is the problem of how there can be many determinate things different from one another but in part determinate with respect to one another. This problem is a powerful motive in the monotheistic traditions that say that the many determinate things of the world are created by a single creator. It is also a motive in the South Asian traditions to say that any diversity has a deeper unified ground. In East Asian traditions, it is the motive for saying that the complex is explained by the simple. In Whitehead, the problem comes up regarding how it is possible that there are many, one, and creativity interacting in the Category of the Ultimate. The Category of the Ultimate might be descriptive of process, but it is itself contingent in the sense that it needs a cause. Whitehead's Ontological Principle requires that any complexity in the world needs to have a cause in some decisions somewhere, but he did not apply that Ontological Principle to the complexity of the Category of the Ultimate itself.

Third, by limiting himself to descriptive philosophical cosmology and avoiding the metaphysics of being-itself, Whitehead failed to analyze determinateness itself. Yet it comes up crucially in the very meaning of manyness, complexity, and the determinacy of eternal objects subject to grading in the Primordial Nature of God. Had he analyzed determinateness as such, I think he would have seen that any determinate thing needs other determinate things with respect to which to be determinate and it has conditional components by virtue of those others. However, any determinate thing has essential components also that are not contained within those others. Moreover, the others have their own essential components not contained within the first. If determinate things did not have essential components external to one another, each would wholly contain the others, and the others could not be determinate things with respect to which the containing thing is determinate. Although there is a cosmological field in which things condition one another, the possibility for externality in that field depends on the things being together in an ontological context of mutual relevance that contains their essential components as well as their mutually conditioning conditional ones. This ontological context cannot be determinate itself, for that would simply make it another determinate thing within the context. The only thing that can be this ontological context is an ontological creative act, the end product or terminus of which is the entire world of determinate things, related to one another but in part external to one another. This is my version of creation ex nihilo.

Fourth, Whitehead's failure to address this point opens him to the interpretation that there in fact is only one thing in the universe, the concrescing occasion. Although not the only interpretation of Whitehead and surely not his intention, his claim that, given his doctrine of transmission, the real is always only from a perspective can mean that the past has no reality except when prehended into something presently concrescing, and the same for the future. On this interpretation, all real externality is lost. The world has no reality independent from God, as panentheists are wont to say, and God has no reality apart from a finite prehender from that prehender's standpoint. Only an ontological context of mutual relevance would allow the externality among things that prevents reduction to an absolute monism. Even to distinguish a move from this perspective to the next according to the Category of the Ultimate presupposes the ontological context of mutual relevance, that is, creation ex nihilo.

Fifth, the metaphysical engine that brings Whitehead to affirm the reality of God as he conceives it is the necessity to account for the initial subjective unity in a concrescing actual occasion, which is given by the divinely constructed subjective aim or lure. Because, for Whitehead, all reality is from a perspective, a beginning concrescence needs a perspective to determine which other occasions are in its past, future, and so forth, and this is subjective unity. God's provision of a subjective aim provides the perspective for any given finite occasion as its subjective unity. When fully concresced or satisfied, an occasion has subjective harmony. Assuming a Whiteheadian cosmology, however, the ontological act of creation ex nihilo can equally well give the subjective unity to an incipient occasion. In fact, this makes more sense than Whitehead's account, which, paradoxically, cannot say how an incipient occasion can prehend a subjective lure in God so as to get the subjective aim before it has the perspective from which to prehend. So the creation ex nihilo theory does away with at least this metaphysical reason for the finite process God.

Sixth, nevertheless, if there are other reasons to believe in Whitehead's God as an everlasting actual entity, the ontological creative act could create that God along with the world of finite occasions, both sides being in determinate parallel with each other. Or the creator ex nihilo could create the world plus Hartshorne's God as a society. Or, if one is worried about the problem of evil, the creator ex nihilo could create the world plus a good God and a bad God. Or, if one wants to be a Roman Catholic process Trinitarian like Joseph Bracken (SJ), you could have the creator ex nihilo create the world plus a Trinity of interpenetrating divine societies. The point is that one needs to have reasons over and above those accounting for why there is anything determinate at all to explain why certain determinate things are to be affirmed, such as determinate divinities relating to other determinate things. Those reasons could be something like Whitehead's philosophical cosmology.

Seventh, it has often been complained by Whitehead's friendly opponents, such as I, that the process God plus the world is more worshipful than that God alone. Now we see why. The ontological creative act of everything determinate is awesomely free, gratuitous, surprising, and undeserved from our standpoint. That is the object of worship. Any created demigods within creation can be praised for their goodness and booed for their nasty behavior. Or we can save theological language for the creator ex nihilo and treat the demigods as idols. Let the whole of determinate things be described plainly naturalistically. This requires a very healthy understanding of religious symbols, as from the Bible, and how they might be both affirmed and broken. From the standpoint of creation ex nihilo, the process God looks very domesticated and subject to being interpreted with special pleadings. God, the ontological creative act of everything determinate, is as wild as the creation itself, which is God's only nature. So I say in opposition to Whitehead.

History of Philosophy

Whitehead was famous, or notorious, or amusing for claiming that Descartes was the great empiricist, Locke the great metaphysician, and Kant the great dead-end. He had a rare generosity of mind and empathic understanding with regard to reading his tradition. But he recognized that for the philosophical issues dominating his own era, only some of that tradition is useful and figures might be useful in ways hitherto unexpected. At stake is the identification of the best resources for wise guidance in the direction of interest, attention, inquiry, living, action, and communal life. How did Whitehead see his own situation?

He claimed that a new set of philosophical categories, what we might call a metaphysics and he called a philosophical cosmology, is needed to account for the background of modern science. The old Aristotelian metaphysics-turned-to-common-sense assumptions understood that the world consists of substances that bear properties. Modern philosophy exhibited great creativity in modifying the theme of substance. Think of Locke's, Descartes's, Leibniz's, Spinoza's, Hume's, Kant's, and Hegel's widely divergent theories of substance. For all their brilliance, those modern conceptions of substance simply cannot model a world defined by modern physics mainly in terms of mathematical relations. The cosmological scheme that Whitehead worked out in *Process and Reality* is unlike anything conceived by his modern predecessors. Whitehead did liken his scheme to that of Leibniz in certain respects: Whitehead's actual occasions are a little like Leibniz's world of monads except that the occasions have "windows" on one another whereas the monads do not. His windows include the mathematical relations.

What Whitehead liked from Locke, and the reason he called him the great metaphysician of modernity, is Locke's conception of a substance having force that can be felt. This registers in Whitehead's system throughout the doctrine of prehension and up to the doctrine of the vector force of feeling in nature and in human symbolic reference. Whitehead resisted Locke's so-called empirical theory of primary, secondary, and tertiary qualities of experience, which is what nearly everyone but Whitehead associated with empiricism.

What Whitehead liked from Descartes, and the reason he thought Descartes to be the great modern empiricist, was Descartes's appeal to experience. Negatively, this was Descartes's rejection of authority in church and philosophical antiquarianism. Positively, it was his insistence on inspecting the content of experience, either in the intuitive inspection of mathematical and purely logical relations or in the experimental method of taking things apart to see what they really are. Whitehead's Descartes cautioned against imposing one's ideas on what one thinks one knows or experiences without actually looking. Whitehead rejected Descartes's cosmological dualism of corporeality and mentality, though he strongly affirmed that what one finds when one intuitively and experimentally looks has to include everything that shows up in either side of the mind-body dualism. For Whitehead, the initial physical prehensions of an actual occasion are material, the process of concrescence is all mental, and its completed satisfaction is all physical again. Of course, Whitehead's cosmological conceptions of matter and mind are wholly unlike anything Descartes would have imagined. Whitehead replaced Descartes "looking" metaphors with "prehending" and "feeling" metaphors.

Another part of Whitehead's situation as he knew it was that it was largely bereft of philosophical cosmology that might cope with the changes in assumptions demanded by twentieth-century physics. This was Kant's fault in two ways. First, for Kant, only the sciences can give us objective knowledge of the world, and philosophy is limited to critique and the construction of conceptions of human subjective according to which the sciences are possible. Philosophical cosmology, Kant thought, would necessarily breach the sharp divide between empirical reality, a construct of consciousness, and transcendental ideality, the misplaced attempt to talk about things apart from the self. Of Whitehead's great philosophical contemporaries, Wittgenstein, Heidegger, and Dewey, only the last made any attempt to talk about nature. And Whitehead thought Dewey's philosophy of nature in *Experience and Nature*, for instance, did not take seriously the rigor needed for a new philosophical cosmology.

Kant's second fault, according to Whitehead, was his whole conception of transcendental subjectivity that limited scientific knowledge to knowledge of representations rather than knowledge of things represented. Whitehead thought that Kant should have developed a naturalistic critique of pure feeling, elaborating the doctrine of the Aesthetic in the First Critique and skipping all the rest, that is, the transcendental logic and dialectic. Whitehead would have wanted the analysis of feeling to follow a Lockean "historical plain method" and give a genetic, non-transcendental account. Kant himself noticed that the first version of the transcendental deduction of the categories was much too genetic and Locke-like, and he completely rewrote that section for the second edition in a purely transcendental mode.

Yet a third element that Whitehead noted about his situation was that much modern philosophy was far too reductive in scientific ways and therefore obscured the task of giving a philosophical account of what he called "the breadth of civilized experience." The main plot of *Science and the Modern World* is that science is the creative breakthrough of modern intellectual life but that the romantic poets and others called attention to what is left out. For Whitehead, the broad problem of value, specialized in poetry, the visual arts, music, architecture, the politics of high civilization, and religion, needed to be integrated with the world as reductively analyzed by the sciences. Whitehead was not big on morals as a part of high civilization. This is where Whitehead appealed to Plato and counted himself a Platonist. Plato had a strong grasp of the breadth of civilized experience and at the same time looked to mathematics as the conceptual key for holding much of this together. Whitehead appropriated this and in many ways and places argued for the cultivation of the *appreciation* of things, not just the ability to model them scientifically. This led Whitehead to thematize the necessary simplification of infinitely dense concrete reality and to insist that one of philosophy's tasks is to be the critic of abstractions. Beware the fallacy of misplaced concreteness!

The most important contemporary change from Whitehead's situation to ours, a change that he would most certainly recognize based on his own position, is the transformation from a Western to a more nearly global public. He did discuss other religions than Christianity from time to time, most especially Buddhism. But I doubt he ever thought he was writing for thinkers in those religions imbued with the motifs and texts of those diverse traditions. He was writing for the European/North American Anglophone world. In the more than a century since Whitehead began to formulate his philosophy, there has been a radical transformation of the intellectual background in which a philosopher such as he might write. For one thing, there has been a century of translations into European languages of the basic writings of the other great intellectual and religious traditions than the Euro/Christian. Although most American philosophy departments do not train students in the background paideia of non-Western cultures, they could and should. Whitehead would certainly agree. Moreover, there has been a vast outpouring of secondary scholarly works interpreting these works in their historical and social contexts. That kind of historical and social contextualizing is becoming important in academic philosophy.

This globalization of the public within which philosophy is written should surely relativize the Western philosophic tradition in ways Whitehead would not have imagined. He would have thought it quaint if someone would have said it is enough to relate to philosophy that is only German, or only French, or even only British, ignoring the rest. In our time, the whole of the Western tradition is seen as one among many, and surely not the only tradition to define what the interesting philosophical problems and methods are. Perhaps David Hall and Roger Ames exaggerated or epitomized and stylized the difference between Western and East Asian cultures. But their lesson was that the Western philosophic tradition is not only flanked by the Chinese but turns out to be not as good in their view. The limitation of their reading is that things are even more complex. And then add the comparisons with the South Asian and Muslim traditions.

A second factor would cause Whitehead now to supplement his reading of the history of philosophy if he were with us today, namely the increased recognition of the importance of semiotics, the theory of signs. I have two points to make about this.

First, Whitehead's own theory has a strange and ironic lacuna between his appeal to the breadth of civilized experience and his modeling of how actual occasions can give rise to consciousness. The former is detailed in its historical reference and eloquent in its evocation of civilized consciousness, as in *Science and the Modern World*, *Adventures of Ideas*, and *Modes of Thought*. The latter, in parts two and three of *Process and Reality*, labors mightily to build up a model of consciousness as a complex of propositions that achieve an affirmation/negation contrast. Whew! And that's all. Part four presents the mathematics for analyses of parts and wholes in vectors of feeling, but there is precious little there about conscious human feeling. In between the vast riches of civilized experience and the emergence of consciousness as an affirmation/negation contrast is the whole topic of interpretation, the use of signs, or hermeneutics. It is ironic that Whitehead says almost nothing about this except to give the philosophical cosmology of what he called "symbolic reference."

Semiotics was the brainchild of Charles Sanders Peirce, who was eighteen years Whitehead's senior and who died about a decade before Whitehead moved to Massachusetts. Whitehead surely knew about Peirce because Whitehead was a colleague of Charles Hartshorne and taught Paul Weiss, who began editing Peirce's philosophical papers while they were graduate students. Like Whitehead, Peirce thought of himself as a mathematical logician who developed a naturalistic philosophy of everything that was so bizarre it was ignored by most of the philosophical establishment, at Harvard and elsewhere. Whitehead would have been fascinated by him if Hartshorne and Weiss had clued him in. Volumes two, three, and four of the *Collected Papers of Charles Sanders Peirce* focus on semiotics, and Whitehead would have been one of the few philosophers who could read them with immediate understanding and delight. He seems not to have, for if he had, he would have picked up on the emergence of semiotics in European thought from Ramon Lull to Saussure and thence to Peirce.

Peirce's chief advance on Saussure and other European semioticians was to insist that interpretation is triadic rather than dyadic. The Europeans, down to Derrida and Eco, stress the relation between the signifier and signified. Peirce said there is no signifier except insofar as there is an interpreter who takes the sign to be a representation of its object in a certain respect. European semiotics lends itself to mapping signifier-signified relations within a semiotic system or within a field of consciousness. It is possible to say that nothing signified is anything except itself a conscious sign, with no real reference beyond the signs in interpretation. But for Peirce, a sign within its semiotic system can be used to engage something beyond the system. Perhaps some interpretations are interpretations of things within the semiotic system at hand, but most need not be. For the Europeans, the paradigm case of interpretation is interpretations of texts. For Peirce and his pragmatic followers, the paradigm case is interpreting the wilderness of nature, with scientific experiments as the organized methodological way to go, not the intermingling of horizons of meaning in a hermeneutical circle. Interpretation for Peirce is not a play of consciousness alone but, more basically, a natural physical process, just as Whitehead would need. Like Whitehead, Peirce developed novel conceptions of physical nature. For Peirce, an effect is an interpretation of its cause by means of the general law or habit of nature that the interpreting effect takes to stand for the object-cause in a certain respect. Whitehead's cosmology in *Process and Reality* can be read as one exemplification of Peirce's theory: the satisfaction of an actual occasion is the interpretation of the initial data by means of the intermediate stages of prehension functioning as signs. None of this is to say that Whitehead would have accepted Peirce's philosophy of nature. He worked on a much more specific, non-metaphysical level of generality than Peirce. But at least the opening is there to graft the whole enterprise of Peirce's semiotics onto Whitehead's theory of actual occasions, giving Whitehead the vast riches of the pragmatic theory of experience.

The second point, about what Whitehead might learn from the semiotic traditions he neglected, has to do with the experiential issues of focusing attention, that is, of focusing on foreground objects interpreted against a background that is already part of the interpreting. Peirce was deeply concerned with issues of intellectual and emotional control, not thinking that it is sheer will or that it is identifying objects that really are objects adventitiously set within backgrounds. More and richer work has been done in the phenomenological tradition that carries on European semiotics but corrects it with a reading of experience through the body. Merleau-Ponty and Edward Casey are phenomenologists who carry this out with rigor, and because Whitehead should be able to incorporate their work, he should acknowledge their antecedents in Hegel, Husserl, and Heidegger. The control of attention is a teleological move, something rejected by most scientists (except when it comes to their own work). Whitehead today would like to adopt the historical antecedents in evolutionary biology and neuroscience.

An offshoot of this point gives yet another resource for Whitehead's potential antecedents. Beginning in the 1960s, the psychologist James Gibson developed a theory of what he called "affordances," namely the organized value-structures in the environment that allow interpreting animals, particularly human beings, to grasp and appreciate largescale interpretations as a whole. Instead of summing up zillions of little interpretations of natural causal antecedents, the natural environment offers affordances for human integrative interpretations in which the multitude of values of things can be grasped holistically. We can "read" situations, this ecological biologist says, without a computer-like summing up of algorithms. Whitehead surely would reject computer analogies of mental activities and their mechanistic antecedents going back to Descartes and Hobbes, and this tradition of ecological psychology offers a way.

Ecological Thinking

The various points I have made about Whitehead's unusual reading of the modern Western philosophical tradition lead me to some final observations about Whitehead and ecological thinking. Much of the Western philosophic and religious tradition, broadly speaking, has set a high contrast between the human and the rest of nature. The Bible makes humankind the crowning achievement of creation and asserts that human beings should have dominion over the rest of nature. The classical Greeks distinguished sharply between teleology in nature and human teleology that reflects human purpose. The early modern period in the West depicted nature as mechanical objects and human beings, at least in part, as subjects. Nineteenth-century evolutionary theory ran against the prevailing view that humanity is above nature when it claimed that humans descended from lower natural forms, and yet still supposed that human kind is the crowning achievement of natural evolution. As naturalists, Whitehead and the pragmatists were anomalous in the Western tradition and very carefully reconceived nature to show how the highest achievements of civilization are complexifications of natural processes.

A new resource that Whitehead could now read into his background is the metaphoric system of South Asia that emphasizes the community of all sentient beings united by processes of reincarnation. This is not the place to do more than acknowledge the many different versions of reincarnation in South Asian history, most notably Hindu and Buddhist ones, as well as Jain; in each of those traditions are multitudes of divergent and contradicting schools. Some involve karma and some do not. Moreover, for many forms of Buddhism and Hinduism, the lives of reincarnation express a proximate truth that is superseded by a more nearly ultimate one but all together create an enormous sense of community among all sentient things. Whitehead distantly appreciated the metaphysics of Hinduism and Buddhism, especially the latter. But he did not attend much to the community aspects of the multiple lives of sentient beings. As we explore a Whiteheadian ecological sensibility, we can encourage a positive reading of those traditions fostering a community, with various appropriate responsibilities, of sentient beings. They remind us also that ecologies should not be thought of as static harmonies of elements but as constantly changing mixtures.

Nevertheless, the cultures of communities of all sentient beings still make a sharp division between such communities and non-animate or insensate elements of nature. It takes a stretch to get Buddhists or Hindus to have fellow-feeling for mountains and streams. In light of this, we should note that the Chinese traditions, especially Confucianism, has at least since the days of the *Yijing* thought of the breadth of nature as including human societies and individuals within it. In those traditions, there is no distinction except in the ways changes are put together among human life, sentient life, social institutions, rituals relating individuals and communities to mountains and streams, and natural things far removed from anything human. The Confucian traditions are more valuable here because the Daoist traditions sometimes cordon off much of human institutional life and pretenses at high civilization as "artificial" and un-Dao-like. At any rate, Whitehead today would be greatly strengthened to read the Chinese traditions as resources for his ecological philosophy. In principle, he already argued in the first half of the twentieth century for a cosmological continuum between actual occasions, human individuals as societies of occasions, and human groups as societies of societies and thence to the puff of existence in far-out space. He also had argued that any occasion anywhere and in any nexus of occasions is a bearer of value, a point about which the Chinese never doubted. Deference to the heavens, the mountains, and the seas, as well as to people in relation to oneself, is parsed on continua among all these things with exacting, if sometimes contradictory, attention to how differently to observe deference. China is a more natural cultural home for Whitehead's vision than the West, which he had to read so oddly.

Much American and European environmentalism and ecological thinking for the last century has argued for the protection of natural resources because they support human life; their destruction will be bad for human life. This reflects the view that nature is for the sake of humankind. Perhaps some make this argument because they think that only by appealing to human selfishness could people be moved to care for the environment. Whitehead would read this as a great mistake. Rather, all of nature, including the human and our high civilizations but also the heavens, mountains, and seas as well, bears values of specific sorts determined by things' internal and external relations. The aesthetic sensitivity to appreciate a great breadth of nature as well as a great breadth of high civilization needs now to be cultivated upon the resources of all civilizations. Peirce said this in the nineteenth century in his claim that aesthetics is the master discipline and that the law of the universe is to extend and better integrate harmonies of all sorts. The Chinese have had major thinkers who have articulated this splendidly, for instance Xunzi. And Whitehead presents a worldview that at the cosmological level makes sense of this point about the aesthetics of being human. There is no reason to think that specifically human interests are the most valuable things to defer to and support, although most of our deliberations are about things in the human sphere. Whitehead would agree with Peirce that although all human experience is guided in part by human purposes, the most important purpose is that of discovering the purpose most worth having. This might move far beyond what is good for human beings. In fact, for Whitehead, value is characteristic of any occasion whatsoever. Whether one believes in occasions or other versions of philosophical cosmology, I believe value is that broad. And deep.

Chapter 13

On Robert Corrington

The Unconscious

Hail to the Unconscious!
How great thou art!
Deeper than subconscious flow,
More original than ego,
Tethering us as separate selves,
Spreading into distant nature,
As effective in us now as
Binding to the primal state.
But only part of what we know now,
Obscuring what the mind reveals.

Psychoanalysis

Robert Corrington and I have had a very long philosophical and personal conversation, dating at least from the 1980s. We have talked about nearly everything in our philosophies, agreeing on most things and disagreeing in agreeable ways about others. Nevertheless, I have steered away from one major component of his philosophy, his devotion to psychoanalytic thought. Unfortunately, from my perspective, this is an absolutely central element in his philosophy. His whole theory of the self turns on it, and the self is itself central. So at last I turn to it.

Psychoanalysis is important in Corrington's first book, *The Community of Interpreters*.[1] It also occurs in his *Nature's Religion*, for which I wrote a foreword.[2] In fact, it occurs in nearly all of his books. But most of all it is the main topic, or theme, of *Nature's Sublime: An Essay in Aesthetic Naturalism*, which is dedicated to me.[3] So I guess he really wants my views on his use of psychoanalysis!

Corrington wants psychoanalysis to be not only the analysis of the unconscious and the conscious within human beings. He also wants it to be a characteristic of the world, the unconscious of nature and the becoming conscious of nature. His overall scheme is nature's unconscious, the collective unconscious, personal unconsciousness, personal consciousness, and nature's consciousness. That is the rhythm he works out in *Nature's Sublime*. All this movement is what he calls "selving" and it operates in nature as well as personal selves.

Of course, he needs to baptize all these elements with his own twists. His fundamental distinction is between *natura naturans* and *natura naturata*, or nature naturing and nature natured. "*Natura naturing* can be defined as, 'nature perennially creating itself out of itself alone,' while *nature natured* can be defined as 'the innumerable orders of the world,' which have no collective outer shape or contour."[4] Spinoza, drawing on medieval sources, distinguished *natura naturans* and *natura naturata* slightly differently. For Spinoza, *natura naturans* means an eternal making of *natura naturata* but only the latter is temporal. For Corrington, *natura naturans* is itself part of time. I agree with Spinoza in the sense that the distinction should mirror something of that between the act of creation and the created. More on this later.

Justus Buchler's ordinal metaphysics is the main inspiration for Corrington's analysis of nature natured.[5] Corrington expands this notion of ordinality into ordinal hermeneutics and ordinal metaphysics and gives his own version of the latter in "The Categorial Schema," a truly brilliant essay.[6] Ordinal hermeneutics studies nature natured while ordinal metaphysics studies both nature natured and nature naturing, to put the matter roughly. Ordinality runs through Corrington's arguments here and elsewhere.

Corrington analyzes psychoanalysis in much this way. Freud, of course, is the genius founder, but Corrington finds him supplemented greatly by Jung, Rank, Reich, Kohut, and Kristeva. All of them deal in their ways with the unconscious and its relation to the conscious. Moreover, all of them deal in their ways with sickness, with pathology, with ways of impeding or distorting the unfolding of consciousness. Finally, all of them deal in their ways with more than the human patient, with primal forces or unconsciousness. Psychoanalysis generally rests upon or derives from the larger philosophy of Schopenhauer's Will; Schopenhauer, like Corrington, dealt with both the universe and the personal, using the category of Will in a larger and stranger sense than the clinician.[7]

After a long and informative introduction, Corrington begins *Nature's Sublime* with a chapter on "selving," the becoming a self that is the interesting order for a human person. The background for selving, for him, is the universal unconscious. This is the underlayment of all of nature with its unconscious structures. He might have called it simply "nature" insofar as it is unintelligent, nonconscious, and somewhat unknown by later thinking. But he wants to emphasize that it has powers and processes that are ongoing and that sweep up the infant in their forces. This leads to infants' own developing unconscious, something that begins with their birth and develops by natural processes and by accident. Here, he follows pretty much Freud's development of the oral, anal, and oedipal or sexual stages. These always play out on the unconscious processes of nature in various ways. They also develop, or are developed by, a collective unconscious. Corrington stresses the various ways by which the movement through these unconscious stages can be thwarted, diminished, misguided, and arrested. He is attentive to the ways by which therapists address these faults and attempt to bring the person around, more or less, to normalcy.

All this time, of course, infants are also developing consciousness with its conscious thoughts and superego (in one sense or other). The therapist's entrance to the personal unconscious is through consciousness mainly, although Rank and others operate on a much larger scale. Although there are many variations on this, generally a healthy person is one who has a good balance between personal unconscious and superego's sexuality. Having a good sex life is just part of maturity. Sex is so important because it has so many unconscious, collective unconscious, personal unconscious, conscious, and super-egoistic levels.

Chapter two of *Nature's Sublime* is about the social maturation of the self. Corrington is dead set against putting private selving first and its social dimensions second. Maternal figures are present prior to birth and many other figures and institutions enter very quickly. The ways by which people establish eye contact are early and are learned, with different cultures teaching differently. Languages enter at the prelinguistic stage and so do other sounds as in music. There in fact are communities of interpreters in which infants are brought up and that have their destructive as well as constructive components. Corrington follows psychoanalysts in depicting these and correcting them more or less. Communities of interpretations are where consciousness flourishes and conceptions of the self are developed and furthered. Communities of interpretation are where the superego's dictates to consciousness, however different they are culture by culture, show up.

Chapter three, "God-ing and Involution," draws an important distinction between evolution and involution. The first two chapters deal mainly with the infant evolving to be a participating mature person in communities of interpretation. Involution, by contrast, looks less to external standards and more to internal ones. The internal standards come into play rarely and with something of a shock to the external ones. They consist of images that provide new and different orientations of the self or part of the self. Most of us ignore them or are not even aware of them. But sometimes something does come into us from the outside that is shocking and that reorients the whole. It is usually the self who responds to this, or sometimes even a social self (an idea that is appreciated by many). Perhaps Jonathan Edwards represents involution most strongly, although Sri Aurobindo also represents it. For them, their lectures can open people to entirely new ways of seeing things. Corrington calls these experiences of "god-ing." By god-ing he does not mean the encounter with a divine being, a god, let alone a major God. Rather, he means that nature or society "gathers" itself in new ways to call forth a new response in the person. It is perhaps strange to call such a gathering of nature and society by the divine name "god-ing." Nevertheless, there is something uncanny and often a lot like a real God about this experience. Edwards and Aurobindo did not hesitate to apply divine language to this experience and in fact do take it to involve a real God.

Chapter four, the conclusion and the final chapter, is about "Genius, Art, and the Sublime." Corrington begins by pointing out that the true genius creates art. The rest of us, to some degree or another, appreciate it. The creation of art is one of the most important mature expressions of a self, and the better the creation, the better the self. He follows Aquinas in his interpretation of beauty, noting that it has special *integritas*, *consonantia*, and *quidditas* (not that Corrington has studied Aquinas—he gets this from James Joyce's *A Portrait of the Artist as a Young Man*).[8]

Beauty, of course, is to be found in nature as well as in humanly made products. The sublime abounds at the limits of our horizons and has the capacity to overwhelm our finite selves. Citing Otto Rank, Corrington links the sublime to a mature version of the birth trauma, something wholly unsettling to what has gone before. Experiencing the sublime is not only individual but also social. The sublime is the culmination of nature in human beings: as the unconditional in nature was our beginnings, the sublime is nature at our endings.

Limits of Psychoanalysis

There is no denying the power in Corrington's use of psychoanalytic figures for his development of the self, nature, and the sublime. It allows him to be sensitive to personal development of people as natural selves and also to see how this is related to nature in larger senses. I would not want him to give up these insights. But they do have limits.

The perspective of psychoanalysis is far too narrow for phenomenology and metaphysics to frame our current situation and its larger setting. It starts with personal psychological problems and expands from there. From Freud to Kristeva, its expansion has been tremendous but nevertheless far too worried about the self. Schopenhauer and Jaspers are mentioned, but their work is interpreted by Corrington largely from the standpoint of psychoanalysis. Charles Peirce is discussed with great approval but mainly in terms of his development of personal semiosis, with some attention to its larger reach.[9] For a book on *Nature's Sublime*, which might very well be Corrington's theory of the universe, this book focuses far too much on a narrow view of the self.

When it comes to the self, Corrington rightly notes that its career is one of maturation, that is, change, so that interpersonal relations are always shifting. He also rightly notes that maturation has to do with relating properly to the world in various stages. For Corrington, the world influences the infant as a precondition, but only pushing it to relate to things. Only the unconscious and conscious drives discover the obligatoriness of the world. But I think that, because of his psychoanalysis, he does not see the dualism involved in the very idea of self. Is it not the case that the obligation to do right by the environment (including the self as an environment) is a *precondition* for the development of the self? Is it not the case that the obligations of the world call to the person to take them up? He misses the priority of obligation.

Corrington's stress on psychoanalysis leads him to something of an imbalance between his ordinal hermeneutics and ordinal metaphysics. Of course, he is right to see that we need both. And it does not make much difference where one begins, with hermeneutics or metaphysics. Nevertheless, in one sense metaphysics needs to take priority, namely the sense in which it needs to be true regardless of whether his hermeneutics is true. Hermeneutics describes *our* experience, and that surely needs to have its metaphysics. But metaphysics needs to be true regardless of our experience in the sense that there might be no experiencers around. To be sure, we would not be asking these questions if we were not, but at least that possibility needs to be open.

Buchler's ordinality as such also needs to be questioned, although this is much less dependent on the psychoanalytic stress. Ordinality, in Corrington's sense, studies the forms of nature natured in hermeneutics and the forms of nature naturing as well as nature natured in metaphysics. In the latter sense, it traces the emergence of forms. But I think that the tracing of forms, metaphysically as well as hermeneutically, is at best cosmology, not metaphysics. Corrington's "The Categorial Schema" begins as follows: "0.0 The One is the Prior of all Priors. 1.0 The sequent Prior is the greater Nothingness. 1.1 From the greater Nothingness the potencies unfold via the infinitesimals (the first positive Prior)." But the infinitesimals are either indeterminate or determinate. If indeterminate, no progress is made toward potencies. If determinate, then the greater Nothingness is an act that already includes the determinate potencies. Therefore, there is no One or Not-One Prior to all Priors. There being no One Prior to the ontological act with its plural potencies, the most radical thing is the contingency of the act plus its products. Nevertheless, this contingency is not on a par with anything else in ordinality and the ordinal scheme can at best describe orders, not the absolute origin of order, which is indescribable. Order just happens.

Why would Corrington make this mistake, if it is a mistake? To be sure, he traces the dialectic of metaphysics nearly all the way back. But he keeps it within a constant chain of ordinal forms and does not answer the question of how that ordinality comes to be. This is because he begins, in his basic thinking, from psychoanalysis. He expands from Freud *et alia* to a cosmic psychoanalysis to ordinal metaphysics but not to metaphysics per se. This is the way it seems to me.

My Contrary Hypothesis

At this point, it is important for me to attempt to make my contrary hypothesis plausible. After all, we are dealing with fairly high-powered stuff here. I shall begin by restating my last point about metaphysics and then work my way back through the objections.

What is the ultimate reality in the world? The world consists of a plurality of things. These things are at least partly determinate with respect to one another. One determinate thing is determinate with respect to another determinate thing by virtue of containing a relation to that thing; otherwise, it would have no relation to it. Nevertheless, that determinate thing is not totally inclusive of the other nor is it totally included in the other; otherwise, there would only be one thing. Therefore, a thing that is determinate is a harmony with two kinds of features, conditional and essential. The conditional features connect it with other things and the essential features constitute its own identity. Ordinality (although I don't use that word) relates the harmonies by conditional features, and I call this cosmology. But what makes the determinate harmonies be together with their essential as well as conditional features? I say that this is the ontological creative act that creates all the determinate things with all their modes of togetherness, including their essential ones.

Given the creation of a spatial and temporal world, such as ours, the ontological act is unmeasurable and eternal, that is, creates things that are spatially external to each other and temporally before and after. Much more specific cosmology would have to be undertaken to say just what spatiality and temporality are and to say how the ontological act is inclusive of them.

The ontological act is singular but not One. Its singularity consists in its creating all the created things with whatever kinds of unities and relations they have. The singularity of the act is a character of its various products. It has no overarching Oneness, however, that is more unified than the plurality of things with their various unities and disconnections.

Apart from its creating of the determinate world, the ontological act is not real and has no structure, potentialities, or anything else. It can be viewed as the ontological togetherness of the determinate things so long as it is not confused with mere cosmological togethernesses. It can be viewed as the *existence* of all things so long as it is not confused with one thing existing over against the others; it is all existing together. It is the *ontological* togetherness of all things that would not exist without it.

The argument that I've given here and that I would go on to give for more cosmological details is filled with necessities. But we know from it that these necessities are contingent upon their being the determinate things together. This is a contingent surprise.

Although it does not matter where we start, from the ontological creative act through many layers of cosmology to the issues of the future of the cosmos or the curing of the COVID-19 virus, the logical relations among these do matter. They move from the most vague to the less vague. Most vague is the metaphysical speculation about the ontological act and the bare bones of determinateness. Less vague is my cosmological speculation about form, complexity, relations among many things, and value. Less vague than that is my speculation about a temporal cosmology with spatial things. Then the vagueness goes in different directions, to the limits of the cosmos (very speculative, though conceived mathematically) to the details of the virus and what we should do about it. The more vague should be specifiable by the less vague, but alternatives to the less vague should be possible. The less vague should specify the more vague but may well allow for completely contradictory alternatives that also specify the more vague level. Corrington does not order his levels of generality as more or less vague, although surely they are in part.

In my cosmology, fairly far down among less vague things, I discuss the nature of the self. Selves, so far as we know now, are limited to earth and are of great concern to us because we ourselves are selves. A self is in a dyadic relation with four things, giving rise to beauty, truth, righteousness, and virtue. This dyadic nature is an obligation, in my view. It is part of the nature of things; people find out about it and mature in taking on the obligations. There are zillions of triadic relations in these dyadic ones, but they are dyadic because obligation marks meeting it or missing it. Hardly ever do we fully meet an obligation, but we can approach it more or less well, more or less maturely, more or less singularly or in cooperation.

Rituals play a large role in my philosophy and do so differently from their roles for Corrington. For Corrington, rituals are the more or less dead ways by which interpretive groups are organized and get along. It takes extra energy to involve oneself with evolution and involution, with art and the sublime. For me, rituals are the building blocks of societies and even of a singular person's relations with things. We learn them very early and continue to learn them the more we learn about the world. Anything that can be interpreted semiotically, that is with Peirce's triadic sign relations, is a ritual because it is learned. Rituals are shared with nature, institutions, and other participant individuals. Yet they are never the whole of experience. Even when we are experiencing as we have done before, the generality of rituals is specified and the rituals changed. A small child has relatively few rituals but already goes way beyond rituals to imaginative games. A society is built up out of rituals piling upon rituals piling upon rituals, all of which are slightly changing while people attend to specific beauties, truths, issues of righteousness, and the search for virtue. Most of all, we learn to be conscious of our civilization and attend to various parts of that, most of which are not rituals. As we are aware of our civilization, we are conscious more of what is wrong with what we have and how rituals and other conditions need to be changed. These views of mine call for much more attention to ritual in thinking about human individuals participating in societies and civilization than Corrington would think. He celebrates getting beyond rituals. I celebrate their highly interwoven functions at building societies and civilizations.

How Do We Compare?

Let me begin by stressing once again how Corrington and I agree that all our philosophies are speculative and hypothetical. They are speculative in the extreme as we both reach for categories that encompass metaphysics. By speculative, we both mean that we take ordinary ideas and stretch them to deal with the most general, abstract, and far-reaching issues. Corrington stretches to make ordinality of sufficient metaphysical generality and I stretch the notions of Ultimacy. Concretely, he stretches the notion of the aesthetic to bear the weight of Ultimate reality and I stretch the notions of God, the gods, and the heavens to the greatest extreme in religions, taking a final step into sheer contingency.

Our philosophies are also hypothetical in the sense that Charles S. Peirce developed that notion and the idea of vagueness. We both reject a priori reasoning in metaphysics and deal with the best categories we can find. We both know that in the future, philosophers will take our theories to be too narrow and expand them, if they don't just start over with entirely new categories. We both know that even our embodied theories now might give way to theories in the far future that are embodied in very different ways, or perhaps are even disembodied. Nevertheless, we both know that philosophy does not advance if we do not put forward our best theories now.

We both regard our metaphysical theories as "vague" now in Peirce's sense, and also much of our cosmological theories. This is to say, our theories are arranged hierarchically with the higher ones being vague with respect to the lower ones. For Peirce, a theory is vague if contradictories can specify it; a theory specifies a vaguer one if it can add details to it. My theories are arranged more specifically to exhibit this level of vagueness than Corrington's, although his are vague too.

Second, we agree that our approaches to philosophy are naturalistic. Since we both appeal to gods, or perhaps even God, this requires some explanation. By naturalism, I mean that we both reject any sense in which the whole of nature is the result of a creative act by a God (or gods) who are beyond nature. For Corrington, this is a fairly simple matter that is explained above. For him, all gods are bits of god-ing within nature and nature itself is the subject of metaphysical ordinality. When he tries in 0.0 to postulate an absolutely Prior One, it does not work, as I showed above. For me, the ascending levels of vagueness can follow a track of personal intentional creation, a track of personal creation that transforms itself into pure consciousness, a track of natural phenomena, a track of some combination of these, or perhaps of some other metaphorical base. But most of them agree that the end is indeterminate because of the dialectic of creation. Some of them say, in one way or another, that this dialectic leads to a fullness of being that is infinite and creates the rest. I say that a consistent dialectic leads to saying that the whole of the created act, both its source in non-being and its products in creation, is contingent. For both of us, the more transcendent, the more abstract, and yet also the more intimate. The created act is an *act*, not a thing, and thus has no traits of its own. Corrington and I agree that any determinate thing, even a determinate infinite creator, is determinate and thus not the real creator. He thinks there is no real creator, whereas I think it is the contingent ontological act.

Third, despite our general agreement on the speculative, hypothetical, our rather Peircean epistemology, and our naturalism, we are widely divergent on the actual means by which we do Ultimate philosophy. For Corrington, the means are through the development of his psychoanalytic story. Starting from the corrections of personal psychopathologies to the healthy development of the self, to the connections between the unconscious of nature and collective unconscious to personal consciousness, to the achievement of personal and social greatness in the arts, the psychoanalytic story is present and developed. This means that intimacy is cultivated throughout his system and expanded to its connections with the extent of *natura naturans* and *natura naturata*. Because we philosophers are nearly always borderline crazy, we generally have a good connection with psychoanalysis, even when we don't use it philosophically.

My own metaphysical categories are friendly to his psychoanalytic ones but are not psychoanalytic. Rather they arise from a cross-cultural study of philosophies and religions and build up to a mixed bag of categories. My treatments of space and time, for instance, are vague with regard to our own experience of space and time. My treatments of form, components formed, relations, and value are vague with respect to our own temporal cosmology, and their roles within my metaphysics deal with classical Platonic and Confucian terms, however much I redefine them in my way as contingent.[10]

I would say, then, that my own theory is more plausible as a philosophy of the whole, connected to Ultimacy. On the other hand, I would say that his theory is more plausible as an intimate philosophy that expands directly on our experience without leaving it behind. Mine quickly leaves personal experience behind and works to reconnect with it only by leaping down to the descriptive level.

Fourth, we differ on the most general level as to the purpose of philosophy. This might not be obvious. Corrington and I agree that the purpose is aesthetic, to create systems that are pleasing to behold and that astonish and delight. We agree that, in a peculiar sense, it is better for our philosophies to be interesting than to be true, a lesson we both learned from Whitehead. In this, we take our satisfaction more like Beethoven's than like Bertrand Russell's, in creating something that enlightens and enlarges the visions of people. Our visions aim to be true, but not exclusive. You can begin his way or my way and will end up with valuable philosophic vision in both cases, different but valuable. I would never say that his philosophy is false and am confident that he would not say that mine is.

Corrington's philosophy is shaped like a funnel with a long downspout, or up-spout since his funnel is upside down. Ecstatic Naturalism, the name of his whole philosophy, takes into account many contexts of nature, including but not limited to that displayed in psychoanalysis. As he comes closer to metaphysics, he opts for ordinality and provides his revision of Justus Buchler. In "The Categorial Schema," he runs from the top down and very quickly moves from *natura naturans* and *natura naturata* to the sacred and the non-sacred. He then deals with the sacred alone in its modalities: sacred folds, sacred intervals, providingness, and the unruly ground. Finally, he moves to the sacred in human experience. It's the sacred almost the whole way.

My philosophy, by contrast, looks like an upside-down stack of cake pans fitting inside one another, with the very top pan, the largest one, being an ontological act that includes the determinate things of all sorts held together by the act itself. As I say, the top pan is the ontological act, the next pan down has my speculation about determinateness itself, the next one down has a temporal and spatial cosmology, and the rest go off in all sorts of directions, but all more specific than the temporal and spatial cosmology. That last level might consist of many different cosmologies, entirely separate from one another, continuing to fit in one another, or a combination of the two. So I can bring in a lot more for free, as it were, than Corrington can.

This is particularly apparent with regard to beauty. For Corrington, beauty and the sublime are constitutions of nature that are of the outermost reaches of experience, and in the case of sublimity they transcend even that reach. For this reason, he can say that the goal of philosophy is to be beautiful or sublime. For me, however, beauty is the outcome value of any harmony in its subjective form. This is a limited case of value that, for me, is what you get with these particular elements combined with this form in these relations so as to have this harmony. For me, value is the largest normative sense and it applies to the highest cosmology that defines determinateness. I believe all determinate things have value because each embraces both its own characters and its influences on other harmonies that themselves take into account that influence. Beauty, for me, is on the same level but is a universal trait of any harmony's subjective form. The subjective form is how a harmony relates its own components and this excludes how its influences are integrated by other harmonies. Any harmony has beauty in itself.

For Corrington, beauty and the sublime are always in connection with their human appreciation, either in hum-drum, fancy, spectacular, or sublime ways that negate the experiencer. The sublime belongs to nature, not to persons, but it is still related to persons. For me, things are beautiful by virtue of having determinateness, which everything has. Of course, to make this claim plausible, I have to jump down to human experience and show how it relates simply to determinateness. In fact, I even have to give an account of art and its appreciation, where art is humanly made beauty. Nevertheless, what we appreciate in art is its special kinds of determinateness. What we appreciate in nature is larger kinds of determinateness. It is the determinateness, not our appreciation, that constitutes its beauty. This is so even on the highest level where we know dialectically what determinate things are, namely harmonies with many components integrated by their form with their relations with other harmonies, thus constituting their value. Their beauty consists in the determinateness as such. Corrington would find it very hard to admit this.

Fifth, a final point of comparison needs to be made, illustrating most of the previous points. How is it that we know something? For Corrington, this is an extremely complicated process that involves sensation and many levels of interpretation. The interpretations (following Peirce) are of interpretations that are of other interpretations. Moreover, they quickly pick up on nature and its unconscious, and issue sometimes in great beauty and the sublime.

For me, however, knowledge involves a relation to its object with a situation. A "situation" is the extraction of a limited set of conditions that allow for a transition from the object as a whole (whatever that is) to the observer as a whole (whatever that is) of some traits that carry the observer's appreciation of the object's nature and beauty. The observer does not know the whole of the object, only those traits that are carried across an array of conditions that mediate the object. The object, the observer, and the mediating conditions all have relations with many other things that are irrelevant to the situation, at least not immediately relevant.

Consider a sunset seen by observers on our sunset-viewing platform. The sunset itself is a meteorological set of conditions of which some traits are mediated to the observers. These include the shapes, movements, and colors of the sunset as these are carried over the miles to us on our deck. At this distance, we cannot pick up on the winds in the object, or how it looks as a sunrise from the other side, but we do get the moving colors from our perspective. The observers have to have their attention on the sunset, operative faculties for picking out shapes, movements, and colors, and capacities for interpreting the sunset with regard to others of the observers' experiences. This constitutes the "situation" for the sunset viewing. The situation is determined by the conditions of the observers, for instance being at the right distance and angle to the object, having no clouds or trees in the way, and the like. The beauty is in the object in the situation, however, not in the observer or in the media. Therefore, we can say in some situations that there is a beautiful sunset there and then where the observers' conditions are all "if there were real observers there." Any real observers with the right conditions would see the sunset, even if none actually does.

With this concept of a situation, my philosophy explains a lot at a higher level than Corrington's. His philosophy mainly cites instances of knowledge, assuming that we know what knowledge is. My philosophy provides an analysis of what the knowledge is and how it relates to the various levels of cosmology.

This chapter began with a study of Corrington's employment of psychoanalytic materials from Freud to the present. It lauded his careful but highly imaginative expansion of the materials to deal with a psychoanalytic interpretation of all of nature. For all my appreciation, Corrington's work still seems to me to have a certain failure of intent. He intends it to be a philosophy of the whole when combined with his modification of Buchler's ordinal philosophy. Yet for various reasons noted above, it is smaller than that intent.

I elaborate a bit of my own philosophy that puts his in perspective. In particular, I developed my notion of metaphysics as the dialectical study of determinateness and its complete and absolute contingency on an ontological creative act that gives rise to the determinate things and includes them as termini of its creativity. Corrington has nothing like this and in fact reaches the top of his ladder of creativity with the same old emergence of things by infinitesimal increments from a pregnant nothing.

Nevertheless, we agree that our philosophies are both contributions to the global conversation that are valuable, each in its own way. They are more like different composers' making symphonies, both good. His is like Brahms' Fourth Symphony: grand, eloquent, the outcome of his string of symphonies, finally experiential. Mine is like Beethoven's Ninth Symphony: grander, more eloquent, suddenly out of nowhere.

Chapter 14

On Stefan Alkier

Does a scripture's authority
Come from the past?
Begin as a vague truth
And slowly gather meaning?
Or does its authority
Grow from the future,
Enticing interpretation,
Slowly becoming plausible?
Authority from the past diminishes.
Authority from the future is
Never stronger than our fallibility.
Have we authority?

Pragmatists

As a humanistic American Confucian pragmatist, I am delighted to see Charles Peirce's ideas become influential in German theology. He has been known in German philosophy for a long time, but it was not until Hermann Deuser in the mid-1990s translated Peirce's writings on religion into German and wrote his brilliant monograph, *Gott: Geist und Natur: Theologische Konsequenzen aus Charles S. Peirce' Religionsphilosophy*, that Peirce began to stimulate German theological thinking.[1] Deuser has continued to develop his own philosophical theology with Peircean inspiration to this very day. I want to thank his student and colleague

Stefan Alkier and to call attention to his book, *The Reality of the Resurrection: The New Testament Witness*.[2] Alkier uses the pragmatic semiotics of Peirce to provide a new hermeneutical theory for interpreting the New Testament witness to the resurrection both of Jesus Christ and of Christian believers. In my remarks, I want to extoll this approach and raise some further issues.

First, however, I want to point out an important irony. European semiotics, from Spinoza and Schleiermacher to Gadamer, Ricoeur, Eco, and Derrida, has taken the business of hermeneutics to be the interpretation of texts, very often biblical texts. Pragmatic semiotics by contrast takes the business of hermeneutics to be the interpretation of nature. For Peirce, a controlled scientific experiment in a laboratory is the prime analogate for interpretation. The interpretation of texts played a small role in Peirce's semiotic theory of interpretation. Now, Alkier is turning Peircean semiotics away from the laboratory to the interpretation of the problem of resurrection in the New Testament texts.

The significance of this is that Alkier, with the pragmatists, takes the interpretation of texts to be natural processes. Human writing, reading, and interpreting are natural processes by which people engage their environment. That environment, for pragmatists, includes human society, religion, and the venues for spiritual cultivation. Peirce and Alkier (and I) construe the social character of religion as processes within nature. The conscious and unconscious aspects of religious experience and the content of psychology of religion, all count as elements of nature. Pragmatism rejects the transcendental turn that would construe religion and the reading of religious texts in terms of human subjectivity. Alkier is making pragmatic hermeneutics attend to the European topic of hermeneutics as it rarely has before. What can pragmatic naturalism bring to the understanding of the New Testament witness to resurrection?

Over the first half of Alkier's volume is a meticulous analysis of all the New Testament texts, book by book, with regard to what they say about the resurrection of the dead and the resurrection of Jesus. They say different things, as we know, yet cumulatively they depict God as a loving, just, and merciful creator who responds both to sin and to the victims of oppression and suffering by raising them from the dead, according to Alkier. The resurrection of Jesus Christ both (1) establishes a community with him as Lord for raised people to join and (2) serves as a sign that allows people to be raised after death into that heavenly community.

The Peircean substratum of this interpretation is in Peirce's theory of categories, Firstness, Secondness, and Thirdness. Firstness is what things are in themselves, and the biblical images and ideas, from the Hebrew Bible to the New Testament writings, are Firsts. They are given to the community that is aware of them. Secondness is difference, opposition, surprise, the unexpected, shock; it is the mark of real existence in contrast to what is merely expected, the correction of expectations. The relevant New Testament Secondness is the resurrection of Jesus in contrast to the experience of defeat. Whether Jesus was raised as an empirical matter, for instance, whether the tomb was empty, is not the point. The point is that the early Christians took the witness to Christ's resurrection to be a reality check, a contradiction to their expectations, and made them believe that Christ's resurrection changes things for them, promising their resurrection. Thirdness is the interpretive web of signs, the mediators connecting things, and the New Testament. Thirdness is the interpretive theological story that constitutes the belief in Jesus's resurrection and their own, plus the songs, rituals, and community organizations that allow life to be lived in their convictions both of Christ's resurrection and their own. From the pre-resurrection culture of Israel and the surrounding Hellenism, the early Christians and New Testament writers developed an enriched culture based on Jesus's resurrection and the new hope for the eschatological resurrection that allowed people to understand the justice of God being served through the mercy of resurrection. So much for the ways the early Christians wrote and read their scriptures.

We all know the problem for us, however, and Alkier states it starkly:

> Without creation theology, without an understanding of sin, without questions of theodicy, and without apocalyptic eschatology, the coherence of the plausibility structures of New Testament discourse about the resurrection of the dead would collapse. The universe of discourse the New Testament writings present, however, no longer corresponds in an unbroken fashion to the conceptions of reality assumed by post-Enlightenment societies. Angelic bodies of light are now at home in fantasy films. Apocalyptic scenarios are understood as natural catastrophes based on the law of cause and effect. The resurrection of the dead is hardly looked upon as a serious question in the discourse of the humanities. The

question of sin is dismissed as moralizing ecclesial theology removed from real life.[3]

Alkier's question then is how it is possible, if at all, to read the New Testament as scripture in our own time. He puts the point sharply: How do we express the Christian faith today to people who are dying or recently bereaved, if "the coherence of the plausibility structures of New Testament discourse" are broken or simply missing? Here is what he says about the content of the Christian faith: "The faithful answer of the New Testament writings to these decisive questions about the future is that God shall make everything well."[4] It would be quick and easy to say this if there were contemporary plausibility conditions with which you could say God will make everything well. Something like this was Bultmann's strategy of demythologizing, translating the biblical language and symbols into the persuasive language of existentialism. Nevertheless, how many Christians today facing death for themselves or loved ones are accomplished existentialists? Furthermore, Bultmann's strategy is a way of doing away with the Bible in the late modern world, whereas Alkier is committed to making sense of it.

We are accustomed to thinking of this problem in terms of European hermeneutics that would say it is a matter of relating or overlapping different cultural horizons, ala Gadamer. Nevertheless, continental hermeneutics is under Kant's thrall to say that experience is wholly constructed. Pragmatic naturalism says, rather, that experience is a matter of engaging the real world with signs. The signs are culturally or imaginatively constructed, and so pragmatism is historicistic in this sense. Nevertheless, the process of interpretive engagement with the signs is human engagement with real things, for instance ultimate human reality in the case of the resurrection problematic. Alkier adroitly lays out a Peircean rendition of interpretive engagement.

Now, I want to stress a pragmatic point more decisively than Alkier does. The basic symbols in religious discourse address real problems, problems of what is ultimately important. I define religion as the human engagement of Ultimacy in cognitive, existential, and practical ways. Serious religion engages real ultimate matters. Its language has reference, indexical as well as iconic, as Peirce would say. Every society lives with the climate of their surroundings and develops cultural ways of engaging that climate. Every society needs to find food in its environment and develops cultural ways of getting nourishment. Similarly, every society lives within the Ultimate conditions of life and over time develops cultural ways of engaging those Ultimate conditions. All this is to say that theology is not merely a matter of consistency regarding fundamentals of a discourse. It is not merely a matter of connecting alien discourses by overlapping their horizons. Religion needs theology to guide its actual living responses to the Ultimate conditions of human life.

Ultimate Conditions

Let me propose here a hypothesis about the Ultimate conditions of human life. Five such Ultimate conditions exist, plus multitudes of Ultimate dimensions resulting from their combinations. The first Ultimate condition is the radical contingency of the world on some kind of creator. The second is the condition of having to make choices among alternatives that have different values, giving rise to the religious problematic of righteousness: how to discern differences in value, how to choose, how to handle mistakes, guilt, and alienation from a moral community. The third is the condition of having to make up a whole self out of all the diverse and often conflicting and broken components of life. The fourth is the condition of having a location within a larger created world, with dimensions of relating to other persons as others, to our natural environment, and to our social structures; this is the problematic of place in the whole, estrangement, and reconciliation. The fifth Ultimate condition is finding a meaning to life, of having an identity in reference to the creator and creation that has some significant goodness.

These five Ultimate conditions are conditions for life anywhere in any society. Every culture needs to find ways, perhaps multiple and conflicting ways, of engaging them in religion. These five conditions, I submit, are the preliminary foundations for comparative theology among religious traditions and movements, because careful, detailed, critical, and self-correcting interpretations can exhibit to us the diversity of responses to these five Ultimates as well as the power of each response to engage the Ultimates in its own ways. Every religion has symbolic problematics for engaging contingency and ontological creation; for engaging righteousness, discernment, choice, guilt, and moral judgment; for engaging the search for wholeness out of brokenness and disarray; for engaging the need to relate to the whole, especially other people, from one's place within creation; and for engaging the question of the meaning of life.

These differences in symbolic systems not only mark differences among the great traditions. They also often have parallels within a given tradition that carries diversity. Alkier's reading of the New Testament, in light too of the Hebrew Bible, emphasizes the personal character of God as loving, merciful, and just. When the author of 1 John says that God is love, he jumps to a non-agential metaphoric system, although he also uses agential metaphors. When the author of Colossians says (1:15) that Jesus Christ is the first visible image of God, we can read this as saying that God is not literally a person, that God is only imaged as a person. Later theologians such as Augustine and Aquinas who identify God with Being-itself purify that conception of all traits of personhood, except by analogy. To interpret the outlier symbolic usages by assimilating them to dominant or preferred ones is always possible. But it is also possible to see the diversity of alternative symbols as having merit. Each symbol might lift up something in ontological creation and contingency that helps engage it better for the context in which the interpreter, or interpreting community, engages it. Religions, including Christianity, exhibit similar diversity and parallels, not unanimity, regarding the problematics of righteousness, wholeness of the self, place and relations with the creation, and meaning.

This leads me to propose that we abandon systematic doctrinal interpretation of the symbols, including the Bible, in any strict sense. Instead, we should engage in what Ray L. Hart calls "systematic symbolics," the interpretation of how symbols work to engage people in their diverse contexts with Ultimate matters.[5] Pragmatists know that interpretations of things are always contextual, given the historical, social, and situational contexts of interpreters, with their diverse needs, purposes, values, and resources. One person might engage the ontological creator in one way with a symbol but another person might use that same symbol for a very different kind of engagement. The symbols mean different things to different people in different contexts. Each symbol has its own network of meanings, often several different networks. What makes sense in one context might not make sense, or might make different sense, in other contexts. The theological practice of systematic symbolics allows the symbols to function realistically in engaging people with Ultimate matters in their different contexts. To try to make the symbols in their diverse engagements consistent is to abuse the text.

Consider the New Testament symbol of Jesus as sacrifice, an aspect of some of its interpretations of Christ's resurrection. John the Baptist said, in John 1:29, "Here is the Lamb of God who takes away the sin of the world." The Lamb of God reference is to the Passover in which the sacrifice of the lamb prevents the killing of the firstborn Israelites; it has nothing to do with their sin. Taking away the sin of the world refers to the Levitical placing of the sins of the people on the scapegoat so that the people can become pure enough to approach God; it has nothing to do with death in particular. The Baptist (or at least the Evangelist) wanted to associate sin with death, which neither of the Hebrew Bible texts did explicitly, and so mushes the different symbol systems together. Matthew 20:28, Mark 10:45, and 1 Timothy 2:5–6 add the ransom symbol to interpret the sacrifice of Jesus. Hebrews 7 identifies Jesus as sacrifice with Jesus as High Priestly sacrificer. Why not understand all of these symbolic uses of Jesus as sacrifice on their own terms in their own contexts without distorting them to fit together? A splendid example of systematic symbolics is Alkier's nearly two-hundred-page discussion of the different New Testament writings, showing how different authors writing to different communities parse the resurrection language differently. Alkier, however, also wants to generalize the upshot of New Testament witness to the resurrection of Jesus Christ and the apocalyptic resurrection of his believers to get a common story, as I quoted earlier. He moreover wants to limit the context of his reading of the New Testament to Protestant Christianity, as if Eastern Orthodox, Roman Catholic, and Anglican Christianity were different contexts, not to speak of non-European forms of Christianity. He, of course, can pick and synthesize what he wants to go together from his own particular context. Nevertheless, I commend attending first to how the symbols work diversely from many contexts of interpretation.

Permit me now to make one more general point about the dynamics of signs relative to the fact that we always interpret from a specific context of our own. In fact, there are contexts within contexts. Alkier focuses on reading the New Testament on resurrection from the context of pastoral leadership (including preaching) in contemporary worshipping Protestant Christian congregations. Within such a context, there are pressures in various subcontexts to interpret the symbols along different places on two continua.

One continuum is between a maximally transcendent interpretation and a maximally intimate one. Talking with the more intellectually critical people in the congregation, the pastor/preacher might interpret God more toward the transcendent end of the continuum, something like transcendent Being-itself, or at least as something higher than personal. Talking with simpler folk, the pastor/preacher might interpret God as a king on a throne who rules the world as a kingdom. The God as king symbols weigh heavily in the liturgies of American Protestant worship. Think of all the variants in between. To take another example, think of the transcendent images of Jesus as Cosmic Christ in comparison with the intimate images of him as your friend.

The other continuum is between maximally sophisticated interpretations and the interpretations that define popular religion. Alkier reads the New Testament on resurrection with a superbly sophisticated and careful hermeneutics. Many people today, however, at least in American Protestant churches, believe in local angels and frequent miracles caused by divine intervention. In many American worship services, we pray to the Trinity, one of the most sophisticated conceptions of God ever, for favors in business, love, and health, a shamanistic practice. All of these different contexts of interpretation, regarding needs for transcendence versus intimacy and sophistication versus popular culture, interact in most congregations. Every seminary-educated preacher worries about this, as does every pastor dealing with death, religious education, or interpreting the sacraments, topics at the heart of Alkier's hermeneutical concerns.

Resurrection

Turning to the reading of the New Testament specifically about resurrection, the fundamental issue for theological interpretation is to identify the real problems that those religious symbols engage. As Alkier says and does, we need to read the underlying reality philosophically and through the symbols and the contexts we have at hand.

We face two connected questions here. The first is what the resurrection problematic really is about. The second is whether the New Testament discourse addresses this question so well, when properly read, that we can rest with it as our Sola Scriptura. I shall consider these together.

Consider first the New Testament concern for life after death. Many ancient theories and assumptions about this existed in the early Christian world. Some thought that the soul is naturally immortal and thus will go to some heaven, hell, or middle ground after death. By medieval times, this was the dominant Christian assumption. Others thought that the soul naturally dissipates a short while after death and that there is no long-lasting afterlife, the common assumption of the Hebrew Bible and of the Sadducees. Others believed in a resurrection after death, either immediately or in some distant apocalyptic eschaton. Those who took to Christianity believed human salvation to depend upon an afterlife in a good place, and that death with no resurrection is disaster. Hell was worse than final death for those who believed in natural immortality, as Jesus apparently did in his Luke 16 parable of Lazarus and the Rich Man. Note that this set of ancient Near Eastern cultural assumptions did not hold strongly in the ancient world for people in South Asia who believed in reincarnation. Being born to a next life, on and on, is the very condition from which enlightenment promises escape or liberation. Resurrection would be religious failure for South Asian religions.

What would be the assumptions about life after death and salvation in the twenty-first century? Speaking for American Protestantism, I suspect that most congregations of any size would have believers in each of the versions of the afterlife I just mentioned, with variations. You would find many different beliefs about heaven and hell, with maybe purgatorial or limbo places in between. However, you would also find some more sophisticated people who understand everything we attribute to soul to be dependent on biological processes that require a functioning brain and body, and so would not believe in any life after death whatsoever. I do not know of any American Protestants who hold to the old belief that God transfigures a dead body into a new, improved, and living body, the early reason for insisting on burial rather than cremation. Everyone knows that bodies decay and usually remain in place until they do so. The exception for some people might be belief in Jesus's resurrection as a quick thirty-six-hour transformation of his old body before it had a chance to decay.

What is a preacher/pastor to do with the biblical passages about believer's resurrection when interpreting the New Testament today? For the believers in various forms of afterlife, the preacher/pastor can take the biblical passages about resurrection pretty much at face value, so long as we do not look as closely at the differences as Alkier does. For the others, I recommend the resurrection passages be interpreted as metaphors for eternal life in God, not literally everlasting afterlife. The creation of the world includes the creation of time and temporal things. Therefore, the ontological creative act, however symbolized, cannot itself be in time. It is eternal or in eternity. Although human temporal days pass away, each is what it is eternally as part of the terminus of the creative act. Our real lives are eternal in God, and we live somewhat abstractly within time's flow in which all days pass.

The biblical symbols concerning the afterlife are good metaphors for an eternal relation to God. So too, however, are the South Asian symbols stopping the passage of time in an enlightened death, although they are very different symbols. For Christians with the New Testament, the resurrection language can be very effective for metaphorically signaling the point that what counts is one's relation to God; this is in contrast to getting a reward for oneself that should be denied from the metaphor. The eternalist transfiguring appropriation of temporalist resurrection symbols requires shifting from a mainly narrative theological frame to a more metaphysical one. In the metaphysical frame, one engages ultimacy by virtue of relating to the eternal God in life, not by playing a role in a cosmic narrative. The Bible contains both points of view. The Pentateuch, the historical books, Daniel, the authentic writings of Paul, and perhaps Revelation mostly situate relating God to the people through narrative. Much of Psalms, Proverbs, Ecclesiastes, Song of Solomon, the parables and preaching of Jesus, Colossians, and Ephesians emphasize that what matters ultimately is how you and your people stand in relation to God now. Karl Barth was a narrative theologian whereas Paul Tillich was metaphysical one. Barth would have a hard time with Christians who reject a literal afterlife and look for it to be a metaphor for eternity. Alkier adopts the language of narrative rather strongly.

Contemporary Congregants

Alkier points out that the New Testament connection of resurrection with salvation depends upon a double assumption that (1) we are sinners under judgment by a personal God who is just and (2) who must punish sinners. Many American Protestants are comfortable with those uncomfortable assumptions and can take the biblical setup without difficulty. Many of the more sophisticated Protestants, however, have difficulty with both. The divine command theory of right and wrong is not commonly plausible to many of these people. Most moral issues are superlatively complex and ambiguous. Many people believe that those who do bad things, once you know what that is, are to be understood as ill, ignorant, or caught in a situation not of their own making. Complicated as it is,

I believe to the contrary that differences between right and wrong do exist and that to be human is to lie under obligation. Not to be judged as under obligation is not to be taken seriously as a person. Therefore, I would claim that the biblical insistence on the reality of sin is a lesson we should keep, even if we treat the content of New Testament ethics as something that deserves continued reflection.

Many American Protestants also have difficulty taking the personifying metaphors for God too seriously. As I said earlier, this is nothing new. For our time, I would take the personifying symbols of God as metaphors for the eternal ontological creative act. Other traditions have different, non-personifying metaphors for that creative act. We can use personifications as metaphors because we find them in our scriptures. Nevertheless, we should reject the literal understanding of divine intentionality that gets us into trouble with theodicy. The creative act does create human beings in a situation where they face possibilities of different value; their moral character comes from what they choose. Created this way, we are under obligation whether or not there is a personal creator who has intentions to create us this way. We do not need to believe literally in a judging, wrathful God because each of us has the moral character we achieve as part of our eternal nature in the divine creative act. The metaphor of a judging God encourages us to take our obligations seriously. Nevertheless, it should not lead us to assume that God is a person who is also under judgment, as in theodicy.

Another aspect of divine personhood to which Alkier rightly calls attention is divine mercy. Although God justly ought to punish sinners, and it would be unjust for God not to do so, God's merciful love arranges a way out through Jesus Christ. The mercy of God can bring us into community with Jesus the Resurrected One in our own resurrection; the faith in this is what allows us to live before God now as redeemed sinners. Alkier applies Peirce's semiotic scheme as follows. The experience of the risen Christ as described by Paul and other New Testament writers is a precritical First. Whether they were right in perceiving what they thought they perceived, or instead were hallucinating, is beside the point. The interpretation of that experience to give rise to the idea of acceptance into the community of Christ's resurrection as the New Testament lays that out is Thirdness. The shock of Jesus's crucifixion and subsequent resurrection, given the expectations the disciples had previously, is the Secondness that breaks the old expectations and inaugurates the new eschatological one. Thus even if the story of

Jesus's resurrection were empirically false (and Alkier is clear that the story is not an empirical claim), the witnesses who had those precritical perceptions of the risen Christ, and those who believed their witness, enter into the new community with eschatological expectations. They have a new and shocking interpretation of the mercy of God and of the transformed status of their old and continuing sins.

For those of our contemporary congregants with a precritical acceptance of the New Testament witness, that story is their interpretation of their own situation. Nevertheless, for our contemporary congregants who understand those biblical resurrection perceptions to be precritical, and are skeptical that they can withstand criticism, the biblical accounts are no longer perceptions shared through witness across the centuries. They accept that the witnesses might be hallucinating, or projecting, or succumbing to mutually reinforcing wishful thinking. What can our skeptics do? They can make a fideistic move and will to believe the story as if it were true, with the consequences for their own lives. Theological sophistication is not kind to that simple fideism, however. Alternatively, the skeptics who are no longer precritical can also say that the story, with its emotional impact of Firstness, Secondness, and Thirdness, is a metaphor for something else, not about redemption in a resurrection community. The resurrection community is a metaphor for some other way of living before God.

As I understand Alkier, this last is his position, as it is mine. The real point of the New Testament story is that under God, everything is somehow well. What it meant for everything to be well for the early Christians who believed in a personal, judging, loving God was redemption from condemnation for their sins by being brought into a resurrected community with the resurrected Son of God. Nevertheless, what does it mean for the more skeptical Christians among us today to be well? This question needs answering at length. I have hinted here at my own suggestions in this regard, namely that (1) God is a nonpersonal creative act, (2) that we are created to be under obligation to choose well, (3) that our choices determine much of our character, and (4) that among our obligations is a quest for wholeness, engagement with the rest of creation, and resolution about the meaning of life. The perception of the world with this metaphysics gives rise to profound peace and gratitude, even when things locally are terrible. Of course, I have not made this case here.

To interpret the New Testament witness as a true but metaphorical story, about something other than what it seems to be about, requires a philosophical route to point to that something other. Otherwise, the gospel that under God everything is well cannot be preached to the sophisticated skeptics with the New Testament witness. One might hope, as Alkier seems to do, that the dynamic quality of the New Testament witness will cause a contemporary conviction that everything is well, which in turn causes a contemporary interpretation of what being well means. This reflects Peirce's theory that some objects are signs that cause signs interpreting them to come into existence, which in turn causes the interpretation of the object by the signs. Nevertheless, not all objects cause the signs that interpret them, and even when that dynamic motion of interpretation does take place it often is deflected in some other direction. Secondness, such as the shock of modern science, deflected contemporary New Testament faith quite decisively for many people. For the sophisticated skeptics in our Protestant congregations, we need to say what "everything being well" under God means for them and how understanding the New Testament witness as a good metaphor is a way of affirming their faith that God makes everything.

The result is that Scriptura cannot be Sola if this would mean that we can interpret, preach, and teach the New Testament effectively today without philosophy and without the interpretation of religion more generally. My own conviction is that the New Testament witness is a massively good metaphor for the human condition and God's creation in which, despite the worst, everything is still well. When we ask, symbol by symbol, what the Bible truly means for engaging reality, it is far more penetrating than most modern, late modern, and postmodern symbols for the Ultimate. When it comes to the reading of scripture in church, those who still live in the cultural world of the Bible can take it at face value. Those who do not live in that world, but pretend by an act of will that they do, can take it at face value but should be prepared for an abrupt loss of faith. These strategies give rise to powerful convictions of living in the resurrection community. However, they do not say much about how to live in that community in the conditions of our own time. Those of us who read the biblical witness metaphorically with critical sophistication can come to see the good grace of creation in the depths of our own situation. This is proper Thirdness for modern Christian congregations.

Chapter 15

On Nancy Frankenberry

There was a young singer from Dartmouth
Who sang out her views with conviction.
But her crowning achievement,
Contingency regnant,
Supposed the whole show was
Resplendent.

Nancy Frankenberry and I have disagreed about what is good in pragmatism for many years. She holds that the advance to neo-pragmatism of the sort found in Richard Rorty and Donald Davidson is the best and has developed an entire epistemology for religious symbols based on this. Namely, she holds that religious symbols do not exist legitimately and works to get along without them. I, of course, like the older pragmatists, which I label paleo-pragmatists to distinguish them from the neo-pragmatists. Like Frankenberry, I have an elaborate epistemology comings from my pragmatism. Whereas hers is based on taking the object being interpreted to be a proposition or set of propositions, mine is based on taking real objects to be the objects. And I, to be sure, just love religious symbols, whole trajectories of them from popular religion to the symbols of nothing.

When Frankenberry retired from Dartmouth a few years ago, I gave a paper at her symposium that was published later in the *American Journal of Theology and Philosophy* and, in a different version, in my *Defining*

Religion.[1] She responded in that same issue of the *American Journal of Theology and Philosophy*, and so I wrote the first version of this chapter, which was published in the *American Journal of Theology and Philosophy*. The topic is contingency.

I distinguish two kinds of contingency, cosmological and ontological. Regarding cosmological contingency, I wholeheartedly applaud president Frankenberry's theory of contingency that she derives from Whitehead, Buddhism, and neo-pragmatists such as Richard Rorty and Donald Davidson. She is so good on contingency that I have urged her in print to have more of it, namely ontological contingency.[2] Her response in part has been to convene this meeting of the Metaphysical Society on the topic. Her presidential address, which comes next in the program, develops her Buddhist and neo-pragmatic roots, and perhaps she will slip down the slope to embrace the ontological dimension of contingency; here is another friendly nudge.

Let me begin by giving preliminary definition to two kinds of contingency, although I shall argue that the distinction between them gets too complicated to sustain in the long run. Cosmological contingency is the contingency of things within the world upon other things within the world, plus perhaps their own temporal spontaneous creativity. Ontological contingency is the contingency of everything in the world that is determinate in any way upon an ontological ground. That ontological ground cannot itself be determinate, and you can recollect Plotinus's One, Thomas Aquinas's pure Act of To Be, Brahman without qualities, or the Ultimate of Non-Being in Zhou Dunyi's philosophy for sample conceptions of such an indeterminate ontological ground. (I shall offer yet another conception.) In this brief discussion, I want to sketch an abstract theory of each kind of contingency but to focus mainly on their connection or interaction. My thesis is that we cannot conceive cosmological contingency thoroughly without ontological contingency and we cannot conceive ontological contingency thoroughly without cosmological contingency if there is any cosmological change.

Cosmological Contingency

For purposes of this discussion, I shall give a generalized statement of cosmological contingency, derived in part from Whitehead, Peirce, and Paul Weiss, the founder of this Society. Like many process philosophers, I treat things as events, occasions, or changes, all of which we can characterize as harmonies happening in space-time. An event is cosmologically contingent in three ways.

In the first way, an event is contingent on past or environing actual events that it takes up within its own-being. They are the actual components out of which an event makes itself up. (That locution is not as bad as "the grocery bill up which I have run.") I equivocate on actual things in the past and in the environment because of the complexities of defining simultaneity relative to past and future, an issue I want to finesse here.

The second way in which an event is contingent is that the possibilities for what it can do with its actual components limit how it can make itself up. Those possibilities exist in a field with possibilities for other events, and the constant changing of things makes those future possibilities constantly shift. One thing's future possibilities are contingent in part on what other things do. I believe, but will not argue here, that the future contains alternative possibilities and that part of what an event does when it happens or comes to be is the selection among the alternatives of those to actualize. Pretend for the moment, if you will, that these characterizations of contingency on the past and on the future are more or less true.

The third way in which an event is cosmologically contingent is upon some spontaneous creativity in how it comes to be. Paul Weiss was brilliantly insistent upon this point, more forceful than his mentor, Whitehead. For an event to happen, something must be added to all the actual things that are past and potential causes. If nothing were added, then the past would just be what it turned out to be and nothing more would happen. Whitehead's account appealed to general creativity at this point, saying in his theory of the Category of the Ultimate that whenever there is an actual many, creativity forces the creation of a new one integrating that many and adding to it. True, but something has to show up in the emerging new event that is more than the past, namely creativity creating something new. From the standpoint of the past, this novelty in the event is spontaneous, that is, not accounted for by anything in the past. I would say that this creative spontaneity in the emergence or present existence of an event is a third way in which the event is cosmologically contingent. Pure spontaneity in present emergence is quite abstract and not very interesting. In human beings, however, it can be interesting when it is the spontaneous adoption of one out of several actual motive impulses. We give ourselves the moral character of being the one who adopted this motive rather than those others, along with whatever justifications there are that go with that motive. Contingent spontaneous creativity relates to the contingency of the actual past by adding something to it so that change happens. It relates to the contingency of the future by selecting for actualization a set of possibilities for which there might be alternative possibilities. As William Desmond would say, a contingent event is "in the middle" between past and future, constituting a connection between them. If his philosophy does not persuade you yet at this point, say it in Greek, which adds authoritative plausibility: all contingent things in the world are "metaxologically" located.[3]

Let me suspend the discussion of cosmological contingency for now and pick up ontological contingency. Because so many philosophers nowadays associate ontological contingency with religion, which they reject, it takes an argument to make the issue between the contingencies even plausible. Those hypothesizing ontological contingency do so, historically, out of two main problematics, the problem of the one and the many, and the problem of being- itself or being versus beings. Philosophers in the Western traditions influenced by Neo-Platonism, including Thomists, often hunt for a primordial One as the ground of the being of the many. Philosophers from South Asia often attempt to diminish the reality of the many with their distinctions, leaving an undifferentiated ground, but often without a unifying center of intention. Philosophers from East Asia construe the one and many problematic to be a search for something that does not need explanation, noting that anything with order or determinateness needs explanation; so only a generative nothingness can be the ontological ground. Philosophers who quickly reject some notion of ontological ground for a contingent determinate many need to solve the problems of the one and many and of being-itself some other way. For now, I want to sketch an argument for the ontological ground as an act of creation, the terminus of which is everything that is determinate. Everything determinate is ontologically contingent upon that act. After the sketch, I shall return to the connection of ontological with cosmological contingency.

Ontological Contingency

The place to begin is with an analysis of determinateness, that is, of the many things or events that are different from one another. To be different, they need to be determinate with respect to one another. If one thing is determinate with respect to another, that other must condition it in some way, giving it what I call conditional components. In my Whitehead-like cosmology, the real conditioning others enter into a thing, although they might be transformed in order to fit in with the other real conditioning others in the thing. How one thing conditions another is a matter of cosmological contingency, either of the actual past sort or of the limiting future sort. The mutual conditioning of things constitutes an existential field in which things have locations relative to one another, an existential field that is dynamic and temporal for temporal things. The existential field is a kind of cosmological togetherness.

A thing cannot consist only of conditional components however, because it has to be something to be conditioned. It has to have its own-being in order to receive and integrate into its own determinate identity all its conditioning components. That own-being comes from what I call essential components. For Whitehead, all the creative subjectivity in the genesis of an actual occasion would be a matter of essential components. In my earlier sketch of cosmological contingency, the essential components would be at least the creative spontaneity of the present that adds to the past, selects the future, and actualizes the new event or thing.

Now you might think that one thing that conditions another thing becomes wholly contained in that other thing, losing its independent own-being reality. Sometimes John B. Cobb Jr. thinks this. But if this were so, there would be no real others with respect to which the conditioned thing could be determinate. There would be only the conditioned thing, one thing, which could not be determinate with respect to anything other than itself. If there is a multiplicity of determinate things, then the conditioning thing with its own-being is in part external to the thing it conditions. If you say there is no multiplicity, as some Advaitins do, then you disagree with me, demonstrating multiplicity (thanks, Rene). Therefore, things that are determinate with respect to one another relate internally to one another but also remain at least in part external to one another. Although the network of conditionings constitutes a cosmological togetherness, there must also be an ontological togetherness in which things are together in their separateness with their own essential components. If there were no ontological togetherness, there could not even be the cosmological togetherness and nothing could be cosmologically contingent upon anything else.

What might this ontological togetherness be? It cannot be something determinate over and above all the determinate things, such as a totalizing whole or a One that is determinately full of being, for then it would be just another determinate thing for which a more encompassing ontological togetherness is needed. My hypothesis is that the ontological togetherness is an ontological creative act, the terminus of which is all the determinate things in their mutual relations, related both internally and externally. The ontological creative act is a strange notion with many associations from which it needs to be refined.

The Ontological Creative Act

First, the ontological creative act is immediate. It has no stages that could be mapped. It is the immediate, sheer making of the determinate things. So the analogy with an act of a person or other agent does not hold.

Second, the ontological act has no nature of its own save for what it produces. It can have no antecedent potentials for acting, no rationality, no goodness, no divine nature, just its making of the determinate things. The act has no possibilities for acting but creates all such things as possibilities. It has no innate powers but creates all such things as have powers.

Third, the ontological creative act is thus absolutely contingent, constrained by nothing, necessitated by nothing. This is to say that the world of determinate things is absolutely contingent. Ontological contingency is not contingency on some cause. It is the contingency of all things that cause upon the radical, root act that makes them. This is the contingency that I think Professor Frankenberry's contingency needs more of.

Fourth, while you might think that the ontological creative act cannot explain anything because it is indeterminate, it explains in a different sense. It explains how the ontological togetherness of the determinate many is possible. The ontological creative act, making the things together, is their togetherness. The recognition or acknowledgment of the ontological creative act is the same as acknowledging the radical contingency of there being a world of determinate things at all.

Fifth, the ontological creative act is singular in the sense that it is the creation of all determinate things together. But it is not one in any ontological sense from which the many things are derivative, for instance as Neo-Platonists say. The world contains many unities, and some of its spread has pockets of order. But there is a lot of disunity in the world, lack of mutual conditioning or connection. What kinds of unity the world has is an empirical matter we determine by inquiry.

Sixth, the ontological creative act is eternal in the sense that it creates time by creating temporal things and hence cannot itself be in time. The act is not at the beginning of temporal process, nor a lure at the end, nor an act of present spontaneity, for all of those locations of the act presuppose temporal location. Even Augustine's *totum simul* notion of God based on expanding the present to include past and future is a temporal notion.

Seventh, the ontological creative act is immense in the sense that it is unmeasurable; that is, it has no location whatsoever. It is nowhere except in the determinate things it creates as their ontological togetherness.

Enough strange claims about ontological contingency from the perspective of the ontological creative act. Let me now explore more about ontological contingency from the standpoint of cosmological contingency.

Eternity and Temporality

We have just seen that my hypothesis about ontological contingency plays very hard with notions of eternity and immensity. But this means also that there is a special relation of ontological contingency to eternity. What, then, is temporality? This raises new questions.

First, if we could think of the present moment of an event in its coming to be, the spontaneous creativity in what it adds to the past and with which it selects what future possibilities to actualize is a primary locus of the ontological act creating. It creates temporal beings in the temporal location of their coming to be. Some mystics focus on cultivating the experience of sheer present creativity. This sheer being-created-here-now for a thing is the ontological creative act in that part of its terminus that is that event in its present happening.

Second, that present event is conditioned by all the past actual things with respect to which it is determinate. Two senses of ontological contingency are involved here. First, each of those past events had spontaneous creativity when it was in its own present moment, and so the ontological creative act is creating the present event along with the past events that are external to it and had their own moments of coming to be. Second, each of those past conditioning actuality enter the present moment as conditions and thus have ontological as well as cosmological standing within the present moment. Some mystics cultivate the experience of other things being such as they are, in relative irrelevance to the present moment. Other mystics cultivate the experience of things as not being other but as being unified within the present moment.

Third, the present event is conditioned by all the relevant future possibilities that it might actualize. Because the determinate structure of the future possibilities, including the alternatives within them, comes from the need to make coherent or unified the diverse previously actualized things, the present faces the future as radically contingent on diversity. This is the ontological creative act in making the many, as relevant to facing the future. Because the determinate nature of future possibilities comes also from the conditions for unifying what the future can be, the present faces the future as radically other than the need to be unified in the becoming of the present moment.

Fourth, the identity of a contingent event in time is both temporal and eternal. It is temporal because each date in a thing's existence has a moment in time with a particular past and future, and this is always changing for the temporal thing. Its "now" is a procession through present moments that is always changing and cosmologically contingent. Nevertheless, each of a thing's dates has a present moment, a series of past actualized moments, and a series of future moments. The ontological identity of a temporal thing is eternal in the sense of being the togetherness of all its dates as present, all as future, and all as past. Because we are accustomed to thinking of ourselves as being only in the present, enjoying and suffering, it is hard to develop the symbols to appreciate eternal identity. But most great religions have such symbols.

Fifth, within time, in a present moment we experience our being as what we are in this way: we are spontaneously becoming the next move on the past and the delimiting power on the future. Our being is to be with the past and future things with respect to which we are determinate. Our being is not exhausted in the moment but is in the moment in ontological togetherness with the past and future, even though mostly the moment is brought to consciousness.

Sixth, things are beings, to use Heidegger's expression, that have relations to others internal to their natures but also have their own-being. The being-itself of beings is their all being created together in an eternal togetherness as well as in their temporal relations. To put it in the active voice, being-itself is the creating of all the beings together. Being-itself is not something over and above the beings. It is the beings together. The beings could not be themselves in their relations without being together.

Seventh, being-itself can be experienced only as the togetherness of the beings. As temporal experiencers, we experience the ontological togetherness of beings only insofar as we have signs to do so. Sometimes this is no larger than experiencing the relevant past and future as involved in present change, with the signs for interpreting that. However, most philosophical cultures have sign-systems for symbolizing and thus potentially experiencing larger swaths of the togetherness of beings. Some cultures symbolize a cosmic narrative, such as the South Asian theory of *kalpas* of expansions of *hiranya garba*, the East Asian ever-flowing Dao, or the modern scientific theory of one or more big bangs. Other cultures symbolize a fundamental underlying reality such as Nirguna Brahman that we can engage experientially through meditative processes of eliminating distinctions. Some, but not all, Buddhist conceptions of emptiness, of which many exist, provide alternative symbols of ontological togetherness on a cosmic scale.

Eighth, the complicated abstract dialectical argument to which I have subjected you intends to be a complex indexical sign that allows us to engage ontological and cosmological contingency. Following through and understanding the argument, and filling in its gaps, is supposed to allow for a kind of perception of the contingencies, an interpretive engagement of the contingencies as they are found in things. To be sure, this is a funny kind of perception, not something framed just in the signs of our neural sensations. It is a mental, or better, Chinese heart-mind perception, appreciating the positive and negative values in the contingencies as well as the contingencies in their places.

Ninth, I submit that the experience of ontological contingency in cosmological contingency is not uncommon and has been registered in many cultures. The interpretations of these experiences, of course, have differed, and I propose my interpretations as the best hypothesis. I remember Jacques Maritain once saying that Thomas Aquinas (St. Thomas to him) was the first and the last of the great existentialists. By that he meant that Thomas pointed to the experience of the "act of to be" delimited in our own finite situations; we experience not only what we are in our situation but that we are, being "in act." This is a very sophisticated interpretation of the experience of existing that I call experiencing ontological contingency. I myself do not like Thomas's Aristotelian act-potency interpretive scheme and much prefer the more process-oriented scheme I've sketched here. But we are describing much of the same experience, I think.

Tenth, if the same general kind of experience can be interpreted more or less well with different philosophical theories, then appeal to the experience cannot be proof for one interpretation over another. Other considerations will have to choose among the interpretive theories. Nevertheless, appeal to the experience can partly justify the claim that there is ontological contingency in cosmological contingency. To those philosophers who deny ontological contingency, I point to the reality as experienced. That indexical pointing is through the dialectical argument I have sketched. One can argue for different interpretations from my explication of ontological and cosmological contingency, but that argument has to defend itself by showing how it can interpret the experience of engaging ontological contingency. In this sense, all our interpretive theories are empirical hypotheses for making sense of experience.

So, Nancy, does this move you to accept ontological contingency? An ontological creative act? The apparatus of eternity and immensity?

Chapter Sixteen

On Charles Taylor

Modernity is a local term used in many ways,
Mostly oriented to Western Culture beginning with
    Descartes.
Western Culture has no inside and outside, however,
So we ask how modernity affects the other cultures as well.
Western modernity overcame the medieval.
Chinese modernity the Neo-Confucian.
What does Wang (Yangming) get over
That Descartes does not?
Wang advanced subjectivity, re-editing the *Great Learning*.
Did not Descartes do precisely the same thing, writing the
    Meditations?
Wang began by meditating on a grove of trees.
Descartes contemplated the stove.
Is this not what modernity is about, the focus on the
    subject?
But is not modernity's metaphysics deeper than subject and
    object?
Is not transcendence within late modernity
The deepest pool of all?
Modernity's lauding of the only secular
Is based on the metaphysics of Nothingness
That opens our eyes to the
Freedom of Creation.

I have been asked to reflect on Charles Taylor's complex thoughts about a Catholic modernity, especially concerning transcendence, from my identity as a "Confucian (and Christian)," to use editor Hellemans's phrase. Let me explain. I was raised as a Methodist in Missouri, am an ordained Elder in the United Methodist Church, and taught in a United Methodist theological school at Boston University from 1987 to 2018 where I was dean from 1988 to 2003. Thus I have a Protestant identity in relation to Taylor's Roman Catholicism with a serious spiritual life and a career of institutional commitment. In the late 1960s I became interested in Confucianism along with many other philosophies and other religions of East and South Asia. My degrees in philosophy from Yale (BA 1960, MA 1962, PhD 1963) had involved only Western materials and I was schooled in the pragmatism that was so well taught there. The more I studied and taught these new sources, the more I became convinced that Confucianism was a set of traditions with which I wanted to identify. I began to practice Confucian ways of life as I helped raise a family and taught philosophy and theology at American universities. In the early 1970s I began the serious study and practice of taijiquan, a Confucian as well as Daoist exercise-art with deep spiritual dimensions. Although I do not read or speak Chinese, I began publishing, not as a scholarly interpreter of Confucianism but as a contemporary Western Confucian philosopher.[1] I have held many offices in the International Society for Chinese Philosophy, including the presidency and the chairmanship of the board of officers, and publish regularly in the *Journal of Chinese Philosophy* and other journals of Chinese philosophical and religious studies. Currently I am on the consultative committee of the International Confucian Association. Thus I have a Confucian identity in relation to Taylor's Ricci-oriented Christianity with a serious spiritual life and institutional commitment.[2]

Confucianism had a bad time of it in China in the twentieth century. At the beginning of the century it was associated with the antiquated and weak imperial dynasty and was rejected by the Westernizing, or modernizing, reform movements, especially Communism. Mao's Cultural Revolution included deliberate persecution of Confucians and Confucian ways of life. Most important Confucian scholars fled to Taiwan, Europe, or America; Tu Wei-ming at Harvard and Cheng Chung-ying at the University of Hawaii have been prominent in preserving Confucian philosophy and bringing it to the West. When I first traveled to Beijing in 1986 I was told by government officials that Confucianism was a discredited feudal philosophy and not a religion at all. When I traveled from Beijing to Urumqi in 2001 I was greeted everywhere as a harbinger of a new Confucianism (my *Boston Confucianism* had just been published). When I traveled to Confucius's birthplace in 2010 it was to take part in a Confucian/Christian religious dialogue, and the Chinese government paid my way. Now Confucianism is touted by the government of the People's Republic as China's native contribution to world culture in religion and philosophy, and many Confucian scholars in the West are worried that Chinese Confucianism is being debased for nationalistic and patriotic ends.[3]

My own Confucianism is no more Chinese than my Platonism is Greek. My 2001 book, *Boston Confucianism: Portable Tradition in the Late Modern World*, argued that Confucianism arose at the end of the Zhou dynasty as a philosophy and religious way of life in dialectical, critical relation to the culture of its chaotic period and that it can be transported to Western social conditions as a worthy philosophy and religion in dialectical, critical relation to social conditions well outside of China. One of the intellectually important events in the modernization of China was John Dewey's two-year tour there from 1919 to 1921, giving lectures across the country.[4] In the 1950s, the newly victorious Chinese government attacked Dewey's influence almost as much as it attacked Confucianism. In 1999, Roger T. Ames and David L. Hall published their extraordinary volume *Democracy of the Dead: Dewey, Confucius, and the Hope for Democracy in China*, arguing that Confucianism and Dewey's pragmatism have very much in common and are a far better set of resources for the future of China than Karl Marx and Mao Tse-tung.[5] They provide a deep and philosophically sophisticated interpretation of modernity in China, citing Thomas Berry's "Dewey's Influence in China."[6] Though he became better known for his ecological philosophy, Berry was my Roman Catholic colleague at Fordham, where I taught for six years, who turned me on to Indian and Chinese thought; he was also my Sanskrit teacher. So I am a Protestant philosopher and theologian with deep roots in Plato, pragmatism, and Confucianism, sharing also a long-term involvement with Roman Catholicism. I am not your standard Confucian dialogue partner for Charles Taylor as a Roman Catholic thinker and I apologize for the need to explain myself at such length.

Agreements with Taylor

Taking a judicious long view, Taylor deeply appreciates modernity's project of achieving universal prosperity, equality, freedom, and flourishing across the globe, no matter how uneven, spotty, and sometimes backsliding its results are in our time. (In my long years as an academic administrator, I have come to appreciate the great power for good of creative hypocrisy.) The very fact so many people in somewhat modern cultures have these ideals is new in the history of the world and astonishing. This modern project is congruent with Taylor's history of the West regarding the self in which the modern era prioritizes the importance of ordinary people; he points out that the erstwhile dominant heroes, the soldiers, the sages, and then the saints, are valuable in modernity according to how they serve the ordinary common good.[7] With all this I agree, although I believe that writing only about Western history is an abstraction from real global history that does violence to the very real interactions among cultures.[8] I shall return to this point.

Taylor asks whether, under the conditions of modernity, we can still be open to religious transcendence or must rather be limited to what he calls exclusive humanism or exclusive secularism. He has written the biggest, most complex, and thorough book I know on secularism, and any summary on my part of his sophisticated account can only be crude.[9] Crudely stated, by exclusive secularism he means the social philosophy that says human flourishing is the limit of legitimate political aspirations and that religious aspirations for anything transcending human flourishing is not politically legitimate. He writes:

> The development of modern freedom is then identified with the rise of an exclusive humanism—that is, one based exclusively on a notion of human flourishing, which recognizes no valid aim beyond this. The strong sense that continually arises that there is something more, that human life aims beyond itself, is stamped as an illusion and judged to be a dangerous illusion because the peaceful coexistence of people in freedom has already been identified as the fruit of waning transcendental visions.[10]

Taylor wants to counter this by arguing for the legitimacy, within conditions of modernity, of human orientation to, worship of, and love of the transcendent. In his lecture "A Catholic Modernity?," Taylor takes advantage of an explicitly Roman Catholic venue to name the transcendent with the Catholic doctrine of God as Holy Trinity. But he is clear that any Christian doctrine of God provides meaning for his question about the transcendent in modernity, perhaps any theism, and perhaps nontheistic notions of ultimate reality. I shall revisit Confucian notions of transcendence later. Here I want to register my own solid agreement with Taylor that relating to the transcendent, however we define it, is good and legitimate within the conditions of modernity.

In his "Concluding Reflections and Comments" to the volume *A Catholic Modernity?* Taylor acknowledges that "transcendence" is an awkward term, and I agree. It supposes that there are boundaries, in this case boundaries to human flourishing, that the transcendent goes beyond. To the extent that Taylor assumes a traditional Roman Catholic worldview, for instance, a Thomistic one, transcendence might suppose for him a bounded realm of nature beyond which is the supernatural including the Trinitarian God, perhaps heaven, other supernatural beings, and perhaps an eschatological condition for human beings. To my knowledge, Taylor has not developed at length a metaphysical system that would sort these things out with plausibility in the modern world. Perhaps this is because of his associations with anti-metaphysical analytic philosophy in his early work, or perhaps it is because so many thinkers in his Catholic audience have affinities for anti-metaphysical postmodernism. I shall return to the topic of metaphysics shortly, but here note that the lack of a metaphysics in Taylor's treatment of transcendence in modernity is a huge lacuna. He cannot say with much exactitude what is alleged to transcend what.

I myself am a happy metaphysician and say that the best hypothesis (to be explained more shortly) is that the world, nature including human persons and societies, consists of everything that is determinate and that it is dependent for its existence on an ontological creative act that itself is not determinate except as creating the world. Call that ontological creative act "God" if you like personifying theistic symbols. Or call it "Brahman" or "Emptiness" if you like consciousness-oriented symbols, or call it "The Ultimate of Non-Being" or "Dao" if you like spontaneous emergence symbols. Because the ontological creative act is not determinate itself except as creator of the determinate things, no literal iconic knowledge of it is possible. It can be referred to metaphorically, however, by taking ordinary things and pushing them to transcend their ordinariness in the direction of ultimate creation. Roughly speaking, the West Asian religions have used metaphors of personhood and agency, the South Asian ones metaphors of consciousness, and the East Asian ones metaphors of spontaneous emergence. Only a metaphysical system that allows each of these symbols or metaphoric systems to be registered fairly can allow of a comparison of them with respect to being ontological Ultimates. The determinate things are related to one another and together they are the terminus of the ontological creative act; each thing is part of the terminus of that act. No way is possible for a thing, for instance a person, to be separate from that act. Therefore that ontological creative act cannot be transcendent of the nature and existence of the thing, the person, except in the sense that it creates other things too.

"Transcendence language" can usefully be used, but not to refer to something apart from the world or us. The transcendent Ultimate is always with us as creative act. But there exist many ways by which it can be engaged that we have not yet engaged, and we transcend ourselves when we come to engage the ontological act in new ways. The ontological act is "transcendent" in the ways in which we have not engaged it yet. Perhaps Taylor would agree with me that modernity's critique of classical religious symbols, Christian and others, has made it harder for many to engage the ultimate ontological creative act than it was in earlier times. Perhaps, however, modern science has provided new ways of engaging ontological creation. Surely, "exclusive secularism" has made it difficult to engage the ontological grounds of human flourishing as defined in the ways advocated by modernity.

I myself claim that human flourishing includes not only the social, educational, and civilizational conditions for a good life but also engagement of the ultimate conditions of existence. Sometimes these ultimate engagements set priorities for quotidian life that amend or transform the priorities that come from social and economic concerns. Sometimes, even more, these ultimate engagements call for human flourishing to empty itself out of the narrower priorities of human life for its own communal and individual sake. Christians say things such as that the first will be last and the last first, and that whoever seeks to save his or her life in the worldly sense of flourishing will lose it, and that whoever loses that life will find it in an eternal sense. I would like to promote *eternal* flourishing of human life, individually and communally, as an extension and contextualizing of "secular" life. Exclusive secularism is a violent abstraction from the fullness of human flourishing.

I am convinced that Taylor would agree with me, especially if we stay this vague about eternity and other conditions of existence, an agreement I will risk when I get more specific shortly.

Meanwhile, I fully share Taylor's frustration with the forces of exclusive secularism and their truculent sidelining of religion into some private sphere where it can be ignored by sophisticated people. The distinction between the public and the private is surely problematic, both historically and in terms of contemporary institutions. To take just the example of academic philosophy, a profession Taylor and I share, the study of first-order theological questions is almost entirely debunked now, except to debunk them. In the first half of the twentieth century, Boston University's philosophy department was the center of Boston Personalism and had a robust program in philosophy of religion. Now no one teaches philosophy of religion or first-order topics about God or ultimacy; I did myself before I retired, but my courses were centered in the School of Theology. The religion department recently excluded all philosophy of religion in favor of the critical (in the "critical theory" sense) study of texts and traditions. Although exceptions exist, the general ethos in the University outside the School of Theology is that people positively concerned with the questions and practices of first-order religious issues are unsophisticated. To say I have felt marginalized in professional academic philosophy is to speak more politely than I am wont. Taylor early earned respect among analytic philosophers but more recently has often been marginalized into the group of Roman Catholic philosophers.

Finally, I want to express my enthusiastic agreement with Taylor's willingness to do philosophical history, especially his monumental projects in *The Sources of the Self* and *A Secular Age*. Hegel did it, of course, and Karl Jaspers's *The Origin and Goal of History* was a masterpiece. Jaspers's work was criticized as being unempirical by empirical historians, and it did not fit into the programs of analytic or continental philosophies.[11] But it is gaining new attention these days, especially because of Robert N. Bellah's *Religion in Human Evolution: From the Paleolithic to the Axial Age*.[12] Philosophical reconstructions of and reflections on history are extremely important for understanding our places in modernity and what openness exists for the transcendent.

Broadening the Field of Modernity

My first job as a Confucian conversation partner in the discussion of Charles Taylor's Catholic Modernity project is to broaden our attention to modernity to take into account its impact on the cultures outside the

West; Taylor's focus mainly has been limited to the West. Excepting a few isolated tribes, the Internet, money and credit economy, medicine, science and technology, and Western-style education and inquiry are affecting just about every society on the globe. Most societies anticipate significant social change with downsides for traditional cultural forms and have a penchant for comparative self-understanding. Modernity arose in Europe but it has become a cultural fabric woven somehow into the garments of every nation. Outside Europe, modernity has been invested in by radically different civilizational traditions.

South Asia has long been dominated by British rule, and so modernity in the nineteenth and twentieth centuries in India had great continuity with European modernity except for the very sharp class differences in South Asia, which has made modernity sit on top of extremes of poverty long since overcome in Europe. Before the British, South Asia was the field of contestation between "native" political regimes and the Muslim Moghul empire. Centuries before the Moghul empire, South India had been the field of contestation between the early Dravidian peoples and the Aryans coming from the north. The Aryans also went west to Iran where its culture was encountered and conquered by the Arab Muslims.

Modernity seems to be coming latest to sub-Saharan Africa through financial investments of the contemporary Chinese in the African nations recently born after the overthrow of European colonial powers whose cultures are still influential. European colonialization of Africa was laid down on a rich mix of early Islam and Christianity with tribal religions, a mix stirred by the centuries-long Bantu migration. The Chinese had made a few massive trading expeditions to East Africa from 1405 to 1433 during the Ming dynasty, led by an admiral, Zheng He, who was a Muslim and a eunuch, but the Chinese at that time explicitly decided not to set up trade connections with Africa and did not go back, banning the construction of ships large enough for profitable trade.

Modernity in China perhaps began with Matteo Ricci prompting a bit of curiosity about the West but did not become serious until nineteenth-century encounters with the American and European military powers, who forcibly opened trade. Then in the twentieth century China was conquered by Marxist ideology, a European philosophy that imposed on Chinese political thinking its fundamental distinction of classes based almost exclusively on ownership of the means of production. That was far more simplistic in its understanding of social order than the highly nuanced traditions of Confucianism. China now has fully appropriated modernity, even capitalism, but in ways that combine both its imported European Marxism and its non-European past. That non-European past includes both its native Daoism and Confucianism and also the foreign import of Buddhism that dominated China during the Dang dynasty and had been incorporated into Neo-Confucianism. The story I told earlier about the shift in People's Republic government attitudes toward Confucianism from my first visit to my most recent illustrates the complexities of Confucian-Marxist contemporary Chinese modernity.

I have jotted down this very brief discussion of international modernity as uniting the globe in so many ways. In each area of the globe, however, modernity rests upon different cultural traditions. Moreover, as illustrated, those traditions themselves are amalgams of earlier traditions, often crisscrossing the Eurasian-African landmass. This global history is vastly more complicated than I have indicated.

Nevertheless, I believe that we need to supplement histories of the rise of modernity in the West, like Taylor's, with global histories that show how the many different contemporary civilizations, to use that term in Samuel Huntington's way, have come to their places in modernity.[13] We are accustomed to thinking of modernity as arising in the West and then being globalized through European colonialization. We need also to understand how the different civilizations were ready for modernization and thus embody it in ways perhaps peculiar to themselves. Then we can ask how their various approaches to transcendence fare.

In order to understand the culture or cultures of modernity on a global scale, three important philosophical tasks need to be undertaken. One, of course, is philosophical history broad enough to encompass the interactions of the world's historical cultures and the reasons why they change. This is what Jaspers attempted in *The Origin and Goal of History*, and we need to do this on a much more massive scale, with alternative philosophical histories in critical debate with one another. We also need to keep updating our global philosophical histories with new findings and suggestions in many other domains of history and philosophy.

In order to develop better global philosophic histories we need to perfect, practice, and produce the arts of comparative philosophy/theology, the second philosophical task I commend here. Two major approaches to comparison of this sort exist now. The first is to root the comparativist solidly in one's own philosophical and/or theological tradition and then see how the philosophies and theologies of other traditions look from that standpoint. In Christian theology, this is often called "theology of religions" and can take either sweeping reads of other-than-one's-own tradition or double down of close readings of the texts of those others (or approaches in between that do a little of both). This is often associated with Roman Catholic comparative projects following the important leads of Francis X. Clooney (SJ) and Catherine Cornille.[14] Because of his frank Roman Catholic commitments, Charles Taylor might be tempted to this approach. But I hope to persuade him to take the other.

The other approach is to center the subject matter to be compared, for instance kinds of modernity or kinds of transcendence, and then carefully develop categories for comparison that are fair to all the positions being compared. This involves two kinds of related developments. On the one hand is the work of getting more and better details about the things being compared. On the other hand is the continual modification of the categories according to which comparisons are made to eliminate bias as much as possible. This requires perhaps distancing the comparativist somewhat from home traditions that set up the initial conditions of comparison, as I have done with the Western notion of modernity and will do shortly with Western notions of transcendence. Whereas the first approach to comparison is willing to give biased and distorting representations of the other traditions because its real aim is to supplement its home tradition, the second insists on the pursuit of fairness of representation.

To be sure, any comparativist is historically and socially located. Nevertheless, it is possible to be serious about lack of distortion and bias, building the correction of comparative categories into the ongoing inquiry. To work collaboratively with others is also a good way to check for bias. To develop decent philosophical global histories, the struggle for fairness in comparative philosophy/theology is crucial.

The third philosophical task I commend here is likely to be a disappointment to many, namely the long work to develop metaphysical perspectives, a point I raised earlier. By metaphysical perspectives I mean systems of categories that can be intended as literally as possible and that do not have to be changed when moved from context to context. Surely no complete escape from metaphorical language is possible and every metaphysical category has a parochial history that biases it. Nevertheless, the effort has been made in nearly every civilizational tradition to develop such categories, and in our time the effort is necessary to develop categories with comparative reach, categories with regard to which the symbols of each tradition can be registered as specifications. In relation to comparative philosophy/theology, a metaphysical system would include the comparative categories among its metaphysical categories. A metaphysical system, however, needs also to develop the categories that connect the categories. It needs to develop categories inventing new perspectives from which questions can be asked. As Paul Weiss used to say, the only protection against dogmatism in philosophy is the systematic critique of the philosophy from as many angles as possible. Some of those angles of critique come from the perspective of doing justice in the metaphysics to the insights of all the cultures that can be compared. Other angles of critique come from practical needs in life for which metaphysics should give guidance. Yet other angles of critique come from the aesthetics of systematic thinking itself. At any given point in time, a metaphysical system is a grand hypothesis in process of being tested and amended. As both pragmatists and process philosophers say, all thought is fallible, even that which is framed to hold steady when applied from one context to the next.

Shortly I shall say something more about the metaphysics I have to offer as a hypothesis in the discussion. Before that, however, I want to address the disappointment that my call for metaphysics elicits among most philosophers today. Analytic philosophers are so anxious to have something to analyze that they recoil from the need in metaphysics *imaginatively* to invent new bridging and connecting categories, particularly when they are needed to bridge radically different civilizations. A century ago analytic philosophers rejected "grand metaphysical systems" as too arrogant: philosophy should stick, they thought, to humble work that can clearly state its meaning. Postmodern philosophers also prize humility and think they have it by limiting their work to reflecting on the history of their own discourse. They are hostile to both metaphysics and large-scale history and have no use for cross-cultural comparative philosophy/theology. Most postmodernists reject all logo-centric stories except their own, which is based on liberating the oppressed from the oppressors. Their favorite oppressor is European (and American, but not Japanese) colonialism and they allow non-Euro/American cultures into the conversation only in the roles in which they are victims of colonialism. Ironically, this further marginalizes those other cultures, quite the opposite effect from what anti-colonialist theory has intended. A reasonably unbiased understanding of the competing hypotheses of the world's cultures, and the global significance of modernity and transcendence, is possible only if all voices are given a fair hearing, which requires both comparative philosophy/theology and metaphysics.

A further disappointment for most philosophers in my project is that both analytic and continental philosophers work within a professional venue in which they write for other professionals in their respective projects, accept peer review by others in their respective projects, and so forth. Taylor's work, and mine, aims at a larger intellectual audience and does not have any steady peer review system. To undertake global philosophical history, comparative philosophy/theology, and metaphysics at the present time is not to be narrowly professional but rather to be amateurish in the best and most imaginative sense.[15]

I fear that my advocacy of metaphysics puts me at odds with the way Taylor has shaped his philosophical career.

A Metaphysical Mediation

I want now to engage Taylor with a comparative Confucian vision of modernity, or at least with part of one. Confucianism is as diverse in its traditions as Christianity, and the one I present here represents the one I stand for, as developed in *Boston Confucianism* and *The Good Is One, Its Manifestations Many*. In order to do this, however, I need to present a metaphysics in which I can represent both Christian and Confucian categories as alternative specifications of Ultimate Reality about which transcendence in modernity might be alternatively concerned. To find the categories for comparing Confucian and (Catholic) Christian interpretations of modernity and relative senses of transcendence, it is necessary to be able to refer to cross-cultural metaphysical categories that aid the comparisons. The following is the hypothesis I offer. For thinkers accustomed to thinking with Taylor about social realities, such metaphysics might seem a stretch, a very abstract theory the relevance of which is obscure. Nevertheless, the relevance is that it makes possible a fair comparative vision of Confucianism and Christianity and a way to get beyond postmodern insistences that we treat "other" traditions only according to the roles they play in the histories of our own discourse.

The fundamental metaphysical idea is that everything determinate is created by an "ontological creative act" that has no nature of its own save what comes from creating the world. Our world can be described many different and mutually incompatible ways. Nevertheless, whatever claims are made about the world are compatible with that world being created by the ontological act. For instance, we have a temporal and spatial world. The ontological creative act therefore creates time and space and is not itself temporal or spatial except insofar as the temporality and spatiality of the world are among its created products; they are elements of the termini of the act.

Part of this fundamental idea is my metaphysical hypothesis that every thing is a harmony that is determinate with respect to some other harmonies. To be a determinate thing is to be a harmony with two kinds of components, conditional and essential. The conditional components are those that derive from the things with respect to which a given harmony is determinate. Those other things thus in one respect are internally related to the harmony that contains them as conditional components. The essential components are those that integrate the conditional components and one another so that the given harmony has its own being. By virtue of its own-being, a harmony has its own nature and existence that can be in relation to other things with respect to which it is determinate. Thus those other things, having their own essential components, are in another respect external to the given harmony. Therefore harmonies are both internally related insofar as they are determinate with respect to one another and externally related insofar as they have their own essential components.

The conditional components by virtue of which harmonies condition one another constitute an existential field in which each harmony is located relative to the other things with respect to which it is determinate. Nevertheless, because those existential relations would not be possible if the harmonies did not have their own essential components over against one another, the harmonies must also be together in an "ontological context of mutual relevance" that embraces their essential components as well. If that ontological context of mutual relevance were determinate, then it would be just another harmony and would need a deeper ontological context of mutual relevance to relate to those it contains. The only thing that can be the ontological context of mutual relevance, I argue, is the ontological creative act, indeterminate in itself but creative of all the things that are creative. The world as it exists is simply the terminus of the ontological creative act.

To put the point in other language, the world consists of *beings*, mainly processes and changes, that affect or determine one another but that do not reduce to their mutual influences. *Being-itself* is the togetherness of the beings as the terminus of the ontological creative act. It would not be possible for the beings to be together unless there is a context in which their respective essential components, their own-being, their inner core, can be together while still being outside the being of the others. Being-itself is the existential act in which all beings have their being. In a sense, this is an upside-down version of Thomas Aquinas's theory of God as the pure Act of To Be, infinite act with no internal delimitations and no potentialities for doing something not yet actualized. Thomas says God is infinite act and that the creatures of the world are finite delimitations of actuality, determined by their essences. Like the Neo-Platonists, Thomas says that the created world is a limited version of the infinite divine nature created by the imposition of negations or boundaries on infinite act. I find this odd—that creation is the introduction of negations on infinite act. I would rather say that creation is the making of something new, not the delimitation of something that was already there. For my hypothesis, the ontological creative act creates anything that is a thing as novel. Without creating the things, the ontological act is not even an act.

The ontological creative act has no phases: its creation of the determinate things is immediate, and all intra-world intelligibility and structural necessity is contingent on the fact of that creation. The ontological creative act is singular in the sense that all things are created together insofar as they are determinate with respect to one another in the ontological context of mutual relevance; thus the ontological act is the One for the Many of the plural things making up the world. Because the world has temporal things in it, the ontological act is not in time but embraces the earlier and later within it with all their dynamisms. All the moments of time are contained within the ontological act as the ontological context of mutual relevance as they are future, present, and past together; they are not temporally together but eternally together. Because the world is spatially spread out, however that is understood, the ontological creative act is dimensionless but contains spatiality and temporality within its product.

Earlier I said that the ontological creative act cannot be described literally but must be pointed to with the dialectical argument that would make sense of the previous paragraph. I also mentioned that three families of metaphors have been developed to point to it: personal agency in the West, consciousness in South Asia, and spontaneous emergence in East Asia. I shall elaborate these in the next section. From the points made here about the ontological creative act, it is apparent how each of those metaphorical systems might point to it and how the act can be metaphorically specified by each system. This is important for introducing the Confucian approach to transcendence to Ultimacy later.

Because any determinate thing is a harmony, it has four traits: form, components formed, existential location relative to the other things with respect to which it is determinate, and the value achieved by getting its components together according to its form in its location with respect to the other determinate things. The philosophical analysis of these four traits is extremely complex and here I shall just assume it can be done. These four traits, form, components, existential location, and value-identity, are transcendentals that would be true of any determinate world whatsoever.

With regard to Ultimacy, the ontological creative act is obviously Ultimate because any determinate world depends upon it. Without the act, there would exist no determinate harmonies. Nevertheless, the four transcendental traits are also Ultimate relative to the Ultimate ontological creative act. The act could not create anything unless the act created it with form, components, existential location, and value-identity. Thus there are five Ultimate conditions for the existence of a world of determinate things: the ontological creative act of all determinate harmonies, form, a plurality of components of each harmony, existential location of each harmony relative to the others, and the value-identities of them all. My metaphysics here is a hypothesis about five Ultimate conditions for existence.

Relative to human existence within the world, the metaphysics displays five Ultimate conditions for human life. The ontological creative act or ontological context of mutual relevance bears the radically contingent character of all existence and provokes human responses of awe, gratitude, wonder, surprise, or the negation of these and like fundamental responses to existence as such. Confucians have these responses just as Christians do.

Form bears upon human life as possibilities for human choice and action, possibilities that often contain alternatives with different values. Human choices determine a powerful part of what the character of the chooser is, and thus all choosers lie under obligation to choose well. All civilizations have problematics of choosing, knowing what to choose, dealing with failure, and the like. Confucians have an even more elaborate problematic of righteousness than Christians do, or so at least it seems to me.

The plurality of components in any human being constitutes a problematic of making a self, of integrating the components in ways that recognizes their values, of overcoming the suffering of brokenness, and so forth. Every civilization has problematics of achieving selfhood, however that is understood. Whereas the Western approach to selfhood has been backgrounded by the importance the West sees in substances, the Confucian approach is backgrounded against its appreciation of changes, about which I shall speak more later.

The fact that every person, throughout constant changes in life, has existential location with respect to other things, every civilization has problematics of engaging others: other people, especially people in other groups than an individual's ingroup, and other things such as social institutions and the natural environment. Confucianism has its version of the Golden Rule. Confucians emphasize the integrative role of rituals in relation to nature, social institutions, and other persons more than most Western cultures.

The fact that every person achieves value, for better or worse, individually, with others, in families and social institutions, or in nations, histories, and civilizations means that concern about the worth of what one does and is constitutes an ultimate condition of human life: this concerns little things as well as issues such as the meaning of life. Confucians discuss the meaning of life in many ways, from the domestic to the cosmic. But they have never suggested that it consists in getting to Heaven (unlike many Daoist schools).

These Ultimate conditions obviously interact in human life. They all involve choice, they all affect the self of different individuals, they all involve social and natural relations with others, they all involve issues of meaning and value, and they all affect just what kinds of radically contingent conditions make us exist rather than not.

Every civilization has problematics, usually many of them, that deal with these Ultimate conditions of life. They can no more escape those problematics than they can escape having to deal with their climates. But civilizations are vastly different in how they deal with these problematics, with different cultures, different historical developments, different geographical locations and movements, and the like. Thus my metaphysical hypothesis is both "realistic" and "historicistic." It is realistic in the sense that human beings respond to Ultimate conditions of existence, no matter when and where they are on the earth. Thus it can sustain a robust commitment to real reference in human life, including philosophy, over against postmodernists and linguistic-turn analytic philosophers who think discourse is mainly or only about discourse. It is historicistic, however, in the sense that all signs are human constructs, all belong more or less well to human semiotic systems that are constantly changing, and all interpretations, including metaphysical ones, are fallible and bear the particular histories of their formation and local use.

I define religion, heuristically, as human symbolically shaped engagement of Ultimacy in cognitive, existential, and practical ways. By ultimacy I mean the five Ultimates of the ontological creative act or radical contingency of existence, form, components formed, existential location relative to others, and value-identity. By engagement, I mean that religion engages the Ultimate conditions as such in relation to the things of the world. Morals and aesthetics engage choices, but religion engages the condition of being under obligation and having to choose. Psychology, medicine, history, and the like engage the various processes of building a self, but religion engages the project of having (or losing) a self as such. Politics, social work, environmentalism, and so forth engage the particulars of building good relations with others, but religion engages the Ultimate condition of having to be with others itself. All sorts of things are involved in our attention to the things of value that we can make or destroy, at many levels, but religion engages the fact of value-ladenness itself. The joys and sorrows of sheer existence operate at many levels of life, but religion engages the issues of radical contingency on the ontological creative act itself. Of course there are vastly different cultural ways of being religious. All this bears on transcendence in Taylor's sense.

Confucian Modernity

The metaphysics I've so briefly sketched serves as a framework for comparisons necessary for a global philosophical historical perspective on modernity and transcendence. We might ask, in some book bigger than Taylor's, how the different social groups of the world come at modernity with their own histories of how they variously have developed problematics relating to choice, integrating selves, relating to others as others, achieving (or losing) value, and dealing with the surprise of the world. We can compare all the different ways in which modernity has been approached and embodied, and how it is being developed and changed differently. But that is not the task for now.

Now I want to take up the task of the Confucian comparativist and engage Taylor concerning transcendence.

The ontological creative act is immediate in its creation, on my metaphysical hypothesis. This means it is not like a temporal act that goes through stages that might be described. It has no antecedent character such as goodness or rationality that can be known apart from the goodness and intelligibility in things created. There can be no icon of the ontological creative act, only understanding of what is created and what that radically contingent created status means. Nevertheless, people need ways to refer to the act, to the ontological context of mutual relevance, to the radical contingency of the world. I have proposed that there are at least three families of strategies for referring to the ontological creative act that have been developed at least in West Asia (the Near East and Europe), South Asia, and East Asia. I shall discuss the first only briefly because it is familiar to Taylor and his audience; I shall discuss the second briefly because it is not to the point of a Christian-Confucian comparison; I shall discuss the third at greater length in order to bring Confucian transcendence into the conversation. Each of these strategies takes a familiar thing in quotidian experience and transforms it into metaphors for the ontological creative act.

The West Asian approach (generalizing brazenly) has been to treat the ontological creative act as God or several gods modeled on our understanding of a person. The personal traits emphasized are usually agency intentionality, action, creativity, rationality, emotion, desire, and goodness. In some West Asian mythologies, there are numerous gods with sometimes conflicting personalities. Of course, God is not an ordinary person, particularly if God is supposed to create persons. By the first century, Platonic ideas of the Form of the Good and Aristotelian ideas of Thought Thinking Itself were common and were used to fix up the idolatry of popular theological anthropocentrism. Within a few centuries some Christian (and Jewish and Muslim) theologians said God transcended personhood as the One beyond the Dyad, or the pure Act of To Be, or Ein Sof. Nevertheless, there was a trajectory of the metaphor of personal agent that led to more transcendent concepts that carried over into the official conceptions, a trajectory that could be followed back down. Thus the highly anthropomorphic depictions of God in various scriptures could be affirmed, with the qualification that they applied only metaphorically. Even Thomas Aquinas, who said God cannot be related to anything, could give analogical interpretations of God as a person.

The hope in this approach to referring to the ontological creative act was to find some character in God, for instance rationality, goodness, or purpose, that could help illumine the human condition. Thus, Christians can be deeply concerned to know the will of God when they know also that God cannot have a will, that is, an unfulfilled intention. Taylor is at home in all these issues and knows the profundities and traps in the doctrine of the Trinity.

The South Asians also began with the person but pushed the metaphorization in a different direction. Instead of infinitizing intentionality, action, desire, and creative rationality, they regarded those personal traits as precisely that which gets human beings into trouble. They infinitized the purity of consciousness, rather, beginning with easy meditative clear-headedness and learning to separate the contents of consciousness from the act of being conscious. The Vedic tradition developing into Hinduisms conceived consciousness as pure atman, and purified atman into Brahman without qualities. The Buddhists turned that upside down, denying any kind of underlying reality, including continuous consciousness in most senses, and said that only the dharmas arise and cease. Dharmas have no own-being or lastingness and for most forms of Buddhism, enlightenment is being able to just let things be. South Asians have believed in lots of gods, but the gods as individuals are subject to karma and thus are not ultimate. The ontological ultimate is imagined as some kind of pure consciousness that entertains determinate harmonies without being dependent on them.

The East Asians quite explicitly abandoned the metaphoric use of persons for referring to the ontological creative act about the time David took the throne of Israel. Prior to that time they had believed in a high God, Shang Di, who was a storm god rather like Yahweh. They used non-personalistic metaphors of spontaneous emergence instead, like springs burbling up from the ground or blossoms opening in the spring. Like the Platonists and Buddhists, the Chinese from before Confucius's time believed that things are changes. So, a harmony in the world, to recall my metaphysics of determinateness, takes the form of a change from one thing to another. The fundamental form of change is a shift in yang and yin. Yang is extension and yin is relaxation or contraction; these notions have a wide range of related meanings. Yang and yin are like waves, which have amplitude (how high the yang goes and how deep the yin) and frequency (how fast waves of one thing go relative to the waves of something else). Since ancient times, two lines of thought have been prominent about measuring yin-yang changes. One is the set of hexagons in the *Yijing* where the solid lines signify yang and the divided lines yin; the sixty-four hexagons contain all possible patterns of six changes of yin and yang. The other is a theory of how the yang-yin patterns constitute the Five Agents: water, fire, wood, metal, and earth; these are not exactly Aristotelian elements but are known for how they change each other—water puts out fire, fire burns wood, and so forth.

On the one hand, the Chinese have emphasized constant change, with differing views on how much is completely determined in advance and how much is spontaneous. On the other hand, the Chinese have said that this process of change—imagine horizontal movement—is also dependent on the arising of change from non-being (imagine vertical creation). The *Daodejing* makes this point. Perhaps it is best to say that there is one Dao with two dimensions. In the temporal dimension, the antecedents "mother" the consequents in patterns that are somewhat intelligible. In the eternal dimension, any duration of changes is to be appreciated as arising out of the creativity of non-being. This latter is a Chinese way of specifying the ontological creative act giving rise to temporal harmonies but not separable from them.

Another way of expressing the spontaneous emergence of processes of change from what is nothing, not even change, is from the eleventh-century Neo-Confucian philosopher Zhou Dunyi in his *Explanation of the Diagram of the Great Ultimate*: For him, the Ultimate of Non-being and the Great Ultimate arise together, and from them come yang, yin, their alternation including time, and the ten thousand things. Commentators have debated whether the Ultimate of Non-being and the Great Ultimate are two things or one. I read them as two dimensions of the process of changes, the unity of which is the Great Ultimate and the source of which is the arising spontaneously of the Great Ultimate from that which has no characters, the ontological creative act in my sense. These metaphors of spontaneous emergence from nothing have no predictive value as to what emerges. You just have to look at the mothering Dao or the state of the changes among the Five Agents to see what the world contains. This Chinese version of ontological creation is not as interesting as the personal agent model of the West for predicting much about human life, although Confucians meditate upon it. It is not a common topic in Confucian philosophy.

What changes according to the Confucian (and broader Chinese) tradition is a primordial stuff, called *Earth* in ancient times and *qi* (Wade-

Giles *ch'i*) in Neo-Confucian times. The processes of changes in this *qi* range from the very steady, regular, and repetitive, such as mountains, through more subtle forms, such as living things, and to the very subtle things such as human minds and hearts, the springs of perception and action in human beings. All the processes of *qi* are natural, and the human parts are just toward the subtler end of the spectrum of patterns of change. There is no dichotomy of the human from the rest of nature, and the components of human life include the mountains and seas. The patterns of change themselves are a function of the source of coherence or form, called *tian* (Heaven) by the ancients and *li* (Principle) by the Neo-Confucians. *Li* as Principle is what makes multiple changes of yin and yang cohere into patterns, especially patterns of changes. If there were no multiplicity of changes to be made coherent in patterns, Principle would not be determinate. If there were no *li* as the source of patterns, changes could not take place in patterns of yin-yang movements. The moving Dao requires both *qi* and *li*, which are ultimate conditions in the Chinese cosmology. Of course, these very general terms have been given many different and often conflicting interpretations.

Human beings are parts of nature whose most central subtle part is what the Confucians call *xin* (heart-mind). The heart-mind is a kind of change that perceives the surroundings and the person according to the kinds of values that are embodied and responds in an appropriate ways. We would say that the heart-mind harmonies are changes that involve aesthetic perception, aesthetic interpretation relative to response, and aesthetic responding. Of course, a human being is a lot more than heart-mind and has to be trained to perceive accurately and act effectively. Confucians more than nearly any other large-scale tradition emphasize the importance of education of the whole person to be able to exercise the central human heart-mind. The whole person is a harmony within which all the world comes as conditioning components, hopefully to be accurately felt in appreciation of the embodied values and responded to appropriately. Instead of conceiving of the self as a subject to which the world is object, the Confucians conceive the self as a moving harmony within nature that can, at its best, exercise the harmonies of heart-mind perceptions and responses. The medium through which the heart-mind works is not only the person's body but also ritualized institutions of life, personal and social habits. Most rituals involve other people as players in a more or less coordinated dance. So the Confucians would not recognize much of a distinction between individuals and groups because each individual is already playing with others in a ritual group. The group is internal to each individual player. *Li* provides patterns not only for the things to which the heart-mind responds but for possible responses to those things; these are possibilities for choice, each with its own value.

Please forgive my vast generalizations about Confucian philosophy. Each point requires a thousand qualifications. Nevertheless, with a generous spirit you can understand in general how Confucian philosophy gives its own specification of the Ultimate conditions of human life. It engages the ontological creative act as spontaneous emergence from nothing to changes. It takes possibilities to be forms for response to the things of the world. It takes the problematic of selfhood to be the cultivation of the self to be effective in perception and response of the heart-mind. It takes the problematic of relating to others to be the development of appreciative perceptions of those things and responding to them appropriately. It takes the problematic of value-identity to be the building of personal capacities, social structures, and interactions with nature so as to achieve value in life and make the Dao flourish.

The ways by which Confucians receive and live within modernity reflect the themes of the Confucian tradition. I do not know the exact shape of modernity in China now, nor do I know just how genuinely Confucian the government is. But here are some points by which Confucians would adapt to the conditions of modernity in their own way regarding transcendence and Ultimacy. Whereas Taylor framed the issue of transcendence in modernity in terms of transcending the limits of human flourishing as defined by exclusive secularists, we Confucians define it in terms of engaging matters that relate to Ultimacy, indeed the five Ultimates. Transcendence is not reaching out to something non-quotidian but rather engaging the Ultimate dimensions in the quotidian. Confucians say that human flourishing itself involves engaging those Ultimate dimensions. Here are some way by which contemporary Confucians would embody modernity in a Confucian way and through that engage Ultimacy.

First, a Confucian modernist would suppress or severely limit the fact-value distinction that comes from early modern European science. Everything that is a harmony, especially a harmony of changes, such as a person, has multifaceted value. Only under highly restricted and self-conscious conditions can things be treated as facts only. This emphasis on the value-laden character of everything is ancient in Chinese culture. When Confucianism became deliberately metaphysical in the

Neo-Confucian period, one of its great concerns was to account for this value-ladenness, which it did in terms of Principle (*li*). The recent importation of Western modern science poses a challenge for Confucianism because of its separation of fact from value. Contemporary Confucians would insist that modern science be received in ways that accommodate the appreciation of the values of things. At the present time, it seems to me, the situation is not at all clear whether the Chinese cultural heritage regarding value will be able to withstand the easy fact-value distinction that makes it so convenient to exploit people and nature for selfish ends. Confucians insist on maintaining the aesthetic basis of human life while learning and advancing modern science. To deny the ubiquity of value-ladenness, for the Confucian viewpoint, would be to deny a transcendent element of Ultimacy.

Second, and following from the first point, a contemporary Confucian modernist would suffuse social behavior of all sorts, especially economic, political, and global communications behavior, with an intentionality of cultivating better appreciation of the values of things and how they interconnect. Sometimes we think this can be accomplished by embedding humanities requirements in scientific and technical education, which surely is a good thing. But it is not enough. Confucians would insist on adding aesthetic considerations to the construction of daily life and the adventures of high civilization. Attempts to consider the values of things along with everything else need to be sustained as habits in our ritual plays. Confucians believe that the ultimate of selfhood is the cultivated capacities of heart-mind (*xin*) to perceive with appreciation and respond with appropriate tending to the values at stake in the situation. The cultivation of heart-mind is an Ultimate norm for human selfhood.

Third, a contemporary Confucian modernist would be highly suspicious and critical of any attempt to draw a sharp line between human flourishing and the flourishing of nature and social institutions. All of these are simply different configurations of nature and are interconnected. Human flourishing means the life of enhancing the values of things we might affect. This includes enhancing a person's personal life but also that of family and community; that of large-scale social institutions such as education, the economy, and the government; and also that of nature near and far, short run and long run. In Confucian modernity, no dichotomy should exist between enhancing human flourishing and enhancing environmental flourishing, although there are countless important interventions in environmental inertias to stabilize and enhance the human habitat, social institutions, and other aspects of nature. Special attention to the continuities within nature is a transcendent experience of the Ultimacy of the existential field.

Fourth, a contemporary Confucian modernist would recognize that among the valuable characteristics of other people are their own choices and heritages regarding culture, their own attempts at building selfhood, their own engagements with others, and their own senses of life's value and meaning. Therefore, because of the modern global kinds of interactions, a cultural pluralism needs to be sustained. Confucians would recognize that Confucianism is only one of many traditions being developed and relating now to modernist conditions. Confucians would insist on treating people of other cultures as appreciable "others" while engaged in modernist interactions. This treatment of the Ultimate importance of cultural pluralism, recognizing and appreciating other cultures on their own terms, is something new within the traditions of Confucianism that had usually taken Confucian culture to be superior to all others. Now Confucians can interact with other forms of high civilization and appreciate them for what they stand for. This is not to say at all that all the cultures are equally good, as if we could calculate equality. Detailed comparison of the various values found in different cultures, with appreciation and relative assessment, is extremely difficult and the world's intellectuals are only beginning to work on that task. Nevertheless, to engage in an existential field with other cultures requires respecting them for their achievements and failures in their place.

Fifth, a contemporary Confucian modern person would see that a primary task in global modernity is to invent, build, and practice rituals of interacting across cultural boundaries in economics, politics, military dispositions, and all forms of communication. Whereas Western anthropologists tend to interpret rituals as the creation of boundaries around social groups, legitimating the borders of ingroups, Confucian ritual theory emphasizes ritual practices as bridging the boundaries among social groups, for instance among different social classes in a geographical locale and among different cultures. A practiced ritual accomplishes something through the human, institutional, and natural interactions, such as economic production, political governance and negotiation, military conditions, and communication. To accomplish those things, the players need to do their part in the ritual, but they do not have to like one another or even know one another outside the ritual play, or share common values and aspirations except insofar as that is involved in making the rituals work. A shorthand way of saying this is that the global social interactions involved in modernity should be made courteous, which means fostering the rituals of courtesy that recognize cultural pluralism. This point builds on the previous one but emphasizes the Confucian conviction that engagement with others, including other institutions and other parts of nature, is primarily through rituals for which human beings can take responsibility. Rituals allow people to be respected as selves in the existential field through which they interact and thus have an Ultimate dimension.

Sixth, a contemporary Confucian modernist would see that part of human flourishing is engaging Ultimacy in all its forms, including versions of form itself, components to be formed, engagement with others, the value and meaning of life, and recognition and response to the radical contingency of existence—the Dao that cannot be named, the Great Ultimate arising from the Ultimate of Non-being. All of these engagements go beyond or transcend exclusive humanism that limits human flourishing to what is served in "an affirmation of universal human rights—to life, freedom, citizenship, self-realization—which are seen as radically unconditional."[16] These religious engagements of Ultimacy are not over and above human flourishing, but part of it. This point makes explicit that human flourishing requires what Taylor would call transcendence to something beyond exclusive secularism. Confucians would insist that life in modernity is deeply rooted in engaging Ultimacy in at least the five ways I have defined ultimacy. No doubt should exist that Confucianism is a religion!

The next five points single out attention to the five Ultimate realities I have described as conditions within which modernity can be embodied in Confucian ways. The previous points have stressed their interactions.

Seventh, beyond getting people to choose and behave well, surely a seriously important goal defining much of Confucian culture, a contemporary Confucian modernist would stress the religious importance of living under obligation as an Ultimate condition of human life. Because of the Ultimate condition of form, regarding which people need to make choices among alternative possibilities, part of personhood or selfhood is being under the obligation to choose well. I believe that modern Confucians would insist on four dimensions of choosing well: choosing to inquire and know truly, choosing what to actualize in specific choices, choosing to conform one's life's patterns to the realities of one's situation with appropriate critical and reinforcing pressures, and choosing to be a virtuous person who enhances the situations in which one lives. This is a religious condition for oneself, and it is part of the dignity with which other people should be regarded: others are to be regarded as living under obligation as well.

Eighth, beyond doing the things that seem right for selfhood, such as the universal rights quoted from Taylor above, a contemporary Confucian modernist would transcend the efforts at selfhood and see the responsibility for building a self to be a religiously Ultimate condition of human life. A person's life has many parts that need to be integrated, including inherited DNA, health, age, family situation, community location, and institutions such as education, healthcare, and economic structure; a person also has to integrate a political and historical environment into selfhood, and all the accidents of friendship, love, and social intercourse. A person must also integrate matters of suffering relative to conditions such as these. All this is to say that a person needs to harmonize the essential and conditional components of life, an Ultimate condition of life. This is so regardless of how a person in a culture defines the ideals, ways, and means of building a self. Building a self is part of human flourishing, and Confucians would insist that it is an Ultimate condition of life. Confucians can accept modernity only insofar as it respects the religious ground of the necessity of self-building.

Ninth, beyond engaging other people, institutions, and elements of nature as others, a contemporary Confucian modernist would see that the obligation to respect things from their own perspective is an ultimate religious condition of human life. Not only should modernity allow for the appreciation of the values of other things but it should also foster the abilities of people to take up those other perspective as their own so as to be respectful. This is so even when the occupation of those other perspectives is temporary and inevitably mistaken in many ways. Because so many of the ways by which human beings engage others are carried by ritualized institutions, an ultimate obligation exists to care for and minister to the institutions and ritual practices involved in engaging others in the deepest respect. This gives a religious dimension to respecting differences in global pluralism and focuses several of the points made above.

Tenth, beyond doing things to achieve value in one's personal life, community, and historical place, a contemporary Confucian modernist engages finding the meaning of life as an Ultimate religious condition. The meaning of life is to live life well, and much debate has taken place regarding what this consists in. This debate and quest is a religious Ultimate. A crucial aspect of the question of the meaning of life, of course, is how to live it under the conditions of modernity. Modernity means many things in many places, as I've argued. Confucian modernity in Beijing will continue to be quite different from Confucian modernity in Boston.

Eleventh, engaging the radical contingency of existence, which means engaging the act by which all things in fact exist in mutual determinations, is over and above engaging the things in the world, even our own achievements and failures. Confucian meditation on the Non-being at the heart of the sheer fact of existence in the Great Ultimate is a kind of deep piety that is the subtle, quiet glory of human flourishing. All the other aspects of transcendence involved in engaging Ultimate conditions, mentioned in my previous four points, determine priorities for life that are set on top of and penetrate through the priorities of non-ultimate engagements of life. Engaging the Dao that cannot be named in the Dao that can, a version of engaging the ontological creative act, sets human priorities aside or makes them penultimate. The pinnacle of human flourishing is giving up human flourishing as a concern to live in awe and gratitude for the radically contingent world of things existing eternally together in this changing world. Confucians and Christians alike point out (at least some of them do) that despite the hurt, disappointment, and evil in the world, its very existence constitutes goodness.

In this chapter I have tried to replay the adventure of Matteo Ricci in China to which Charles Taylor alluded to get both distance and accessibility on our situation. In my replay I have argued that not just the West but the rest of the world, including China, is the situation on which we need analytical distance and participatory accessibility. As Taylor made clear, in our time Catholics, indeed all Christians, need to accept the existence of respectability of other religions and world cultures. This need also holds for contemporary Confucians in global modernity. My Riccian trip to China has crossed through the philosophical needs for global philosophical history, comparative philosophy/theology, and metaphysics that can be specified by at least Confucian as well as Christian culture, all within the conditions of modernity. Though outrageously simplified, I have tried to present the cultural and philosophical background that Confucianism brings to the historical duration of living in modernity. And I have defended Taylor's claim that genuine religious transcendence is possible within the conditions of modernity, in Confucian terms that can be compared through the metaphysics to the Christian versions of transcendence to which Taylor alluded. With how much of this can Taylor agree? I suspect very much.

Chapter 17

On Ray L. Hart

You've published your first books together,
Both too difficult for easy readership.
Yet our hearts are joined about the Ultimate.
We never agree, but we never disagree or give up.
We struggled with each other to mature our philosophies,
Neither agreeing nor disagreeing.
After many years, he returned to retirement to Montana
 and I took retirement here.
He published his last book, again too difficult for easy
 readership.
I keep publishing aiming to reach agreement.
What else can you do with a friend?

Ray Hart and I have been friends since before his first book came out in 1968 (my first book came out the same year). Although we both had gone to Yale University, he was in theology and I was in philosophy. Nevertheless, we dealt with many of the same topics: God, *creatio ex nihilo*, being-itself, nothingness, parallels between God and human development, and the special qualities of language about God analyzed after it is used, not in prospect. Given those topics and our time, it is unlikely that one of us would have undertaken them, let alone both. We also share the fate of being hired for our administrative effectiveness, not for our theological ideas or writings. For both of us, the administration has passed and our writings continue to raise the deepest questions.

Why is it, then, that I still have questions for Ray? Here they are.

1. Is all thought temporal?
2. Can God be perceived?
3. Does eternity set the conditions for temporality?
4. Is *creatio ex nihilo* a surprise?

Is All Thought Temporal?

Aristotle thought that perfection is the most excellent thing and that perfection consists in a thing's potentials being completely actualized with nothing left to do. He thought that we human beings recognize this and strive for the experience of contemplation as the best we can do. But contemplation, thought knowing its object thought completely, is still hedged around by other considerations. We get tired of sitting and go off to dinner. At best we might glimpse this quasi-divine identity, although most of us do not do that, and "one swallow does not make a summer."

Ray and I recognize Aristotle's assumed limitation and agree in rejecting his actualization theory of thinking. For us, thinking is always changing. For some of the Hindu philosophers, the ideal is to reach a constant steady state with no change, but no one that I know of would say that our thinking really stops except with death. Ray and I agree that thinking is always interpretation, and one of the meanings of interpretation is always to point toward a future that involves change.

For me, thinking consists in interpretation, following rather much along Peirce's line. Everything is a sign that points to its object when interpreted by another sign that takes the sign to stand for its object. The interpretant is itself a sign that calls for further signs. Within the course of nature, things prompt signs to interpret them. Even when a course of signs is interrupted, any sign within it still anticipates its being interpreted. Some courses of signs are so esoteric that we say they are all within a person, this person's thinking, although the person is constantly bombarded with signs from other things.

For Ray, all this is true but elementary. Real thinking consists in those esoteric signs that are interior to a person. We are both realists, with signs coming from outside and reference going to things outside, even to God. But he is far more sophisticated than I in his account of multiple layers of signs upon signs upon signs, and thinking of God in all those ways at once. Part of his realism is in thinking God, *creatio ex nihilo*, being, nothingness, the relation of the human to the divine unfolding, and the thinking of all this all together, all at once. He cries for the inevitable privacy of all this thinking. Nevertheless, he also knows his own thinking is part of, participates in, and contributes to the larger thinking of philosophy. But I think he also would say that all this interpretation, including the thinking that learns from what it says, can never stop saying and learning.

Admitting all this, and standing in awe of Ray's mastery of it, I want to acknowledge a sense in which thinking nevertheless grasps eternity and does so once and for all. Suppose we have a person who grasps a multitude of levels of reflection, from a simple God as a Good Guy in the Sky, to Thomas's lover who does not move and is the pure form of what we have in finite ways, to Thomas's pure Act of To Be, to the transcendence of this to the simple recognition of the givenness of the world of determinate things together. According to this person, the transcendence of the personal still gives an "agency flavor" to the trans-agency last few steps. This is a dialectic of agency. Suppose also we have a person with multiple layers but whose layers construe the first person's agency flavor as the very thing that must be rejected in favor of the flavor of consciousness so that toward the end the goal is pure consciousness or something that still has that flavor. This is a dialectic of consciousness. Suppose finally that we have a person whose signs of the Ultimate are no longer at all personal in any sense but natural, who moves from springs and budding trees to the Dao of nature, to the Dao transcending change and making it possible, to nothingness or something like that. For this person, the flavor at the end is not human at all—human beings are within the created order—but natural. Here is a dialectic of nature. This scheme of three persons is mine, not Ray's, although he might not disagree with it. All three supposed persons differ in their flavorings but agree that the last step is surprise that there is a whole world of determinate and partly indeterminate things. This surprise, upon reflection, is that it is reached by the pursuit of what is Ultimate among any of the three routes, or a combination of them, or of some other route.

Now any of these dialectical routes has its twists and turns, each being different. Ray's route can be stated quite roughly by me: the indeterminate Godhead takes infinitesimal steps toward a determinate God by facing off against nothingness in making determinate things that start and stop. How we understand this depends on where we are in our dialectic, with the whole orthodox Christian tradition missing the beginning in the Godhead (according to Ray). But is not any position in the dialectic vaguely correct? The orthodox position is right even though what it says is seriously wrong: it is at least aiming at what is ultimate. The heterodox imagining of the infinitesimal steps of the Godhead becoming God is more nearly right in what it says, but is still so vague in its truth that we would have to read the whole of Ray's last book to get it more nearly right. Perhaps Ray would like to emphasize the negative and say that the heterodox position has a great deal of error, my simple statement of his heterodox view less error, and his book even less, always backing up. But why then do we say that the dialectic takes us closer to the truth? I believe the resolution of the negative and positive interpretations of the dialectic turns on the sense in which we interpret any saying that we say. If we take it to be the last word, literally true, it is just wrong. If we interpret it as needing more work, not being the last word or literally true, it is true as far as it goes.

The problem with "as far as it goes" is that at some point it is as far as we get. We can always say that whatever we say will need further interpretation, as Ray proclaims so eloquently, but still we ourselves can get no further than here. "This" is the dialectic of signs we understand so far and any further interpretation is not for us. We just live with the last step for us. Can we say that this is at least true *for us*?

Can God Be Perceived?

I want to claim myself that this dialectic as a whole, however shortsighted it might be, can be an indexical perception of the ultimate. This is to say, God can be perceived. To explain this I need to develop Peirce's distinction of three kinds of signs, the iconic, the conventional, and the indexical. This distinction concerns how signs refer to their objects. It marks three kinds of reference.

Iconic reference is by virtue of a similarity between the sign and its object. So, for instance, a traffic map is an icon for a territory by virtue of the similarity between what it says are the roads and the roads in the territory. Most of us learned to read road maps when we were younger, and many of us still can read them on the dashboard of our car. The map might also be iconic for the terrain of the territory, marking out hills and valleys, streams, and other elements of the terrain. Architects are particularly good at reading terrain from the maps. Or the map might also mark out population, indicating where the population is dense, nonexistent, or of varying degrees of density in between. Population density can be indicated by circles of different sizes, by filling in areas with colors, or by a host of other means. Town leaders are good at reading maps of population density, or any other kind of density, for instance chiggers, piles of waste, or taxable value to property, not just population. There is one terrain here with many kinds of icons. The use of maps records human interests in iconicity. It also understands iconicity from the standpoint of its interpretive third term, its interpretant, to use Peirce's language.

But iconicity also obtains when there is a flow of natural processes that maintains a continuity of similar structure, like a mountain that remains pretty much the same. Even a mountain does not remain exactly the same, however, and the changes can be measured in movements of iconicity. Sometimes, for instance during an earthquake, there is significant change. Iconicity in nature is also interpreted by many onlookers, including animals and human beings; this continuity or dissimilarity of pattern is noted by interpretants. Natural causation is governed, when it is and to the extent it is, by natural laws that determine that the effect is the way the cause is interpreted. The natural law might be strictly deterministic such that, following Kant's rule, every feature of the effect is determined by a feature of the cause. Or it might be vaguer, saying, for instance according to the laws of gasses, that the overall shape of the gas might be determined but that the behavior of the molecules is not. Or it might be that some aspects of the effect are determined in the above ways and other aspects are not determined at all; perhaps free will is constituted this way. Or it might be that nothing is determined and there is no regularity at all between cause and what comes after. The tightness of determination and its absence can be determined empirically, although it is very difficult to determine complete absence. The complexity of nature is truly astonishing. Whereas the population of squirrels in a given territory might be constant, the activities of the squirrels might involve much novelty. Nature is like this.

Conventional reference depends on the conventions of language. Languages have histories with branches. So, the word "three" shows its evolution from "tres," "drei," and so forth. But it is quite different from the Chinese "san," which contains none of its letters. Borrowing words from one language to another can be strict or sloppy. The objects of conventional words can be other words, as in a book, or it can be nonlinguistic. You can hold up three fingers, or point to three people, and pretty soon your interlocutors will learn what you mean by "three." Some philosophers, for instance Sri Aurobindo, believed that there are natural words, words that have deep natural connections with things. Aside from simple examples, such as "ba-ba-ba" for three things, this is doubtful. Words come to refer to other words according to systems of semantics, syntactics, and pragmatics, perhaps reflecting even deeper structures. There might be many deep structures. Babies are introduced to language by indexical pointing to objects while saying their names in your language, and then learning how these connect in vast ways through the organized, more or less, structures of language. If you count within language gestures, songs, symbolic objects, and a variety of other modes of communication, the complexity of language becomes apparent.

Indexical reference is pointing at the object of the referring sign, like using the index finger to point. A crude case of pointing is to have your neighbor point out a bear approaching. Most of the time, we take our language to carve up our environment so that we notice what the language tells us to notice. Our experience is a constant moving responsiveness to the environment that mostly works with what we know, that is, what we have words for, plus a little uneasiness, sometimes fear or great joy, at what we do not yet have words for or understand the structure of. For the most part, we take our conscious experience to be in very close touch with our perceptions of the world and responses to what we perceive. Nature so often calls to us to pay attention to its traits; as I write this, the rains and winds are very loud and demanding of attention. Other times our purposes guide more of what we perceive and respond to, but all within an ordinary worldview that we take to be indexical. The more sophisticated of us are aware of different shadings of language, of different languages, of different stages of learning language, even of different experiences of language. This is especially important with people who know firsthand several languages and use them all to carve up their environment and interpret the accidents of life. How odd it must be for small children to know both Chinese and English and learn to treat their parents according to which language is spoken at the time, which rituals, which habits!

The occasions in which we cannot take our experience to be indexical of the world are in dreams, hallucinations, and some kinds of play. In dreams, for instance, we know that reality is not what we perceive in our experience, or at least not much. The interpretation of dreams long has hunted for indirection connections, such as predicting the future, or functions of deeper levels of experiential processing. The use of imagination is particularly perilous in treating indexical materials, sometimes allowing for more subtle interpretations of real things and sometimes distorting it a bit, or a lot, or wholly. Signs that usually are both iconic and indexical might turn out to be only iconic.

The perception of the Ultimate is a very advanced and difficult indexical sign to manage. Regardless of our responses to it, being able to rest in that perception is something some people pursue strenuously. Resting in the Dao, or in some simple Western, culturally fleshed out version of God, is not complex and might not really be useful. It is just what we take to be a perception of the world, and we know it is literally false. It is constructed by connections with the rest of what we know and holds little that is Ultimate unless we think about it. But when we do think about whether those signs of Ultimacy are good perceptions of it, we are in some dialectic or other. By dialectic here I mean the entire argument of analysis, criticism, imaginative speculation, and juxtapositions of diverse lines of thought that constitute our views of the Ultimate, for better or worse. The dialectic contains many features, integrated more or less well. Here is the point: without the dialectic, we would be stuck with some previous interpretant; with the dialectic, we have a new interpretant, however confused it might be. With no dialectic whatsoever, our interpretant of the Ultimate is just what we get from our friends. With an immature dialectic, we have learned something new, but there is far more to learn. With a mature dialectic, such as Ray Hart's, we have an amazing new way of thinking about God.

Let's assume that we get as far as reading, understanding, and coming to believe in Ray Hart's complex dialectic. This is a massively complex idea of God, the whole of which we never think at once. We always approach it from the many arms and new conceptions of the dialectic. Perhaps we refer to it as "the dialectic" and then can follow out is parts. Or perhaps we refer to it as the dialectic of Godhead and God, the eternal and the temporal, or the immanent and economic conceptions, although to get into any one of these is to change our conceptions of the others. There are levels upon levels upon levels of many different avenues to the new conception.

The perception of God made possible by this dialectic is never had at one moment. Rather it is general and is had in many moments as directed by the connections of the dialectic and the environments within which we think. How well we "have" that new conception depends on how often and well we think of its parts and overall structures. This is to say, the perception of the Ultimate is never an icon, although it has many iconic elements. It is an index that always points us to the Ultimate. When we try to say what that conception is, we resort to icons and usually break them. The point of the dialectical argument is to get us in the position of perceiving what is pointed to.

Why not rest with Ray Hart's dialectic? Why go on to mine? This requires a return to the dialectical argument between us, and for that I need to make an excurses into the distinction between eternity and temporality.

Eternity and Temporality

Let us begin with determinate things and Ray's agreement with me that they are all created. I have an argument about what determinate things are, which I shall give here; Ray does not have such an argument, at least not in detail.

A determinate thing is a harmony with two kinds of components. Some components relate it to other things with respect to which it is determinate, and other components give it its own-being. I call the former components conditional and the latter essential. With the conditional components, a thing can be determinate with respect to some other thing; it is not determinate at all without this. With the essential components, a thing is determinate on its own over against the other things. Having conditional components entails having essential ones and having an essential one entails having conditional ones.

Each determinate thing is created with both its conditional and essential components. This means it is created in itself as an independent thing with relations. But each is also created in a matrix of other things from which it gets its conditional components. The whole is created together. Thus the creation of the determinate things is both the creation of the individuals and the creation of them together. The creation of them as individuals includes the creation of their conditional components with the other individuals functioning as components, or parts of components, of the first things. The creation of them together includes the creation of them as individuals with essential features functioning to make each individual. The creation of the determinate things includes both the individuals with their essential and conditional components and their ontological togetherness in which they condition one another, and their essential features are independent. If one thing is completely included within another thing, its essential features still must be included within the essential and conditional components of the inclusive thing. Thus the ontological togetherness of the determinate things contains them as external to one another and also as internal. They are external insofar as their essential components are not the essential components of the others and they are internal insofar as their conditional components do make reference to the others, directly or indirectly.

Notice that this creation of determinate things involves all the things together. This togetherness is not temporal in the sense that temporal togetherness also involves non-togetherness—the past is gone, the future is not yet, and the present is moving from one form of affairs to another. It is also not the togetherness of merely the conditional components of each thing. Rather this togetherness consists in the being of the independent things in relation. So I call it ontological togetherness.

Ontological togetherness is purely eternal in the sense of not being at all temporal. Temporal togetherness is all at a moment. Contemporaries are temporally together. The past is not together with the present because it simply is not present: it is past. Similarly with the future. When the present exists, the essential features of the past and the future do not exist. And yet temporal passage is real. There is no time in which the three modes have their essential features together, but they do have them together. They are together in eternity that is not temporal at all. Eternity contains temporal relations within it as abstractions. The abstractions have all the dynamisms of time—past constantly growing, future shifting kaleidoscopically, present moving decisively from one form to another—because those abstractions are real only within the eternal frame that gives equal reality to all moments with their essential components.

We who live within the present moments of time experience the past as slipping away and then being gone. We are no longer together with it. In different ways we experience the future as not yet, but slipping into the present moment. We experience the present only as existent, and yet the present is dynamically slippery, losing to the past and gaining from the future. We would not experience this slippery dynamics, however, if in another sense the past did not exist yet as past and the future as future. The past, present, and future must be equally real for the dynamics of our experience to obtain, equally real in their being. This is their ontological togetherness.

What is the ontological togetherness of time? Each mode of time—past, future, and present—must have its essential components and also its conditional components coming from each other. Essentially, the past is fixed and actual, the future is pure unity, and the present is spontaneous. These essential components would be impossible if they were not harmonized with conditional ones. The past receives from the future its specific possibilities and from the present the spontaneous activity of specifying which possibilities will be actualized. The future receives from the past the diversity of thing that make its unity into diverse possibilities and from the present the readiness of its possibilities to be actualized. The present receives from the past the diversity of actual things to be integrated into its whole and from the future the lures for possible novelties. Every present moment is a spontaneous pulse that receives the actualities from the past and responds to them with possibilities luring from the future.

Thus each mode of time has its own dynamic changes. The past is constantly growing, although it cannot change what has grown. The future is constantly shifting because its possibilities are sensitive to the present. The present has the dynamism of spontaneity, constantly making something new out of what was old and finishing with a newly old novelty. These three dynamisms are not temporally related because they constitute time. Rather, they are ontologically, eternally related. The heady dynamics of time are possible only because they are constituted eternally.

What is our own identity? Let us take as examples really old people such as Ray Hart and myself, people who have been friends and co-workers for about sixty years. In the creative act, Ray has a great many moments and so do I; these moments are all future, all present, and all past. These make up our eternal identities. But let's take a particular moment to be present within Ray's life, say, during his forty-ninth year (when Aristotle said a person reaches their acme). That year I would have been thirty-nine, and it would have been 1978 in the larger world.

Ray was teaching at the University of Montana that year and was in charge of a committee in New York State to establish a statewide religious studies program. I had been hired to run that program at SUNY Stony Brook and moved to Long Island in 1978 from Yonkers for that purpose. There was a lot of communication between him and me that year. Our respective pasts gave us loads of conditional components, many of which we actually shared. Also, in 1978 we looked forward to a dynamic conditional future, his future and my future but also considerable common elements. We both were making many present decisions then, some of which had to do with our relations, and all those decisions, plus many other things, were our essential conditions for 1978. But our essential conditions marked off our different identities. All through his life, Ray had been making decisions of various sorts and these made his past *his* past, not mine. The same would be true of his future from then until now. Our interactions in 1978 had his decisions and also my decisions that distinguished us. My own decisions had given me my past up to 1978 and my anticipations and resolutions for the future; since then I have made yet many more decisions. In this way, we were independent but related and mutually conditioning people. I hope this chapter continues that temporal relationship with a response from him.

Within time, I heard a lot from Ray in 1978, and he heard a lot from me. I thus entered into his reality and he into mine. But what he did with me in his reality was up to him and I can only get indirect evidence of that. I also am responsible for how I responded to him. His essential conditions did something with my objective reality (not subjective) and my essential conditions did something with his. His subjective identity controlled everything his essential features integrated into him, and my subjective identity did the same for me. But this means that my objective identity was his responsibility, and his was mine. Our subjective identities were very important. Yet Abraham Lincoln's objective identity for Ray and me and everyone else is more important now than his subjective identity. Our subjective identity dies with our last breath. Our objective identity lives long afterward.

Eternally there is Ray's moments from birth to death and mine, each of them future, present, and past. That eternal moment is not now, it is eternal. We are also related to all the other circumstances of our lives, our families, works, friendships, and enmities, both temporally in which they are not completely over and eternally in which we are simply together. From within time, Ray and I see the goods and evils of the world from our own perspectives at the time, and from those of our different pasts and different futures. We agree on many of these goods and evils. But we have not the slightest degree of knowledge of the goods and evils of the universe in which we are eternally together, with each other, our families, jobs, philosophies, and all the other things in far off distant space, whatever that is. Evil is where the good of one thing inhibits the good of another. Who knows what evil there is? All we can know, ultimately, is that the God's creation of all determinate things in relation has just the good it does, all interconnected, none of it Ray's or mine.

Does Ray object to this rather exaggerated view of eternity that I have?

Is Creatio ex nihilo a Surprise?

My last question to Ray is a rhetorical one: of course *creatio ex nihilo* is a surprise, a huge one, that which nothing greater can be conceived. You can't begin to imagine how great the surprise is until you follow my argument to see why the existence of any created things is a surprise. Or Ray's argument. We agree that creation is a surprise. But for different reasons.

For Ray, the movement from Godhead to God is utterly free. God is always bound to the past and limited regarding the future. But Godhead creates God in this situation with no bounds on freedom whatsoever. Ray's sense of temporal creation is to preserve God's ability to respond to us (and everything else) and for us to respond to God. I have only a truncated sense of temporal creation. Whereas Ray's sense of God is very limited in freedom, his sense of the Godhead is perfectly free.

For me, abstractly, at a finite point within time, God has created the past as fixed, the future as a still-unfolding panoply of forms, and is at the moment creating the present as a movement from one form to another. In this present, God has created *only* the past. The future is still unfolding and the present is still not finished. The creative part of God, however, is in no way within time. The fullness of time within God has all its moments counted as past, present, and future. The abstraction of time within God, in which we live apparently, has God as finished creator only of the past and not of the present or the future. The abstraction of time within God counts God only as real within time, real in different senses for the past, the present, and the future.

The fullness of time within God does not have only this abstraction to a given moment when only the present exists. The past and future moments also are determinate as present moments, each with its own past and future. The eternity of the fullness of time within God contains an infinite number of different present moments when determination is a passage, an infinite number of those same moments when they are past and fixed, and an infinite number of those same moments in which they are various kaleidoscopes of forms.

Of course, we cannot get an icon of this triple-infinity of senses of determinateness. Rather, my dialectical argument, though persuasive, I think, only points to the phenomenon. It can only be an index.

I would do away with Ray's distinction between Godhead and God. Neither of them exists without the creation of determinate things. With that creation, God is the ontological act that creates them together, externally independent and internally related. The eternal act of creation is entirely free except insofar as some of its determinate products inhibit others. Within the determinate world, things are partly determinate and partly indeterminate with respect to one another, and this gives the world its appropriate senses of freedom. God is entirely free only in the sense that its being as act has no antecedent causal determinates. The creator creating is totally surprising, I think.

Ray would say, I believe, that the distinction between Godhead and God is needed to preserve the distinction between economic and immanent creation. The immanent creation is how Godhead overcomes nothing to create God who then within time creates the world economically. Only when Godhead takes an incremental step does it encounter the difference between nothingness and positive being and overcomes it to create God. For Ray, God can exist only when being-itself has encountered nothingness and prevailed. That prevalence is the action of Godhead, which itself is antecedent to being and nothingness.

This contest between being and nothingness is Ray's great insight and his grounds for transcending the orthodox view of Christianity. I admit in my view that the creative act is a move beyond nothingness. I think the creative act results in determinate things that are positively in being. Ray, however, says that there is something prior to the creative act, namely Godhead, and I deny this. For Ray, Godhead is eternal, with which I would have to agree were Godhead to exist. But I think Godhead does not exist and that the creative act creating is the first and most ultimate thing.

For Ray, the reason he posits a Godhead is that he thinks that from a really real nothing, nothing can come. There has to be a something. He believes in *creatio ex nihilo*, and he believes that the Godhead is completely indeterminate. Yet he believes that Godhead has the enormous task of overcoming nothingness and establishing being, that is, God. So, for him, the Godhead is not exactly positive, since that would put it on a part with being, but rather antecedently positive, a deep mystery.

I think this is a mistake. If the incremental appearance of God overcoming nothing is a surprise, as I believe we agree, then let there be only one surprise. That surprise is the appearance of the creative act creating the determinations. The creative act creating does not appear from anywhere, not even from nothing. It is just here, and it is a total surprise for us. For it to be a surprise, we had to be thinking of something else, had we not? I suppose we had been on the dialectical track of the ultimate, expecting something like Ray's cause beyond all causes distinguishing being and non-being. His cause beyond all causes in itself has no effects; it just is. But then beyond itself it has the incremental effects of overcoming nothingness and resting in positive being, even if only incrementally. The slightest infinitesimal move beyond the Godhead is still a move into being and against nothing. To say that Godhead creates even in infinitesimally small, itsy bitsy increments is to say that it is oriented outside itself and thus creates something else. To have an inside and an outside is for Godhead to be determinate. So, I would say that this just strings things out indefinitely. It is better to say that there is only one surprise, that of the creator creating determinate things.

Our surprise here is not really a disappointment of expectations. We need to give up the expectations of our dialectical search. Rather our surprise is simply the ontological shock of discovering the determinations to exist ontologically because of being created. Doubtless we have the icons of a dialectical search. But they amount to an ontological shock of a perception of the creator creating the determinations. The ontological shock is not of there being something rather than nothing, but simply of there being something—the creator creating the determinations. The ontological shock is not of there being just the creator creating without the determinations—the creator is creating only with the determinations. The ontological shock is not that of grasping some determinations from our perspective—that partial grasp of determinations is dependent on a deeper ontological grasp of all of them independently and together. The ontological shock is not that of discovering for the first time that the creator is creating the determinations—we always have known that, but have not known that we have known it. The ontological shock is not a drastic shake-up—it is rather a sudden settling into what we really are as parts of the terminus of the creative act creating.

After the shock, everything is different. We remain committed to our ethical projects, with as firm a commitment as we have to anything, or we are ambivalent about those projects, or dubious. We have no greater tasks than pursuing those projects. Of course, they mean different things at different stages in life—not so much at first, passionate adolescence, confused pulls in many directions, sorting into hierarchies of priorities, and relinquishing of projects to people in old age. Although this is not the place to argue the point, our very being as persons is to be in a dual relation with our environment: we have duties to truth, to morality, to living rightly, to being virtuous, and to contributing in various ways to our flourishing in our civilization. We have ways of being wrong in any of these areas. Nevertheless, because we are persons we have obligations to pursue them, hoping that we are more or less on the right track. Despite all of this, we are also simply creatures of the creative act, and the shock of this lets us rest in the created world of determinate things being created. To experience this ontological shock the first time sets us back on our heels, but we need also to get back to attending to our duties. If we are lucky, we can experience it again and again, growing more comfortable in that rest. If we are very lucky, we can focus more on this shock in our death, resting more and more in its peace, coming to accept more and more of our beauty in light of the beauty of the whole world. If we are very, very lucky, we can employ our icons of dialectic to embrace something more of the world of determinations, not just our familiar environment. We never get too far with this, but we can make some advances.

So long as we perceive the creative act creating with indices, there is a duality. This duality is part of what makes an index an index. The more we rest in this perception, the closer it comes to unity but always as perceived. The more we grow more comfortable, the closer yet, the more we rest in peace; even closer, the more our icons include within our perceptions the closer we become. But we never give up the perceptive mode, the dualism of indices. Because of this dualism, we are always surprised.

I have gone on a bit about my sense of ontological surprise in order to make it clearly different from Ray's. We have radically different conceptions of God. His divides into a quasi-temporal God to whom we react and to whom we pray (because that God reacts to us and sets up our tasks) and a Godhead who is eternal, indeterminate, and who creates through the difference between being and nothing. For Ray, we respect and love God, and we go through the abyss toward Godhead.

For me, God is only the creative act creating determinations of being. So I would give up the external reality of both Godhead and a God who creates independently of creation. My God is an ontological act of creation that terminates in the created determinations. From the standpoint of any determination, my God is eternal because it is not in time, and singular because God ties together anything determinately different from anything else. For me, God is the world eternally being created together as independent related entities. For me, the appreciation of God is an abyss because of the duality of the perception of this situation in which we find ourselves as created by the creative act.

Of course, the dialectic of seeking the Ultimate through Ray's theism is not the only one, although I have adopted it here. Obviously, there is a dialectic through the alternative theism of south Asian religions according to which consciousness, not agency, is the mark of God. And there is the dialectic through wholly natural, nontheistic means characteristic of China. I think that were we to pursue those alternative dialectics, we would end up in the same spot, my creative act creating determinations. This gives me confidence that my way is best. But then perhaps Ray would argue also that his way is best, that Buddhism, Hinduism, Daoism, Confucianism, and all the rest have iconic dialectics that in the end come down to a perception of Godhead, if in fact he would agree to a perception-theory.

I have worked to advance the friendly argument between Ray Lee Hart and me here by dealing with four questions.

First, I asked whether all thought is temporal. Although most thought is temporal in most senses, I argued that certain dimensions of thought are not temporal. Even though all signs are in time, their relations to one another in perceptions in a sense are not temporal. Does Ray agree?

Second, I asked more specifically whether God can be perceived and argued that God can be perceived. However, God is perceived in different senses for Ray and me. Does he agree with my characterization?

Third, I asked whether the eternity of created determinations alone is fully real whereas the temporality of them is partially an abstraction, and I answered with a long account of our friendship, saying, Yes. Does Ray agree with this, or does he hold to his Kantian view that says temporality embraces eternity?

Fourth, I asked whether Ray and I agree that *creatio ex nihilo* is a surprise and say that it is a surprise for both of us. Nevertheless, for him, the surprise consists in what Godhead does in creating God, whereas for me it is in the sudden appearance of the creative act with its creatures. I believe that my sense of surprise is more surprising than his. Does he agree?

Ray, I salute you with these questions.

Chapter 18

On Wesley Wildman

Wesley J. Wildman's theology can be understood from reading his writings, from being his student, and from being his friend. Although I've read his writings and have learned many new things from him as a student (especially how to manage my computer), my understanding of his theology comes most profoundly from being his friend for more than thirty years. We have been colleagues in curricular matters at Boston University, collaborators on projects such as the Comparative Religious Ideas Project and the Science and Religion Program, and I even had a role in setting up his Center for Mind and Culture. But most importantly we have been friends, sharing families, and the adventures of children, traveling together, crying and laughing together, and being mutual shrivers. Although I cannot express it well, I know a lot about how his theology feels for him and how he feels the world through it. For all our theological similarities and differences, we have come to relate to one another with mutual love. Of that I am more confident than I am of my own theology.

    In this chapter, I aim to articulate some of the main lines of Wesley's theology. I aim also to give a critical reading of his philosophy, indicating where I disagree with him. Because our conversation has gone on for many years, this involves elaborating a bit of my own theology as he has criticized it, exposing our back-and-forth for a wider audience. For those interested in the public record of this conversation, the place to begin is Wesley's "Neville's Systematic Theology of Symbolic Engagement."[1] As he and I have often said, despite the differences between us, those very differences stem from our separate enterprises of artistic intellectual creativity. We offer our systems as different works of theological art, both to be enjoyed as enriching the theological world. To ask which of us "wins" the theological debate is a category mistake. In Wildman's language, we put forward two systematic ways of effing the ineffable.

Although Wesley is an ordained minister in the Uniting Church of Australia, from the Methodist branch of that union (I am an ordained United Methodist minister), his theology is not aimed at Methodists, or Christians of any sort, in a confessional way (nor is mine). Rather, as he argues in his 2010 *Religious Philosophy as Multidisciplinary Comparative Inquiry: Envisioning a Future for the Philosophy of Religion*, he writes theology for the secular academy.[2] "Religious philosophy" is the word he used in that book for "theology," "philosophy of religion," "systematic theology," and "philosophical theology," all of which are more or less synonymous for him, although some might be more natural in certain contexts.[3] More recently, in his 2017 *In Our Own Image: Anthropomorphism, Apophaticism, and Ultimacy* and *Effing the Ineffable: Existential Mumblings at the Limits of Language*, Wesley uses "philosophical theology" and sometimes "systematic theology" for what he does.[4] Basically he and I are both philosophers who focus often on first- and second-order theological topics as they arise in religion, religions, secular culture, and personal life. We are both systematic, having been influenced in this by Paul Tillich. Like Wesley, I have not known exactly what to call myself until recently when I settled on "philosophical theologian," a title supposedly invented for Tillich.[5]

Theology in the Academy

When Wesley claims that theology in the sense of philosophical theology should be addressed to the secular academy, he means two things. One is that its arguments and methods of inquiry should be those that would be respected by the academy. This entails that confessional appeals to special revelation or religious identity are not to be part of academic theology because not all members of the academy could hold to them. This point sets Wesley (and me) apart from a great many Christian theologians who believe they are thinking for the sake of the church with the assumptions of the church taken for granted.[6] Other religions also have confessional theologians from whom Wesley is distinct. Theology as "faith seeking understanding" is *not* what Wesley does (nor I), although it is what Tillich did. Of course, we have both had some form of religious faith since childhood, and for many years that faith has not been exclusively Christian. Perhaps for us the relation between faith and theology is best expressed as "theological inquiry seeking the best faith." Theological inquiry should be respectable to anyone in the academy, regardless of their faith (or non-faith) position.

The second thing Wesley means by the claim that theology should be addressed to the academy is that the academy itself should be interested in academic theological inquiry into first- and second-order religious and theological topics, which it often is not. Many in the academy today think of theology as exclusively confessional, even overtly or covertly Christian, and work to purge it from the academy. Wesley's own university, Boston University, recently has purged him and his theology (as well as me and mine—I then retired) from any of its units except the School of Theology.[7] Where then will the academy treat serious inquiry into what Wesley calls the big questions of theology, for instance the nature of God or Ultimacy, why there is something rather than nothing, the grounds of value and obligation, the nature of the self and its ideals, how to engage others beyond self-interest, the meaning of life? These might be addressed in philosophy departments, in which case they would be philosophical theology, but most philosophy departments reject such questions these days in favor of small questions and with the suspicion that *any* theology is confessional theology. Wesley's limitation of theology in the academy to what would be respected according to academic norms of inquiry carries with it an important normative implication of what the academy *should* be interested in, namely the big theological questions. Denominational schools of theology are not likely to be trusted to represent the best of academic thinking because they are subject to accusations of confessionalism.

I would add two additional points about academic theology that he does not stress but with which he might agree.

First, academic philosophical theology should write for an audience that potentially includes anyone with an interest in the outcome of the inquiry. This would include all sorts of confessional theologians who would be interested even if they could not bring their "confessions" to bear on the inquiry in a trumping way. In this sense, philosophical theology should be at home in denominational seminaries and they should look to learn from it. So should secular or nonreligious thinkers who wonder about the big theological questions. This means that philosophical theology should develop discourses that connect with this interest that is broader than the academy alone.

Second, I would be almost as suspicious of the norms of inquiry in the academy as many in the academy are to the trumping norms of confessional theology. Centuries-old traditions of humanistic thinking have existed in the academy of which philosophical theology is a natural part. But these increasingly are being squeezed out or shrunken in these days when the academy principally trains students for jobs and is coming to think that science, technology, engineering, and mathematics (STEM) are the only truly legitimate forms of knowledge with legitimate methods of inquiry. More than any other theologian I know, Wesley has worked to bring the natural and social sciences into the heart of theology, but he knows that their methods of inquiry are not the only ones needed for theology. Although he is clear about the limits of scientific reductionism and appeals to humanistic inquiries of many sorts, he is not as suspicious as I of the negative effects of STEM for the policing of the academy.

An obvious implication for philosophical theology for the academy is that it should be erudite in a wide range of religious traditions so as to be able to address their ideas and concerns. Wesley was involved during the late 1990s in the Cross Cultural Comparative Religious Ideas Project at Boston University that over a four year period compared some of the big ideas of Buddhism, Chinese religions, Christianity, Hinduism, Judaism, and Islam on the topics of the human condition, ultimate realities, and religious truth. There were six historians of religion and their graduate assistants plus four generalists including Wesley and me.[8] All of us received crash courses from the specialists on their traditions and we all participated in discussions of methods of comparison. Wesley and I collaborated on nine essays spread throughout the three volumes, publishing our findings, mainly on methodological issues and comparative conclusions.[9]

The comparative method on which Wesley and I agreed and that guided the project compares religious ideas as various specifications of explicit comparative categories. The comparative categories themselves are vulnerable to correction as inquiry proceeds, aiming at fairness and lack of bias. This responded to the common criticism of comparison that it employs the categories of Christianity to compare all the other traditions. When the ideas compared can be expressed as different specifications of the constantly improved comparative categories, the ways the ideas compare can be stated. Wesley himself has gone far beyond the explorations of that project in the development of comparative categories. For instance, in *Religious Philosophy* he concludes that there are six theological traditions or categories of historical development that cut across all the major world religions: the ontotheological, the cosmotheological, the physicotheological, the psychotheological, and axiotheological, and the mysticotheological. I shall return shortly to his categories for comparing concepts of God or Ultimacy.[10]

Wesley is one of the few philosophical theologians who insist on broad erudition in the world's religions as the experiential and cultural base from which to do theology. He also insists that theologians need to be able to address the ideas and concerns of thinkers from all religious traditions and from various secular arenas. He himself is astonishingly expert in both of these conditions for philosophical theology.

An important implication of this approach to global religious erudition is that the primary focus in the study and comparison of religions is the logic of the ideas, not close readings of particular texts. Of course, no one would encourage sloppy readings of texts. Nevertheless, many postmodern thinkers believe that only close readings of particular texts are legitimate, rejecting large theories that express and sometimes compare the logic of ideas and rejecting also philosophical readings of history that are needed to bring distant religious cultures into relation. Wesley and I reject those postmodern limitations to large theory and philosophical history and are suspicious that "close readings" can be blind and naive about their own prejudices without them. Wesley has a fascinating discussion of postmodernism in *Religious Philosophy*, chapter three.

Hypothesis and Understanding

Wesley approaches theology with a Peircean method of inquiry that he sometimes describes as problem-solving.[11] Nevertheless, the bulk of his theological writing is in setting up the problems to be solved. This is to be expected, because he has to tie his theological conceptions to the historical traditions of theology and also to the other disciplines that bear upon them. The remarkable thing about *In Our Own Image* is that he does bring the discussion to a well-formulated problem, presents alternative hypotheses, and probates them according to criteria he spells out. I will sketch his argument in *In Our Own Image* to illustrate and comment on his method.

The topic of *In Our Own Image* is the nature of what is Ultimate, if anything is. It aims to set up alternative hypotheses that can be so clarified and distinguished in relation to one another that they can be referred to with acronyms. He finds, after much careful historical and conceptual discussion, three Ultimacy (U) models: U1, U2, and U3. U1 is the class of models of the Ultimate as an agential-being, God as a being who acts in some sense or other, and some kinds of personal theism. U2 is the class of models of the Ultimate as the ground-of-being, Tillich's phrase but a class in which Wesley would put perennial philosophies. U3 is the class of models that have no coherent conception of Ultimacy but that would include theologies of finite Gods, such as Whitehead's in which God plus the world is Ultimate, with Ultimacy rejected as a theological category, and anti-theologies of eliminative materialisms that also reject the category of Ultimacy. U1, U2, and U3 are to be considered as candidate hypotheses about Ultimacy.

Wesley supplements these hypotheses about Ultimacy with philosophical cosmologies that are hypotheses about how human beings might relate in the world to the possible Ultimates. Again, he finds three cosmological (C) models. C1 is supernaturalism, in which supernatural beings might be found within the world and in which the Ultimate as agential-being is taken to be supernatural ("supranatural" Tillich would say), for instance as creator of the world of nature.[12] C2 is cosmological naturalism that denies the existence of any supernatural beings and any supernatural God transcending the world but that finds Ultimacy within nature itself, under some construction or other of "nature." C3 is any philosophical cosmology that denies the theological importance of any conception of Ultimacy. Obvious linkups exist between the Ultimacy and cosmological models. U1 agent-being models easily go with C1 supernaturalism to produce certain kinds of personal theism. U2 ground-of-being models easily go with C2 naturalisms to produce religious naturalisms; they also can go with C1 supernaturalisms that believe in supernatural beings within the world. U3 no-coherent-model Ultimacy views go with C2 naturalistic models such as Whitehead's that have a subordinate-deity theism with a naturalistic theory of the world; they go as well with C3 models that reject any notion of Ultimacy within the world. Wesley's discussions of the various internal complexities of these several hypotheses and the possible combinations of them are subtle and display his comparative and historical erudition. He has an astonishing sensitivity to conceptual affinities and allergies.

Wesley is eminently worth teasing about his love for denotative acronyms and numbered hypotheses. Therefore, I shall refer to *In Our*

Own Image: Anthropomorphism, Apophaticism, and Ultimacy as IOOI-AAU, pronounced *yuu-ee-ow*, or IOOI (*yuu-ee*) for short. IOOI has three magnificent, long chapters on U1, U2, and U3, respectively, with the last devoted to the examination of theologies of subordinate deities such as those in process theology, William James, and others.

How does a philosophical theologian evaluate these hypotheses of Ultimacy? Wesley is insistent on the process of evaluation, not content to leave the hypotheses distinguished and logically interrelated. Strangely, Wesley claims that the criteria for evaluation are rather personal, reflecting the interests and commitments of the theologian. The following are the criteria at which he arrives after long discussions the content of which you can guess:

1. Be not less than personal in the conception of Ultimate reality.
2. Include a conception of God.
3. Define God as unambiguously, definitively, good.
4. Provide a robust metaphysical basis for the hope for life after death.
5. Demonstrate a high degree of internal coherence in relation to Ultimate reality.
6. Eliminate the problem of divine neglect.
7. Eliminate the problem of suffering.
8. Eliminate the problem of divine incompetence.
9. Treat Ultimate reality as the object of religious reverence and worship.
10. Comport well with the Central Result of the scientific study of religion (supernaturalism as an evolved cognitive default).
11. Comport well with the natural and social sciences.
12. Support a fair and non-parochial interpretation of religious diversity.

13. Be amenable to both theistic and nontheistic interpretations.
14. Resist the Rational Practicality dimension of anthropomorphism.
15. Resist the Intentionality Attribution dimension of anthropomorphism.
16. Resist the Narrative Comprehensibility dimensions of anthropomorphism.
17. Support robust apophaticism in relation to God.
18. Support a powerful solution to the problem of the One and the Many.
19. Captivate the hearts and minds of large numbers of ordinary people without specialized training.
20. Support robust religious institutions.
21. Specify a metaphysics that helps to resolve outstanding problems in philosophy.[13]

Note that these criteria for hypotheses about Ultimacy are not easily made consistent with one another. But they do reflect the interests of large numbers of theologians in each case and will determine, among other factors, what each theologian seeks to articulate and defend. Preference is not entirely subjective, however. Wesley assigns high, medium, or low scores to each of the Ultimacy hypotheses coupled with cosmological hypotheses, U1-C1, U2-C2, and U3-C2 (subordinate deity) for each of the twenty-one criteria. Weighting high as 3, medium as 2, and low as 1, agential-being models (U1-C1) get 44 points, naturalistic ground-of-being models (U2-C2) get 53 points, and subordinate-deity models (U3-C2) get 40. Weighting each of the twenty-one criteria equally, "objectively" the naturalistic ground-of-being models (U2-C2) are most plausible, and they are most plausible to Wesley for reasons I shall develop. Nevertheless, different theologians weight the criteria differently, so the plausibility scores do not stand as merely objective.

Here I want to draw a major distinction between Wesley's philosophical theology and mine, regarding how we treat hypotheses. I call Wesley's approach an "external" one in the sense that he as theologian mostly stands outside the array of hypotheses about Ultimacy as if he could delineate their contours as logical on their own and comprehensible to anyone as at least neutrally different. When he comes to his own theological affirmations, he brings his own preferences for criteria in from the outside. IOOI has many very moving passages about his own theological and spiritual development regarding how to evaluate theological issues. He also has accused me for some decades now of merely having personal preferences for the criteria that count heavily in my theology, for instance, number 18, solving the problem of the One and the Many. He thinks it is perfectly legitimate for a theologian to dismiss that criterion and hold to a hypothesis that simply cannot solve the One and Many problem. (To which I answer that someday someone will raise the question of the One and the Many and the very raising of the question will create havoc for theologies who cannot solve it.)

My own philosophical theology I would call "internal" in contrast to Wesley's "external" one. My treatment of hypotheses is "internal" to a philosophical theological system that I have been developing since childhood. Because we have talked about them in depth for over a quarter century, Wesley and I treat pretty much the same Ultimacy and cosmological hypotheses, as well as criteria for evaluating them, even when we frame them a bit differently. Nevertheless, I arrived early at a hypothesis about determinateness in the world and how it demands what I call an "ontological creative act." I have elaborated this hypothesis from many directions over the years, relating it to alternative hypotheses about Ultimacy, the cosmos, ethics, the nature of the self, relations with others, the meaning of life, and so forth. Wesley was a naturalistic ground-of-being theologian from very early years as well, but he has always defended it as the best hypothesis among many, given his criteria-preferences. I have defended my comprehensive systematic hypothesis and its many components hypotheses relative to their alternatives, but with the alternatives considered as within the development of my system. Moreover, I have defended the criteria by which I evaluate the hypotheses within the system in many ways for a long time. My criteria have been vulnerable to correction within the system and are not applied only at the end. Like Wesley, I recognize my particular historical location but try to control for its influence on the elaboration and defense within the theological system.

Wesley sometimes says that this difference between us is a matter of temperament. I say that my way provides a better means for making the whole array of one's arguments vulnerable to correction. Furthermore, I think my way provides a more solid commitment to seeking truth rather than what serves one's interests. One major strength of Wesley's externalist approach is that it allows others to get into it just by following the logic of his analysis. A major weakness of mine is that one slowly has to buy into the system to see how it unfolds, even if one rejects it in the end. Another strength of Wesley's approach is that he can frame his hypotheses in clear, univocal language friendly to denotation, as in the "operational definitions" of the natural sciences. An opposite strength of my approach is that it uses language dialectically, changing meanings by contexts, playing upon odd resonances and connotations rather than strict denotations, thus possibly avoiding the reductionisms that so easily attend scientific operational definitions. Wildman thinks of his philosophical theology, in its approach, as an extension of Peirce's scientific inquiry into theological matters. I think of mine more as the creation of a work of art, the inhabitation of which makes you see differently and understand more of what the world is. My theology comes out to be a non-supernaturalistic ground-of-being naturalism, but a different one from Wesley's. I also share his apophaticism, a point to which I shall return shortly.

Anthropomorphism in conceiving ultimacy is a basic notion signaled in the subtitle of Wesley's IOOI-AAU. Many religious traditions, especially in the West, conceive of Ultimate reality as a God who has something like human agency, intentionality, rationality, perhaps emotions, and perhaps a moral character. No sophisticated theologians would employ crude anthropomorphisms such as that God is a Big Guy in the Sky, as Michelangelo painted him symbolically on the ceiling of the Sistine Chapel. But a great many would develop more transcendent conceptions of divine personhood, claiming that God is "at least personal" if also "more than personal," according to some meaning or other of that "more." Such transcendent conceptions of personhood usually are correlated with human personhood to allow personal relations between God and human individuals (e.g., in petitionary prayer) and groups (e.g., in covenants). "Personal theisms" might take the form of belief in subordinate deities or belief in super-transcendent agent-beings.

Wesley and many other scholars in the scientific study of religion believe that anthropomorphism has a kind of primacy in the founding of religion because it is an evolutionary default response to many things. For evolutionary reasons, people came to attribute anthropomorphic traits to all sorts of things, even things that have no real anthropomorphic structures. People attributed supernatural personhood to trees, storms, and pools and believed in all sorts of supernatural beings, ghosts, living dead ancestors, demons, angels, gods, and demigods. "Hyperactive agency detection" is a kind of cognitive error, but it had its evolutionary advantage. To hear movement in the bushes, attribute it to a tiger, and run like mad is far more adaptive in the long run than stopping to investigate whether it is a tiger or only the wind.[14]

Among many scholars of religion in the West, it is fashionable to *define* religion as belief in supernatural beings and to *explain* the origin of religion as a result of hyperactive agency detection, an evolutionary default behavior.[15] To the contrary, however, what the evolutionary story explains is primitive science. It explains why people who are not aware of such cognitive errors would believe that the world is populated with all sorts of supernatural beings. Modern philosophical, scientific, and scholarly thinkers about science recognize the cognitive errors for what they are and can develop techniques not to be caught by them (hyperactive agency detection is only one of several such tempting cognitive errors). Modern science has banished supernatural beings from its categories of things that exist and interact. Those sophisticated people who identify religion with belief in supernatural things banish religion from its list of true beliefs. I myself think these people mostly are criticizing primitive science when they think they are criticizing religion; vast numbers of people today do indeed hold to primitive or "popular" science.

Nevertheless, whether anthropomorphic belief in supernatural beings is relevant to religion depends on whether those beliefs function to orient people to Ultimacy, Wesley and I agree, making exceptions for sophisticated beliefs in subordinate deities of the process theology sort. Surely it is the case that Western religions have developed anthropomorphic conceptions of gods and a monotheistic God. But Plato's Form of the Good is not at all personal; Aristotle's Thought Thinking Itself has more to do with his theory of actualization relative to potentials than with personal agency (it is pure, non-agential contemplation). But Judaism, Christianity, and Islam have developed increasingly transcendent conceptions of personhood in trajectories that reach to conceptions that are beyond personhood, such as Thomas Aquinas's conception of God as the pure Act of To Be. That trajectory allows for thinking of God as an agent, at least as an intentional creator of the world if not an actor within it, although the end of the trajectory—God as pure Act of To Be—cannot act or intend. Anthropomorphism is surely an issue within Western religions such as Christianity.

In the South Asian traditions around Hinduism and Buddhism there has been no lack of belief in supernatural beings. Just try counting the supernatural sentient beings enlightened in the *Lotus Sutra*! Nevertheless, all such sentient beings were considered subject to karma, and hence not Ultimate. Metaphors for Ultimacy in those traditions focused rather on consciousness, cultivating pure forms of it, distinguishing consciousness itself from its contents, and extinguishing intentionality, agency, desire, rational commitment, and so forth as having any Ultimate reality. Indeed, the very intentional agency the West personified in the most transcendent ways often was taken in South Asia to be the root of the human predicament from which religion seeks liberation and enlightenment.

The Chinese in East Asia also believed in thousands of supernatural beings but very early rejected notions of a High God (Shangdi) for nonpersonal metaphors for Ultimacy such as Dao, Heaven, and the Great Ultimate; the Chinese metaphors center around spontaneous emergence. Sophisticated contemporary Buddhists and Hindus, Daoists and Confucians, by and large have abandoned the primitive science of their forebears and practice their religions with no significant anthropomorphic figures except for teachers and cultural legends that are recognized as merely metaphorical.

Ultimacy

Wesley's theological approach begins with the assumption that religion historically and for most people now is based on anthropomorphic conceptions of God as an intentional agent. The default anthropomorphism stems from evolved hyperactive agency detections, which in most instances is a cognitive error built in to our bio-cultural makeup. Ways exist to control for this cognitive error, as well as others, and careful modern science helps. Because we now know how so many of the capacities for intentional action depend on the biological structures of the body, especially the brain and nervous system, disembodied supernatural beings are increasingly implausible. Nevertheless, he gives the anthropomorphic U1-C1 approach 44 points as scored according to his list of criteria, compared with 40 points for the U3-C2 for the subordinate-deity model, which might very well be anthropomorphic too, and compared with 53 points for his own preferred naturalistic ground-of-being U2-C2 model. In the long run, his greatest complaint about the agential-being models of ultimate reality is that they cannot handle the problems of theodicy if they say that God is good as well as Ultimate. For Wesley, the trajectory of theology is from anthropomorphism to non-anthropomorphic naturalism (sliding off into apophaticism).

For me, by some possible contrast, the trajectory of theology begins with a glimpse of Ultimacy in the orders of things, including the wonder why anything exists at all, and moves through different symbol systems for Ultimacy, including personification, pure consciousness, and spontaneous emergence, finding perceptual satisfaction in seeing the world as embraced in an ontological context of mutual relevance that is best named an ontological creative act.[16] Hyperactive agency detection is important for understanding the development of science but not so much for the development of religion except in the personified theistic West. I am annoyed by thinkers who define religion itself as belief in supernatural beings both because it privileges the West over East and South Asia and because it pays too much attention to the cognitive side of engaging Ultimacy at the expense of existential determination of selfhood and religious practices and institutions.

Wesley's flight from anthropomorphism to naturalism is by no means an attraction to scientific materialism. Quite the contrary, he is extremely clear that science picks up on only certain aspects of nature, which is permeated by values of many kinds. He describes nature as structured by "axiological folds," a term he develops, I think, from Robert Corrington's "sacred folds."[17] Axiological folds are structures that yield values of various sorts, values that can be appreciated in human experience and even more greatly appreciated with increasing scientific sophistication about natural structures. I agree with him thoroughly in this and give my own account of axiological folds as relations among densities of being.[18] We agree that the Ultimate reality is a ground-of-being that gives rise to a world filled with value.

In his "Neville's Systematic Theology of Symbolic Engagement," Wesley points out as if it were a problem that my view of the ontological creative act is that it has no nature of its own apart from what comes in the creating. This is indeed my view. What is created includes the determinate world that in turn includes whatever characters the ontological act has by virtue of creating. I reject *creatio* or *emanatio ex deo*, which Wesley defends in relation to Plotinus in chapter three of *Effing the Ineffable*, and hold strictly to *creatio ex nihilo*, as he says. This might sound odd if you begin by assuming that creation language supposes a creator with a nature.

I am urging a purification of that assumption: the nature of a creator is the result of creating. Another way of putting my view is that the world exists only insofar as it is in an ontological context of mutual relevance; that ontological context of mutual relevance consists in the ontological creative act with the determinate things of the world as its terminus. So it makes sense for me to say that the ultimate is just the world so long as by "the world" you include the ontological creative act creating the world in the ontological context of mutual relevance. In *Ultimates* I became clearer than I was before that it is fair to call my theology a "theism" only when dealing with the personification metaphors of West Asian religions. It is not a theism when dealing with the basic consciousness and spontaneous emergence metaphors of South and West Asia, respectively.

Wesley, by contrast, in chapter three of *Effing the Ineffable*, defends the thesis that there is a theogony by which God develops a character by infinitesimal steps of creating determinateness, which he likens to Plotinus's One giving rise to determinateness. To this, I would ask whether there is any difference whatsoever, no matter how small, between the infinite One and the first step toward determinateness. If there is not, then no step has been taken and the One is alone. If there is, it is a determinate difference, bringing the One into finite relation with the end of the step, and thereby demanding a yet deeper ontological context of mutual relevance to contain the One plus the step, which is my position. If there is a series of infinitesimal steps from the indeterminate or infinite One to full-blown determinateness, either a finite series or an infinite series, each step is a cheat, feigning determinacy and yet denying it. Because any step from an infinite One toward determinacy comes by inserting negations or limitations in the infinity of the One, each cheating step is an addition of negation, or nothingness relative to Infinite Oneness. Therefore, the series of infinitesimal steps, finite or infinite, is just the accumulation of negations. Since any move away from the infinite One is through the creation of negations, why not just call it *creatio ex nihilo*? All that is added to the One to achieve determinateness is negations: the One creates things by creating negations of infinity. Is it not much simpler instead and in conformity to common sense to say that the ontological creative act creates positive determinate things with all their reality, including determinate negations and relations with one another? I admit, with Wesley, that we have two hypotheses here: his, with *creatio ex deo*, moving from the infinite one to determinations by infinitesimal steps, and mine, with *creatio ex nihilo*, a total surd, moving from nothingness to the determinate world in the ontological creative act that is the existence-dimension of all the related things in the world.

Whereas he often speaks graciously of balancing these two hypotheses, claiming they are two ways of construing the abysmal ground-of-being, I recommend taking the better one (mine!). He concludes chapter three of *Effing the Ineffable* in reference to the claim that the two hypotheses are balanced alternatives for construing the abysmal ground by saying: "It is a slender case. And I may not be a wholly impartial evaluator. But the Abysmal ground view of ultimacy looks significantly better to me than the alternatives. Long live symmetry! And long live the playground where we philosophical theologians perpetually attempt to eff the ineffable" (93). His argument that the two hypotheses themselves emerge from the ineffable abysmal ground is by analogy with the story of the big bang in which there was a period when the electromagnetic and weak forces could not be distinguished, followed by a cooler period in which they become distinct. But he already knows that a temporal story is precisely *not* analogous to the eternal theogony of which time is a result. Is he not pleading for a "rational floor" in which the utterly arbitrary, absurd givenness of the ontological creative act creating the world as its terminus is made to seem more understandable in temporal terms? Long live the asymmetry of the ontological creative act that gives us a world with its pockets of order!

In some places, including chapter three of *Effing the Ineffable*, Wesley accuses me of being an occasionalist, thinking that for me the eternal ontological creative act creates each temporal thing in its own time, relations along with the things related. He says this "profoundly obscures the rational conditions for scientific inquiry and human freedom, among many other things."[19] To this I answer that my analysis of determinateness as such applies to any world whatsoever and is vague with respect to whether the world is temporal. But our world is indeed temporal, and so the ontological creative act creates the temporal things in all their connections, with causation as known by science, freedom as known by the pursuit of responsibility, and a whole host of other conditions. We simply have to look to see what the characters of the temporal world are. Great temporal distinctions, changes, and connections suppose that all their elements are eternally created together in an ontological context of mutual relevance containing all temporal transitions.

Apophaticism

Let me now attempt to articulate another subtle contrast between Wesley's philosophical theology and my own, close as they are, beginning with mine this time. I practice theological inquiry in order to develop concepts that guide our engagements with Ultimate realities so that we become aware of what is important or valuable in the Ultimates and respond appropriately. For all its dialectical twists, turns, and interpretations of the histories of religions, the point of my philosophical theology is to be an index that connects us with Ultimate realities and enables appropriate responses. I believe that truth is the carryover of what is important or valuable in the object interpreted into the interpreter such that the interpreter can comport to the object appropriately.[20] I claim my philosophical theology is true, however fallibly, in this sense. Having a philosophical theology means living within the system so as to engage Ultimate realities with guidance as to what is valuable and important for the living. Selections among theological hypotheses are just steps for composing the living system and inhabiting it as vulnerable to correction.[21]

For Wesley, the truth of his theology lies in inference to the best explanation among the hypotheses considered. Of course, vast work goes into the framing and contextualizing of the hypotheses, and the identification of relevant criteria for choice. But for him, I think, truth consists in the claims made for the best hypothesis. Given the roles for preferred criteria, his appeal to truth is as existential and "subjective" as mine. Nevertheless, for him the truth of his final hypothesis (subject to revision) is external to his living in it, whereas for me the truth is internal to the living in the hypothesis. The existential quality of his theology lies in living with the balances of the hypothesis. This is very close to the position I take on "religionless religion" in *Religion*, part four.

Accordingly, for Wesley apophaticism is the denial of the final stability of any hypothesis about the ultimate. Part of this is the general Peircean commitment to fallibility. Wesley holds that the world gives us feedback regularly, if very slowly, to correct our Ultimacy hypotheses. Another part of Wesley's apophaticism is that the criteria by which we judge hypotheses about Ultimacy are inevitably subject to personal preference.

Apophaticism for me, beyond the general point about the fallibility of all hypotheses, consists in the hypothesis that the ontological creative act is immediate, with no intervening steps of creation that might be plotted in a hypothesis. The ontological creative act is not a thing with a structure beyond what it creates; rather it is the ontological context of mutual relevance containing all existing things by containing them. The act contains no reason why it creates this or that, or why it creates at all. Though fallible, my hypothesis explains *why* the ontological creative act cannot be known except by what it creates.

Behind our differing approaches to apophaticism is a deep puzzle between us. I would like to quote extensively from the third chapter of his *Effing the Ineffable* for the bulk of his argument against my position. In that chapter he has established the character of a fallibilist pragmatist like the two of us as a laid-back surfer dude who counts on nothing solid but is hyper-attentive to the waves and swells around him.

> Consider self-identified fallibilist pragmatist Robert Neville. The philosopher responsible for the only significant advance in the theory of *creatio ex nihilo* since medieval philosopher Duns Scotus, Neville reduced the problem of the One and the many to its purest form—the ontological conditions for determinateness. In *God the Creator*, he demonstrated that there is a best account of the One behind the many using this pure form of the problem as the leading criterion. He gets a solution to the rational floor of inquiry for free, having solved the problem of the One and the many.
>
> But there is a trick in the argument. In Neville we have a fallibilist pragmatist who believes a rational floor of inquiry is indispensable for any type of intellectual activity. But he actually invokes as a premise of the argument that there is a rational floor for inquiry. He doesn't make a big deal about it; the premise is not made explicit. But it is a functional premise nonetheless. If the idea of an ontological ground and the concept of a rational floor are as tightly correlated as they seem, Neville's argument begs the question. It presupposes its own answer. His One is fated to be the triumphant solution because the criteria active within the inquiry are freighted in its favor. He might appear to get a rational floor as a result of identifying an ontological ground, but in fact it is the other way around. His uncompromising demand for a rational floor guides his inquiry and yields his *creatio ex nihilo* answer to the problem of the One and the many, eliminating competitor views along the way. Neville's

argument is very strong, and possibly logically valid (it is a complicated comparative argument and so validity is difficult to assess). But the rational-floor premise is deeply questionable.

I think this rational-floor premise is worth fighting about. I reckon Neville functions here only partially as the fallibilist pragmatist surfer dude. It might be the characteristic suit and tie that gives away his incomplete commitment to the surfer lifestyle—though I do admire the way he dresses down when working in the garden or on sabbatical. It seems as though he is ruling on the issue of whether we need an ultimately rational floor for inquiry without considering the relevant evidence. Surfers are always patient and rarely surprised. It is part of the spirituality of waiting for waves and noticing their endlessly varying shapes and potentialities. Neville might have given more patient thought to whether we truly need his One-style rational floor.

I think we can get by without an ultimate rational floor for inquiry. In fact, about half the time I think we are getting by without it. The other half of the time I lean toward thinking that Neville is correct, that the rational floor, and the grounding One that goes with it, really are there. And this raises a question I find stunningly interesting: What if the question of whether there is a rational floor can't be decided?

Very big questions can be answered only by examining the qualities of inquiry to see whether rationality or irrationality dominates—an infuriatingly circular process that provisionally presumes rationality and depends on irrationality appearing as failures of putative rationality in the interstices and at the margins of inquiries. When we do this, what do we find? Well, here comes that generalization than which no more outrageous can be conceived: we see a mixed bag of successful and frustrated inquiries. And we must acknowledge the difficulty of deciding whether inquiries are frustrated because we didn't organize them optimally, because the feedback on which we rely to correct hypotheses is absent or weak, or because there is irrational absurdity at the root of reality. If the latter, we must further acknowledge the distracted genius of irrationality: reality supports the very possibility of constructing inquiries that we are prepared to call rational but now manifested as teasingly rational surds within an irrational ambit having no boundaries, no intelligible features, and no possibilities of final comprehension. Even judgments of rationality necessarily must be merely functional declarations.[22]

Even after all these years of arguing about this, I still do not understand why Wesley believes that I presuppose a "rational floor" for my argument about the One and the Many. Certainly it is not a term that I myself used, and "floor" language sounds terribly foundational in a way that pragmatists reject. In fact, my position is that intelligibility is radically contingent on the existence of determinate things. That there is any rationality at all is a radical surd. No reason exists for why there are determinate things. The ontological creative act is absurd in the sense Wesley means. Sometimes he explains his position on the ground-of-being as its being symmetrical, giving physics the need to account for the breaking of symmetry. This comes from his mathematical sense that basic rationality is symmetry—things balance across the "equals = sign."[23] By contrast, I call my ground-of-being view asymmetrical in the sense that whatever symmetry exists needs to be created: it is an order that needs explanation, and the only explanation is the absurd, arbitrary, gratuitous, ontological creative act whose terminus is whatever is determinate. The ontological creative act is asymmetrical in the sense of moving from nothing to whatever rational somethings there are, an immediate move of sheer creating; "nothing" is intelligible only after the fact of something. I celebrate the title (and arguments) of Tyler Tritten's book *The Contingency of Necessity*, where rationality is included in what he means by necessity.[24]

Given determinate things, however, and I believe there is a given world, the question remains what rationality consists in. Charles Peirce said that it is pointless and immoral as part of inquiry to entertain a hypothesis that says its topic cannot be explained. Wesley agrees, I think, but points out that many inquiries do not work out. They might fail because the inquiries are ill-formed or the circumstances of inquiry are not right. But they also might fail because there is no rationality in what they are trying to understand. In this case, if we could ever tell that this is the case, the inquiries would be right in saying that their topic is irrational.

My own view is that an analysis of determinateness as such might yield a hypothesis about determinateness that would apply to any possible world. I have such a hypothesis and argue that it is a good one.[25] It is not deductive, but it is dialectical and it depends on step-by-step internal persuasion that this is the best way to think about determinateness. We also can inquire into just what determinate world we have here, and this is an empirical as well as dialectical inquiry. My own hypothesis is that the world is temporal and spatial and that determinate things in it are harmonies, which themselves can be analyzed. This hypothesis needs to be argued from the inside. My general guess about the rationality of the world, given the small sample we know, is that there are pockets of tight order with lots of internal rational connections within seas of very little order, vast seas of space-time with very few complex metaphysicians such as Wesley and I and with little order besides some laws of motion. I don't see how this view of mine supports Wesley's view that I presuppose a floor of rationality. Rather, I aim to work argument by argument, on the inside of philosophical inquiry about how systematic the world is, with mini-inquiries taking their form as we understand the contexts and powers, which in turn calls for the development of larger contextual hypotheses.

To summarize my view of rationality, that there is any determinate world with any rationality to it is an absurd fact, simply given. This is explained in the hypothesis about the ontological creative act creating determinate things within an ontological context of mutual relevance. There are characteristics we can hypothesize to apply to any set of determinate things. There are the particular determinate things we can know, fallibly and hypothetically, by various means. And there is a great deal that we find ourselves not grasping by any modes of inquiry so far. We might conclude down the road that there simply is no kind of order of the sort we are looking for in this or that area of inquiry. This is what Wesley notes when he says that irrationality shows up around the edges of our inquiries, especially their failures.

Here is what I suspect about the root of our disagreement, a point I made earlier. Wesley takes an external approach to the hypotheses he formulates, looking to adjudicate them by criteria from elsewhere. Therefore, he balances the hypothesis that the world has a rational floor with the hypothesis that the world is permeated by chaos or irrationality; he claims that it is a significant achievement to think of this dilemma. He has no prioritizing criteria beyond splitting his time while believing. Half the time he sides with me in the cogency of my dialectical argument for the ontological creative act as the one for the many determinate things, but I suspect bias here because I know how much he prizes our friendship. The other half of the time he sides with the irrationality hypothesis because so much does seem chaotic or irrational, but I suspect bias here too because I know that he knows that one of the offices of friendship between philosophers is the obligation to push my vulnerability as hard as possible.

I take an internalist approach to hypotheses, developing a system around which to assess and coordinate them. I say that sometimes the failures of inquiry come from faults in the inquiry but other times the inquiry is correct to conclude that there is no rationality of the sort sought in the topic under investigation. Peirce rejected the claim that science presupposes determinism by arguing that just how much rational order exists in the world and of what kinds are empirical questions, not questions about what is to be assumed for inquiry to take place. The traditional, multicultural grand inquiry, for instance to correlate the positions of the stars with the fortunes of human affairs, has by and large concluded that no close correlation can be found—that the impulse for the inquiry was determined by one of the cognitive errors Wesley points out. Wesley says that even "judgments of rationality must be merely functional declarations." Yes, but when the functional declarations are interwoven in an intricate system whose parts are vulnerable to criticism from many angles, they are not so "merely."

Where do we come out in all this? First, Wesley and I agree that all hypotheses about ultimacy, even the big ones worked into systems such as he and I have, are fallible. We probably would agree even more strongly that anything we think now about ultimacy is probably at least a little wrong and will be corrected in the future. Second, Wesley and I agree that the ontological Ultimate (I claim four additional Ultimates) is a ground-of-being, not itself determinate and the ground of everything that is determinate. Third, we have not yet found agreement on what "ontological grounding" means. As I read (and hear) him, he is attracted to something like a Plotinian view in which the primordial symmetry of the One breaks out into determinateness and determinate things, breaking symmetry.[26] I say, somewhat differently, that the one is the singularity of an ontological act of sheer creation, sheer making, that has no nature of its own, One, Many, or Otherwise, except what arises in creating determinate things. The singularity comes from the fact that the act creates all things that are at all determinate with respect to each other by creating them together as an ontological context of mutual relevance;

it does not unify them. So in the problem of the One and the Many, I dismiss the emphasis on oneness and substitute for it the singularity of all relations and relata. The ontological act is asymmetrical, not symmetrical, as Wesley would have it. Fourth, we agree that inquiry often breaks down, perhaps from its own fault and perhaps because it seeks a kind of order that its topic does not have. Fifth, we disagree about how the world simply might lack order. Wesley would infer that it lacks order if inquiries, in the long run, show more instances of irrationality than rationality. This is his hypothesis contrasting with what he calls the floor of rationality. I would say that how much rational order exists in the world is an empirical matter to be decided by further inquiry; the rationality of inquiry in the long run hopefully can show what aspects of the world are rational and ordered, or chaotic and disordered. For Wesley the big question is whether the world is rational or irrational; for me it is how rational it is, in what sense, and where. He would answer his question by assessing inquiries; I would answer mine by looking at cases. Sixth, we differ about how absurd the existence of the world is. Wesley explains the radical contingency of existence itself by minutely absurd infinitesimal steps toward determinacy from a symmetrical infinite One. I say that the existence of the world is totally absurd, without reason, motive, or even a possible alternative apart from what is given in the world. This is why Wesley says I'm likely to be the only philosophical theologian to be to his "left."

Religious Symbolism and Philosophy of Religion

Permit me to root out one last tension between Wesley and me. He, like me, has been deeply influenced by Paul Tillich, including by Tillich's claim that, because of apophasis, all religious symbols need to be broken. Tillich thought that such symbols still participated in what they point to, and Wesley has approved of my systematic elaboration of that claim, calling upon pragmatist insights of which Tillich was unaware. Nevertheless, Wesley sometimes thinks that broken symbols are mischievous and often used for downright evil; this is the moral outcome of his analysis of anthropomorphism. I, by contrast, try to hedge the broken symbols and use them metaphorically, even musically, to enhance participation in the ultimate reality of the ontological creative act. This leads him to criticize my preaching for allowing my hearers to think I believe the symbols in some literal sense when I do not. I, in turn, praise his preaching for using symbols so musically when he should not be able to do that on his theory of symbolism. Indeed, I delight in his *Effing the Ineffable* for using nine avenues of religious symbols and pushing them in trajectories toward Ultimacy, breaking them only at the end.

Wesley rightly notes (along with Tillich and me) that religious symbols are employed to engage Ultimacy in many ways besides intellectual ones. Most of the chapters of *Effing the Ineffable*, except chapter three, are about existential and ecclesiological engagements, not high metaphysics as in *In Our Own Image*. To be sure, unbroken symbols can be mischievous and evil in existential matters and church life. Nevertheless, the "liberal" project of breaking anthropomorphic symbols can be destructive of religious communities and the faith of large numbers of people, Wesley says in chapter six of *Effing the Ineffable*. He believes those communities need anthropomorphism for their own solidarity. The anti-anthropomorphic mystical apophatic theology he espouses can only live on the underside of organized religion. He does say that organized religion depends on the experiential intensity of his kind of mysticism to stay vital, and so he sees a struggle between community solidarity and vitality.

I would like to complicate this picture of symbolism in religious life by pointing out that at least three related continua exist in religious communities.[27] First is the continuum stretching from popular religion to the most sophisticated kind of religious thinking in a tradition. Second is the continuum stretching from the need to make symbols intimate to human life to the need to make them properly transcendent, which for anthropomorphic symbols means breaking them. Third is the continuum from thinking about most of the world in completely secular, non-religious and non-ultimate terms and thinking of the world as suffused with religious meaning relative to Ultimacy. We in the Christian and Jewish traditions are accustomed to thinking of religious communities as congregations in which everyone in a geographical area is mixed together—from the uneducated to the sophisticated, from the existentially needy to the anti-idolaters, from those who take the secular world on its own terms to those who see the sacred everywhere. This has not always been the case, even in Christianity and Judaism. Thomas Aquinas would have spoken differently to his seminarians, to monks in a monastery, to nuns in nunneries, and to aristocrats, tradesmen, peasants, and villains, shifting his symbols and their interpretation to what each group needs. Buddhists also have distinguished theologians from monks and them from laymen, and men from women. Advaita Vedantins and Confucians often have said that their paths to enlightenment and sagacity are only for some individuals in a community, even only for some individuals within a family, with the others handed over to different traditions of discourse. It seems to me that, in nearly all large-scale religious traditions there exist significant groups who would be up for Wesley's anti-anthropomorphic mystical apophaticism (and my ontological philosophical theology) without having to speak that way to other segments of the community. Wesley's worries about the conflict of communal solidarity with intellectual theological honesty are problems mainly for communal organizations in which all kinds of people are mixed together in congregations.

My response to Wesley's dilemma about religious communities is complex. First, I would never fall to the journalistic or sociological tack of identifying religion with religious communities of a social sort.[28] Those communities are religious in a serious sense only when they are venues for engaging Ultimacy, and here I would hope they would be compatible with some mystics in the balcony. Homogeneous monasteries, hermits living virtually by themselves, and theologians collaborating with theologians from other traditions in developing their spiritual lives have different social settings for being religious, not all called "communities." Schleiermacher and Tillich thought there was more authentic religion in coffee houses than in churches in their times, although they also spoke for churches.

Second, I would say that it is possible to educate people who think they need anthropomorphism and a "personal God" when they really can learn to be more sophisticated and follow the breaking of symbols, avoiding the mischief and evil of anthropomorphism. Third, I point out again that not every religious tradition starts out with an anthropomorphism it has to get over. Many traditions need to become more sophisticated about other elementary religious symbols. Fourth, the social situation of religious communities is rapidly changing, and not too much worry should be given to the ones we have now, for instance congregations, because religious life is already morphing into new, non-congregational forms.

Finally, I believe in the importance of socially organized religious communities in our time, but more for their political usefulness than their necessity for religion. To counteract the excessive individualism of much global culture, there is great political reason to strengthen the social infrastructure. We need educational communities, recreation communities, and economic and special interest communities as well as religious ones. Even if religious communities are totally vapid with respect to fostering engagements with ultimacy, they can be extremely useful for building a rich body politic within which people learn and practice the institutional structures of freedom and equality. This means, I think, that we do not need to worry as much as Wesley does about the religious fragility of religious communities under threat from wild mystics like us. We will find each other irrespective of religious communities.

One of the reasons Wesley Wildman is one of the greatest theologians of our time is that he can preach without the symbols of anthropomorphic deity. I wish he would feel free to preach *with* those symbols because sometimes they are the best music and do not have to be mischievous or evil. But what he has in *Effing the Ineffable* is a rhetorical blockbuster of an argument for the God beyond gods. I have to say that he remains on my right because he thinks the problem is to get over gods. For those with that affliction, he is the soma of liberation. What an astonishing surd of the universe that I have him as friend!

Notes

Chapter 3

1. Walter Gulick, "Toward an American Aesthetics," in *American Aesthetics: Theory and Practice*, eds. Walter Gulick and Gary Slater (Albany: State University of New York Press, 2020), 3–35.

2. Wesley J. Wildman, "Axiological Landscape Theory: Uniting Aesthetics, Ethics, and Inquiry," in Gulick and Slater, *American Aesthetics*, 139–56.

3. "Value" is the word most commonly used in discussions of axiology. Its drawback is that it has the connotation of being the product of valuation instead of what valuation is about in things. So I have taken to using "goodness" and the adjectival form "good" to refer to what valuation is about, the value resident in things by their nature.

4. For perhaps the best interpretation of Whitehead's value theory and its relation to cherry blossoms, see Steve Odin, *Tragic Beauty in Whitehead and Japanese Aesthetics* (Lanham, MD: Lexington Books, 2016). The cover of Odin's volume is important.

5. See Dewey's *Experience and Nature* in *John Dewey: The Later Works, 1925–1953; Volume 1, 1925*, ed. Jo Ann Boydston, vol. ed. Joseph Ratner (Carbondale, IL: Southern Illinois University Press, 1981), chap. 3, 69–71.

6. David Tracy, *The Analogical Imagination: Christian Theology and the Culture of Pluralism* (New York: Crossroad, 1981), chap. 1.

Chapter 5

1. Terrence W. Deacon, *Incomplete Nature: How Mind Emerged from Matter* (New York: Norton, 2012).

Chapter 6

1. Chan, *A Sourcebook of Chinese Philosophy* (Princeton, NJ: Princeton University Press, 1963), 98.

2. Translations of the *Daodejing* vary with the philosophy of the translator. Here is the way Philip J. Ivanhoe translates the first stanza:

> A Way that can be followed is not a constant Way.
> A name that can be named is not a constant name.
> Nameless, it is the beginning of Heaven and Earth;
> Named, it is the mother of the myriad creatures.
> And so,
> Always eliminate desires in order to observe its mysteries;
> Always have desires in order to observe its manifestations.
> These two come forth in unity but diverge in name.
> Their unity is known as an enigma.
> Within this enigma is yet a deeper enigma.
> The gate of all mysteries!

This is from *The Daodejing of Laozi*, trans. Philip J. Ivanhoe (New York: Seven Bridges Press, 2002), 1. Compare this with the translation of the same text by Roger T. Ames and David L. Hall in their *Daodejing: "Making This Life Significant": A Philosophical Translation* (New York: Ballantine Books, 2003), 77:

> Way-making (*dao*) that can be put into words is not really
>   way-making.
> And naming (*ming*) that can assign fixed reference to things is
>   not really naming.
> The nameless (*wuming*) is the fetal beginnings of everything that
>   is happening (*wanwu*),
> While that which is named is their mother.
> Thus, to be really objectless in one's desires (*wuyu*) is how one
>   observes the mysteries of all things,
> While really having desires is how one observes their boundaries.
> These two—the nameless and what is named—emerge from the
>   same source yet are referred to differently.
> Together they are called obscure.
> The obscurest of the obscure,
> They are the swinging gateway of the manifold mysteries.

Ames and Hall give a strictly temporalistic, anti-eternalistic, interpretation of the texts.

3. Ivanhoe, *The Daodejing of Laozi*, 323.
4. Ivanhoe, 160.

Chapter 7

1. Peter Jonkers, "Philosophy and Wisdom," in *Wijsbegeerte*, ed. Natascha Kienstra (Amsterdam, NT: Amsterdam University Press, 2020).
2. Wing-tsit Chan, ed. and trans., *A Source Book in Chinese Philosophy* (Princeton, NJ: Princeton University Press), 65–66. This is a widely available translation and remarkably neutral in tone, though a bit archaic. For instance, the Chinese has a neutral word for a person, needing a prefix to indicate male or female, whereas Chan translates it "man."
3. "A Treatise on *Jen*," in Chan, *A Source Book in Chinese Philosophy*, 594. For our purposes, it is not important that the third in the series seems to be different from the list in Mengzi.
4. Chan, 22.
5. Chan, 30, *Analects* 6:21.
6. See, for instance, Stephen C. Angle, *Sagehood: The Contemporary Significance of Neo-Confucian Philosophy* (New York: Oxford University Press, 2009).

Chapter 8

1. See *The Analects of Confucius: A Philosophical Translation*, trans. and intro. Roger T. Ames and Henry Rosemont Jr. (New York: Ballantine, 1998), intro and esp. 45–65. The first line of the *Analects* contains a reference to *junzi*.
2. John Makeham, ed., *Dao Companion to Neo-Confucian Philosophy* (Dordrecht: Springer, 2010).
3. Vincent Shen, ed., *Dao Companion to Classical Confucian Philosophy* (Dordrecht: Springer, 2014).
4. See Cua in Shen, 291–334.
5. Roger T. Ames, *Confucian Role Ethics: A Vocabulary* (Published for North America) (Honolulu: University of Hawaii Press, 2011). Published internationally, Sha Tin, N. T. (Hong Kong: Chinese University Press, 2011).
6. See Stephen C. Angle, "Wang Yangming as a Virtue Ethicist," in Makeham, *Dao Companion*, 315–35. See also Angle, *Sagehood: The Contemporary Significance of Neo-Confucian Philosophy* (Oxford: Oxford University Press, 2009).
7. See David L. Hall and Roger T. Ames, *Thinking Through Confucius* (Albany: State University of New York Press, 1987), 246–49. They discuss *ars contextualis* in reference to cosmology, but it is about the cosmology for virtuous action.

8. See Tu Weiming, *Humanity and Self-Cultivation: Essays in Confucian Thought*, with a foreword by Robert Cummings Neville (Boston: Cheng and Tsui, 1998), esp. chap. 2.

Chapter 10

1. Paul Eduardo Muller-Ortega, *The Triadic Heart of Siva: Kaula Tantricism of Abhinavagupta in the Non-Dual Shaivism of Kashmir* (Albany: State University of New York Press, 1989).
2. Tran. Wing-tsit Chan, in *The Source Book in Chinese Philosophy*, ed. Wing-tsit Chan (Princeton, NJ: Princeton University Press, 1963), 139.
3. Chan, trans., *Source Book*, 202.
4. Chan, trans., 321.
5. Commentary on the *Daodejing*, 40, Chan, trans., 323.
6. Tran. Wing-tsit Chan from the beginning of Zhou Dunyi's *Explanation of the Diagram of the Great Ultimate*, in Chan, *Source Book*, 463.

Chapter 11

1. Josiah Royce, *The Religious Aspect of Philosophy: A Critique of the Bases of Conduct and of Faith* (New York: Houghton Mifflin, 1885; repr., New York: Harper Torchbook, 1958).
2. Josiah Royce, *The Problem of Christianity* (New York: Macmillan, 1918); repr. with a new intro. by John E. Smith (Chicago: University of Chicago Press, 1968).
3. Dwayne A. Tunstall, *Yes, But Not Quite: Encountering Josiah Royce's Ethico-Religious Insight* (New York: Fordham University Press, 2009.
4. Josiah Royce, *The Sources of Religious Insight* (Edinburgh: T. & T. Clark, 1912).
5. Randall E. Auxier, *Time, Will, and Purpose: Living Ideas from the Philosophy of Josiah Royce* (Chicago: Open Court, 2013). For Royce on Peirce, see *The Problem of Christianity*, part 2 but esp. chap. 11.
6. Royce did not use the language of Ultimacy as much as the language of absoluteness. But I find "Ultimacy" language more flexible for Royce's interests; see my *Ultimates: Philosophical Theology Volume One* (Albany: State University of New York Press, 2013).
7. Josiah Royce, *The World and the Individual: First Series; The Four Historical Conceptions of Being* (New York: Macmillan, 1899). Repr. with an intro. by John E. Smith (New York: Dover, 1959); *The World and the Individual: Second*

Series; Nature, Man, and the Moral Order (New York: Macmillan, 1901). Repr. New York: Dover, 1959; *The Philosophy of Loyalty* (New York: Macmillan, 1908).

8. Josiah Royce, *The Spirit of Modern Philosophy* (Boston: Houghton Mifflin, 1892); *Lectures on Modern Idealism* (New Haven, CT: Yale University Press, 1919). Repr. with a new intro. by John E. Smith (New Haven, CT: Yale University Press, 1964).

9. These categories are detailed in *Ultimates* and in *Existence: Philosophical Theology Volume Two*, as well as other chapters here.

10. Royce argued this systematically in *The Religious Aspect of Philosophy* but restated the argument with greater succinctness in his essay "The Conception of God," in *The Conception of God: A Philosophical Discussion Concerning the Nature of the Divine Idea as a Demonstrable Reality*, ed. G. H. Howison (New York: Macmillan, 1909).

11. See Auxier, *Time, Will, and Purpose*, esp. chap. 7.

12. Mathew A. Foust, *Loyalty to Loyalty: Josiah Royce and the Genuine Moral Life* (New York: Fordham University Press, 2012).

13. See Smith's "The Contemporary Significance of Royce's Theory of the Self," chap. 6 in his collection of essays *Themes in American Philosophy: Purpose, Experience, and Community* (New York: Harper and Row, 1970).

14. See, for instance, Royce's critical analysis of Buddhism in *The Problem of Christianity* in the chap. "The Christian Doctrine of Life."

15. Royce, *The World and the Individual: First Series*, 346.

Chapter 12

1. *Religion in the Making* (New York: Macmillan, 1926), 68–69.

2. Theophilus of Antioch, *Theophilus to Autolycus*, chap. 8, accessed from *Early Christian Writings*, https://www.earlychristianwritings.com/text/theophilus-book1.html.

Chapter 13

1. *Community of Interpreters: On the Hermeneutics of Nature and the Bible in the American Philosophical Tradition*, 2nd ed., Studies in American Biblical Hermeneutics 3 (Macon, GA: Mercer, 1987, 1995).

2. *Nature's Religion* (Lanham, MD: Rowman and Littlefield, 1997).

3. *Nature's Sublime: An Essay in Aesthetic Naturalism* (Lanham, MD: Lexington Books, 2013).

4. *Nature's Sublime*, xii–xiii.

5. Justus Buchler, *Metaphysics of Natural Complexes* (New York: Columbia University Press, 1966).

6. Corrington, "The Categorial Schema," in *A Philosophy of Sacred Nature: Prospects for Ecstatic Naturalism*, eds. Leon Niemoczynski and Nam T. Nguyen (Lanham, MD: Lexington Books, 2015).

7. All this is spelled out in *Nature's Sublime*, although it also is dealt with in more or less this fashion in his other works.

8. *Nature's Sublime*, 159–60.

9. Charles Peirce is in fact much discussed throughout Corrington's work. He wrote *An Introduction to C. S. Peirce: Philosopher, Semiotician, and Ecstatic Naturalist* (Lanham, MD: Rowman and Littlefield, 1993) and then developed a Peircean *Semiotic Theory of Theology and Philosophy* (Cambridge: Cambridge University Press, 2000).

10. The legacies of Plato and Confucius are that to which my *The Metaphysics of Goodness* is dedicated.

Chapter 14

1. *Charles Sanders Peirce: Religionsphilosophische Schriften*, Uebersetzt unter Mitarbeit von helmut Maassen, eingeleitet, kommentiert und herausgegeben von Hermann Deuser (Hamburg: Felix Meiner Verlag, 1995); Hermann Deuser, *Gott: Geist und Natur: Theologische Konsequenzen aus Charles S. Peirce' Religionsphilosophie* (Berlin: Walter de Gruyter, 1993).

2. Stefan Alkier, *The Reality of the Resurrection: The New Testament Witness*, trans. Leroy A. Huizenga, with a foreword by Richard B. Hays (Waco, TX: Baylor University Press, 2013); originally published in German as *Die Realitaet der Auferseckung in, nach und mit den Schriften des Neuen Testaments* (Narr Francke Attempto Verlag GmbH + Co. KG, 2009).

3. Alkier, *The Reality of the Resurrection*, 200.

4. Alkier, 201.

5. "Systematic symbolics" is one of the main themes of Hart's *Unfinished Man and the Imagination: Toward an Ontology and a Rhetoric of Revelation* (New York: Herder and Herder, 1968).

Chapter 15

1. See Robert Cummings Neville, "Nancy Frankenberry: Philosopher of Religion, Radical Empiricist, Herald of Contingency," *American Journal of Theology and Philosophy* 37, no. 1 (2016); also *Defining Religion: Essays in Philosophy of Religion* (Albany: State University of New York Press, 2018).

2. Robert Cummings Neville, "Nancy Frankenberry," 5–20. Her response is "Enduring Questions in Philosophy of Religion: A Response to Neville and Godlove," *American Journal of Theology and Philosophy* 37, no. 1 (2016): 36–52. Some of my arguments in the current chapter are in response to her response.

3. See William Desmond, *Being and the Between* (Albany: State University of New York Press, 1995), esp. chap. 5 on determinism and indeterminism.

Chapter 16

1. My explicitly Confucian books are *The Tao and the Daimon: Segments of a Religious Inquiry* (Albany: State University of New York Press, 1982); *Behind the Masks of God: An Essay Toward Comparative Theology* (Albany: State University of New York Press, 1991); also in Chinese is *Boston Confucianism: Portable Tradition in the Late-Modern World* (Albany: State University of New York Press, 2000); *Ritual and Deference: Extending Chinese Philosophy in a Comparative Context* (Albany: State University of New York Press, 2008); and *The Good Is One, Its Manifestations Many: Confucian Essays on Metaphysics, Morals, Rituals, Institutions, and Genders* (Albany: State University of New York Press, 2016). The last book has a drawing on the cover of me taking dictation from Confucius on my Microsoft Surface.

2. In his lecture "A Catholic Modernity?," in *A Catholic Modernity? Charles Taylor's Marianist Award Lecture*, ed. James L. Heft (New York: Oxford University Press, 1999), 13–37. Charles Taylor makes reference to Matteo Ricci's attempt to become at home in Chinese culture in order to communicate persuasively with them; the issue for Taylor was the combination of cultural difference and cross-cultural participation.

3. See Stephen C. Angle, *Contemporary Confucian Political Philosophy: Toward Progressive Confucianism* (Cambridge: Polity Press, 2012). Like me, Angle is a contemporary Western Confucian. See also his *Sagehood: The Contemporary Significance of Neo-Confucian Philosophy* (Oxford: Oxford University Press, 2009) for a much more fulsome account of Confucianism than I give in this chapter.

4. The lectures were given in English from notes and published in Chinese. They were then translated back into English by Robert W. Clopton and Tsuin-Chen Ou as *John Dewey: Lectures in China, 1919–1920* (Honolulu: University Press of Hawaii, 1973).

5. David L. Hall and Roger T. Ames, *The Democracy of the Dead: Dewey, Confucius, and the Hope for Democracy in China* (LaSalle, IL: Open Court, 1999). See also Joseph Grange, *John Dewey, Confucius, and Global Philosophy* (Albany: State University of New York Press, 2004).

6. Thomas Berry, "Dewey's Influence in China" in *John Dewey: His Thought and Influence*, ed. John Blewett (New York: Fordham University Press, 1960).

7. See Charles Taylor, *Sources of the Self: The Making of the Modern Identity* (Cambridge: Cambridge University Press, 1989). See also my *Soldier, Sage, Saint* (New York: Fordham University Press, 1978) in which I explore these three spiritual models for the self but not as characterizing history sequentially, as Taylor did.

8. I obviously have to say this because I am a Confucian. But I was also much moved by William H. McNeill, *The Rise of the West* (Chicago: University of Chicago Press, 1963) that details many of the crossover interactions. The introduction to the twenty-fifth anniversary edition (1988) deals with many fascinating aspects of global history-writing.

9. See Charles Taylor, *A Secular Age* (Cambridge, MA: Harvard University Press, 2007), 874.

10. *A Catholic Modernity: With Responses by William M. Shea, Rosemary Luling Haughton, George Marsden, and Jean Bethke Elshtain*, ed. and intro. James L. Heft (SM) (Oxford: Oxford University Press, 1999), 19.

11. Karl Jaspers, *The Origin and Goal of History*, trans. Michael Bullock (London: Routledge and Kegan Paul, 1953); Routledge Revival edition in 2010.

12. Robert N. Bellah, *Religion in Human Evolution: From the Paleolithic to the Axial Age* (Cambridge, MA: Harvard University Press, 2011).

13. Samuel P. Huntington, *The Clash of Civilizations and the Remaking of World Order* (New York: Simon and Schuster, 1996).

14. See Francis X. Clooney (SJ), *Comparative Theology: Deep Learning Across Religious Borders* (Malden, MA: Wiley-Blackwell, 2010).

15. The important topic of professionalism, especially in philosophy, is intricately discussed in William M. Sullivan, *Work and Integrity: The Crisis and Promise of Professionalism in America* (New York: Harper/Collins, 1995).

16. Taylor, A Catholic Modernity?, 16.

Chapter 18

1. Wesley J. Wildman, "Neville's Systematic Theology of Symbolic Engagement," in *Theology in Global Context: Essays in Honor of Robert Cummings Neville*, eds. Amos Yong and Peter G. Heltzel (New York: T. & T. Clark, 2004), 3–27. We have both reformulated our positions somewhat since then. See, for instance, Wildman's "How to Resist Robert Neville's *Creatio Ex Nihilo* Argument," *American Journal of Theology and Philosophy* 36, no. 1 (January 2015): 56–64; and my response, 65–68. See also his paper on my interpretation of Paul Tillich in the *Bulletin of the North American Paul Tillich Society* (2018), and my response.

2. Wesley J. Wildman, *Religious Philosophy as Multidisciplinary Comparative Inquiry: Envisioning a Future for the Philosophy of Religion* (Albany: State University of New York Press, 2010). See esp. "Afterword: Religious Philosophy in the Modern University."

3. See *Religious Philosophy*, chapter one, for a discussion of the relations among philosophy, religious studies, and theology in "religious philosophy."

4. Wesley J. Wildman, *In Our Own Image: Anthropomorphism, Apophaticism, and Ultimacy* (Oxford: Oxford University Press, 2017). In this volume Wildman summarizes his methodological stipulations from *Religious Philosophy*, often speaking of "trans-religious" rather than "comparative" matters, although the emphasis on comparison across religions is the same. See also his *Effing the Ineffable: Existential Mumblings at the Limits of Language* (Albany: State University of New York Press, 2019). In this chapter, my citations of his work come mainly from *Religious Philosophy as Multidisciplinary Comparative Inquiry*, *In Our Own Image*, and *Effing the Ineffable*.

5. My recent "coming out" as a philosophical theologian is in my trilogy, *Ultimates: Philosophical Theology Volume One* (2013), *Existence: Philosophical Theology Volume Two* (2014); and *Religion: Philosophical Theology Volume Three* (2015) (Albany: State University of New York Press). *Ultimates* is dedicated to Wesley and his *Religious Philosophy* is dedicated to me. I cannot find anyone claiming the title of philosophical theology before Tillich for whom it named his position at Union Seminary in New York beginning in 1940. Many recently have used the title, however, generally to designate the use of philosophy to think about theological topics, in which case it goes back in the Western tradition to Plato and Aristotle. Wesley and I frequently have discussed what to call what we do, and it is no surprise that we both settled on "philosophical theology."

6. One thinks of Karl Barth, of course, as a confessional theologian thinking for the church. But Paul Tillich begins his *Systematic Theology* with the same profession. See my "Theologies of Identity and Truth: Legacies of Barth and Tillich," in *Realism in Religion: A Pragmatist's Perspective* (Albany: State University of New York Press, 2009), 9–21, for an analysis of their texts on this point.

7. Wildman's *Effing the Ineffable* is dedicated to "my colleagues in Boston University's Graduate Division of Religious Studies: A Fond Farewell," and the dedication is explained in the acknowledgments.

8. The specialists and their assistants were M. David Eckel with John J. Thatamanil (Buddhism), Livia Kohn with James Miller (Chinese religions), Paula Fredriksen with Tina Shepardson (Christianity), Francis X. Clooney (SJ) with Hugh Nicholson (Hinduism), Anthony Saldarini with Joseph Kanofsky (Judaism), and Nomanul Haq (Islam). The generalists were Peter Berger (a sociologist), John Berthrong (a Sinologist), Wesley, and me. With the exception only of Haq, the historical specialists were experts in a religious tradition other than their own so as to avoid even the appearance of interreligious dialogue.

9. The volumes were *The Human Condition*, with a foreword by Peter L Berger; *Ultimate Realities*, with a foreword by Tu Weiming; and *Religious Truth*, with a foreword by Jonathan Z. Smith, all edited by Robert Cummings Neville (Albany: State University of New York Press, 2001).

10. See *Religious Philosophy*, chap. 8.

11. See his explicit discussions of pragmatism and inquiry in *Religious Philosophy*, chaps. 6 and 7, and in *In Our Own Image*, chap. 1 and *passim*.

12. For Tillich's distinction between supernaturalism and supranaturalism, see his *Systematic Theology, Volume II: Existence and the Christ* (Chicago: University of Chicago Press, 1957), 5–10. Wesley's discussion of this is in *Science and Religious Anthropology: A Spiritually Evocative Naturalism Interpretation of Human Life* (Burlington, VT: Ashgate, 2009), 19–23.

13. IOOI, 217.

14. See Wildman, *In Our Own Image*, 82–90, for a more elaborate discussion of this "Central Result" of the scientific study of religion.

15. See Robert Cummings Neville, *Defining Religion: Essays in Philosophy of Religion* (Albany: State University of New York Press, 2018), chaps. 1–4, for a better definition of religion.

16. My theory is spelled out in detail in *Ultimates*, with the last part of *Religion* as the extreme statement of my apophaticism.

17. See Robert S. Corrington's *Nature's Religion*, with a foreword by Robert C. Neville (Lanham, MD: Roman and Littlefield, 1997).

18. See my *Metaphysics of Goodness: Harmony and Form, Beauty and Art, Personhood and Obligation, Flourishing and Civilization* (Albany: State University of New York Press, 2019).

19. *Effing the Ineffable*, 83.

20. See my *Recovery of the Measure* (Albany: State University of New York Press, 1989), divisions 1 and 4, for an explanation and defense of this approach to truth.

21. See my *On the Scope and Truth of Theology: Theology as Symbolic Engagement* (New York: T. & T. Clark, 2004). Compare this to Wesley's *Religious Philosophy*.

22. *Effing the Ineffable*, 65–67.

23. See *Effing the Ineffable*, chap. 3.

24. See Tyler Tritten, *The Contingency of Necessity: Reason and God as Matters of Fact* (Edinburgh: Edinburgh University Press, 2017). Tritten argues his case from late antique and German Idealist authors, especially Schelling, whereas I argue mine from medieval and pragmatic authors.

25. It is spelled out in my *Ultimates*, part three, and many other places.

26. See his discussion of symmetry and asymmetry in *Effing the Ineffable*, chap. 3.

27. These are explained at length in *Ultimates* chap. 4.

28. See the argument in chap. 1 of my *Defining Religion*.

Index

Abhinavagupta, 157–58, 164–65, 173
Absolute, 11, 33, 59, 125, 155, 158, 179–83, 191–92, 196–97, 203, 218, 222, 246, 326
Act of To Be, 10, 70, 85, 92, 151, 167, 173, 183, 198, 200, 242, 249, 264, 268, 281, 307
Aesthetics, aesthetic, xiii, 5, 22, 30, 31–52, 90–91, 97, 120, 127, 141, 188–89, 192, 194, 206, 212, 214, 221, 223, 261, 267, 271, 273
Age, mine, xi; undergraduates, xii
Alkier, Stefan, xv, 228–39
Al-Kindi, 146
Ames, Roger, 117–20, 207, 253, 324
Anderson, Victor, 126
Anselm, St., 147
Aquinas, St. Thomas, xxxii, xxxiv, 10, 70, 74, 85, 93, 147, 149, 151, 167, 173, 198, 200, 216, 232, 242, 249, 264, 268, 307, 319; Thomistic, 9, 59, 85, 92, 183, 159, 200, 244, 255
Aristotle, 6, 19, 70–72, 84–85, 112, 145–49, 280, 286, 307, 331
As-Razi, 146
Augustine, xxxii, 26, 75, 149, 151, 199–200, 232, 247
Aurobindo, Sri, 284
Auxier, Randall, 178–79, 183

Averoes, 146
Avicenna, 146

Barth, Karl, 200, 236
Being, being-itself, xiii, xxii, xxxiv, 3–17, 26, 29, 36–37, 39, 41, 50, 59, 62, 74, 83, 87, 93–94, 97, 149–51, 157, 159–65, 167, 170, 183–84, 191–92, 197–202, 211, 216, 222, 232, 234, 244–50, 255, 263–64, 279, 281, 288, 291–94, 302, 307–309
Bellah, Robert, 257
Bellarmene, Robert, 200
Bracken, Joseph, 201, 203
Bradley, F. H., 33
Brahman, xix, 6, 10, 56, 64, 79, 93, 155–56, 182, 242, 249–50, 255, 269
Brandom, Robert, 126
Buddhism, Buddhist, Buddha, the, Buddha-mind, xix–xx, 6, 10, 17, 21–22, 57, 64, 79, 92–97, 117, 130, 145–49, 152–57, 162–67, 179, 181–82, 187, 189, 207, 211, 242, 249, 259, 269, 294, 300, 308, 319, 327

Cahokia, 146
Cajetan, 200

Index

Calvin, Jean, xxv, 33, 149, 200
Carroll, Anthony J., xvi
Casey, Edward, xiv, 128, 130, 209
Chan, Wing-tsit, 95
Chapter, xii, xviii, xx, xxix, 32, 45, 54, 82, 94–95, 117, 173–74, 178, 215–16, 226, 242, 301, 303, 309–14, 318–19, 331
Cheng, Chung-ying, xiii–xiv, 116, 118, 128, 130, 252
China, Chinese, xiv, xxxiv, 17–18, 27–30, 56, 79–80, 84, 86–97, 99, 101–103, 106–108, 110–12, 115–16, 121–22, 130, 132, 134–43, 145–46, 148, 153, 159–67, 207, 211–12, 249, 252–53, 258–59, 269–73, 277, 284, 294, 300, 308, 329, 231
Christianity, Christian, xii, xx–xxi, xxv, xxviii–xxxv, 85, 122, 148–52, 163–64, 179–81, 183–89, 195–201, 207, 228–39, 252–53, 255–59, 262, 265, 268–69, 277, 282, 291, 298–300, 307, 319
Clooney, Francis X, 260
Cognitive science, xii, xiv, 70, 77
Complexity, 7–8, 13, 27, 36–38, 40–41, 73, 78, 85–89, 93, 96, 103, 129, 132, 140, 143, 158, 160, 181, 185–87, 189, 192–93, 198, 202, 208, 210, 220, 236, 243, 249, 254, 259, 265, 283–85, 302, 316, 320
Component, 4, 7–8, 13–14, 19–27, 33–41, 44–49, 54–55, 63–66, 72–78, 82, 88, 135, 171, 181, 184, 187, 190, 202, 213, 216, 223–25, 231, 243–45, 263–67, 271, 275–76, 286–89
Conditional, 7–8, 13, 25, 33, 40, 72–74, 171–72, 202, 219, 245, 263, 276, 286–89

Confucianism, Confucius, xiv–xiv, xix–xx, 17, 26–27, 32, 39, 62, 88–92, 95–97, 105–13, 114–23, 126, 130–44, 145–49, 159–69, 211, 223, 227, 252–59, 262–77, 294, 308, 320, 328–29
Conner, David E., xv
Contingency, contingent, ix–xvi, 4, 27–28, 54–59, 129, 158, 172, 181–94, 199, 201–202, 218, 220–23, 226, 231–32, 241–250, 264–68, 275, 277, 314–15, 318
Cornille, Catherine, 260
Corrington, Robert S., xv, 213–27, 309
Courage, xxxi, xxxiv–xxxv, 117
Creation, creativity, creating, creative, (God's) xiv, xvi, xviii–xxx, 4, 10–13, 15, 20, 24, 26–29, 34, 41–42, 50–54, 56–59, 72, 74–75, 81, 85–86, 95–97, 139, 150–51, 157–58, 161, 168, 170–72, 181–83, 187, 194, 195, 197–205, 210, 214, 219, 222, 226, 229, 231–36, 239, 242–45, 247, 249, 255, 262–65, 268, 270, 279–81, 287–95, 309–18
Culture, xii, xiv, 32, 45, 49–50, 55, 59–67, 78–82, 87–91, 96, 99–101, 112, 116–19, 126, 132, 134, 137–38, 142, 153, 158, 162, 173–74, 182, 187, 189–91, 201, 207, 211–12, 215, 223, 229–31, 234–36, 239, 249, 252–54, 257–63, 266–67, 272, 274–77, 285, 298, 301, 308, 317, 320, 329

Dalai Lama, 146
Dao, Daoism, Daoist, xix, 10, 17, 25, 56, 58, 62, 79, 89–97, 107, 117, 136, 140, 146, 148–49, 156,

159–62, 167–68, 182, 211, 249, 252, 255, 259, 285, 294, 308, 324
Davidson, Donald, 126, 241–42
Deacon, Terrence, xiv, 69–72
Derrida, Jacques, 208, 228
Descartes, Rene, 22, 70–71, 85, 147, 173, 201, 204–205, 210
Desmond, William, 244
Determinations (as created), xii, xxxv, 59, 70, 85, 138, 173, 183, 198, 200, 277, 283, 291–95, 310
Deuser, Hermann, 227
Dewey, John, 5, 45, 47, 51, 125–26, 130, 138, 183–84, 188, 206, 253
Duns Scotus, 313

Easter, xx–xxv
Eco, 228
Ecstatic Naturalism, 223
Elegance, 37–41
Emergence, emergent, xiv, 30, 59, 69, 71, 75–83, 93, 161, 167–68, 182, 208, 218, 226, 243, 255–56, 264, 269–72, 308–10
Emerson, Ralph Waldo, xi–xii, 51, 125, 179
Emptiness, empty, xxxiii, 4, 6, 10, 16, 22, 56, 93, 150, 152, 156–57, 164, 173, 182, 249, 255–56, 259
Essay, *see also* chapter, xi–xiii, xvi, 117, 152, 184, 214, 300, 326–32
Essential, 7–8, 13, 19–21, 24–25, 27, 33–34, 40–41, 73–74, 171–72, 183, 188, 190, 202, 219, 245, 263–64, 276, 286–89
Eternity, eternal, xiii, xvi, xxv, xxviii–xxx, xxxiv, 4, 17–30, 74–75, 94–95, 151, 155–56, 159–61, 171, 202, 214, 219, 235–37, 247–50, 256, 264, 270, 277, 280–81, 286–91, 294–95, 311, 324

Experience, experiential, xiii, xxxii, 22–23, 27–29, 39, 42–52, 54–67, 70, 81–82, 108, 117, 125–34, 137, 142, 164–66, 194, 200, 205–209, 212, 218, 221, 223–26, 228–31, 237, 249–50, 268, 274, 280, 284–85, 287–88, 293, 301, 309, 319

Feld, Alina, xvi
Felt, James, 201
Firstness, 72, 129–30, 229, 238
Form, 4, 6, 11, 13–16, 19, 24, 26, 33–41, 44–46, 49, 51, 54, 57–60, 64, 72, 74, 78–82, 85–87, 98, 104, 112–13, 129, 132, 138, 146, 149, 151–52, 159–60, 180–83, 186–88, 194, 197, 218, 220, 223–25, 258, 268–78, 281, 287, 290–91, 307–308, 313
Francis, St., 61
Frankenberry, Nancy, xvi, 241–50
Friend, xii, xvi, xxi–xxii, xxv–xxvi, xxxi–xxxii, 11, 42, 62–63, 100–101, 107–108, 116–18, 120, 127, 130, 132, 181, 187, 192, 199, 204, 223, 234, 242, 276, 279, 285, 289, 294–95, 297, 306, 316, 321
Future, xi, xxii, xxviii, xxx–xxxi, xxxv, 4, 18–30, 56, 60, 62, 74–75, 84, 115, 122, 137, 160, 163, 169, 181, 184–86, 191, 203, 220–21, 230, 243–49, 253, 264, 280, 285, 287–91

Gadamer, Hans-Georg, 228, 230
Gibson, James, 210
Glaude, Eddie, 126
God, xviii, xx, 35, 4, 9–10, 25, 30, 41, 47, 56–59, 70, 75, 77–79, 85–88, 92–94, 138, 148–58, 162–68, 173, 179, 183, 187–88,

336 | Index

God (continued)
194–204, 216, 221–22, 228–39, 247, 255, 257, 264, 268–69, 279–86, 290–92, 294–95, 299, 301–304, 306–10, 313, 320–21
Gospel, xviii, xxi, xxiii–xiv, xxix, xxxi, xxxiii, 146, 197, 239
Grange, Joseph, 201
Gu, Linyu, xiii
Gulick, Walter, xii, 31

Hall, David, 120, 207, 253
Hallman, Joseph, 201
Hamzah Fansuri, 146
Harmony, harmonious, xiii, 6–9, 13, 14, 19–25, 29, 31–54, 57–58, 63–67, 72–74, 77, 81, 85–90, 102, 112, 138–44, 157, 160–72, 181, 203, 211–12, 219, 224–25, 243, 263–65, 269–73, 276, 286, 288, 316
Hart, Ray L., xvi, 232, 279–95
Hartshorne, Charles, 15, 86, 203, 208
Hayes, Richard B., xv
Hegel, Georg, 129, 147, 179, 196, 201, 204, 209, 257
Heidegger, Martin, 6–7, 16–16, 129, 206–207, 209, 248
Hellemans, Staf, xvi
Hill, Robert Allen, xx
Hinduism, Hindu, xix–xx, 10, 22, 64, 138–56, 163–66, 179, 189, 211, 269, 280, 294, 300, 308
Hobbes, Thomas, 201, 210
Hopkins, Gerard Manley, 57
Huizenga, Leroy, xv
Hume, David, 201, 204
Husserl, Edmund, 23, 129–30, 209

Ibn al'Arabi, 151
Immediacy, xxvii–xxix, 4, 11–12, 27, 47, 49, 59, 91, 105–106, 108, 129–30, 208, 225, 235, 246, 264, 268, 312, 315
Indeterminacy, indeterminate, xiv, xxxiv, 4, 10–11, 19, 24, 40, 72, 74, 79, 84–87, 91–94, 96–97, 150–51, 156, 161, 168, 170–72, 180, 182–83, 218, 222, 242, 246, 281–82, 291–94, 310, 329
Islam, 122, 145–52, 196–97, 258, 300, 307; see Muslim

Jabir ibn Hayyan, 146
James, William, 80, 125, 129–30, 178–79, 184, 188, 303
Jesus, xviii–xxxv, 228–29, 232–38
Jews, Jewish, xxi, xxiii, xxvii, xxix, xxxi, 85, 150, 163, 165, 268, 319
John (biblical writer), xviii–xix, xxiii–xxiv, xxix, xxxi–xxxv, 197, 232–33
Judaism, xix–xx, xxiii, 149–52, 197, 300, 307, 319
Justice, xxiv, xxix–xxx, 79, 137–38, 261

Kant, Immanuel, 18, 22, 84, 118, 128, 147, 185–86, 201, 204–207, 230, 283, 295
Kienstra, Natascha, xiv
Kohn, Livia, 162
Kraus, Elizabeth, 201

Laozi, 88, 145, 159
Lazarus (biblical character), xxi–xxii, 235
Leibniz, 14, 36, 85, 147, 173, 201, 204–205
Lincoln, Abraham, 289
Literature, xii, 86
Liu Zhi, 146
Location, existential, 4, 8, 13–14, 26–27, 33–37, 43, 54, 65, 76–79,

165, 181, 189–90, 231, 245, 247, 265–67
Locke, John, 201, 204–206
Lonergan, Bernard, 200
Luke (biblical writer), xviii, xix, xxi, xxiii–xxiv, xxvi, xxix–xxxi, 235
Luther, Martin, xxv

Mar, Gary R., xiii
Mark (biblical writer), xviii, xxi–xxiii, xxix, xxxi, 233
Martha (biblical character), xxii
Martin, Jerry, xiii, xv
Mary (biblical character), xxii–xxiii
Matthew (biblical writer), xviii, xxi, xxiii, xxix, xxxi, 233
Mengzi (or Mencius), 99, 101, 104–106, 112, 118, 122–23
Mercier, 200
Mercy, merciful, xxv, xxix, 228, 232, 237
Merleau-Ponty, Maurice, 129, 209
Metaphysics, xxiv, xxxii, 5–7, 14–16, 18, 27, 30, 66, 70–73, 77, 81–82, 95, 117, 121, 130, 135, 147, 170, 172, 191, 200–204, 211, 214, 217–21, 223, 226, 238, 251, 255, 261–64, 267, 269, 277, 304, 318
Michelangelo, 306
Moss, Gregory, xiv
Muller-Ortega, Paul Eduardo, 157
Muslim, 84–85, 146–47, 150, 163, 165, 207, 258, 268; *see* Islam
Mysticism, mystics, mystical, xix, 9, 16, 55–81, 151, 183, 188–89, 247–48, 301, 319–21

Nagarjuna, 152–55, 164
Narrowness, 34, 41, 44–50
Neo-Platonism, xxxiii, 10, 59, 85, 92–93, 151, 156, 183, 197–99, 244, 247, 264

Neville, Beth (my wife), ix
Niemoczynski, Leon, xv
Non-being, 10, 27, 79–80, 93, 97, 139, 151, 155, 159–61, 167–68, 172, 182, 222, 242, 255, 270, 275, 277, 292

One (in an ontological sense), 4, 25–26, 59, 85, 88, 92, 142, 149–51, 159–60, 167, 171, 173, 183, 196–200, 202, 218–19, 222, 237, 242, 244, 264, 268, 270, 304–305, 310, 313–18
Ontological creative act, xii, xxv, xxviii, xxx, 4–5, 9–16, 24–30, 54–59, 64, 66–67, 75–80, 96, 139, 168, 170–72, 180–83, 190, 193, 200, 202–204, 219–22, 226, 235–38, 246–50, 255–56, 262–70, 277, 288, 291–95, 305, 309–18
Ontology, ontological, xi, xii–xvi, 4–9, 11–12, 14–16, 25–29, 41, 54, 59, 74, 79, 84–97, 131, 139, 154–55, 164, 171–72, 180–82, 188, 193, 198, 199, 202–203, 219, 231–32, 242–50, 256, 263–65, 268–70, 287–88, 292–94, 309–11, 313, 316–17, 320

Paganism, pagan, 85, 149, 152, 167, 200
Park, Iljoon, xv
Past, xxviii, xxx, xxxiv, 11, 18–29, 41, 43–49, 56, 59, 74–79, 84, 96, 121, 137, 160, 203, 243–49, 259, 264, 287–91
Pastor, pastoral, xii, xx, 233–35
Paul (biblical writer), xxiv–xxxi, 186, 236–37
Peirce, Charles Sanders, 10, 15, 51, 71–72, 125–30, 138, 178–79, 184, 188, 191, 208–12, 217, 221–22,

Peirce, Charles Sanders (*continued*)
  263, 225, 227–30, 237, 239, 242,
  280, 282–83, 301, 306, 312, 315,
  317, 326, 328
Peter (biblical character), xviii, xxiii
Philosophy, global, xii, 51, 97, 116,
  141, 146–47, 169, 173, 259, 262,
  267, 277
Philosophy, philosopher, ix, xi, xvi,
  xx, 6, 8, 10–11, 14–15, 17–30,
  31–35, 42, 45–46, 51, 59–60,
  70–71, 74, 77, 84–86, 91–92, 95,
  97, 101, 112, 116, 119, 127–32,
  138, 141–74, 178–88, 191, 194,
  197, 199–209, 212, 213, 215,
  220–26, 227, 234, 239, 242, 244,
  249–50, 252–62, 265–67, 270, 272,
  277, 279–81, 284, 290, 297–307,
  311–13, 317–18, 320, 330–31
Physics, xxiv, 139, 197, 205, 315
Plato, Platonism, 6, 11, 14, 17, 32,
  72, 75, 84, 87, 112, 145–51, 206,
  223, 253, 268–69, 307, 328, 331
Plotinus, 85, 95, 149–51, 167, 173,
  197–98, 242, 309–10
Poet, poetry, xi, xxii, 15, 28, 34, 117,
  206
Polke, Christian, xv
Pragmatism, pragmatic, xiv–xv, 46,
  71, 81, 125–44, 178–79, 209–10,
  227–30, 241–42, 252–53, 261, 284,
  313–15, 318, 332
Present, xxv, xxviii–xxix, xxxiii–
  xxxiv, 4, 18–29, 70–71, 74–76, 84,
  95–97, 135, 158, 187, 203, 226,
  243, 245, 247–49, 264, 287–91
Pseudo-Dionysius, 151
Psychoanalysis, 213–23

Rahner, Karl, 200
Religion, religious, xi, xiii, xvi, xviii–
  xxxiv, 16, 18, 32, 47, 54–57, 60,
  67, 71, 75–82, 93, 122, 136, 139,
  143, 147–53, 157–73, 178–89, 194,
  197, 200–201, 204, 206–207, 210,
  221, 223, 227–35, 239, 241–42,
  244, 248, 252–60, 267, 275–78,
  289, 294, 298–312, 318–21,
  331–32
Ricci, Matteo, 112, 146, 152, 158, 277
Ricoeur, Paul, 228
Rorty, Richard, 126, 241–42
Royce, Josiah, xv, 125, 178–94

Schleiermacher, Friedrich, xxxii,
  xxxiv, 149, 228, 320
Scott, Robert H., xiv
Secondness, 72, 130, 229, 238
Seibert, Christoph, xv
Sermons, xii, xiii, xx, xxxi, xxxiii
Shankara, 164
Shults, F. LeRon, xvi
Simplicity, 36–37, 41, 183
Slater, Gary, xiii
Space, spatial, 4, 11, 13, 26–27, 35,
  41, 48, 51, 65–66, 74–75, 103,
  134, 157, 171, 199, 211, 219–24,
  243, 263–64, 290, 316
Spinoza, Baruch, 147, 173, 201, 204,
  214, 228
Spontaneity, xiv, xxxiii, 6, 11, 20–30,
  34, 41, 59, 76, 79, 91, 93, 96–97,
  104, 139, 161, 167, 182, 242–48,
  255–56, 264, 269–70, 272, 288,
  308–10
Strange, Strangely, viii, xi–xiv, xxvi,
  3–5, 9–10, 14, 17–18, 26, 30, 36,
  42, 67, 67, 138, 172, 185, 200,
  208, 215, 246–48, 303
Sure (about the future), ix, xi–xiv,
  xxiv, xxx, xxxiii–xxxiv, 66–67, 94,
  97, 111, 158, 180, 207, 275, 307
Surprise, or Surprising, vii, xi–xii,
  xviii, xix–xx, xxiv 3, 5, 12, 27, 49,

59, 83, 153, 181, 220, 229, 265, 267, 280–82, 290–95, 314

Taylor, Charles, xvi, 252–77, 329
Thirdness, 72, 130, 229, 238
Tillich, Paul, xxxii–xxxiii, 59, 85, 149, 197, 236, 298, 302, 318–20, 331–32
Time, xi–xii, xiv, xxi–xxiv, xxvii–xxiii, xxxii, xxxiv, 4, 11–15, 17–30, 34–35, 39, 41–43, 49, 51, 56–62, 64–66, 70–71, 74–78, 88, 90, 95, 97, 101, 110, 121–22, 133–34, 136, 140, 142, 145, 150, 153, 156–57, 160–61, 179, 187, 189, 199, 207, 214, 223, 230, 234–37, 243, 247–48, 254, 256, 260–64, 269–70, 277, 279, 287–91, 294, 311, 316, 320–21
Tracy, David, 50
Transcend, transcendence, transcendent, transcendentals, Transcendentalist, xi, xiii, xix–xxi, 4, 6–7, 12–14, 18, 54–67, 75, 79, 89, 92–96, 126, 129, 150–52, 155, 157, 163, 166, 182, 185, 189, 197, 200, 206, 222, 224, 228, 233–34, 252, 254–57, 259–68, 272–77, 281, 291, 302, 306–308, 319
Tritten, Tyler, 59, 315, 332
Tu, Wei-ming, 252
Tunstall, Dwayne A., 178

Ultimate, ultimacy, xiv–xv, xxxiv–xxxv, 4–6, 10, 22, 27, 29–30, 54–56, 60–64, 67, 77–82, 92, 95–95, 138–39, 147–53, 157–91, 194, 196, 202–203, 211, 219, 221–23, 230–32, 236, 239, 242–43, 255–57, 262, 265–77, 281–82, 285, 286, 291–94, 299–321

Vague, vagueness, 7, 12, 20, 34–50, 70–72, 120, 132, 161, 168, 184, 191, 220–23, 282–83, 311
Value, xiii, 4, 13–15, 19–20, 32–38, 47–48, 54–79, 90–91, 103, 126–130, 134–35, 138, 141–43, 165, 181–87, 190–94, 206, 210–12, 220, 223–25, 231–32, 237, 239, 265–67, 271–76, 299, 309, 232

Wang Bi, 93, 95, 160
Wang, Yang-ming, 86
Weiss, Paul, 20, 208, 242–43, 261
West, Cornel, 126
Wheeler, Damian, xv
Whitehead, Alfred North, xv, 6, 11, 14–15, 18, 20–21, 26, 34–37, 42, 45, 71–75, 80, 87, 125, 130, 147, 195–212, 223, 242–46, 302, 323
Width, wide, 34–41, 43–50, 80, 108, 205, 269
Wildman, Wesley J., xi, xii, xvi, 32, 50, 297–32
Wind-egg, mere, 18
Wisdom, wise, xiv, xxxiii, 4, 14, 21, 97, 99–113, 117, 137, 171, 197, 204
Wittgenstein, Ludwig, 206

Xunzi, 101, 104–105, 112, 118–19, 123, 131, 136, 159, 212

Yin/yang, 7, 161

Zhou, Dunyi, 10, 27, 93, 95–96, 160, 172, 242, 270–75
Zhu Xi, 105–107, 112
Zhuangzi, 159

www.ingramcontent.com/pod-product-compliance
Lightning Source LLC
Chambersburg PA
CBHW031703230426
43668CB00006B/93